Front cover:
Aberystwyth from the North
Sketched by Capt. R. G. Roberts. Published by John Cox

Back cover:
Aberystwyth Harbour c. 1850
Sketched by Capt. R. G. Roberts

Born on a Perilous Rock

Aberystwyth Castle, built, according to a 13th century cleric, "on a perillous rock by the sea".

Born on a Perilous Rock

Aberystwyth Past and Present

By

W. J. Lewis

Cambrian News (Aberystwyth) Ltd.
Aberystwyth
Dyfed

Printed and Published by The Cambrian News (Aberystwyth) Ltd., Aberystwyth, Dyfed.
1980

I.S.B.N. 0 900439 04 1

To my wife, Heather, Gwenda and David

Contents

Preface

For much of the past thirty years I have been engaged in studies which have often touched upon the history of Aberystwyth. The work on lead mining, in particular, revealed much of the history of the port, transport and industries while some of the mining promoters whose lives were examined—Sir Thomas Bonsall, Job Sheldon, John Taylor and others—were also important men in the town. It also entailed the study of family papers, especially those of Gogerddan and Nanteos, papers which contain a great deal of information about the town which the Pryses and Powells dominated for centuries. I often felt the need for a history of Aberystwyth and occasionally considered writing one myself, but the nearest I ever came to this was a few articles written for *Ceredigion* and other journals. Then, almost two years ago, I was asked by Messrs. Henry Read and Eric Evans of the Cambrian News, both natives of the town and very interested in its past, to write a history of Aberystwyth and offering to publish it, a generous gesture in these days of high and rapidly rising costs in printing. I agreed and this book is the result.

Most of it is concerned with the post-1800 period when the town spread rapidly and the population increased from 1,758 in 1801 to 5,189 in 1851 and to 8,074 in 1901. It is now about 11,000. In the interests of readability there is some repetition, particularly in street and other names which have changed, and in the last chapter which, it is hoped, will help readers to identify features of historical interest and to place those which have disappeared.

The writer of a local history tends to be remembered as much for his errors and omissions as for his contribution, and it is too much to hope that this book is free from such faults. Whatever its failings, I hope that this work will induce others to add to the story so that the history of the ancient town of Aberystwyth will, in time, be as fully recorded as it deserves to be.

A piece of information which has just come to the writer's notice is that before it was branded as sinful by the Methodists, there was much open-air dancing to the music of the violin and harp on Sunday evenings in summer, at Pen Craig y Wig now occupied by the Theological College, and at Pen Craig y Nos near Graeg Goch.

The writing of a book such as this involves putting one's sickle into other men's corn, a process made much easier by J. Lewis Jones's *Bibliography of Cardiganshire*. Three writers in particular have yielded a considerable amount of information—David Samuel, George Eyre

Evans, and C. Howard Jones who contributed "Wireless Whispers" to the *Cambrian News*. Much of this and other information has been gleaned from local newspapers and other material at the National Library of Wales, and I am grateful to the staff there for their ready assisatance. Some material came from the Aberystwyth Public Library and I am particularly grateful to the staff of the local history section. In addition, I have drawn on the works of Prof. E. G. Bowen, Islwyn Beynon, Mary Brown, Dr. B. G. Charles, Lewis Cozens, Fr Kiely O'Carm, Gwennant Davies, Dr. E. L. Ellis, Dr. D. I. Evans, Evan Evans, Madge Hughes, D. B. Hague, Dr. E. D. Jones, Prof. I. G. Jones, T. Wyn Jones, Iwan Morgan, Janet Kyffin, T. M. Merchant, Llewelyn Morgan, Lieut. Bryn Owen, R.N., B. G. Owens, Irene D. Rees, George Rees, Rev. T. E. Roberts, Dr. I. J. Sanders, J. Beverley Smith, C. J. Spurgeon, Dr. Clare Taylor, Rev. Geoffrey Thomas, Sir Ben Bowen Thomas, Dr. A. L. Trott, E. R. Horsfall Turner, Sidney and Beatrice Webb, Dr. R. F. Walker, Emlyn Williams and Emrys Williams (Peter of *Cambrian News*).

Others who have helped by word of mouth are J. E. R. Carson, Cyrus Evans, Alun Edwards, Sarah L. Jenkins, T. R. Jones, Bryn Morgan, G. C. Suff, J. Pryce Thomas, Hywel Watkins, Mrs. Basil Williams, Harry Williams and Dr. Moelwyn Williams. I have also been fortunate in drawing on the excellent memories of some of the town's senior citizens, particularly John William Jones, Llewelyn Jenkins, Arthur Miller and Johnny Chamberlain.

The work was made a lot easier by the aid given so readily by Dr. John Owen of the Ceredigion Museum. Not only did he put me right on some matters of fact but he also read the manuscript and some of the proofs. I am grateful, too, to Prof. E. G. Bowen for reading the work, making valuable suggestions and writing the foreword.

The older illustrations are almost all from the collections at the National Library and Ceredigion Museum ansd I wish to thank the people concerned. I am also grateful to Peter Henley, David Jenkins and Norman Jones. The photographs of present day Aberystwyth are the work of Eric Evans of *Cambrian News,* by whom I was given an enormous amount of assistance both in and out of working hours. The credit for the orderly arrangement and presentation of the text belongs to him. I would also like to thank my wife for her forbearance and for her assistance in reading the proofs.

Place names have been spelt in the modern, recommended manner; the only one likely to puzzle readers is *Pumlumon* for "Plynlimon".

Foreword

Emeritus Professor E. G. Bowen,
M.A., D.Litt., Ll.D., D.Univ.,
F.S.A.

The literature on towns in prodigious both in volume and variety and for a town of its size, Aberystwyth is no exception. The literature on the town during the present century has included much diverse approaches as a transcription of the records of its Court Leet, a classical academic treatment of selected aspects of its history to celebrate its sept-centenary, and, more recently, a pictorial record. The present work, however, is the first to present a comprehensive history of the social life of the town on the lines of Lord Briggs' well known *Victorian Cities*.

This, of course, is no easy task, for the author has had to engage upon very considerable research. This is due to the fact that the most illuminating courses of information are buried away in the most unlikely places. Local newspapers and periodicals provide an indispensible record of contemporary views and accounts of the progress, or otherwise, made in providing improved social facilities such as public offices, hospitals, schools, gas, electricity and water works. In addition, Aberystwyth as a sea-side resort has an excellent collection of local *Guides* to the town and neighbourhood some of which (like those of T. O. Morgans) are of a very high standard for their day and age. The author needs to consult all this material and much else besides including, for instance, the Minutes of the Town Council and other public bodies such as the old Board of Guardians. Other records such as the Parish Register, the Census Returns and the special Religious Census of 1851 have all to be examined together with concert and other programmes and letters of social interest in our libraries and in private hands, while in the end comes the even greater task of digesting this material and arranging it all in a scholarly and attractive manner.

Mr. Lewis has correctly selected the year 1700 as his starting point and after a brief section on the origins of the Bastide Town, the social story unfolds itself. The choice of such a starting point is important because the early eighteenth century saw the beginnings of the Industrial Revolution in Britain which brought in its wake what is generally known as "the Urban Revolution", when new towns and cities arose in the most spectacular manner while older ones grew immensely in size. When Queen Victoria came to the throne in 1837 there were only five towns in England and Wales with over 100,000 people. At present there are fifty-six. While Aberystwyth had several small industries, it had nothing to compare with these giants.

Nevertheless, we must remember that during the last two centuries Aberystwyth has passed through similar social changes, but obviously on a very much smaller scale.

Social change during the period under review can best be visualized in the realm of transport where changing conditions have provided for the ever increasing mobility of the population and all that follows from it. We pass from the stagecoach, riding horses, pack horses and highwaymen to the coming of the railways, the motor bus, the commercial and private motor car, and ultimately to the more rapid movement on land, sea and air provided by the change from horse power to that of steam, gas, oil and electricity. It is usually agreed that the coming of the railway marked the real watershed between the past and the present. The railway reached Aberystwyth in 1864.

The great changes involved in the above summary affected the social and economic life of the town primarily in its rôle as a market centre for the surrounding countryside and the important part the harbour had to play in the life of the town. The people came to town no longer by horse and cart but first by train and then by bus and in their own motor cars. The market place and the fairs, we must remember, were the traditional centres of social intercourse. At the same time the sea-faring community with its long tradition of sail saw many of their little ships vanish, to be replaced by those of steam. Even so, the sea-faring community and its associated trades has left a unique and distinctive mark on the social life of the town—evidence of which is still visible for all to see.

The Victorians, whatever may have been said of them in the past, raised a vast accumulation of social capital usually by voluntary or municipal effort. Much of the voluntary effort went into church building which, in Wales, followed upon the great Methodist Revival in the eighteenth century. The chapel became virtually the centre of the social life of the community, and attendance at Sunday Services and associated week-night meetings was for many their sole social contact with other members of the community outside their immediate family relations. Church membership in late Victorian and Edwardian Aberystwyth represented a very high percentage of the total adult population; possibly as high a percentage, if not even higher than that of any other town of its size in the whole country. In consequence, the Ministers and Clergy ranked highly in the town's list of 'Worthies'. While it is true that some of the week-night meetings threw off branch societies that were not necessarily connected with the church or chapel and dealt with cultural matters including English and Welsh literature and politics, they offered no challenge to the chapels themselves. Neither did the intermittent theatrical performances in the town's Theatre.

The vast accumulation of social capital represented by the Churches was augmented in these years by municipal effort. This again represented a national tendency. Towards the middle of Queen Victoria's reign, a few leaders and prominent men in the great towns and cities, themselves often prominent Nonconformists, made the discovery that a strong and able Town Council might do almost as much to improve the conditions of life in the towns as Parliament itself. The story of what happened in this respect in cities like Birmingham and Manchester is outstanding, but in a small way a similar view was taken in many other towns large and small. The old Improvement Commissioners and similar bodies were jogged into greater activity and often from their midst the abler members were encouraged to seek selection to the local Town Councils. In this way in the years towards the close of the century, and before the First World War, we had what may be called the Golden Age in local politics. Many of the smaller towns were served by able and prominent citizens whose names have since been added to the list of "Worthies". During this period, too, efforts were being made all over the country for the local Corporation to gain possession of the gas and water supplies—essential services in any attempt to raise the local standard of living. Great efforts were made by intelligent mayors and councillors to sweep away streets in which it was not possible to live a healthy and decent life. The slums of Trefechan and other courts and alleys were slowly cleared away and soon it was apparent that prominent Town Councillors were foremost in dealing with all the complex urban problems associated with Health, Housing, Education, Law and Order.

There is one very important way in which Aberystwyth differs from almost all towns of the same size in Wales. It possesses several institutions and central headquarters of national organizations which in most countries would be located in the capital city. This, of course, is due to the fractionation of national institutions in Wales. The presence of the University College of Wales and the National Library of Wales come immediately to mind and their impact on the social life of the community since their inception has been great indeed. It is true that they are "very big frogs in a very small pond", yet they add dignity and variety to the social scene. All this is extremely important in a small town where every person is known and all his or her movements are liable to observation, the slightest irregularity becoming a matter of local notoriety. This book takes full advantage of this feature and, in consequence, has much to say about colourful local characters and "Worthies" who have stood out in the social scene.

Furthermore, the aim of the promoters of this work was to ensure that the social picture should be placed on record in such a way that it would be of interest not only to local people and those who once lived in the town, but to its many visitors as well. We must always remember that there is a visible as well as an invisible legacy in social life. The one concerns the buildings of the sites of former buildings where great social gatherings took place in the past, the other, of course, is the memory of (and the written record, sometimes) of the ordinary conversations that took place day by day between individuals or groups. Special attention, therefore, has been given to buildings of importance and sites where great events took place in former years. They are listed in gazeteer form with some valuable cross references, together with a similar treatment of the town's "Worthies", forming thereby an admirable conclusion to the volume.

Aberystwyth to 1700

Aberystwyth, now the largest town in Mid Wales, was created over seven hundred years ago when, on 28 December 1277, King Edward I issued a charter making the settlement near the new castle into a free borough with a ditch and a wall, a guild of merchants, a Monday market which is still held, and two fairs, one at Whitsuntide to last for four days, and the other at Michaelmas to last for eight days, also still held.

But while there had never been a town on this site before, there had been people living in the area for thousands of years. Pendinas, the hill to the south of the town, with its memorial column, had been an important, well-fortified Iron Age hill fort in pre-Christian times. Its earthen ramparts are still clearly visible and excavations have revealed, among other things, the sunken hut circles on which round, thatched dwellings were built by primitive men before the birth of Christ. This fort was probably the *Rhiw Faelor* or *Allt Faelor* of Celtic poetry and was certainly the *Dinas Faelor* or *Castell Maelor* of the 15th and 16th centuries.

But there is evidence of a much older settlement on the narrow coastal plain to the west of Pendinas, south of the harbour. Here are to be found the remains of a flint-chipping floor where a colony of hunters and fishermen of the Mesolithic Age made weapons and tools from the flint deposited here by the glaciers of the Ice Age moving down the Irish Sea.

The column on Pendinas is of a very much later date. It was erected in 1852 as a monument to the Duke of Wellington at the suggestion of Major Richardes of Bryneithin who had fought in the battle of Waterloo. It represents a cannon pointing skywards and was meant to carry a statue of a man on horseback, presumably the Duke, whose death revived some fears of another possible French invasion. To persuade people to subscribe to the monument it was even suggested that the sight of the Iron Duke, even in effigy, would discourage invaders.

The first castle to be built in the area was not on the site of the present ruin. At the beginning of the 12th century, Ceredigion was in the hands of Cadwgan ap Bleddyn, who had a very unruly son, Owain. In 1107 Owain met the beautiful Nest, wife of the Constable of Pembroke Castle and a former ward of Henry I. Two years later Owain raided Pembroke Castle and carried Nest away. This so enraged Henry that he sent Gilbert of Clare, nicknamed Strongbow, with a strong army into Ceredigion and caused so much destruction that both Cadwgan and Owain had to flee the country. Cadwgan was soon reinstated and Owain returned secretly

Excavations at Pendinas

1

only to fall foul of the Normans once again and to kill some of the King's men. News of this came to Henry while Cadwgan was at the court and the king, convinced that the latter was neither able to rule his territories properly nor to control his son, deprived Cadwgan of his lands and gave them to the most famous of his barons, Gilbert Fitzgerald of Clare in Suffolk. To strengthen his hold on his territories in 1109, Gilbert built two castles in Ceredigion, another in Cardigan and one "opposite Llanbadarn", not far from the mouth of the river Ystwyth.

This was the first castle, an earthwork and timber structure of the ring and bailey type, built near Tanybwlch on the south side of the Ystwyth and therefore correctly named "Aberystwyth Castle". It was not a strong fort, it proved difficult to defend and changed hands many times in the fighting between the Normans and the Welsh and between the Welsh themselves.

The 12th and 13th centuries saw the rise of two great leaders in Wales. Rhys ap Gruffydd—the Lord Rhys—who ruled Ceredigion wisely for many years and was recognised by the English king as the most important Welshman of his day and the leader of the minor princes of South Wales. He died in 1197 after ruling Ceredigion for at least thirty years. The other great Welshman was Llewelyn ap Gruffydd—Llewelyn the Great—who was all-powerful in North Wales and became so influential in the remainder of the country that in 1258 he was formally vested with the title of Prince of Wales by Henry III.

But Henry was succeeded by Edward I, a seasoned warrior who had no intention of allowing Wales to become independent of England. He launched a carefully planned campaign designed to conquer Wales and was so successful that by 1277, Llewelyn the Last had reverted to being a power in Gwynedd only. To retain his hold on the conquered territories, Edward's policy was to build large, stone castles to which were attached walled towns populated by people faithful to the English king. Such settlements being in a hostile country, had to be carefully sited; the place chosen in northern Ceredigion, described by a Llanbadarn cleric as "a perillous rock near the sea", was well-suited for the purpose. The hill on which Aberystwyth Castle was built had a good view of the countryside, was backed by the sea, was surrounded on three sides by marshy ground and was alongside a small harbour by means of which the settlement could communicate and trade fairly safely with friendly areas elsewhere, as well as receive military aid when necessary. A work force of about 1,300 men was recruited, some from the south west of England, raw materials were imported from Bristol, Carmarthen and Milford and the castle was built. Initially the little town which grew up around it probably had only the protection offered by a wooden stockade and ditches, but by 1280 the borough was surrounded by a stone wall having four gates. At first the townsmen were probably all English but in 1310, of the 144 men holding privileged tenures of land within these walls, over 50 were Welsh, a higher proportion than in most, if not all of Edward's other castles. Further growth received a severe

C. J. Spurgeon's drawing of Aberystwyth Castle as it was built by Edward I.

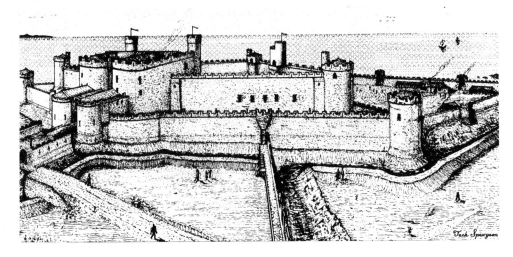

set-back later in the century, when the castle and town lost half of its population during the Black Death.

Though near the mouth of the Rheidol, the fortress was not named after that river. It was known officially as Llanbadarn Castle until well into the 15th century. There were a few, however, who transferred to it the name "Aberystwyth Castle" given to the Tanybwlch fort by King John some sixty years previously. As early as 1277 one of the compilers of the *Chronicle of the Princes* (Brut y Tywysogion) wrote "Edmund, the King's Brother, and a host with him came to Llanbadarn and began to build the castle of Aberystwyth." The name was also used for the castle by Owain Glyndwr, but he described the walled borough as the "new town of Llanbadarn". According to tradition however, the town was known in the locality as Llanbadarn Gaerog (fortified Llanbadarn). By Elizabethan times "Aberystwyth", though geographically incorrect, was widely used and misled Humphrey Lhuyd, the Welsh mapmaker who drew the map of Wales for Abraham Ortelius's *Atlas* in1584, into giving the name "Rheydol" to the river Ystwyth and "Ystwydth" to the Rheidol.

The castle was frequently under attack but it appears to have changed hands only four times in its history. One of the successful attackers was Owain Glyndwr who began his siege of the fortress early in 1402. To finance the resistance to the attack, Prince Henry, later Henry V, was forced to pawn his jewels and to appeal for reinforcements. In April of the same year, Lord Berkeley, Admiral of the Fleet West of the Thames, was commanded to equip three to four vessels for the protection of the King's subjects at the castles of Llanbadarn and Harlech and to supply them with corn, wine etc. Money was sent to Bristol to equip five vessels with men at arms and archers, victuals and stores, and to convey them to the said castles where they were to compel the French, who were aiding Owain, to raise their blockade of the castles. But Glyndwr was too strong, and in 1404 he succeeded in capturing Aberystwyth castle and set fire to the town. This victory was important to Owain for it gave him a status which justified his playing the part of a ruling prince and, while at Aberystwyth, concluding a treaty with Charles VI of France in a princely manner. But it lasted only four years, the recapture of the castle by Prince Henry in 1408 heralded the complete collapse of the Welsh movement. It is interesting to note that in this attack, Henry used cannon, one of the first examples of their use in Wales. One of the cannon, a famous piece named "Messenger", burst during the siege. A great deal of damage was done to Aberystwyth castle, much of which was never fully repaired.

Henceforth the fortress remained firmly in English hands. In 1415 Henry V used it to accommodate a few of the many French prisoners captured at Agincourt, and William Vaughan, the grandson of Sir Roger Vaughan who had fought at Agincourt, was made constable of the castle and mayor of Aberystwyth in the time of Edward IV.

In the reign of Henry VII the fortress was entrusted to the care of Richard Herbert who was later knighted by Henry VIII. Others who were constables or captains of the castle in the latter's reign were Sir Rice (Rhys) ap Thomas and Wilham Herbert of Pembroke Castle. The custodian's annual fee was then £18 5s. and he was allowed twelve archers for the defence of the castle and town. Small as this force seems, it was probably adequate, for the castle's function of protecting the English king's subjects became progressively less important after the accession to the English throne of the Welshman Henry Tudor, in 1485. Also, the Act of Union which united Wales to England in 1536 deprived the castle of most of its administrative functions and gradually it became an object of antiquarian interest only. In 1561 it was stated that "At Aberistwth is a castell of the King's decayed but the hall remeyneth yet covered with leade". Tradition says that much of the building's lead served to pay the marriage dowry of one of its constable's daughters.

In the 17th century, however, the castle again became prominent in affairs and a centre of strife. The silver from the silver-lead ores mined locally was extracted and refined at Ynys-hir, now known as Furnace, and sent to the Tower in London to be minted. Highwaymen, pirates and stormy seas often made this a troublesome and dangerous business. In 1637 Thomas Bushell, who leased the mines from the Mines Royal Society, with the strong support of local landowners, who wanted a more regular supply of ready money, petitioned the king for the right to set up a mint near the mines. In July 1637 the king signed the indenture granting Bushell the right to the coinage of silver in Wales, and the place chosen for the work was Aberystwyth Castle. Bushell was made Warden and Master Worker assisted by a regular staff of five among whom was the Comptroller, Edmund Goodyear, or Goodier, who received a salary of £40 per annum. All the officers were Englishmen except Humphrey Owen, the Clerk to the Mint, and a native of Aberystwyth. One difference between coins minted at Aberystwyth and those minted from Welsh silver at the London Mint was that the Aberystwyth coins of higher denominations had feathers marked on both sides while the older ones had the feathers on the reverse sides only. On the coins of lower denominations, the feathers were placed on the reverse side only. The general Aberystwyth mint mark was an open book and the coins produced were the halfcrown, shilling, half-shilling, twopence and penny, to which were later added the groat (4d.), threepence and halfpenny. According to one report some angels were also produced, coins worth about ten shillings and previously made only of gold.

During the Civil War Bushell fully repaid his king for the right to mint silver. He is said to have supplied King Charles with large amounts of money with which to pay his soldiers, to have raised and equipped a regiment of Derbyshire miners to act as Royal lifeguards and to have clothed three other regiments at a total cost of £36,000. Bushell also struck some silver medals for the King to award soldiers showing exceptional bravery in battle, possibly the forerunner of the V.C.

Despite the Civil War Bushell continued to mint money at Aberystwyth until 1643. In that year, London having declared for Parliament, King Charles lost control of the Tower mint and, to assist his Royal master, Bushell moved the Aberystwyth Mint first to Shrewsbury and then to Oxford, continuing to supply it with silver from Cardiganshire. The Civil War provided some people with a good excuse for helping themselves to the produce of the mines. Cargoes of lead destined for the Royalists and others were seized on the high seas or in ports of call. Thomas Deacon who claimed to be a Parliamentarian, boarded a ship at Swansea and carried away 12 tons of lead belonging to Bushell. A year later he seized 400 tons at the same port. On one occasion, warning of an intended attack on the lead-carrying ships was received after they had sailed. A mounted messenger galloped down the Aberystwyth-Cardigan road until he was able to signal the ships to return. The ships turned back and stayed in Aberystwyth harbour for three weeks before setting sail for Bristol once again.

The silver was sent overland and the carriers were always subject to attack, especially after war was declared. John Williams, a bullion porter, was set upon and robbed of silver worth £107 at Llandeilo on his way to meet Bushell at Bristol. Another was robbed of two ingots of silver worth £77 in Swansea by men who claimed to be Cromwellians. Though the war had a depressing effect on mining, work did not cease and there must have been a considerable amount of silver bullion in the castle at times. An informer of the period described

how, in 1647, a lead factor from London, John Port, broke into the castle and took away coin and bullion to the value of over £30,000. The same man was also credited with having stolen 500 tons of lead awaiting shipment.

During the Civil War the castle was garrisoned by Royalists. In January 1644, Sir William Myddelton, one of Cromwell's men, sent a company of soldiers to Machynlleth. From there they entered Cardiganshire and set up a base at Llanbadarn Fawr from which to attack Aberystwyth Castle and to plunder Trawsgoed and other houses. During their stay, thirty Royalists from the castle garrison, hoping to surprise the fifty men at Llanbadarn, made a dawn attack on the base but were repulsed. Thirteen of the Royalists were drowned in a mill pond near the town, probably part of the mill leat which then flowed down what is now Alexandra Rd. One of the dead was a Lieut. Powell.

In November 1645 the Parliamentarians laid siege to the castle; among the attacking force were many Cardiganshire men, including John Vaughan (later Sir John) of Trawsgoed and Colonel John Jones of Nanteos. The latter's presence can be explained only by his having a personal grudge against someone inside the castle, for not only was John Jones a staunch Royalist but he later suffered heavy fines for his beliefs. He probably used in the siege the regiment of foot which he had raised in the district to fight for the King. In April 1646 Col. Whitely (or Whitley) yielded the castle to the besiegers.

Stories differ as to why the castle was

subsequently destroyed so completely. Some attribute it to Cromwell's men, others to the stores of gunpowder left by Bushell for use in the lead mines. One absurd story is that it was shelled from Pendinas, a feat which was beyond the powers of the cannon of that time. The delay in destroying the building—it was not badly damaged until 1649—may either have been due to the need to continue to store silver bullion there, or supports the story that it had then to be made unusable because it had become a den of thieves, demobilised soldiers who attacked and robbed innocent townspeople and preyed on the nearby market.

In 1652 the town was described by a casual visitor as follows:

"I got into Cardiganshire to a miserable market town called Aberystwyth where before the late troubles there stood a strong castle which being blown up fell down and many fair houses (with a defensible thick wall about the town) are transformed into confused heaps of unnecessary rubbidge."

The damage done in 1649 was rendered much worse by the townspeople's habit of using castle stone for building purposes, a practice which was made illegal in 1835 but continued for a few years afterwards.

Little or no interest was shown by the Corporation in the castle until the reform of the municipal corporations began in 1835. Then some attempts were made to preserve the old fort, such as the repair and propping up of some walls. The castle well, which was known to exist, was found during some excavations in 1844 and, in the interests of safety, was covered over. It proved quite

difficult to establish the ownership of the castle but after negotiations which lasted almost 30 years, the Corporation bought the old ruin and the grounds for £254 in 1881.

The town's growing popularity with visitors and the latter's interest in the old fortress, led to more attention being paid to its appearance. The castle grounds were laid out with walks and flower beds in the 1820's. Much later, the moat was filled in and light entertainment presented on the level sward. To the disgust of some antiquarians, entertainers were even allowed to perform inside the castle walls. The circle of stones within the inner ward is a Gorsedd Circle set up in preparation for the National Eisteddfod of 1915 which, because of the war, was

The Castle in 1740

postponed for a year.

Excavations have shown the wall surrounding the early town to have been a well-mortared structure, six to eight feet thick. Using the modern street names, it ran from the castle along South Rd. to the gate at the bottom of Bridge St., and followed the line of Mill St. and Chalybeate St. to the Great Dark Gate at the lower end of Great Darkgate St. It then ran up Baker St. to the Public Library, having a small gate (the Little Dark Gate) at the lower end of Eastgate. Behind the library it turned south and followed the cliff top, parallel to the sea shore, to the castle. It is not known whether there was an opening at the end of Pier St. which contained very few houses indeed

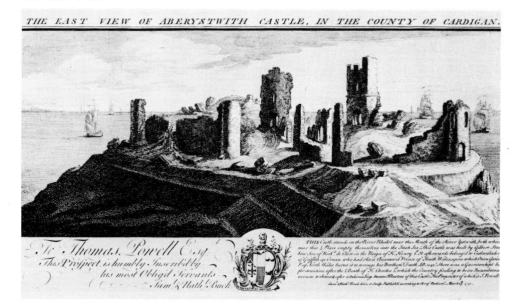

THE EAST VIEW OF ABERYSTWITH CASTLE, IN THE COUNTY OF CARDIGAN.

until the early 18th century.

There was also a fortified medieval mansion near Aberystwyth, Plas Crug, which was said to have been used as a base by Owain Glyndwr during his siege of Aberystwyth Castle. In the 16th century it was the chief residence in the Manor of Llanbadarn Fawr. Its remains were demolished in 1967 to provide a site for a new primary school.

Camera obscura and cannon on the Castle grounds

Plas Crug c. 1880

The Castle ruins

The Growth of Aberystwyth

If those who planned the town in the 13th century thought to attract enough people to fill the space within the walls with houses, they must have been very disappointed. It remained more than half empty for five hundred years. Aberystwyth in the 1570's was a very small place, having no more than three or four score of inhabited dwellings and as many if not more uninhabited ones, most of them in ruins. Nevertheless, it was at least as big as Cardigan, for in 1553 it was ordered that the shire court be held alternately at Aberystwyth and Cardigan, instead of only in the latter. By 1595 the former was the most populous town in the county and in 1605 the Justices of the Assize in Cardigan were instructed to keep an assize or Great Sessions in Aberystwyth once a year at least. Any growth in the town at this time must have been almost entirely due to the development of the lead mines, and under Sir Hugh Myddelton and Thomas Bushell this continued and increased until the Civil War, when the town suffered much damage, many of its houses being reduced to "rubbidge".

Seventeenth century records refer to the following streets, usually giving the Welsh names—*Heol y Porth Tywyll* or *Heol y Porth Mawr* (Great Darkgate St.), *Heol y Weeg* (Pier St.), Castle St., (Upper Great Darkgate St.), *Heol y Bont* (Bridge St.), *Heol y Bwlch Bach* (Eastgate), and Barkers Lane (Queen St.). Great Darkgate St. and Bridge St. appear to have been full of houses, but Pier St. was flanked by arable land along most of its south side. There were very few houses in Castle St. and

Barkers Lane, and not many in Eastgate. Trefechan, too, contained very few houses. In 1636 that part of the town lying between Barkers Lane and the town wall to the south, was called *Gerddi Gleision* in Welsh and the "King's Lands" in English. Mill Lane was almost certainly in existence, a cart track running between the wall and what was called *Tan-y-dref* (Under the Town). There were no buildings on it apart from the corn mill near Trefechan Bridge.

The first half of the 18th century was largely one of disappointment and stagnation in lead mining in North Cardiganshire and this was reflected in the development of the town. A comparison of what is known about Aberystwyth in the late 17th century with what is shown in Lewis Morris's crude map of 1748 shows little or no further growth in the town. William Morris's map of Aberystwyth *c.* 1750 tells the same story.

The Aberystwyth of this period, and until late in the 18th century was far from attractive. Writing in the 1720's Defoe said "This town is enriched by coals and lead which is found in the neighbourhood, and is a populous but a very dirty, black, smoky place, and we fancied [the people] looked as if they liv'd continually in the coal or lead mines." There were no coal mines in the neighbourhood but there was dirt in plenty in the town. Until late in the 18th century, most of the inhabitants threw household refuse into the streets and even kept dung-hills in front of their houses. Drains were open and even stinking fish was allowed to lie in the street.

Food was cheap but wages were low. In 1755 the cost of meat, per pound, was beef

Lewis Morris's Map of Aberystwyth 1748

2½d., mutton 1½d., veal and pork 2d. or less. Meat was never sold by the pound but by the piece and was rarely bought by the common people because they could not afford it. Also the meat market was then in Llanbadarn and it was difficult to buy meat in Aberystwyth. Other prices were, a goose 8d. to 1s., a duck 6d., a chicken 2d. or 3d., a barndoor fowl 4d. or 5d. Butter was 3d. lb. and cheese 1½d., while eggs were 10 a penny. The Rheidol was rich in trout, salmon and lampreys at this period, but the last named were never eaten by the towns-people because they were thought to be poisonous. Eels were plentiful but were rarely eaten.

Both peat and coal were used as fuel, the latter being imported from Neath and Deeside at a very high price—14s. ton. Most people used peat, which was bought in panniers slung on horses, or on drag carts, from Cors Fochno (Borth Bog) and sold in the streets of the town at 3d. or 4d. a load of 150 lbs.

Slates for building cost 6s. to 7s. a ton, but until well into the second half of the 18th century, most of the houses were thatched. The slates were thin slabs of dark grey stone held in position with pegs; moss was stuffed into any cracks to make the roof draught-proof, for there was no lime available for "parching". The source of most of the slates was the old quarry below the Edward Davies Chemical Laboratories.

Rents ranged from 16s. to 21s. a year. Men earned 6d. a day in the 1750's and had to supply their own food. In summer and in the autumn they might get 8d. because there was competition for labour from the fishing boats. Carpenters earned 1s. a day while masons received 1s. 6d., or less if he ate at his employer's table. Tailors were usually peripatetic and received on average 6d. a day and their food.

After about 1770, though the town in general did not improve much in any aesthetic or sanitary sense, it did begin to grow again, especially after the Customs House was transferred to Aberystwyth in 1763 and the port was free to grow. Aberystwyth was then exporting some 3,000 to 4000 tons of lead ore a year, and had a considerable fishing fleet. In the absence of a reliable map, details of the town's growth at this time are difficult to describe but an examination of records such as those kept by the Overseers of the Poor reveal new street names. In 1785 there is reference to Castle Green (High St.), Butcher's Row (Castle Lane), Mill Lane and Rosemary Lane (Princess St.), but according to these records, there were very few living in these streets at this time. Later appears Back Lane (Grays Inn Rd.) which was just a cart track across an open space with a house or two near its junction with Bridge St. By this time Shipwrights Row (South Rd.) was in existence and in 1792, Bonsall's Row appears. Eastgate in 1755 was almost entirely free of houses on its seaward side and its inhabitants could dispose of their rubbish by throwing it over the low cliff on to the beach. By the end of the century this was no longer possible for the street was full. One of the houses built there was "Crynfryn", Sir Thomas Bonsall's town house. An examination of the drawing of "Aberystwith" c. 1790 shows growth also in Barker's Lane and Trefechan. It also shows the first St. Michael's Church, and Castle House, almost rivalling the castle in appearance.

The Court Leet had always been opposed to the erection of buildings on the town commons but late in the 18th century there

Aberystwyth c. 1790

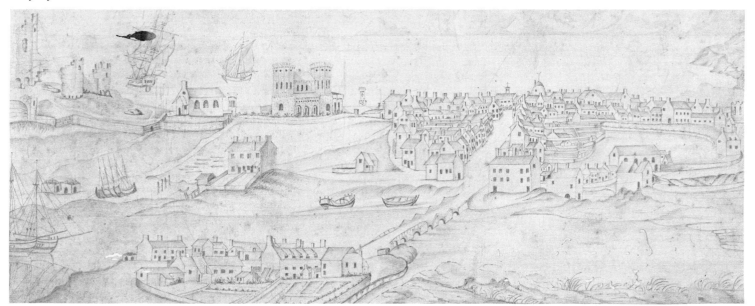

was much more demand for permission to do this. The first surrender was in 1788 when Uvedale Pryce of Foxley in Hereford was allowed to build Castle House facing the sea on a piece of open ground lying between the ancient castle and Weeg St. A few years later John Jones, a prominent man in the town and a grocer, was allowed to enclose another piece on payment of one guinea a year for a 99 year lease. His business was in Castle Lane opposite St. James Square.

The stage was now set for the assault on Penmaes-glas common, where attempts at enclosure had often been made and where, according to the overseer of the poor's records, two or three houses had already been built in 1785, in what is now High St. In 1792 in return for permission to demolish a house known as Parry's House which projected well over the pavement in Great Darkgate St., its owner John Parry was given a strip of land on Penmaes-glas on which to build houses. A Thomas Jones was leased another piece in the same area on which to build 7 houses "of the same Sieze and Dimentions" as those built by John Parry. Single plots were leased to others at a rent of 7s. 6d. a year, and a new street was born. First known as Castle Green, it became New St., then Castle Lane and, finally, High St.

In the meantime, houses were springing up elsewhere, especially in some of the half empty streets. Powell of Nanteos granted a few leases for building plots in Eastgate and in Church St. The leases were for two lives and the rent was to be paid partly in the form of two dozen of the earliest fresh herrings caught off Aberystwyth.

There was now considerable pressure on the Court Leet to allow building outside the town walls (*Yr Hen Gaer*). The first to get permission to do this were the Baptists; the first Bethel was built on its present site in Baker St. in 1797. In the same year a lease of a piece of ground 33 ft by 55 ft was granted to an ironmonger, Dafydd Jenkins y Nailer, for 99 years at 5s. *per annum*. John Williams, Saddler, was granted the next piece, and Evan Humphreys, Mariner, the third plot. Jenkins built his house below the old town wall on the site now occupied by the National Westminster Bank. Once started, building proceeded rapidly, but the name *North Parade* was not given to the street until about 1815.

It is not surprising that some of the town's inhabitants wanted to live outside the line of the old walls, for despite its growing popularity as a seaside resort, Aberystwyth in 1800 was still unattractive, with irregular, steep, narrow, ill-paved streets lined with poor, low-roofed houses covered with thatch or dark grey slates. Sanitation, while better than in the 1750's, was still bad, but the town's growth, limited though it was, had created a medley of ill-ventilated dwellings with yawning archways leading to the many narrow courts. Much of this was to be swept away in the following century; in 1801 there were 350 houses in the town, most of them of the type described above, in 1900 there were 1,800 houses including many that were a credit to any town.

In 1800 the Court Leet decided to allow building on Penmaes-glas, the greater part of which was leased to Job Sheldon, then a prominent citizen. Most of the houses in this part of the town were built between 1822 and 1840. High St. and Penmaes-glas Rd. were complete by 1832, Prospect St. by 1838 and both Sea View Place and Custom House St. were in being, but not complete, in 1834, the former being then called Beach St. and the latter Sea View Place. The Customs House was built there before 1834.

Then the Court Leet began to permit more development of land outside the town walls, a policy which led to the revival of of an old claim by the Powells of Nanteos. In the town's early days the Crown claimed certain rents and tolls; the right to hold fairs and markets and to trade cost the town £1 a year. Five score of the first herrings brought into the port went to the Crown's representative, this was afterwards commuted to a payment of £1 10s. a year. These rights were held for centuries by the Pryses of Gogerddan but about 1700 they were leased to the Powells; the payment of the tolls of herrings was then revived and the fish continued to be sent to Nanteos until well into the 19th century.

But Nanteos claimed that their lease from the Crown gave them other rights, and in 1724 a conflict arose between the Powells and the inhabitants of Aberystwyth. Powell claimed the right to hold Court Leets in the town, to admit burgesses, and to appoint the Mayor and other officers. The town disputed this, litigation ensued and the verdict went in favour of the town. But the Powells did not give in easily, on another occasion, when it was known that the Court Leet had squandered most of its money on feasting and other things, Nanteos, knowing that the town could not afford to go to law, threatened another action concerning some land over which the Powells' claimed manorial rights. But they were thwarted by the Pryses who offered to lend money to the Corporation. On hearing this the Powells withdrew their claim.

When the town began to extend beyond the line of the old walls early in the 19th century, Nanteos put forward a claim to parts of the common and waste lands concerned, and there was again litigation, which again went in favour of the town. But the costs of the action proved heavy-£3,729, and the town authorities were forced to sell off parts of the common in a number of places, particularly on the lower slopes of Pendinas. It was also decided to let land on long leases on the payment of substantial "fines".

The land to the north of North Parade was let in plots on lease and by 1834, as the map on page 13 shows, a large number of houses had been built in that area. There were then 60 houses in Terrace Rd., Portland St. was over half-full, Corporation St. (called Alfred Place on the map) was full on one side, and North Parade was complete except for the north-east corner.

Land on the south or "pool" side of North Parade from Chalybeate St. to the tollgate was leased in 1805 to John Jones for 99 years at £1. 1s. *per annum*. When granted, part of it was under water and there was almost always a pool in one part of this area, a fact of which Cambrian St. is often well aware. After spending some money on drainage, Jones or his widow, Jane, sublet most if not all of it to David Lewis who, between 1820 and 1830, built Lewis Terrace

Old Prospect Street

(that part of Alexandra Rd. now running from Terrace Rd. to Chalybeate St.), Chalybeate Court and Thespian St. He then began building Moor (Cambrian) St. and lower Terrace Rd., then called Mary St. after his daughter, and by 1840 there were 39 houses in these two streets while Chalybeate Terrace, now Chalybeate St., was complete. Building then gradually extended eastwards to the new Chalybeate Terrace, that part of Alexandra Rd. between Brewer St. and Thespian St., opposite the Chalybeate Well, and John Jones's land was

completely built up.

The expansion of the town was rapid in the first half of the 19th century, especially from 1831 to 1841 when 254 houses were built. The number of dwellings in the town increased from 350 in 1801 to 1,020 in 1851.

In anticipation of a marked increase in population when the railway came in 1864, there was another spurt in building, 60 houses had been completed in Queens Rd. by 1860 and Newfoundland St. (Bath St.) was completed between 1870 and 1880.

The last quarter of the century saw not

Chalybeate Terrace, corner of Alexandra Road and Thespian Street

Floods in Cambrian Street and Place

only a continuation of building, but also a considerable amount of rebuilding. The whole of the northern side of North Parade from, and including the Y.W.C.A. building eastwards was rebuilt, the present tall, well-built houses taking the place of "mean and paltry buildings". The Temperance Hall was demolished by the man who built it, the Rev. John Williams who, having already built Stanley Terrace, was completing the north-east corner of North Parade and a neighbouring portion of Queen's Rd., using new methods of building foundations so as to defeat the treacherous, unstable sands of Morfa Swnd (Sand Marsh) which gave Seilo Chapel so much trouble.

Much of all this building and rebuilding was being undertaken by local business and professional people. In addition to the Rev. John Williams, there was William Rowlands, butcher, no novice in building, who was busily engaged in erecting the lofty structure at the junction of North Parade and

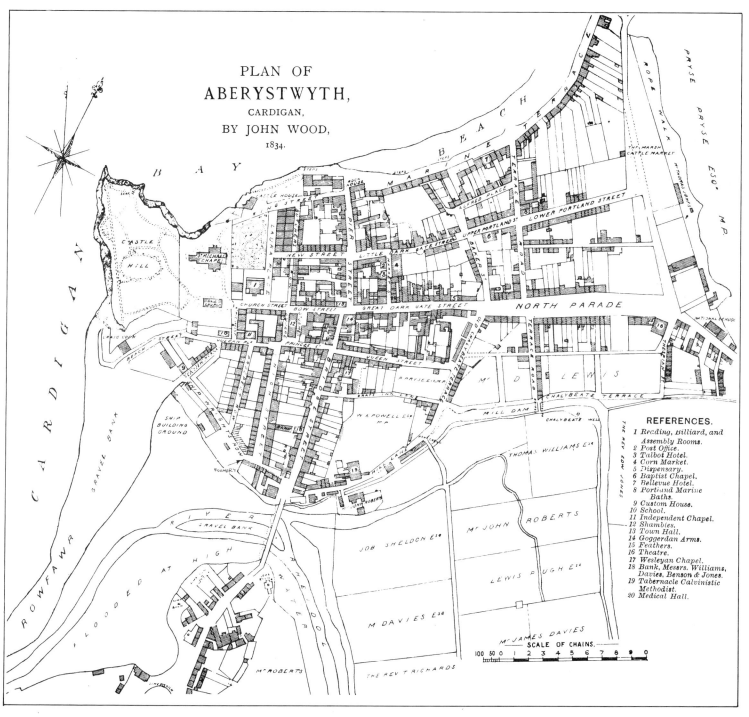

PLAN OF
ABERYSTWYTH,
CARDIGAN,
BY JOHN WOOD,
1834.

REFERENCES.
1 Reading, Billiard, and
  Assembly Rooms.
2 Post Office.
3 Talbot Hotel.
4 Corn Market.
5 Dispensary.
6 Baptist Chapel.
7 Bellevue Hotel.
8 Portland Marine
  Baths.
9 Custom House.
10 School.
11 Independent Chapel.
12 Shambles.
13 Town Hall.
14 Goggerdan Arms.
15 Feathers.
16 Theatre.
17 Wesleyan Chapel.
18 Bank, Messrs. Williams,
  Davies, Benson & Jones.
19 Tabernacle Calvinistic
  Methodist.
20 Medical Hall.

SCALE OF CHAINS.
100 50 0 1 2 3 4 5 6 7 8 9 0

The interior of Temperance Hall

Houses in North Parade built by the Rev. John Williams

Chalybeate St. now occupied by Morgans the Jeweller and its neighbours. Houses were being built for sale around Bryn-y-mor Dingle in the 1890's by David Phillips and Powell the grocer. Queen's Rd., too, was becoming built up, Alderman Palmer, Mayor in 1891, not content with his greenhouses, gardens and hotels, was building another terrace of "well built houses", i.e.

Cambridge Terrace, which, with the Roman Catholic Church, the Life Boat House moved there from the end of Rofawr in the 1870's, and Dr. Bonsall's house, "added immensely to the appearance of this thoroughfare". Dr. Bonsall's house, now the office of the Royal Commission on Ancient Monuments (Wales) was built in 1896, apparently to serve as a nursing home. It is an attractive and unusual colonial-style building, with a two-storeyed, cast iron veranda. The Town Hall was built in Queen's Rd. in 1845/6, the present building, which has received a Civic Trust Award, is an attractive reconstruction of the old building which suffered severe fire damage in 1957.

Another amateur building contractor of the 1890's was William Thomas, coal merchant, and Mayor of the town in 1892. No sooner had he bought Banc Sion Rees, the hillside area behind the Town Hall, than he began to sell freehold plots. Building began there in the late 1890's and parts of North Rd., Loveden Rd., Trevor Rd., and Lisburne Terrace soon made their appearance.

Cae Charles, the field lying between Plas Crug and the Buarth (then known as Buarth Mawr), was completely transformed in the late 1890's. When the lease expired and the field reverted to the Corporation, they filled the lower part of it in with quarry waste, raising its level above that of Plas Crug. It was then considered as the site for the new County School, but Ardwyn House came on to the market before a final decision had been made. The Cae Charles lease was then auctioned and acquired by T. E.

Salmon who set about developing the area. Building began in 1896 and soon part of the southern side of Alexandra Rd., Elm Tree Avenue and Stanley Rd. were built, followed by other streets in the area around Holy Trinity Church. It is interesting to note that the first name given to Edgehill Rd. was *Heol y Crefftwyr* (the Craftsmen's Street) Northgate St. was built, or rebuilt, in the 1860's, but building on Penglais Rd. below Sylvan Palace did not begin until about the time that Cae Charles was developed. This was also the time (c. 1900) when Terrace Rd. was widened. The Post Office in Great Darkgate St. was built by Daniel Thomas, the draper, in 1906.

On the other side of the town, on what had once been known as the *King's Lands*, and owned by Nanteos, the need for accommodation for workers on the railways was one of the reasons given for the building, in the mid 1860's, of Powell St., William Street and George St., named after the Nanteos brothers.

David Jones's Central Meat Stores at corner of Chalybeate St. and North Parade

The decline in shipbuilding had affected the prosperity of the timber yards and when those on Rofawr were burnt down around 1890, the owner, D. C. Roberts, decided to use the area for building. In 1894, 18 houses were built on South Marine Terrace, 9 in South Rd., 5 in Sea View Place and 4 in Trefechan.

At the end of the 19th century it was maintained by George Eyre Evans that practically every building standing in 1800 had disappeared, and all the empty spaces inside the boundaries of the old town had been built on. This was largely true and indicates the extent of both the building and the rebuilding in the town during the century. Outside these limits, Morfa Swnd was fully built up by 1904, North Road was almost complete, and housing had crept along Llanbadarn Rd. and its byways as far

Morgans the Jewellers

as Llain y Gawsai, as it was originally called. Similarly, Penglais Rd. had been developed on the south side to well beyond the workhouse but Elysian Grove remained empty of houses until the late 1930's when a housing estate was built there.

The building of Gogerddan Cottages at the bottom of the southern side of Penglais Rd. has an interesting link with Sir John Gibson, the dynamic proprietor and editor of the *Cambrian News*. Before coming to Aberystwyth he lived in Oswestry where he

Old Poplar Row

was a leading campaigner for better housing and had prepared a scheme for building seven houses at Swan Hill in that town. The scheme involved a method of payment whereby the occupiers became the owners of their houses. Gogerddan Cottages were erected on a similar principle by the Town Council after much prodding by Sir John Gibson.

Much of the development to the east of the town was to provide middle class types of houses for prosperous professional and

Mary Street, old lower Terrace Road

business men who no longer wanted to live over their offices and shops. The College, too, was expanding and houses were needed for the staff.

But despite all this development and redevelopment, there was still much to be done. In 1900 the Corporation, in order to secure a loan to effect improvements, prepared a report on housing which stated that out of the 1,800 dwellings in the town, 500 had only 4 rooms each, and in these 7, 8 and even more persons had to live because of the scarcity of houses. Having been granted a loan, the Town Council began to build low-rent houses early in the 20th century. In 1904 they built 24 houses in Greenfield St., six years later 11 were built in Skinner St., 5 in Poplar Row and also some in Trinity Rd. The year 1912 saw 13 houses built in Glanrafon Terrace and 17 in Spring Gardens, Trefechan, all early examples of municipal enterprise.

Very little building had been done in Penparcau during the 19th century or before. Until late in the last century all the houses were of the old-world type, low-roofed and white washed, some with cob walls. Southgate (or Piccadilly as it was then called), was no more than a few houses clustered round the turnpike gate, and the house of Antaron. In October 1894 the area lost its only public house, the Piccadilly Inn.

Between the two wars, however, Penparcau was to get a massive increase in its population, 130 houses were built by the Corporation on Caeffynnon from 1927 to 1939. Trefechan was given 10 on *Yr Odyn* (the Lime Kiln) in the same period.

Since 1945 almost every available space in the town and its environs has been built on by the council and private enterprise, and Penparcau now contains so many houses east and west of Penybont, that it is itself the second largest settlement in

Ceredigion. Housing has spread up the slopes of the hills overlooking the town—Penygraig, Caemelyn and Danycoed, and there has been considerable development on the Waun. The borough boundary was extended in 1914 as far as Llangawsai and Waunfawr but as stated elsewhere, further expansion in 1938 was rejected by the townspeople.

Moving Western Parade to widen Alexandra Rd.

Western Parade today

Local Government

The charter which created Aberystwyth did not refer specifically to any form of government, what was conceded to the settlement by Edward I was the right to hold a manorial court. From that time until 1835 the town's affairs were almost certainly governed to a large extent by a Court Leet of which the chief officer was the Mayor. The town's records go back only to 1689 but it is known that Aberystwyth had a Mayor (William Vaughan) in the reign of Edward IV, c. 1450. The original aim of the Court was to view the frankpledges of the freemen within the liberty who had given mutual pledges for the good behaviour of each other. Besides this, they had jurisdiction for the preservation of the peace and the punishment of certain minor offences against the public good. Records show that from at least 1689, onwards twice a year, the Mayor issued a writ to the borough's two bailiffs instruct-them to proclaim the holding of a Court Leet, and to summon to it 24 (later increased to 30 or 40) of the burgesses whom the Mayor nominated in the writ. These formed what was called the "Grand Jury of the Town, Liberty and Borough of Aberystwyth," probably established in 1380. At these meetings the Jury admitted new burgesses, heard complaints from anyone that chose to make them, and made presentments. At every Michaelmas Leet the Jury also presented the persons to be appointed as officers of the borough for the following year—the Mayor, Coroner, two Bailiffs and two Constables, and the appointments made seem never to have been questioned. Very occasionally, other appointments were made, as in 1708 when, in accordance with a certain law, the Jury presented two "Searchers and Sealers of Leather". From 1736 onwards it became the custom to designate certain people as Aldermen, all apparently former mayors. Nothing is known of how they were appointed or if they had special duties.

In fact, some of the government of the town was in the hands of the Court of Quarter Sessions, which had as much jurisdiction in Aberystwyth as in the rural parts of the county, except that the borough appointed its own coroner and claimed to be exempt from the authority of the county coroner. The Mayor seems also to have acted as High Constable.

The Mayor was not, *ex officio*, a Justice of the Peace and Aberystwyth had no municipal J.P.'s so that when the services of such an official were required, the town had to rely on one of those local gentry who were magistrates. Without their help "the profane swearer could not be fined, the drunkard set in the stocks, or the vagrant whipped." When Dr. Pococke visited the town in 1786 he complained that "the People of Aberystwith" were "a profligate lot who do themselves justice on all strangers". This was after he saw some local men attack visitors outside an inn, and he attributed this lawlessness to there being no magistrate residing in the town. The only offences that could be dealt with by the town's own officers were nuisances such as failing to keep the streets cleared, or failing to observe the many regulations concerning the common pasture. Aberystwyth did not even have its own lock-up, or a prison; the House of Correction in the town was built, administered and repaired by the Quarter Sessions. It did have its own stocks and whipping post, but it did not have the right to licence alehouses or to authorise the performance of plays in the Town Hall. The appointment and supervision of Overseers of the Poor and the fixing of the poor rate was a matter for the County Magistrates, as was the repair of the roads. The Court Leet was responsible for the paving, cleansing, lighting and watching of the streets, but failed to do this well because it lacked money. It also presented people for not clearing dunghills from the streets, or for not cleaning and mending gutters, or for obstructing the thoroughfares with carts etc.

The first scavengers were appointed by the Quarter Sessions, the town did not have its own until 1763 when John Jones and John Lloyd Esquires were appointed to that office. In 1808 these were 8 scavengers, two for Bridge St., two for Great Darkgate St. and four looking after the remainder of the town, a measure of the concentration of population in the various streets. The office must have been profitable, for in 1811 Edward Evans took over Great Darkgate St. from John Davies and paid the Chamberlain (the Borough Treasurer) £8 for the privilege. In 1815, no less a person than Job Sheldon, always on the look out for a bargain, and Mayor in 1814, paid £10 to become a Scavenger. The official Scavengers did not do the work themselves and had to pay others, so they must have extracted a fee from householders to remove their rubbish, some of which was good fertilizer. From 1826 to 1834 the Scavengers were the Overseers of the Poor and Churchwardens,

and they employed paupers to do the work. The comments of visitors on the state of the town around 1800 suggest that the Scavengers did not do their work very well. Being unable to levy a rate, the Court Leet's power to organise services was very limited and a serious obstacle to improvement, especially after 1800 when the town began to grow rapidly.

The greater part of the Court's time was spent on the management of the commons and wastes (see Law and Order). Next in importance came the markets and fairs and the harbour. The Court's ability to ensure fair trading, too, was limited by its lack of powers; the inspection of weights and measures was in the hands of the Quarter Sessions. When expensive works, repairs, or additions were needed in the markets and harbours, the Court had to place these in other hands. To get the harbour repaired and improved, an Act had to be obtained in 1780 authorising the placing of the haven in the hands of trustees empowered to raise loans, something which the Court Leet could not do. Similarly, to get a new meat market in St. James Square in 1823, the site had to be leased to six inhabitants who undertook to build the market.

Burgesses were appointed by the Court Leet and had to pay a fee; in 1833 it was 10s. 6d. They had at least four privileges, the right to trade in the town, exemption from the payments of market and corn tolls within the borough, the right to pasturage on the town commons and, after 1536, the right to vote in the election for an M.P. for the Cardigan Boroughs.

For centuries the most important of these

was the right to trade in the town. "Foreigners" i.e. non-burgesses, were barred. As the years passed the privilege which became most appreciated (and abused) was the parliamentary franchise, the right to vote for the parliamentary candidate for the Cardigan Boroughs. It enabled influential persons who had the right to create burgesses, to exercise control over the court and the elections. In 1788, Pryse of Gogerddan was said to have created a thousand burgesses in order to secure the return of the person he favoured. The same thing happened between 1740 and 1748, and between 1812 and 1817, all just before particular elections. Since each burgess had to pay a fee, and many of those elected could not afford to pay, someone was prepared to spend a great deal of money to get his way. The result was that resident burgesses were outnumbered by non-residents who should not have been accepted as burgesses.

An examination of the list of mayors for the town until about 1730, will show that the Court Leet was dominated by the leading families in the district—the Pryses of Gogerddan, Vaughans of Trawsgoed, Powells of Nanteos and, to a lesser extent, the Richardes of Penglais. Until c. 1700 the Pryses and Vaughans almost monopolised the office of Mayor. After 1730 there was a change, and more was seen of the middle class members of the town. By the 1760's the Court Leet began to give itself both legislative and executive powers. New rules were drawn up, decisions on policy formulated, leases of land granted, and expenditure incurred. New offices were also created, in

1763, in addition to the Scavengers, a Chamberlain was appointed to hold the funds of the *Corporation* of Aberystwyth, and the bailiffs became Sergeants of the Mace.

But these changes were to produce another form of domination, by a small clique of well-to-do merchants and shopkeepers who took it in turn to fill the different offices, summoned the same persons, principally the non-resident tenants of the local squire and M.P. for the borough, year after year to serve on the Jury, and by so doing kept themselves in office to the exclusion of other people until an elected Town Council was formed in 1835. These newcomers to power, almost all Tory in politics and Anglican in religion, supported the old dominating ways because it proved profitable to do so. If gave them control of the town property, it enabled them to dine at the town's expense and it enabled them to acquire long leases of corporation property on very favourable terms indeed, and thereby make considerable sums of money by subletting the land so acquired. The Court Leet of 1780 presented that a lease for 99 years of a plot of land should be granted to the Mayor, John Hughes, without any entry of the presentment being made. He promptly sold the lease for £100 and this sum was never credited to the town. In 1828 it was found necessary to buy back the lease at the town's expense. These accounts were not published.

John Jones, Mayor on at least two occasions, acquired a lease of all the land now covered by the south side of North Parade—Cambrian St., Cambrian Place, Terrace Rd. and Alexandra Rd.—for a rent of a guinea a year. He sublet it to David Lewis at what was probably a substantial profit.

The outstanding example was Job Sheldon, Mayor at least twelve times. The town had cause to be grateful to him for preventing the Corporation from selling land and getting them to grant leases instead, but he made a great deal of money out of the leases he acquired. It is interesting to record what one of the Municipal Corporation Commissioners had to say of him and of local government in Aberystwyth in 1833, when Job Sheldon was Mayor.

"for the last ten years the office of Mayor has been filled by three individuals in rotation (Morris Davies, Henry Benson and Job Sheldon), one of these, Mr. Job Sheldon, has filled that office seven times during the last fifteen years. A majority of the jury has been commonly composed of non-resident burgesses, the tenants of Mr. Pryse, the sitting Member for the Borough, who is of the same political party with the ruling few who have been mentioned. . . . Mr Sheldon is the lessee of two parcels of property, which is now of very considerable value. How far this gentleman may have availed himself of his influence in the Corporation for the purpose of obtaining a beneficial lease of the property in question . . . or how far improvident bargains may have been made on the part of the Corporation in the other leases granted by them, it would now be difficult to determine; the transactions were not conducted in such a way as to be altogether free of suspicion; in most instances no valuation appears to have been made, nor any public competi-

tion invited, prior to the agreement being entered into."

One of the parcels leased to Job Sheldon was most of Penmaes-glas Common, which he subleased to builders at a substantial profit.

This was the state of affairs in 1833 when the Municipal Corporations Commissioners began their inquiry. They found that for many years the Court Leet in Aberystwyth seemed to have been concerned largely with the promotion of the political and other ambitions of the Gogerddan family. In 1726 an action was brought against the Town Clerk and Pryse of Gogerddan for administering an illegal oath to the burgesses of Aberystwyth, to the detriment of Powell of Nanteos. The case was tried in Hereford and Powell was given the verdict. Every burgess on admission was supposed to take an oath to serve the King and the inhabitants of Aberystwyth, to administer equal justice to the poor and to the rich, and to keep all orders for the good government of the town. Powell complained that the oath administered by the Town Clerk in the 1720's was "to serve the King and be faithful to the House of Gogerddan".

The Reform Act of 1832 seems to have had little effect on local government but the Municipal Corporations Act of 1835 brought about a big change. According to this, all the privileges, customs and rights of the old Corporation were abolished, and the town given a new form of government and constitution. The new Corporation was to have a Mayor, Treasurer, Town Clerk and an elected council of 4 Aldermen and 12 Councillors. One-third of the councillors were to retire each year and there was to be an annual election to replace the retiring members. With some limitations, the franchise was extended to include every male person over the age of 21 years who occupied, as owner or tenant, any house or place of business and who paid the rates inside the borough boundary. The old burgess qualification was abolished. To qualify for election to the council, candidates had to posses property or estates worth £500, or occupied land assessed at £15 per annum inside the borough.

Another reform was the setting up by a local Act of the Town Improvement Commissioners in 1835 to deal with sanitation, light and water, functions which the new Town Council did not possess, and services of which the town was in great need. The promoters of the Bill were largely the landowners of the district and leading inhabitants of the town, and it was maintained by some that this was done by the leaders of the old Corporation to retain for themselves the key areas of local government. There was some truth in this, there were 36 Commissioners and together they proved to be a self-elective body. Twelve vacated their seats annually but were invariably re-elected unless they held views different from those of their fellow Commissioners. The town management was largely in their hands, for the Town Council was a weak body which met only four times a year. Many of the councillors were also Commissioners.

Until elections were held, the new Commissioners were Pryse Pryse, Gogerddan; David Davies, Crugiau; Roderick Richardes, Penglais; Thomas Powell, Nanteos; Thomas Williams, Vere Webb, Pierce Evans, and the Rev. John Hunter. On 22 March 1836 the above were replaced by Pierce Evans; John Roberts the Tanner; John Morgan, Watchmaker; John Matthews Senior, Land Surveyor; William Williams, Land Agent; John Jones Atwood, Solicitor; John Williams, Draper; and Abel Powell Davies, Innkeeper. The democratisation of local government had begun. The secretary was a solicitor, William Howell Thomas who was paid £5 a year for his servicess.

These men set to work with a will, the first item on their minutes was a payment to some constable for arresting some vagrants. It was resolved to appoint a watchman to assist the constables and a uniform was ordered for him from Jenkins the Tailor. It must have been a grand outfit for it cost £9. 2s. 6d., an enormous price in those days.

Then the commissioners started tidying up the town. Carts, waggons or other carriages were forbidden to carry any stone, bricks, lime, metal, sand or any other heavy materials along Marine Terrace, except to the houses there. They were ruining the road. It was also ordered that an old boat abandoned on the beach in front of the Terrace be removed, or the owner would be summoned to appear before the J.P.'s. The borough surveyor was instructed to put the Terrace road in proper repair and to see to the repair of the wall protecting it from the sea.

They next turned their attention to North Parade, ordering that its northern end be filled in with quarry waste to provide a "dry promenade". Later the road leading from North Parade to Waterloo Bridge was also ordered to be repaired and a channel formed on the north side paved over and two gratings placed on the covered channel. Waterloo Bridge spanned the leat opposite the entrance to Terrace Rd.

Much later, in 1864, when part of the north side of North Parade was being transformed from a collection of poor houses into a handsome street, the Commissioners had it lined with trees, a gift from the woodlands of Nanteos. It was hoped that they would prove "a great Ornament" to that part of the town. This was also the year when they widened Marine Terrace.

At first the Commissioners found it necessary to continue the Court Leet practice of warning and fining people for throwing rubbish into the streets or using the commons unlawfully, but in time this became a rare occurrence. They also dealt with complaints from people about the condition of roads, as when Capt. Richards of Bryneithin complained of the state of the turnpike road in Trefechan.

The German Band on Marine Terrace

Entertainment, too, became partly their concern. In February 1847 they voted £20 for the services of a German band which then, and for several years afterwards, played on the promenade in summer, conducted by Philip Hurts. The £20 was supplemented by collections. The band later came under the direction of Jacob Leon, whose jeweller's shop in Pier St. was much frequented by the aristocrats of the district and wealthy visitors. He was himself elected a Town Commissioner in 1852.

Much of the town's business was done in the bar of the Lion Royal where the Commissioners often met. A frequent visitor was Dr. Edwards, a severe magistrate who was over fond of his drink. One night, as on many other occasions, he had to be helped home. Next morning he levied a very heavy fine on a sailor brought before him for drunkenness. The sailor protested, pointing out that he was the one who had helped Dr. Edwards to get home. The reply was "I can

afford it, you can't", an odd answer from a J.P. The Lion is now Padarn Hall.

Much of the above was work that should have been done by the Town Council but, as stated above, it was then an ineffective body and many of the councillors were also Improvement Commissioners. The latter's primary function was to provide Aberystwyth with lighting, water and sanitation. The first was accomplished within a few years. In 1838 William Morley Stears was given permission to set up gasworks in the town and these were built on the site now occupied by the Wales Gas Office in Park Avenue. The town had 80 gas lamps by 1840. The history of the concern is described with other industries below. The provision of water and sanitation were expensive undertakings and under the Act of 1836 the Commissioners could borrow up to £12,000 and, to repay this, could levy a rate of up to 2s. 6d. in the pound. They began by applying for a loan of £4,000 and, after much trouble with the Exchequer Office, this was granted. They then levied a rate of 9d. in the pound on every house rated at £10 a year or over, and 6d. on those under £10. In 1837 they had to borrow another £1,000.

From then on the Commissioners were plagued by a shortage of money. They even borrowed from some of their own members; John Roberts the tanner lent them £300 in 1841. In 1848 the work of improvement came to a halt because they had run out of money; £2,000 was needed to open another well near Llanbadarn. Five years later one of their number, Richard Watkins, was in London negotiating for a £5,000 loan from a

Church of England institution to pay off the Public Works Loans. The rate of interest charged by the Church was well below that paid for a Government loan. In 1869 they were again out of money and trying to borrow £3,000 to complete part of the sewerage works.

When the Commissioners took office, the water supply for the town was very poor.

The Lamplighter

Jacob Leon

It is difficult to imagine life without a constant supply of pure water "on tap" at home or, at least, from a nearby standpipe, but that was the state of affairs in Aberystwyth until well into the 19th century, and for many, until the 1870's and later. As Fairholt's drawing of Trefechan Bridge in 1797 shows, water carried in barrels from the rivers and the Mill Leat supplied the needs of some, but there were many more who could not afford to buy water and had to fetch their own from the rivers, streams, springs and wells. Of the last two the best known were the following:

The *Castle Well* was right inside the fortress. When the latter was demolished in the late 1640's the well became covered with debris and was lost until 1844 when it was uncovered during excavations. It was found to be 60 feet deep but the water in it was neither plentiful nor pleasant to drink, and the well was bricked over to prevent accidents. In 1950 it was again opened up and covered instead with an iron grid.

Near the Castle, between it and what became Laura Place, was a well with the unsalubrious name of *Ffynnon Twlc yr Hwch* (the Well of the Pigsty). Nothing is known of it except that it was much in use for centuries and yielded good water.

On the south side of the castle was *Ffynnon Graig Goch* (the Well of the Red Rock) near Graig Goch in a garden at the bottom of Sea View Place. It was believed to have curative qualities and was visited regularly by people suffering from eye troubles. As with other such wells, the water was thought to be most effective early in the morning; it came through a narrow spout and was usually drunk through a straw.

The well which received most publicity was the *Chalybeate Well* which was discovered by accident about 1779 on the common to the south of the Mill Leat where the railway goods yard now lies. Until about 1820 the well was reached *via Tan-y-Dref*, later called Chalybeate St., over *Corry Bridge* which spanned the mill leat, and along Chalybeate Walk. After Terrace Rd. came into existence, the leat was crossed by means of *Waterloo Bridge*. A small square stone building was erected by Thomas Johnes of Hafod over the well, the water from which was raised by a small pump. The water was stated to be every bit as good as that in Tunbridge Wells and there was plenty of it. On the door of the hut was painted the words—

CHALYBEATE WELL
Keys kept by
ANN JONES
No. 7 Brewer St.

The well was never very popular with the visitors and the building was demolished and the well sealed off when the railway company took over the land in 1867.

Trefechan had three good wells. The one behind the Fountain Inn proved very useful indeed to David Roberts when he opened his Brewery. He was also able to draw on a well behind Beehive Terrace, said to be chalybeate and called *Ffynnon yr Ancor*. The third was known as *Ffynnon Gymmyrch*, halfway between Trefechan and Melin y Mor, the corn mill behind Tanybwlch beach.

Penparcau had its best well on *Caeffynnon*, where the oldest group of council houses was built in the late 1920's

At the eastern end of the town, near the turnpike gate, in a field stretching from the gate to the barracks, was another *Caeffynnon Well*. This was believed to yield the best water in the town for making tea, and people from other parts of the town would fetch water from it when they planned a special tea-party. This may have been the same well as that said to be in *Cae Bach y Tyrpeg* (the Little Turnpike Field) which supplied Poplar Row with water:

Further east, on Llanbadarn Rd. and opposite the entrance to the former Vicarage, now St. Padarn's Primary School, was a well which excited much fear. It was said to be haunted by the Llanbadarn goblin, *Bwci Bach Llanbadarn*. Before being built up, the area was well wooded and must have been a frightening bit of road at night. The fear was made all the greater by the reddish colour of the water on occasions—"the colour of blood". In fact the colour was due to the chalybeate nature of the water.

Some houses and hotels had their own wells, there was one at Loveden House, at the Skinners Arms and, so it is said, at the Talbot Inn. There must have been many others also, for the work of carrying water to make beer, or to supply the needs of visitors in a large hotel, would otherwise have been daunting in the extreme. There was said to be a sulphur spring near the Penglais mansion.

To improve this situation the Commissioners' plan was to build a reservoir in Bryn-y-mor Dingle to the north of the town, where water could be collected from the streams, springs and marshy tracts in that area. Reservoirs were also to be built at Elysian Grove and Cefnhendre to supplement the supply, if necessary.

James Hughes was paid £124 for the land in Bryn-y-mor and Roderick Richardes received about the same for Elysian Grove. The latter was later handed back to Penglais at a rent of £5 per annum on condition that it would be available when required. A sum of £3,800 was spent on building the Bryn-y-mor reservoir and on the purchase of the first lot of cast iron pipes for the distribution of the water. The design and supervision of the scheme was entrusted to Richard Page, assistant to George Bush the supervisor of the harbour works. The turncock was Edward Jones whose salary was two guineas a year. The Bryn-y-mor scheme eventually cost £5,000.

Despite all this, the town was still very

Bryn-y-mor Reservoir

short of water. In July 1844 there was such a severe drought that even more water carriers were pressed into service. This was a laborious business and particularly frustrating for people living up steep slopes which the water carriers were loth to climb. The Commissioners then produced a better scheme. With the consent of the owners of Plas Crug Meadows, known locally as the "Flats", a well was dug there and water conveyed by pipe line through Parcyddol to the corner of Thespian St. and there connected to a large tank. Using a hand pump the water carriers and residents were then able to get their water from the tank. Soon afterwards, Griffith Ellis of the Eagle Foundry nearby, loaned his steam pump to lift the water from the tank to the Bryn-y-mor reservoir. This went on for several years.

But the population of Aberystwyth was still growing and there was much building going on. There were always complaints of water shortage in summer; even at its best, the highest point to which the Bryn-y-mor reservoir could supply water was to the door step of Sion, the Congregational Chapel in Penmaes-glas, now the Red Cross headquarters. This and other elevated areas were often without water for weeks on end in the summer.

Some people did not like having to pay water-rates and would have the piped supply cut off in October and re-connected in the early summer. Less legal was the practice in some houses on Marine Terrace of having the supply cut off in the autumn and using a neighbour's piped-supply of water during the winter, and sharing the water rates.

There were many complaints about the purity of the water, for the well on the Flats lay between Llanbadarn Churchyard and the lead-polluted Rheidol river. In 1850 water samples were sent by the "Gloster" coach to William Herapath, a noted analytical chemist in Bristol. Much to the Commissioners' relief he did not find anything wrong with the water and the Flats well continued to be used. But the argument as to whether this was the best way to supply Aberystwyth with water continued.

By the 1850's there was a great deal of dissatisfaction with the Town Improvement Commissioners and, apparently, a considerable amount of pressure brought to bear on the Town Council to exert themselves more. The Commissioners were said to be tyrants and were greatly resented by the rising middle class. The political wakening of the small man was becoming apparent. The revolt against the establishment is believed to have begun on a very small scale in 1832 when it became clear that a wall would have to be built to protect the new St. Michael's church from the sea. Not being in the original plan, it could be paid for only by imposing a church rate on the town as a whole. This was not the first time that such a rate had been levied, and at least one Nonconformist had refused to pay it in 1758. By the 1830's, there was a large body of Dissenters in the town and some of these, led by John Matthews, a Land Surveyor, and Edward Locke the Customs Officer, refused to pay and, on the orders of a local J.P., had their goods distrained and auctioned for the recovery of the payments due. Such opposition was a new feature and, as the century progressed, and the small men became more aware of their strength, the ruling powers were faced with mounting criticism. The weakness of the Town Council and the inefficiency and apparent extravagance of the Improvement Commissioners were frequent topics of conversation, and were regularly debated at such literary societies as the Radicals.

While the Commissioners had succeeded in macadamising the roads, paving the streets, tidying up the town and, at a cost which was much criticised, installed gas lighting, it had failed to give the town an adequate supply of water and was a long way from completing the sanitation system. The passing of the Public Health Act of 1848 and the revelations which preceded it, and the insanitary state of parts of the town led to a great deal of agitation and criticism of the ineffectiveness of the Local Government Board set up by the 1848 Act to enforce the law. It led eventually, in 1866, to the sending of a petition to Whitehall, signed by 32 of the leading inhabitants, praying for the adoption of the Public Health Act of 1858. After much agitation in Aberystwyth, and pressure in London by the borough M.P., it was resolved in 1868 to abolish the Town Improvement Commissioners and to transfer their powers to the Town Council. In 1873 the latter came into full possession of its new powers.

The supply of water now became the concern of the Corporation, which had been made very much aware of the problem in 1870 when, during much of the summer, and the town full of visitors, water was obtainable for only two hours a day for six days in the week. The seventh being the Sabbath, there was no water at all because the turncock, who turned the supply on and off, did not believe in working on Sundays.

The discovery of a good spring on the Flats about 1871 by Haskney, a crockery dealer in Little Darkgate St., may have been the reason for the Corporations decision to purchase Plas Crug Meadows, for £7,000. It was then proposed to erect a pumping station, costing £14,000, to pump the water from Haskney's Well into the reservoir at Bryn-y-mor. The well being on well-used agricultural land and not far from the lead-polluted Rheidol river, John Gibson was strongly opposed to the scheme and advocated bringing water by gravitation from some upland area. He was opposed by George Green, and the argument went on for years, until the townspeople became divided into "Flats" and "Gravitationists".

The Town Council having already spent £7,000 on the Flats scheme, found it difficult to abandon it, particularly as it had been sanctioned by the Local Government Board. Eventually the senior inspector of the board intervened and, after a careful examination of the evidence, he supported the gravitation scheme. During the discussions that ensued, it was suggested that it would be much cheaper if water was brought by gravitation from the neighbourhood of a farm only eight miles away. But Edward Ellis, the auctioneer, produced a bottle of that water and showed it to be so polluted that it was immediately decided to look elsewhere. Dr. Harries, a prominent man in the town, then made the bold suggestion that water should be brought in from Llyn Llygad Rheidol, the source of the Rheidol river. In 1880 this was done for £18,000, including an underground line of pipes, 18 miles long, a small dam to raise the level of the lake, and a small reservoir at Cefn-llan. This remarkably cheap and efficient system was carried out without opposition from any landowner, and continues to provide Aberystwyth with excellent water to this day.

In 1910, another small service reservoir was built alongside the one at Cefn-llan and in 1913 the dam at Llyn Llygad Rheidol was raised to increase the lake's capacity. Treatment works were constructed in 1927 at Llanbadarn Fawr but, for some unknown reason, were soon abandoned.

The scheme continued to work well until the 1930's when the supply became affected by corrosion in the main pipes. At this time the Aberystwyth Rural District Council (R.D.C.) was seriously considering the problem of supplying water to its own area. Aware of the Borough's supply problems, the R.D.C. offered to pay half the cost of renewing the corroded pipes in return for a supply of water, an offer which met with the wholehearted approval of the Ministry concerned. But Aberystwyth, acting on the advice of a firm of water engineers, refused the offer and the R.D.C. decided to seek permission to bring water from Llyn Craig y Pistyll, a reservoir built about 1877 to supply some local lead mines. The Aberystwyth Rural District Council Act of 1937 gave them the necessary power, but not without some objections from Aberystwyth.

When the proposed Act was examined it was found that it embraced four parishes already included in the borough's supply area—Llanbadarn Fawr, Parcel Canol, Melindwr, Lower Vaenor—and the borough objected to this. These were then omitted from the R.D.C. scheme, but the investigation revealed that Aberystwyth had been over-charging the rural areas for water for many years. The Borough Act stated that these areas were to be supplied with water at the same rate as the borough. It is not known whether the areas concerned were reimbursed the extra rate charged to the rural areas.

The R.D.C. scheme was completed in 1939, just in time to help Aberystwyth out of an awkward situation. Once war had been declared, the town began to receive many evacuees, official and unofficial. It also became a training centre for a large number of service men and, because of the corroded supply mains, there was a shortage of water. In 1940 the Town Council was forced to ask for help from the R.D.C., which readily agreed. A new pipe line was then constructed to bring water from the R.D.C.'s main at Bow Street to the upper service reservoir at Cefn-llan. Tappings from this main have been used to supply water to Waun-fawr, Comins-coch etc.

Since the end of hostilities the corroded pipes have been replaced and a new filter plant erected at Bontgoch. One of the Cefn-llan reservoirs has been covered to prevent pollution and the other has been emptied. Both the town and rural water schemes became administered by the Cardiganshire Water Board in 1962 which was itself taken over by the Welsh Water Authority in 1974.

In the 1970's the water authority has again had to consider plans for an additional supply of water to Aberystwyth. Among these are pumping water from the Nantymoch reservoir to Llyn Llygad Rheidol, the further development of the Craig y Pistyll reservoir, the sinking of boreholes in the valley gravels alongside the river Rheidol, particularly in the Lovesgrove area, and the extraction of water from the Cwm Rheidol Regulating Pond some 7 miles away. Most of these would entail the erection of treatment works to deal with possible lead pollution. The Flats versus Gravitationist arguments might soon be heard again.

The Aberystwyth of the early 19th century had no sanitary provisions or schemes for the disposal of refuse, a state of which the records of the Court Leet provide ample testimony. A good sanitation scheme was one of the things expected of the Town Improvement Commissioners. The provision of sewers was one of the first schemes explored by the Commissioners. A public meeting was called to discuss the matter in 1836, where it was resolved to ask for estimates from George Bush, the engineer in charge of the harbour works. But since the Commissioners had no plans prepared for such a scheme, Bush was unable to give the required information. Being, as usual, short of money, they hoped to use the same trenches for both the sewers and the gas

Town councillors and others at Llyn Llygad Rheidol reservoir in 1913, at the opening of the raised dam.

pipes, but this was contrary to accepted practice and the scheme was put aside for a while. A start was made in the late 1840's when the engineer was instructed to get samples of four and six inch pipes in "glazed stone" from a Derby pottery. A sample was sent *via* Pickford's Mail to Shrewsbury, and in Morgan's wagon to Aberystwyth. The pipes recommended, and adopted, were 18 inches long and had no collars for jointing. In February 1849 it was agreed with the masters of the schooners *Omnibus* and *Enigma* to bring the pipes from Liverpool, and within a few weeks work began on the laying of sewers. Shortage of money prevented much being done at a time, there was still much to be done in 1869, but in some parts of the town sanitation had so improved that there were complaints from some people when they encountered bad smells from drains, a state which would have been taken for granted in the 1810's and later.

Some of the early sewers emptied into the Mill Leat but this was stopped and the main sewer was laid in the field to the south of the leat and emptied into the harbour. The Marine Terrace sewers seem to have emptied into the sea. The Belle Vue sewer caused many complaints, for it emptied on to the beach. Much trouble was caused to the authorities during the building boom of the 1860's, by builders who connected houses to the sewers without permission and without giving any thought to the capacity of the system. This meant relaying sewers or laying additional ones. The practice of laying sewers to the mill leat continued. These had to be taken up and relaid to join

the main sewer to the south. Some of these efforts were said to be attempts at being connected secretly so as to avoid the payment of the appropriate rates. The practice of laying sewerage pipes without cementing them together continued for some years. Excavations behind the Marine Terrace houses in the 1930's revealed nine inch pipes which had been laid in this way about the 1850's, if not later.

In 1869 the Commissioners applied for a loan of £3,000 in order to complete the Aberystwyth Sewage Works but do not seem to have received it, possibly because they were about to be disbanded. From that time onwards the work was in the hands of the Town Council whose attitude to it was very casual. It did proceed in a sporadic piece-meal fashion and John Gibson of the Cambrian News was very critical of the Council's failure to get on with the work. The collection of refuse, too, was neglected in some streets and there were complaints of unpleasant, rotting heaps of manure and refuse in parts of the town as late as the 1890's. The big flood of 1886 stressed the need for better sanitation and an attempt was then made to improve matters, but it was not until the 1920's that the towns sewerage scheme was complete and by then there had been much relaying of pipes. Early in the 1920's the Bridge St. sewer had to be relaid and caused an incident which has long remained in the memories of some older inhabitants. While the large trench was open, a young horse drawing a milk float took fright and fell into the trench. Working on that stretch was a well-known character named Tommy Parnell of Glan-

r'afon Terrace, a man of enormous strength and a boxer, but not fond of regular work. The British Legion once provided him with a power saw so that he could set up in the firewood business, but Tommy soon tired of it and went back to casual labour, especially navvying. When the horse was unable to get out of the trench, Tommy used his strength to lift it out.

The Aberystwyth Sewage Scheme comprising the pumping station, storage tanks and sea outfall extension, was completed in 1925 at a cost of £61,000. There were still a few areas not included—Penyrancor, Antaron, Plas Avenue and others, but these too were on the system by the 1960's. The pumping station at Tan y Geulan, near Trefechan Bridge now copes not only with the needs of Aberystwyth but also with the sewage of the former Aberystwyth R.D.C. There is now talk of a new system of sewage disposal for the town.

A milk float of the type involved in the incident described

The sewerage works under construction in the 1920's

During this period the council, in addition to supplying water and making improvements in sanitation, went gradually about the business of improving lighting, providing public baths, library facilities, doing what it could to develop tourism (such as building the King's Hall, providing tennis courts, bowling greens etc) and, after 1900, improving housing in the town. Its attempts to provide decent houses for the poorer inhabitants compare favourably with those of most other authorities of its size.

Until 1920 the Aberystwyth Council was the only authority in the county to erect council houses, an account of its efforts in that direction has already been given. In the inter-war years, in addition to what has been described, flats were erected in Portland Rd. and Riverside Terrace, and

Mr. and Mrs. Daniel Thomas

Until the 1870's local government in Aberystwyth had not been truly democratic, but the Reform Act of 1867 which granted the franchise to the working man, the introduction of the secret ballot in 1872 and the transference to the Corporation of the power of the Town Improvement Commissioners in 1873, did lead to a democratically elected government. The results were not startling, Nonconformists continued to vote for Nonconformists and Churchmen for Churchmen. The men elected to the Council were almost all tradesmen, businessmen and professional people who tended to be Nonconformist Liberals in politics and values. This state of affairs continued until well into the 20th century, but all were democratically elected. Labour party councillors did not appear until the early 1920's and were very few in number until the 1940's.

The Mayor, Town Council and leading officials, 1913.
The Mayor was G. Fossett Roberts and on his left are D. C. Roberts and C. M. Williams.

Proclaiming the accession of King Edward VIII 22 Jan. 1936

old buildings were converted into council dwellings. Nor did it relax its efforts after the Second World War. In 1946 it sought to purchase compulsorily a part of the north side of Penglais Rd. for the erection of 50 houses. The College objected and, after discussions, the council dropped its plan. In return much of the Penglais Estate was presented to the Corporation for a public park. The council then turned its attention elsewhere and has built houses or flats in St. John's Buildings, Thespian St., Trinity Rd., Cambrian Square, and the Harbour Crescent. Flats for old people have been erected in Rheidol Place and North Rd., the old Isolation Hospital has been turned into flats and many more houses have appeared in Penybont East. The authority's most recent efforts are the flats overlooking the harbour. Until 1972, when the Fair Rents Act was passed the Town Council was able to relate rents to earnings, but this is no longer possible. In 1974 when the old borough had to give up its estates, it owned almost a thousand dwellings in the town, a

proud record for a small town.

Over the years the Town Council has conducted some campaigns and tried some experiments. Its attempts to ban Sunday newspapers in 1894 failed and its refusal to allow Sunday boating was brought to an end in 1935 by a town plebiscite. In 1913 it actively supported the Votes for Women campaign and in 1917 was calling for a national effort to ban the sale of intoxicating liquors. It has always supported the move for an elected Council for Wales and tried hard to become its capital, receiving considerable support in the process. Among those given the freedom of the borough are Sir John Williams, Queen Victoria's physician and one of the founders of the National Library, and Sir Winston Churchill who, being unable to visit Aberystwyth, the casket commemorating the occasion was presented to him in London.

The replacement of the Quarter Sessions with the County Council in 1889 greatly increased the interest taken by the town in county affairs and, perhaps, made the town shire conscious for the first time. But it also created tensions which had not existed before. The town, proud of its ancient lineage, its famous institutions, its corporate estate and its public amenities, had high rateable values, and found itself having to contribute heavily to an upstart authority which denied it the representation on the council which was commensurate with its financial contribution. The county finances were very dependent on Aberystwyth.

In 1938 the town council decided to extend the borough boundaries and planned

to promote what was called the Aberystwyth Corporation Bill in Parliament. But before this could be done there had to be a poll of the electors. This was held and the result showed the townspeople to be strongly against expansion. This was an unpleasant surprise for the council, of whom all but one were in favour of extending the boundary. In fact, the committee chosen to consider the matter consisted of every councillor but Andreas Jones, the Penparcau builder, the only one opposed to the scheme.

The borough council remained very much in control of the town until 1974 when there was a great change. During the 1960's when the reorganisation of local government was being considered, and the "big is better" theory was widely held, administrators were so enamoured of size that they had forgotten the importance to the individual of a sense of community.

Faced with the prospect of becoming just a fringe town in a large administrative unit, the Town Council tried hard to produce an alternative to the proposed three-county merger. The most promising plan seemed to be the formation of a county of Mid Wales to include North Cardiganshire, Montgomeryshire, Radnorshire and parts of Merioneth and Breconshire. Such a county would consist of areas of similar interest and be free from the imbalance created by mixing truly agricultural, sparsely populated areas with highly populated, industrial regions. There were also precedents for the Mid Wales county in the Mid Wales Hospital Board and the Mid Wales Industrial Development Association. This plan was strongly supported by the

Aberystwyth Rural District Council but rejected by those counties which would be dismembered. The Cardiganshire County Council refused to consider any plan which split the county, and proposed the creation of a multi-purpose authority, combining the County Council, the borough councils and the district Councils. It argued that it had both the staff and the facilities to administer the whole county. This plan, unfortunately, proved unacceptable to both the boroughs and the Government.

What was created in 1974, therefore, was the county of Dyfed, consisting of the old counties of Cardiganshire, Carmarthenshire and Pembrokeshire, a creation which appeared to please only the planners. Ceredigion has at least preserved its ancient boundaries, but Aberystwyth has lost a great deal of its influence and power. The new Town Council, like the old Borough Council has its Mayor and councillors but it no longer has its housing and public health powers, and it has lost its valuable old Corporate estate with its buildings, staff and equipment. Its legal powers are now no more and no less than those of a community council.

Ceredigion District Council combines the functions of the old boroughs, the urban district councils and the rural district councils, but does not have the extensive powers of the old Cardiganshire County Council which it replaces. These powers now lie with Dyfed. In Aberystwyth the King's Hall is now the concern of the District Council, as are the public baths, tennis courts, bowling greens and most other forms of entertainment formerly organised by the borough council. The council house rents and those of other property owned by the borough an 1974, are paid to the District Council which is both the housing and the health authority for the town.

The Town Council is responsible for lighting and footpaths, its annual income of under £13,000 does not permit it to indulge in many activities. It advises the higher authorities on such matters as planning development and, in general, performs a very useful function in drawing the attention of higher authorities to any difficulties which upset life in the town. There is no doubt that Aberystwyth is now less of a force in local government than in the past. It lies both physically and psychologically on the fringe of Dyfed. The old County Council is now the Ceredigion District and if it carries out its proposal to make Aberaeron its administrative centre, Aberystwyth's role in local government will be reduced even further. Its future now seems to lie largely with tourism, the provision of higher education facilities, and a place in which to locate Central Government offices.

Law and Order

There was no effective system of police in England and Wales until that begun by Sir Robert Peel in 1830. That the town and country generally was able to do without it for so long is a testimony to the average honesty of our forefathers and, in spite of its defects, to the value of the old Poor Law.

Until the 1830's, the preservation of law and order in Aberystwyth was largely in the hands of the constables appointed by the Court Leet, six in number, only one of these being full-time. A watchman was also supposed to aid these when necessary but since the watchmen were usually very badly paid, the office was invariably held by an old or infirm man who would have been of little use in times of trouble. His work was to patrol the streets at night, call out the time at intervals and watch for suspicious characters and behaviour.

The constables were expected to apprehend wrongdoers, and, as ordered by the Court Leet in 1752, "to make diligent search for, and to apprehand all Rogues, Vagabonds and sturdy beggars that frequently beg and wander in and about this towne". This was not always an easy task, one of the first items on the minutes of the first meeting of the Town Improvement Commissioners in 1836 was the recording of £2. 4s. 6d paid to Thomas Griffiths and other constables for "the conveyance of vagrants" to the House of Correction at the bottom of Great Darkgate St. It must have been a rough affair for the clothing of one of the constables was so torn "in the line of duty" that he was paid 10s in compensation. The constables were also ex-

pected to look after, and repair, the pinfolds (pounds), the whipping post, the stocks, and to see that the commons were properly used. Looking after the commons involved considerable work. To supplement their meagre earnings many of the townspeople kept horses, cows, pigs, sheep, and geese and as long as they were burgesses they could graze these animals on the commons which surrounded the town, and on Penmaes-glas inside the walls. With the growth of population the authorities were hard put to it to control the use of these commons; non-burgesses who grazed their animals on town property were fined heavily—horse 2s., sheep 6d., horned beast 1s. The same charges were levied on burgesses who over-stocked the grazing areas. To prevent rooting, pigs had to be wired or their owners were penalised. People with gardens adjoining the commons had to keep their fences in good order or be presented before the Court Leet. As the century progressed, attempts at encroachment, the ill-usage of the commons, and the increase in the number who wished to graze animals forced the authorities to employ more and more rangers to look after the burgesses' interests. In 1772 it was resolved that even burgesses would have to pay for grazing rights—horse 6s., cow 3s. 6d., and to prevent overgrazing, no sheep, geese, or hogs were to be permitted from that time onward. Also, only those burgesses who paid rates and taxes were to be allowed grazing rights, the others had to make an extra special payment for this right. It was becoming increasingly difficult to control the use made of the commons; the increase in population and attempts at enclosure meant that the town authorities had continually to assert their claims to these lands. Occasionally the commons would be let to someone, as in 1755 when Thomas Pryse, Surveyor of the port of Aberystwyth, took all the town commons lying between the rivers Rheidol and Ystwyth for a period of seven years at 20s. a year. Later, the lands lying between the Rheidol and the road to Penparcau were similarly rented for 21 years at 10s. per annum, the money to be used for the "Benefitt of the Inhabitants of the said Town". Others were let on condition that the tenant repaired and erected fences. Thus did the town authorities try to lighten the burden of looking after these commons. The time was not far off when they would be forced to change their policy on some of them.

In accordance with the law, Aberystwyth had its House of Correction, where vagabonds, vagrants and sturdy beggars were supposed to be taught how to live useful lives. One of its punitive devices was a treadmill. In 1663 this building was in Bridge St. but had ceased to be used long before the 1750's. Its location is unknown but a report of a discovery, when building, of human bones buried somewhere near the junction of Bridge St. with either Queen St. or Grays Inn Rd. may, or may not, have been connected with it.

In 1752 it was ordered at the Quarter Sessions that a site for a new House of Correction for the north of the county be found, but nothing was done. Seven years later the Rev. Mr. Powell and Thomas Lloyd were set the same task and a temporary

building was secured in Great Darkgate St. at a yearly rent of 3s. Richard Morgan John was appointed master at a salary of 30s *per annum*. This was almost certainly the building discribed as a house of detention which stood near the site of St. Paul's Welsh Wesleyan Church, probably where the old Liberal Club now stands. It was nothing more than a low-roofed, single storey hut and was quite unsuitable for a House of Correction. It was from this hut that the notorious Morris of Cwmrhaiadr was dragged to the cart which took him to Cardigan to be tried for sheep stealing and other crimes. The gaol was later moved to the other side of the road. In 1784, for a short while, the gaoler was a woman, she was succeeded by Thomas Nightingale.

Complaints about the lack of a House of Correction continued. In 1782, at the Quarter Sessions, it was again said that it

The gaol in the 1770's was probably in the corner of this old building near the old Liberal Club in St. James Square.

was "highly necessary to build a House of Correction in the town of Aberystwyth for the purpose of punishing, keeping, correcting and setting to work Rogues, Vagabonds and sturdy Beggars and other idle and disorderly persons travelling along, residing in, or resorting to this county". Three years later Richard Foy of the Gogerddan Arms (Padarn Hall) was paid £50 for a piece of ground for this purpose but whether this was used for the building which was eventually built at the corner of Great Darkgate St. and what is now Baker St., "near the Darkgate", is not known. What is known is that in 1789 a piece of ground along part of the Town Wall, 51 yards by 60 yards was appropriated and an adequate building was erected there. In 1799 the new House of Correction with Thomas Clayton as master, was ready to receive its first 'guests'.

On the ground floor it had a kitchen and two cells, one containing six beds and the other two. Behind these was the exercise yard and the 'Black Hole', where unruly prisoners and drunk and disorderly persons were housed. The master or gaoler lived upstairs where there were two large bedrooms. Part of the wall of the old exercise yard can still be seen lining the pavement between the Baker St. Congregational Church and the corner of Great Darkgate St.

The best known of the gaolers was Jenkin Humphreys — *Siencin Jail* —who reigned there in the 1810's and 20s'. He was tall, well-built and very strong, able to handle any wrongdoer, few of whom dared fight him. His method of punishing drunk and disorderly persons was the customary

one of putting them in the stocks, where they became objects of derision and were pelted with refuse and rotten eggs by small boys. They were generally left in the stocks all night and then released.

Jenkin of the Gaol commanded much respect in the town not only on account of his physical strength but also because of his independent spirit in an age when it paid to be servile. There were three brothers living in the town at that time, two of them lawyers—James and Horatio Hughes. Between them they held almost every legal office in the county. James was considered to be a very able lawyer and it was in his office that most of the county's business was done. He had great influence and was much feared. Jenkin often ran errands for him and James resented the gaoler's independent spirit. After what appeared to have been a spirited exchange between the two when Jenkin stood his ground, the lawyer decided to teach him a lesson. One day he gave Jenkin a letter to take to a magistrate named Beynon in Newcastle Emlyn as quickly as possible. This involved a walk of over 30 miles but Jenkin reached there the following day. Beynon then gave him a letter to take to Evans, the keeper of Cardigan Gaol, 10 miles away. When Evans read the letter he said to Jenkin, who could not read, "What happened between you and James Hughes? Do you know what you've done? You've brought your own commitment to gaol." He had to go to gaol for a week but, after his return to Aberystwyth, it was noticed that henceforth it was the lawyer who feared the gaoler and he never lost that fear.

The punishment of offenders often took a severe corporal form. In 1739 it was ordered that Rees Williams, convicted of petty larceny, "be at the rising of [the] morning courts stript naked from the Wast upwards and whippt by the Master of the House of Correction until his body be bloody from the Hall Door to the Kings Arms Door". The offender was usually drawn behind a cart for this punishment but sometimes he would be tied to the whipping post outside the House of Correction or the Town Hall as was done with Griffith Hugh, a vagrant, in 1747.

This punishment was not confined only to men. In 1750 Ann Morgan was dubbed an "Idle and disorderly Person to be stripped and whipped in public" first in Lampeter and then whipped again from the Town Hall at the junction of Great Darkgate Street and Weeg Street (Pier Street) to Aberystwyth Bridge and back. To modern ears the punishment seems at times to be out of all proportion to the seriousness of the offence, as when Elizabeth Davies was "stripped naked from her waist up and whipped publickly from the late House of Correction . . . to Aberystwyth Bridge until the Blood flows on her back". Her offence was that she had taken a piece of brown cloth of the value of sixpence from 'William Evans, Farmer'. The same day a Thomas Davies was similarly treated for "taking of a Waistcoat, Breeches, Hatt, Shirt and Stockings of the value of elevenpence" and his whipping was repeated in Cardigan at a later date.

With the growth of Nonconformity the public conscience began to rebel against public whippings and for a time, at least, the punishment took place in private. It was not always as severe as it appeared. When public feelings or those of the one responsible for the punishment were in favour of the offender, red colouring was rubbed on the whip to give the appearance of blood on the victim's back. This was done by the gaoler when an old man was found guilty of stealing peat. Sometimes Jenkin was given ointment by the relatives or friends of the transgressor to rub into the parts to be whipped, this was believed to make the punishment less painful. Such mercy was not always approved by the crowd lining the route, they liked to see the blood flow.

The town stocks were either used a great deal or much neglected, for they seemed often to be out of repair. Their location at different times were St. James Square, in Great Darkgate Street opposite to the Gogerddan Arms (the Lion), and probably elsewhere too. To satisfy the public conscience they and the whipping post were moved in 1821 to the back of the Town Hall near the entrance to the Skinner's Arms, and Rowland Rowlands was paid 7s 6d., to move them. Whether the town ever had a ducking stool is not known but whenever any woman was presented at court for being a common scold there were complaints because the town lacked such an instrument of punishment. The whipping post used instead of the cart on occasions was outside the centre window of the Town Hall, near the stocks.

In 1824, at the Quarter Sessions it was stated that as the House of Correction and gaol at Cardigan were being enlarged, the Aberystwyth House of Correction was no longer needed and would be best turned into a lock-up. It appears that this was not done.

The Municipal Reform Act of 1835 gave boroughs the power to form their own police forces, and there were soon demands that this be done in Aberystwyth. Because of Gogerddan, most of the townspeople supported the Whigs and during an election in 1836, the windows of the Rev. Thomas Richards' house in Bridge St. were smashed by a mob because he voted Tory. He immediately had the windows boarded up and had written on them in large white letters "This is for want of a municipal police". In September 1837 the Corporation appointed two full-time and 33 petty or special policemen, who worked only when needed. The senior full-time man was paid 22s a week and his assistant 14s; the specials received 2s., a day when on duty. Their uniform was a dark blue frock coat, white trousers in summer and a tall black beaver hat.

The Cardiganshire Constabulary did not come into existence until 1844 and the Aberystwyth police remained an independent force until 1857 when the two were amalgamated. The Chief Constable then lived in Cardigan and the superintendent, who lived in Aberaeron, was sent to Aberystwyth to look after the north of the county. This was when the gaol in lower Great Darkgate ceased to have a resident gaoler and did become only a

lock-up. Presumably the superintendent lived there. Aberystwyth did not become the county police headquarters until a new chief constable was appointed in 1876. Five years later the old gaol was demolished and the police station familiar to all Aberystwyth people except the young, was built. This remained the head quarters of the Cardiganshire force until the move to the old Queens Hotel in 1952. The Great Darkgate St. station gave way to offices in the early 1970's.

The first chief constable was a former Army officer, Captain William Charles Freeman who disliked change so much that, despite what was happening all over the country, the police in Cardiganshire continued to wear the old uniform until 1870. During the 1870's, despite the respect they commanded, the policemen were not well paid. In addition to living in a free station house, a sergeant earned 25s a week, while constables ranged from 22s. to 19s., no better than many labourers. As a result, many left for other police forces when given the opportunity.

In June 1875 Capt. Freeman resigned on the grounds of old age after 32 years as Chief Constable. In the following January the Court of Quarter Sessions appointed in his place Major Charles Bassett Lewis, retired army officer and one-time adjutant to the Cardiganshire Militia. During his period of office the county went through one of the most difficult periods in its history, the tithe war.

In the 1870's Wales was suffering severely from an agricultural depression made worse by the financial crisis which followed the

Franco-Prussian War. An even worse cause was the opening up of new countries having vast areas of fertile soil and grass-lands where wheat could be grown cheaply, and cattle by the thousands could be bred to sell in Britain at prices well below those asked by Welsh farmers. The effects were disastrous, by 1879 the depression was very acute indeed, and continued throughout the 1880's.

The farmers of Wales had long objected to paying tithes, the depression and the spread of Nonconformity greatly intensified this dislike, meetings of protest were held and many farmers refused to pay tithes. Attempts were then made to distrain upon the goods of those who refused to pay, but these often failed because of the support given to the victims by the populace. As a result, police in considerable numbers began to be used to protect the auctioneers and bailiffs at these sales. In Cardigan-shire, as the tithe war intensified, it en-gendered a greater degree of lawlesness in other directions. More cases of arson; highway robbery, riotous behaviour and even murder were quoted by the Chief Constable in his quarterly report to the Quarter Sessions. In 1888/89 the county police had to be used frequently to attend levies and forced sales for tithes, much to the annoyance of people who sympathised with the farmers. Some of these sympath-isers were later members of the Standing Joint Committee which ordered an invest-igation into allegations that the police were being used to watch rivers and game preser-ves in the Teifi Valley and elsewhere. When this was found to be true, and that it was done by the orders of the chief constable, Bassett Lewis was dismissed from his post.

In July 1890 the Police Committee app-ointed Sergeant David Evans of the Card-iganshire Constabulary to succeed Bassett Lewis. The Home Office refused to sanction the appointment but before the disagree-ment, could be resolved, Sgt. Evans died and in December 1890, Detective Inspector Howell Evans of the Carmarthenshire Police was made Chief Constable of Cardig-anshire. He too, was faced with the prob-lem of the tithe war and during the period 1891-95, the police visited over 500 farms in Cardiganshire in order to protect from violence those bailiffs seeking to distrain the goods of those refusing to pay tithes. Howell Evans was an outstanding chief constable, he put new life into the force and brought it up to date. He made every policeman learn first aid, and he introduced fingerprinting, which was just starting to be used.

When Howell Evans died in August 1903, another attempt was made by the Police Committee to promote one of their own men, Sergeant Richard Jones, to be chief constable. But again the Home Office would not sanction the appointment and as a result, in January 1904 Inspector Edward Williams was made chief constable. One of his first acts after taking office was to promote Sgt. Richard Jones to the rank of superintendent. Edward Williams, a Flint-shire born man from the Liverpool Police force did a great deal for Cardiganshire

The Old Police Force

policemen and by insisting on a higher standard of education he raised their social status in the community. He also secured much higher pay for his men and succeeded in getting each man 59 days leave a year, including the annual leave.

Edward Williams's greatest ordeal was probably in 1911 when the King and Queen visited Aberystwyth to lay the foundation stone of the National Library of Wales. There being only 40 men in the whole of the Cardiganshire force he had to borrow and house about 100 extra men from the neighbouring counties. All went well except that some windows were smashed in the town by the sound waves created by the Navy's royal salute from the bay.

In Nov. 1921 Deputy Chief Constable Steven Jones of the Breconshire Constabulary became Cardiganshire's chief constable. During his period of office the first Mobile Patrol appeared, in March 1934. His biggest task was probably the Royal Visit to the National Library of Wales in July 1937, when he had to organise the services of 300 additional policemen from other parts of Wales as well as 250 special constables. He later had to organise the Air Raid Precaution service in the county.

The next chief constable was Superintendent J. J. Lloyd-Williams M.C. of the Metropolitan Police, who took up his appointment in May 1939. He was soon faced with the problems raised by the war and had to reorganise the special Constabulary. In March 1940 there were 600 special constables in the county but still only 42 regulars. Lloyd Williams resigned in July 1943 as a result of an inquiry into certain

Prince George at Tanybwlch with Lord Ystwyth, Col. Taylor Lloyd and the Chief Constable, Steven Jones

allegations made about him.

In January 1944 approval was given to the appointment as chief constable of Superintendent W. J. Jones. His first report to the committee expressed concern at the increasing crime rate in the county, and stressed the need for a stronger detective force than the one sergeant and one constable then covering the county. He also recommended the introduction of wireless communication, and increasing the mobile section which consisted in 1946 of one constable only. But the Standing Joint Committee was slow to adopt the recommendations and by 1958 the strength of the C.I.D. in Cardiganshire was still only 5 men, and that of the Mobile Control, six.

As a result of allegations made by Alderman M. Ll. G. Williams concerning the administration, morale and efficiency of the police force, it was resolved that the matter should be brought to the attention of the Home Secretary. As a result, a tribunal was held in January 1957 when some of the

charges brought against the chief were found proved. He was asked to resign but, as a result of an appeal made by him to the Home Secretary, a reprimand was substituted for forced resignation. He continued in office until he retired on pension in November 1958.

In accordance with the Standing Joint Committee's request, the Home Secretary appointed H. J. Phillimore Q.C., to conduct an inquiry into "the administration and efficiency of the Cardiganshire Constabulary and the state of discipline of the Force". It was held at Aberystwyth in March 1957. The report commented adversely on the efficiency of the force, attributed part of its failings to its small size, and recommended that it be merged with a neighbouring county force. The obvious neighbour was Carmarthenshire. Because of the opposition to the merger by both the police authorities, another inquiry was held by I. H. Nelson Q.C. in December 1957 and among his conclusions was one strongly in favour of the amalgamation of the two forces.

The Carmarthenshire and Cardiganshire Police Force came into being on 1 July 1958 with T. H. Lewis as the Chief Constable. On 1 July 1960 he was succeeded by J. R. Jones, who, on 1 April 1968 as the result of another merger, became the first chief constable of the Dyfed-Powys Police Force and responsible for the maintenance of law and order in Cardiganshire, Carmarthenshire, Pembrokeshire, Breconshire, Radnorshire and Montgomeryshire.

The Established Church

In the early post-Reformation period Aberystwyth was ill-served by the Church, for the town had no place of worship at all. The parish church was at Llanbadarn Fawr, a Celtic foundation and the time-honoured eccleseastical settlement for the whole area. But this was a mile and a half from the town and separated from it by a long stretch of damp and marshy land which often made church-going difficult.

During the Middle Ages, the religious needs of the garrison and, probably, those of the inhabitants of the small town, were served by the chapel within the castle, for there appears to have been no other church within the town walls. By the end of the 15th century the castle chapel had become "so much decayed" that a small chapel of ease, dedicated to the Virgin, had been erected north, north east of the castle, on what must then have been firm ground. The remains are marked on Lewis Morris's map of c. 1745 as being in front of the position now occupied by the central portion of the College. There was a stretch of green turf in that area, known as *Y Morfa,* as late as 1830. It was much bigger in former times and known as *Morfa Mawr.* and used for dancing.

According to tradition, there was an even older chapel near this site, dedicated to St. Padarn. A large pool in the rocks in front of the College was known in the past as *Pwll Padarn* (Padarn's Pool), it can only be seen now when the tide is well out. Local people used to bathe in it for curative purposes many years ago. St. Mary's Chapel was never endowed and may not have been consecrated but services were held there and were paid for out of the profits of the corn mill, known as Our Lady's Mill, near Trefechan Bridge. The Pryses of Gogerddan, who held the mill from the Crown, had to use at least part of the profits to provide divine services in the chapel. It is said that the priest-in-charge conducted marriages of the Gretna Green type in the churchyard and that this went on well into the 18th century, after the chapel was destroyed. But the site was ill-chosen, the chapel was undermined by the waves and, with part of its graveyard, eventually collapsed into the sea. It is recorded that human bones and small articles of jewellery, such as rings, have been discovered on the beach in the past. When repairs were being made to a house called Mount Pleasant, the one next to the College and the first to be built on Marine Terrace, many human bones, some skeletons and bits of coffins were discovered there. Similar finds were made near the main entrance to the College. A human skull containing a bird's nest was also found on the beach.

It is believed that the chapel had collapsed or been abondoned by the early 18th century, but nothing was done by the Established Church to provide another place of worship in the town. The plight of churchgoers in Aberystwyth in 1762 is revealed in the following petition, it also indicates when St. Mary's became unusable.

"There are several persons now living who have been married in the Church-yard formerly belonging to the Church at Aberystwyth. The next Church to the said Town is Llanbadarnfawr above a mile distant, and the way to it extremely wet and disagreeable, so that the old and the infirm cannot attend the public worship of God, and that at a time of life the most probable they would profit by it—of a dry pleasant Sunday many hundreds of souls go to Llanbadarnfawr from Aberystwyth, but of a wet day sometimes not two dozen.

We know of no town in Great Britain so large and populous as this, and yet so distant from any Church, and all its inhabitants, without exception, of the Established Church of England."

The petition goes on to appeal for contributions towards the building of a new church.

This was not the first appeal, one was made in 1758 with little success. Many of the townspeople could not afford to contribute and at least one, Walter Jones, possibly an isolated Nonconformist, was presented at the very Court where he sat as a juryman, for refusing to contribute towards the building of an Anglican church. The 1762 appeal was more successful, and a start was made on the building, but by the time the shell had been built the money had run out and the empty building was used for boat building by Gruffydd Dafydd, "a giant of a man", until about 1785 when work on the church restarted. It was completed in 1787 and consecrated by Bishop Smallwood of St. David's. In 1790 it was fitted with a handsome gallery presented by Mrs. Margaret Pryse of Gogerddan and costing £104. 14s.

The refusal of the Diocesan bishop and clergy to help after receiving the above petition may have been their inability to pay an incumbent, but it may also have been due to their reluctance to help a community having such a bad reputation on religious and moral grounds. It was described during this period as "one of the most backward towns in the whole country", and the Rev. David Peters who was born there in 1765 and became Principal of Carmarthen Presbyterian College, said that "the town of Aberystwyth was the seat of ignorance and vice".

Whatever the truth of this, some of the townspeople did not lack enterprise, nor an interest in church worship. After the bishop refused to help them, a group combined to buy a farm at Llancynfelyn and used the income from it to endow the church that was later to be consecrated.

At the new church, dedicated to St. Michael and All Angels, on Sundays, matins were said in English at 10 a.m. and vespers, in Welsh, at 3 p.m. There were no week-day services, Archdeacon Hughes was more interested in the pastoral side of his ministry. The baptismal register opens 1 Jan 1788 and that of burials on 16 August 1971 with the internment of "Twiddy Twiddy, Player's Child".

St. Michaels was proud of its choir, The choristers prided themselves on being "able to sing from notes" i.e. able to read music. They were trained by the sexton, Jenkin Thomas, himself a fine singer and an even better choirmaster. He travelled from parish church to parish church in

central Cardiganshire, teaching choristers the rudiments of music. He lived in High St. near the back of the Old Bank House in Bridge St. After the death of Jenkin Thomas, the training of the choir was taken over by Tomos Jenkin who was rather over fond of strong drink, a habit which, at least once, had unfortunate consequences. When Christmas Eve arrived the choir met at the house of one of its members to practice for the very early morning service, *Y Plygain,* usually held on Christmas Day. There being a good stock of drink on hand, the choirmaster and the choristers so enjoyed themselves singing and drinking that the "practice" went on all night. At 5 a.m. they suddenly realised that it was time for the service and off they staggered to the church. They managed to get through the first part of the service but then sleep had its way. In vain the black gowned parson in the pulpit appealed to the choirmaster and his coadjutors in the gallery, but instead of praise and thanksgiving all that could be heard were snores, grunts and hiccoughs. After 1813, the rehearsals were held in the old grammar school in Penmaes-glas.

The accompaniment to the singing was played on a hand-operated barrel organ, or hurdy gurdy, which could only grind out a predetermined selection of 39 tunes. It stood like a large box in the gallery at the far end of the church, and was the "Gift of Pryse Pryse Esq., Gogerddan", as stated on a brass plate fixed to it. The words of the hymns were printed and published locally.

The first St. Michaels was a small building

60 feet by 26 feet, but it was said to be adequate for the needs of the town. But Aberystwyth was changing in size and attitude. It was growing fast and the number of well-to-do visitors was increasing rapidly. What is more, the area surrounding the church became the most exclusive in the town. By the 1820's it was felt that Sir Uvedale Pryce's Castle House designed by John Nash, and George Repton's Assembly Rooms and Laura Place deserved something better, and that the town also needed something bigger than the small St. Michael's Church. The demand to rebuild began before the arrival of the dynamic Rev. John Hughes, but his zeal and enthusiasm accelerated matters.

Vicar John Hughes, a native of Llwyn Glas, was a man of much promise; while a curate in Doddington, near Oxford, he had become such a popular preacher that his services were attended by a great many cultured and talented men, among whom would occasionally be seen the great John Henry Newman. On his appointment to Aberystwyth, Vicar Hughes set about improving the position of the church in the town, and by vigourous preaching and diligant visitation among the rich and poor he soon strengthened the church's hold on the town and neighbourhood. He certainly increased the number of week-day services. It was said that his appointment to the Aberystwyth district was "to bring back the town to its proper place in the ecclesiastical firmament". It was the vicar's tact and ability, helped by the extreme views held by the Nonconformists on such matters as temperance,

Vicar John Hughes and his wife

that caused the loss to Nonconformity of a large number of families who had pews and were members at the Old Tabernacl Chapel. This combination of a popular vicar, a growing town and the desire for a more impressive church building proved irresistible and the second St. Michael's was built.

The building of a church, always a hazardous business, was made easier in the 1820's by the existence of funds administered by the Church Building Commissioners. Aberystwyth's first application for a grant in 1820 was refused but in 1825 a grant was promised on condition that a certain sum could be raised locally. Land was procured by persuading Sir Uvedale Pryce to relinquish his lease on a piece of Corporation land near the old grave yard. The raising of the money proved difficult

and, as described later, caused some trouble in the town, but eventually, with the assistance of the Church Building Society, there was sufficient money for rebuilding to begin.

The building of a church to match the work of John Nash and Repton aroused considerable interest among architects and tenders were received from such notable people as C. R. Cockerell and Edward Heycock of Shrewsbury. That Heycock was given the work may have owed something to his friendship with the influential Job Sheldon, who took an active part in the rebuilding movement. By 1833 the second St. Michaels and All Angels was consecrated, a mixture of simple Classical and Gothic styles which fitted in well with its surroundings. It was cruciform in plan and was supposed to carry a high west tower, but money became short and what was planned to be the base of the tower became the vestry. But in time the new church proved to be badly built, damp and inconvenient. Worshippers complained that the walls and furnishings were sometimes covered in mould. Though larger than its predecessor, it was not a big church, far smaller than Tabernacl, the Calvinistic Methodist chapel of that time. The second St. Michaels cost £3,778 to build, £1,289 of which was received from the Church Building Committee.

Despite its weaknesses it was regarded with much affection by Aberystwyth people as a whole, but the leading churchmen in the town did not think it good enough. Almost every Nonconformist chapel in the district had either been restored or rebuilt and some of them were much more impressive structures than St. Michaels, which was said to look shabby in comparison. Chancellor Phillips tried hard to get a new church but failed. His successor, the Rev. J. H. Protheroe, who came to Aberystwyth about 1886, was more successful. Laura Gardens were presented as a site by W. E. Powell of Nanteos, largely through the influence of Mrs Powell, and in September 1890 the third St. Michaels, a much grander and bigger church than its predecessor, was consecrated by the Bishop of St. David's. It was designed by Nicolson and Son of Hereford. All that is now left of Heycock's church is the little ruined vestry destined originally to form the base of the tower that was never built. It stands to the rear of the present church and was used for choir practices until early in this century. It is now an empty shell separated from the main building by a car park. When the second St.

Michaels was pulled down in 1894, a large stone was found to have a brass plate embedded in it giving the name of the builder, Richard Jones. In a hollow under the brass plate, several coins—gold, silver, and copper—were found. The church was built on a small green field known as Cae Bach Judith.

Vicar Hughes was succeeded by the Rev. Owen Phillips who became Chancellor Phillips and, later, Dean of St. Davids; he was vicar of Aberystwyth for a quarter of a century. It was he who saw the need for more services in Welsh. By the 1850's the Established Church in Aberystwyth had become so Anglicised that Welsh services were to be heard only on Sunday afternoons. This bothered local churchmen for they were already well aware of the possibility of Welsh-speaking people being attracted to the Nonconformist chapels which were almost all Welsh. In 1862 Vicar Phillips began to

The second St. Michael's Church

appeal for contributions towards the building of a Welsh church. Col. Powell of Nanteos gave the site in Grays Inn Rd. and on 27 April 1865 Miss Morice of Carrog laid the foundation stone. It was built to a design by the renowned Victorian architect, William Butterfield. St. Mair is considered by some to be the most interesting church in the town, its interior, with its unusual corbels carrying the roof, is much admired.

Laura Place, the second St. Michael's is on the right and behind it can be seen the small, first St. Michael's Church

Dean Phillips

Another of Chancellor Phillips' ventures was the building of Holy Trinity Church on the eastern side of the town, where housing was spreading rapidly in the last quarter of the 19th century. The erection

Interior of St. Mair

of Holy Trinity was strongly opposed at first but the vicar persisted and it was decided to build the church in stages. The Rev. Prebendary Williams accepted the living after the move had been completed and with his assistant, the Rev. D. W. T. Jenkins, set about forming a church. He was very successful. The first section, consisting of the nave, cost £2,700 and was opened 10 August 1886. The following year the parish of Holy

Holy Trinity Church

Trinity was carved out of that of Aberystwyth. It was thought that the first section built would be large enough to accommodate the churchmen in that part of the town but this proved incorrect, within only a few months of opening the church was overcrowded and extensions were seen to be essential. After collecting £1,000 towards the extra £4,000 required, a start was made on the base of the tower and the transepts. These were consecrated on 29 November 1888. Even this extra accommodation was not sufficient in summer but it was resolved to leave the tower and any further building until the existing debt of £1,100 had been paid off. Bazaars were held and a fair amount of money collected but the tower was never completed and Holy Trinity Church is still without its lofty appurtenance.

The Bible Society

A venture which engaged the attention of churchmen early in the 19th century was connected with the S.P.C.K. In 1800 the Rev. Lewis Evans, a clergyman living in or near Aberystwyth, wrote to the Rev. Thomas Charles of Bala asking for help in securing a number of Bibles, claiming that without them he was hampered in his work for the S.P.C.K. In 1804 the British and Foreign Bible Society was established in London and one of the first consignment of Bibles came to Wales. A branch of the Bible Society was set up at Aberystwyth in 1812 at a meeting held in the Talbot Inn, with Thomas Jones (possibly the ropemaker) in the chair. The proceedings were in English but the minutes were written in

The original design for the present St. Michael's

Welsh. The originator of the movement was the Rev. Richard Evans, the Vicar of Llanbadarn Fawr. In the first 100 years of its existence the Aberystwyth branch of the Bible Society sent over £26,500 to the headquarters in London.

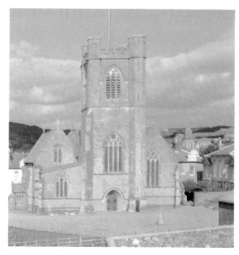

The present St. Michael's Church

Nonconformity

While religion in Aberystwyth was, in general, in a deplorable state until the close of the 18th century, the town was not without a few godly men in the post-Reformation period. Included in these in the 17th century was a small Nonconformist sect, the *Society of Friends,* the Quakers. According to a statement made by Richard Davies of Dolobran in Montgomeryshire, the great apostle of the Quaker faith in Wales, the Friends were holding meetings in Aberystwyth in 1688 and some were sent to prison in Cardigan for doing so, one being a Thomas Ellis. Later, Davies himself attended one of these meetings and Thomas Price (Pryse) of Gogerddan came and put them in the town prison where they continued to hold meetings. But, when they were brought before the Court of Quarter Sessions in Lampeter, they found the magistrates well disposed towards them and discharged them "with great courtesy".

A hundred years later there were still Quakers meeting in the town; at the Epiphany Quarter Sessions in 1775 it was

"Ordered that a certain place or House called ...... situate in the town of Aberystwyth, be set apart for a place of Religious Worshop for those people called Quakers."

Unfortunately it has proved impossible to locate the house.

Nothing further is known of the cause until 1898 when the Society of Friends was allowed to hold services on Sunday mornings in the library, presumably at the Old Assembly Rooms which were then serving as the town library. They were charged half a crown a meeting for the room and the fire. Soon afterwards they moved to their present home, the attractive little chapel in New St. owned by Nanteos. It was formerly the coach house of one of the houses in Laura Place. Because of declining numbers meetings are now held but occasionally.

Quakerism, guided by the Inner Light of the Spirit, "the precious sediment" left after the Puritan pot, with much heat and fury, had boiled away, was too quiet and gentle a creed to arouse the great majority of the people; what was needed was something which generated much more religious fervour and appealed much more to the emotions. Such a creed did not reach Aberystwyth until late in the 18th century when Methodism arrived.

Welsh Calvinistic Methodism

The first Calvinistic Methodist Chapel in the Aberystwyth area was *Gosen* at Rhydyfelin, some three miles away and built in 1770. It was to this that the few Methodists in the town first went to worship. Aberystwyth being then the biggest town in Cardiganshire and only 16 miles from Llangeitho, the birthplace of Welsh Calvinistic Methodism, early attempts were made to penetrate "this seat of ignorance and vice". But this proved difficult, for dissenters were almost unknown there and some of the first Methodist preachers were made most unwelcome and even ill-used. Such Methodist preaching as was done from 1771 to 1774 was in private houses or on the commons outside the town walls. A favourite spot was under the castle wall or, later, in the yard of the Talbot Inn.

The growth of the movement was greatly hindered at first because of the inferior social position of its adherents. Scorn was poured on them by the gentry and their followers and by many of the clergy. Some of the summer visitors treated their services as a form of entertainment, attending to see the worshippers jumping with excitement. They were even known as the *jumpers* to a large section of the townspeople. Their social position was greatly improved when those meetings at the Talbot Inn began to be attended by such people as Bowen, Llwynygwair, who always drove up in a splendid carriage drawn by four beautiful horses, and listened, with others, from their carriages.

In 1774 a Methodist society was formed but it was another eleven years before

The first Tabernacl 1785-1819

there were enough members to build a small meeting house "under the town" in Mill Lane, in an area devoid of any dwellings. At first, for some unknown reasons, it was known as *Capel y Groes* (the Chapel of the Cross) and it had very few members, only ten in 1785, not enough to be able to take communion in their own meeting house; for this they had to go to Gosen. At this time, and for some years afterwards, the devout Methodist made a practice of walking to Llangeitho to take communion once a month. It was not until 1788 that there were sufficient members to form an independent society in Aberystwyth. Once established, however, the cause grew rapidly and Tabernacl soon became an important centre of Welsh Calvinistic Methodism. From 1812 to 1843 the South Wales Association was held there every year, and then every third year until 1864.

The period 1830-40 was known as the "Years of the Great Meetings". They were generally addressed by two of the most famous men in the history of Methodism — Morgan Howells and John Elias. The number attending was so large that the meetings could be held only out of doors, first on Cae-glas behind the chapel and then on Tan-y-Cae, the open area now occupied by South Road and other streets. As this area became built up, they moved to the area stretching from Bath St. to the north. Cae-glas was known for many years as Cae'r Ty Cwrdd (the Meeting House Field), the gate leading to it was near a public house called the Three Horse Shoes. This area, owned by Nanteos and then

empty, now contains Powell St., George St. and William St.

The power of John Elias to stir these multitudes was incredible. On one occasion the meeting was attended by James Hughes, a local solicitor noted for his arrogance, suspected of being unscrupulous, and much feared by the poor. Elias's preaching moved even him and he was heard to say "Let us be thankful that this man is not a solicitor".

In 1823 Aberystwyth was the scene of an important meeting in the history of Methodism. The movement had left the Established Church in 1811 but had not yet formulated its articles of faith. At the Llangeitho meeting in 1822 it was decided that there must be a conference to formulate a Confession of Faith and the following year, at the house of D. Jenkin Davies, a grocer, draper and corn merchant in Great

Unveiling the plaque on the house in Great Darkgate St. where the articles of faith were formulated

Darkgate St., the conference was held, and the articles of faith were drawn up. This house was the birthplace of Welsh Calvinistic Methodism and for many years the room used was kept in exactly the same order as when the articles were formulated. It was known to the ardent members of the sect as the *Jerusalem Chamber of Calvinistic Methodism*. The site is now occupied by the Cooperative Stores which carries a tablet to commemorate that historic meeting.

In the March of the following year, in Tabernacl, these articles were read out to the General Assembly by the Rev. Ebenezer Richards of Tregaron, father of Henry Richard the future MP. who became a member of Tabernacl and learnt the art of public speaking there. The legal costs of drawing up the articles worried the meeting but these fears were dispelled by an offer from a Tabernacl man, Robert Davies, father of Principal David Chas. Davies of Trefecca Methodist College, to

The room where the articles were signed

act as surety for these costs until the money could be collected.

It was at Tabernacl, too, that the location of the ministerial college was discussed and resolved, as so many such problems have been resolved in Wales, by giving one college to North Wales—at Bala, and the other to South Wales—at Trefecca. Eighty years later the two united to form the Theological College—at Aberystwyth.

The setting up of a Foreign Mission, the Sustenation Fund, and the South Wales Reconstruction Fund were all discussed and launched at Tabernacl.

To return to the early years, the church's growth was rapid, a bigger chapel had to be built in 1819, and an even bigger one in 1831, able to seat 1,000 people. While the latter was being built the congregation met at the Thespian St. theatre, much to the delight of the Sunday School children.

The 1831 rebuilding was the outcome of the religious revival of that time, when services were held every day. Invitations were sent to a number of eminent ministers, to come and preach, and such was the religious fervour of the people that crowds would walk some miles to meet the visiting preacher and escort him in triumph through the town.

At one of these early chapels, a space under the gallery had no seating but was provided with a handrail for the use of sailors who preferred to listen to the sermon while leaning on the rail.

In 1878, despite the transfer in 1863 of a considerable number of members to form the new church of Seilo, Tabernacl was again overflowing, and yet another chapel

Robert Davies, Cwrtmawr

The second Tabernacl

was built, with seating for 1,500. Aberystwyth now contained a very large number of Methodists indeed, and their leaders were men of great influence in the town, too influential for the peace of mind of moderate dissenters. But it was a very disciplined cause, partly because of its organisation and also on account of the strength and ability of some of its ministers and deacons.

One of its most powerful ministers was also one of the first, the Rev. Edward Jones. He was born in Borth in 1791 and became apprenticed to Lewis Pugh, a saddler in Rosemary Lane (Princess St.). At Pugh's workshop the Arminianism versus Calvinism argument often waxed strong, with no one able to counter Pugh except one of the workers named de la Hoyde. No attempt was made to influence the apprentices but Edward Jones must have been well versed

The present Tabernacl

in Calvinism when he left to learn the finer points of his trade, first in Bristol, and then in London. He returned to Borth in 1818 and became a deacon in the church there. Soon he began to preach, and in 1825 he was ordained and became the minister at Tabernacl. It did not take him long to make his presence felt and to be looked on as the Archdeacon of Calvinistic Methodism. To the great majority of the sect, his word was law. Edward Jones was a great manager of men as well as of affairs, a kind man to young men wishing to enter the ministry and, being wealthy, ready to help them financially if necessary. But he was a very strict disciplinarian, probably too strict, but he kept the Methodists of Aberystwyth on the straight and narrow path. He died in 1860 and was the first man to be buried in the new cemetery off Llanbadarn Rd.

Until 1837 the Gosen and Tabernacl Churches were served by the same preacher. At first, on every Sunday, two sermons were preached in Gosen and one in Tabernacl, later this was reversed and after 1837 the two churches were treated independently. While Edward Jones was always there after 1825, the sermon might be given by any one or more of the many itinerant preachers passing through the town. Aberystwyth being on the route often used by these travelling ministers, hardly a week went by without a week-day or Sunday sermon from some stranger. Sometimes, when there were a number of preachers staying in the town, there might be a sermon every night and up to four from different men on Sundays.

Among the Calvinistic Methodists, the arrangement of the various services and sermons was in the hands of the senior deacon at Tabernacl, John Davies, who usually tried to announce in advance the name of the leading preacher(s) on the following Sunday. When Thomas Levi first preached in Tabernacl in September 1851 on his way from South to North Wales, he was one of four preachers taking part in the service.

No official pastor was appointed to Tabernacl until 1876 when the Rev Thomas Levi was chosen; he served there until 1903. He excelled in almost every branch of the ministry: not only was he a fine preacher and a good pastor but also an extremely good man of business. It was he who got the people of Tabernacl into the habit of

Rev. Edward Jones

contributing regularly to the Church funds. When he arrived, the church was burdened with a debt of £500, the money paid to Nanteos for the freehold of the chapel ground. He soon cleared this and then set about paying off the £4,000 incurred in building the new chapel. This, too, was accomplished successfully and he next set about getting the church interested in supporting other causes and it is estimated that during his ministry, Tabernacl contributed £27,000 to various causes.

Thomas Levi paid a great deal of attention to the Band of Hope and wrote a number of books for children. His most successful venture was *Trysorfa'r Plant* (Children's Treasury), a religious monthly magazine which he launched and edited for 50 years. Its sales reached 40,000 copies a month and proved very profitable indeed to the Methodist cause. During his ministry, Tabernacl built the Tan-y-Cae schoolroom (1876) and that at Trefechan (1879). His son was T. A. Levi, the well known Professor of Law at the Aberystwyth College.

The opening ceremony of the new Tabernacl church in 1878 was a tremendous affair, it lasted from midday on a Tuesday until late the following Sunday, 19 sermons were preached and 11 ministers took part.

Thomas Levi retired in 1903 and was followed by the Rev. R. J. Rees who was minister until 1922. Soon after his arrival the church experienced the Evan Roberts revival of 1904-06 and reacted strongly to it. He also had to nurse Tabernacl through the troublesome period of 1914-18 and the immediate post-war period with its difficult political connotations. Mrs. Rees had much

to do with the formation of the very successful women's group which, over the years, contributed so much to the finances and well-being of the church. In 1922, R. J. Rees was appointed Superintendent of the Forward Movement and he moved to Cardiff. One of his sons, Goronwy, was later prinicpal of the Aberystwyth University College.

In 1923 the well-known Rev. James D. Evans became minister and, like his predecessor, had to cope with another difficult period, the economic depression of the late 1920's and early 30's. He served with dignity and good humour until his death in 1936.

The Rev. J. E. Meredith was appointed to Tabernacl in 1937 and soon afterwards it was resolved to replace "Capel Bach" in Penparcau with a new "Ebenezer". This was accomplished just before the outbreak of the Second World War, a bleak period for the new minister. Tan-y-Cae and Trefechan schoolrooms were taken over by the armed forces and the Sunday School confined to Tabernacl itself. For four years at least, the church was deprived of the company and service of many of its young people and it says much for J. E. Meredith that he was able to make good the lost contacts when the war was over. In 1976 he retired after many years of good preaching and ministering to the spiritual needs of the people of Tabernacl. He was succeeded by the Rev. J. Elwyn Jenkins.

Tabernacl also had some unusual deacons, some of whom are still remembered in the town, albeit at second and third hand.

John Jones was a tailor from Trisant near Devils Bridge, who walked to and from every service at Tabernacl, a distance of 28 miles. He was a hyper Calvinist whose favourite reading was Witsin on the Covenants and he drew up a plan for salvation which was much discussed and well-known in Welsh Methodist circles. But he was best known and often vilified for his advocation of total abstinence. He was the first to bring up the topic in the society meeting of 1834 which started what has been called the Temperance Revival. With John Evans the schoolmaster he walked many, many miles to preach temperance and it was he who introduced unfermented wine to Tabernacl. His little book, the *Wines of the Bible,* was much read at that time. John Jones emigrated to North America in 1845 and settled at Racine in Wisconsin.

The "holy terror" of Tabernacl was

Some old Tabernacl Deacons

Richard Jones, known locally as Richard Dafydd Shôn, after his father. After a very strict and religious upbringing he rebelled and began to sow his wild oats thickly both at home and during his spell in London. Then he returned to Aberystwyth, a changed man, a fiery Christian. After much heart-searching, the members of Tabernacl made him a deacon, a decision which they must often have regretted. He became the terror of evildoers, his mission was one of fire and damnation as he thundered as from Sinai on lax members of the congregation. He would sometimes get to his feet during the service and rail at members of the congregation, especially young women. His attitude was often deeply resented and he proved an embarrassment to his fellow deacons. He seems never to have missed a service or a church meeting until he died in March 1871 at the ripe old age of 89.

David Jenkins (Dafydd Siencyn y Nailer) was born 6 February 1759 in Llanbadarn and died in 1844. While still a young man he was noted for his handwriting and gave lessons on it at some of the local girls' schools, one being in Pier St. He was once an innkeeper at the Three Jolly Sailors which stood in Upper Great Darkgate St. where St. Paul's Welsh Wesleyan Chapel now stands, and had an open cobbled court in front of it. But Dafydd was a sturdy Methodist, innkeeping did not always go well with his religious beliefs and he became an ironmonger and nail-maker instead. Judging from his subsequent actions the change proved financially worth while. He was one of those who visited

Llangeitho once a month to take communion, was highly respected at Tabernacl and of sufficient standing to have lodged under his roof the famous William Williams, Pantycelyn, on one of the old hymn-writer's visits to Aberystwyth.

The decision by the Methodists to cut themselves adrift from the Established Church in 1811 upset many of the older followers of Daniel Rowlands, some of them the most cultured and most devout of his supporters. They maintained that the only people fit to take the communion service were those who had been ordained by bishops of the Established Church. As a result, quite a number left the Methodists and returned to the Established Church. David Jenkins was one of these, but he believed that he could continue to follow Daniel Rowlands' teaching by creating a new sect, and he was supported in this by several others. He had been granted a substantial piece of land outside the town wall, stretching along what is now called Baker St. On this he had built himself a house but there was still a considerable piece of land unused which he allowed to be used for preaching. After leaving Tabernacl he built an attractive small chapel for the new sect on a piece of land just inside the town wall at the bottom of Eastgate. But when the time came to open the church for worship, his erstwhile supporters deserted him and he was left with an empty building. He then let it for a while, first to the new Congregationalists and then to the militia as an armoury. Some of its remains can still be seen behind J. R. Slater's bakery shop in Eastgate.

David Jenkins was a sturdy individualist, one of the first of a class of men who in the 19th century, eventually broke the hold of the Gogerddan and Nanteos families on the town.

The Calvinistic Methodists in Aberystwyth were also noted for their Sunday schools. They were first held about 1800 when the Rev. W. Williams, Vicar of Glanwenlas near Cilycwm, came to Aberystwyth on holiday. On his first Sunday in the town he saw large numbers of children running about and playing in the streets, especially in Trefechan where he also saw the parents gossiping in groups around the lime kilns. Williams was well acquainted with the Sunday School movement and he resolved to form one in Trefechan. He did this but, having to return home, he was able to look after it for two Sundays only. Before leaving, he set about finding someone to continue the good work.

Living in Aberystwyth at that time was a young man who later became well known in Methodist circles—Robert Davies who became the father of Principal David Chas. Davies and grandfather of Dr. R. D. Roberts, D. C. Roberts and J. H. Davies of Cwrtmawr. Robert Davies took over the Sunday school and sought the aid of his cousin, Owen Jones, an apprentice shopkeeper. Neither was considered particularly religious but they threw themselves into the work so completely that, with the financial help and encouragement of their fellow members at Tabernacl, they produced a very successful Sunday school.

Owen Jones was a talented musician and he set about teaching new songs to the children. They so enjoyed this that singing sessions were held every night of the week except Saturdays.

The school had no fixed meeting place on weekdays, it met wherever there was suitable accommodation, but on Sundays it met regularly at the *Ysgoldy* (Schoolroom) where a day school was kept on week days. In time Owen Jones's apprenticeship came to an end and he had to leave the town. His farewell service was said to be very moving indeed.

Soon afterwards, Tabernacl organised its own Sunday school in the chapel and nothing is then heard of Trefechan for several years. Presumably the children moved to Tabernacl, for Robert Davies was made the superintendent of the new Sunday School and continued in that capacity until 1841.

About 1840 it was decided to restart the Trefechan Sunday School and the middle house of a row of three low-roofed, thatched cottages was taken for the purpose. The superintendent was John Mathews, a gentleman of the old school, and his assistant was John Jones, a young man who later became very well known in Aberystwyth as *Ivon*.

Another who helped a great deal at the Sunday School was Thomas Evans, an interesting character from Blaenpennal. Blaenpennal and Bethel were then well-known hat-making centres, and many families were engaged in the work. Thomas Evans was a hatmaker and, as was the custom, he toured the country selling his hats. Being a very religious man he made a point of arranging his travels so that he could hear sermons from the

leading preachers of the day. Having a good memory and being well versed in the Scriptures, he was able to do full justice to what he had seen and heard, and made a very good Sunday School teacher.

The school again became successful, the rented house proved too small and a new meeting place was found in Spring Gardens about 1844. But this proved unsuitable and another move was made to John Jones the carpenter's shop, between a house called the "Castle" and one known as the "Green". It was entered by steps from the road. Unlike most if not all of the Sunday schools in Aberystwyth at this time, the Trefechan school then consisted almost entirely of children.

But there were still more moves ahead, the first to a house near the site of the old railway bridge, to a long low room which became noted during the religious revival of 1859. The school stayed here until 1887 when it moved at last into a permanemt home, a schoolroom which still stands on the harbour side of the main road. The official opening was a lengthy affair, attended by the town's dignitaries, a number of preachers and others, each of whom had something to say. There were talks on the history of Methodism, on the Sunday School movement, on Methodism in Aberystwyth and on Tabernacl. It was probably interesting for the adults present but it must have been a strain on the children and it is to be hoped that they were rewarded at the end with a sumptuous tea. This schoolroom is now a store for the College Library.

Trefechan Sunday School 1930's

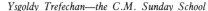

Ysgoldy Trefechan—the C.M. Sunday School

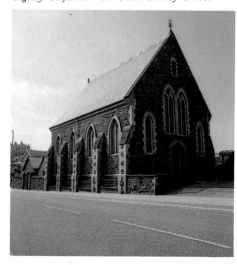

The first Seilo

There are two other Welsh Calvinistic Methodist chapels in Aberystwyth, Seilo and Salem.

Seilo. By 1857 the congregation at Tabernacl had become so large that it was decided to build another chapel at the other end of the town. In December of that year an application was made to the corporation for a grant of a piece of land on the Sand Marsh lately in the occupation of John Hughes, Victualler. Despite opposition from some members of the public and the Town Commissioners, the Corporation sold this land to those responsible for the new chapel for £40. In fact they had no right to do this for Sand Marsh had always been claimed by the Crown. When the Treasury was informed of the sale they refused to permit it. This left the Town Council in a very awkward situation but fortunately for them, as the land was required for religious purposes, the Treasury relented and the church was built there for £2,000. Difficulty was experienced with the foundations of the front of the chapel because of the marshy nature of the soil, a condition which soon proved expensive.

Officially Seilo opened its doors to worshippers in 1863 but despite there being no seating installed, services had been held there during a meeting of the South Wales Association in 1861. In the first half of the 19th century the appointment of a paid minister was unusual

but by the 1850's most of the Methodist leaders felt that a church needed its own pastor and paid him accordingly. Cardiganshire was slow to accept this and Aberystwyth had so many ministers living in the town that it felt it unnecessary to make permanent appointments. The first Methodist Church to appoint an official pastor was Seilo: it invited the Rev. David Saunders of Abercarn to become its first minister but he was unable to accept. Two others were then invited in turn but both refused and it was not until 1874 that Seilo had its permanent minister—the Rev. Griffith Parry from Manchester.

Dr. Parry began his ministry in October 1876 and soon made his mark. He became one of the leading preachers in South Wales and much sought after for preaching festivals. He remained minister until November 1883. After three years without a pastor, the Rev. Lewis Williams, a member of Seilo who had already proved his worth, was appointed minister. His was not an easy task; for some years in the 1880's there were only three deacons in office, two of them strong-willed men who had become so accustomed to having their own way that they would brook no opposition from the new deacons appointed in 1888. The minister had the difficult task of trying to heal the rift, a task made harder by his having long been a young member of the congregation. The unpleasantness created by this discord in the church had much to do with Lewis Williams leaving Seilo for Waunfawr, Caernarvonshire, in 1893.

When the Rev. T. E. Roberts came to

Seilo from Oswestry in March 1895, the church was still in a state of unrest but he had such winning ways that he soon had the full support of his members and there is no record of any serious disagreement during his ministry. His main interest was in preaching, and this, with his handsome appearance and pleasant personality, made him a much sought-after preacher. His evangelical sermons during the 1904-06 revival aroused much interest. During T. E. Roberts's ministry, Seilo emerged fully from under the wings of Tabernacl and became recognized as one of the leading Methodist Chapels in Wales. He retired in 1925. His son, Humphrey D. Roberts, is a well-known solicitor in the town.

Seilo's next minister was the Rev. Dan Evans from Porth, in the Rhondda. His appointment was said to have been partly due to the coming of Henry Morgan to Aberystwyth as manager of Barclays Bank. On his first Sunday in the town, Henry Morgan went to a service at Seilo and was later asked by a deacon if he could recommend someone as minister for Seilo. He suggested his former minister in the Rhondda. Dan Evans was asked to preach at Seilo and agreed to become its minister. It was then said that when Henry Morgan came to Aberystwyth, he brought his chaplain with him.

The Rev. Dan Evans was well loved in Aberystwyth, not only was he a good preacher but also a fine pastor. It was said of him that he had the authority which true goodness confers on a man. After 26 years at Seilo, six of these covering

Seilo with a new facade

the worst war the world has ever known. he left for a smaller church in Llandybie in 1952.

His successor at Aberystwyth, the Rev. H. Wynne Griffith, has already served 28 years there, and during that time has worked hard for unity among churches, and for extending all the aid possible to his fellow men all over the world. Seilo has done a great deal for the Christian Aid cause.

It has been said that the chapel opened in 1863 but the date on the front of the building was 1867. The reason for this is that scarcely had the opening celebrations finished and the humdrum business of running a chapel begun before the cry ran through the town "Seilo's sinking". Many ridiculed this statement but it was true, and it soon became obvious that the front of the chapel was giving way. Those who had objected to the building being located on Sand Marsh were proved right. The wet and sandy foundations were giving way. The town clerk, a true bureau-

crat, said "Do nothing rashly, leave well alone", but the wall continued to crack and the front had to be renewed with much stronger foundations, hence the date 1867.

The new front was handsome, with two attractive towers, one shorter than the other because the foundations were more unstable on that side. In time the instability of the underlying soil again caused concern, for the wooden piles had rotted, and eventually, in 1962-3, Seilo was given a fine looking, modern, perpendicular style front, built so that there is relatively little weight on the weak foundations.

The Calvinistic Methodists of the 19th Century were fortunate in having, as a member, one of the leading choirmasters in Wales. Edward Edwards (Pencerdd Ceredigion) was born in Aberystwyth but left to live in Capel Dewi before going to South Wales. He returned to Aberystwyth about 1836, joined Tabernacl, and began to devote almost all his energies to choral singing. A choral union had been formed there c. 1828; he took charge of this and made changes which astonished everyone at that time. It had long been the custom in Aberystwyth for the tenor parts to be sung by women, Edward Edwards insisted that they be sung by men.

The Temperance movement was then raging in the town and singing played an important part in it so there was plenty for the choirs to do. But Edwards wanted something better than this and under his leadership the singing of oratorios became part of the town's musical life. He had

Seilo with its third front

strong support from such musical families as the Julians, the Samuels, the family of the Rev. Edward Jones of Tabernacl, and that of Williams the organist at St. Michaels. Handel's "Messiah" or Haydn's "Creation" became an annual event and on 1 January 1852 the first "Grand Concert" was given at the Old Assembly Rooms when extracts from the oratorios were sung. Choral singing continued to thrive until the religious revival of 1859 when there was a serious disagreement and split among the Tabernacl choir. His son Jack Edwards was also a musician of note and conducted both the band and many choirs in Aberystwyth.

Later, Edward Edwards moved to Seilo and there he continued the tradition of good singing until he retired. In February 1899 he was presented with an American organ at Seilo, having been conductor of the Aberystwyth choir for almost sixty years.

Seilo was equally fortunate in its choice of young Charles Clements as its organist in 1917. For over fifty years he maintained a high standard of music at the church and, as described elsewhere in this work, he contributed considerably to music circles in the town.

Ysgol Skin. As stated elsewhere, the Poplar Row-Skinner St. area was one of ill-repute in the 1840's to 60's which was probably why Tabernacl chose it for one of its Sunday Schools.

The building chosen was originally a school kept by a John Fiddler. After he retired it was taken by the Rev. William Jones who called it a British School. He also taught navigation and seamanship to sailors who wished to become masters. When William Jones died, aged 92, the owner of the building, the Rev. John Williams who was closely connected with

Ysgol Skin—Skinner St. Sunday School

the Band of Hope movement, allowed Tabernacl to use it as a Sunday School. It began its work in February 1857 and six years later it was taken over by Seilo. Thousands of children and adults have passed through its doors, attendance rarely fell below 100, and evening missions were also held there.

The Skinner St. Calvinistic Methodist Sunday School, as it was officially called, was known locally as *Ysgol Skin* being next door to a skinners' yard. Among its first teachers were John Evans, David Jones the Bank and his brother Ivon. The Skinner St. building was built and first owned by Mary Williams.

As the old hovels were demolished and better houses built, the area lost its bad reputation and became known for the high standards of its Sunday School, especially in choral singing. Its choirs performed many cantatas and even oratorios in the town. They won many eisteddfod prizes and it was the Skinner School choir which gave the first concert designed to provide comforts and Christmas gifts for Aberystwyth men on active service c1915.

The building was also used for adult choir and band practices and strains of Tannhauser could often be heard when passing along Northgate St. when Jack Edwards was putting the Excelsior Band through its paces.

One who attended this Sunday School for many years was William Jenkins, a local photographer who was seen every day in the summer touting for custom on the promenade. As pupil and teacher, beginning in 1881, he gave over fifty years of service

to Ysgol Skin. He helped to preserve into the 1930's the old custom of giving a present of a guinea to any pupil who got married.

As in most Welsh Sunday Schools the pupils included children and adults which is why the Skinner Street and Trefechan Sunday Schools were able to serve as the storm centres of the religious revival of 1859.

Tan-y-Cae Sunday School

Tabernacl also had a Sunday school at Tan-y-Cae (under the field) in what is now South Rd. This name had a special meaning for Methodists for it is said that it was in the field above, part of Penmaes-glas common, that they held their first Aberystwyth Society meeting in the 1780's.

The first Tan-y-Cae Sunday School was held in 1846 at a time when many ships were being built in the harbour nearby. The scholars met in a workshop in John Evans's shipbuilding yard. In 1850 the school moved to a loft in Sam Jones' house in a row of houses off South Rd. with the interesting name of "Bedlam". After 11 years there was another move to a store-house at the bottom corner of Prospect St., possibly part of the extensive timber yards that used to cover this area. The final move was in 1877 to the little chapel of Tan-y-Cae which is still there and thriving. The foundation stone for this was laid by David Davies, Llandinam, who laid a cheque for £60 on top of the stone, a substantial contribution towards the £400 which it cost to erect the building.

There was also a Methodist Sunday School in Sandmarsh Lane (Queens Rd.)

known as the *Morfa* School, in St. John's Buildings opposite the present Life Boat House. It was held in the loft of an old building which was probably used as a brewery for the first few years of the Belle Vue Hotel. Its first teachers were Richard Morris, Jesse Morgan and William Julian. Both Morfa and Skinner St. Sunday schools were established by the Methodists for the "spiritual edification of the lower part of the town".

Tabernacl also established a branch at Penparcau and it was the custom for the Methodists there to send someone on foot into Aberystwyth on Sundays to escort the preacher to Ebenezer, the Penparcau Chapel.

Salem Welsh Methodist Church

Salem near the Town Hall end of Portland St. was formed as a result of a disagreement which began in Seilo in 1890. After Dr. Parry left Seilo in 1883 the church found itself without a pastor and short of deacons. In 1884 three deacons were appointed-- Griffith Williams, William Thomas J.P., and Richard Jones who had a grocer's shop in Northgate St. For the next four years these three were apparently the only deacons, and two of them, Thomas and Jones, were close friends and strong-willed men who were determined to make Seilo as well-known and as important as Tabernacl in the Methodist world. Both had élitist views on who should occupy the pulpit at Seilo and always invited well-known preachers from far afield in order to attract large congregations and to rival Tabernacl.

Their power was all the greater because the church was without a pastor from 1883-86.

In 1888 four more deacons were appointed, David Samuel, Jenkyn Vaughan, W. P. Williams, an accountant with the M. and M.R., and David Watkins. In time the first two began to question the practice of bringing in preachers from far afield but Thomas and Jones would brook no opposition and they had the support of most of the congregation.

The minority maintained that more use should be made of preachers living in the Aberystwyth district, arguing that not only would this be cheaper but it would also show a better community spirit. They also expressed dissatisfaction with the way in which deacons were elected, and complained that because they were a minority their wishes were generally ignored.

In January 1891 the disagreement came out into the open and the church was divided into two parties. Efforts were made by a number of influential Methodist ministers to heal the rift and several discussions aimed at the same end were held at the monthly meetings. But the rift had become too wide, the church remained divided and the minority party declared its intention of leaving Seilo and forming another church.

Though the whole town knew what was going on, the local papers had not mentioned the disagreement until, at a Town Council meeting, Councillor Griffith Williams, one of the Seilo deacons who wished to leave, applied for a plot of land on which to build a chapel. It was obvious from the comments in the newspapers that the

public in general disapproved of the split, pointing out that there was plenty of room for both parties in Seilo and that there were already 20 places of worship in the town, 12 of them Nonconformist.

But the secessionists were determined to leave and while searching for a site they conducted their services and Sunday School at the Old Assembly Rooms. The first site proposed was in the newly-planned Loveden Rd. behind the Town Hall and on part of the old ropewalk. This was opposed and the present one in Portland St. was chosen. Building began and in 1895 the church was opened for worship.

The outgoing party then added fuel to the blaze by claiming that Seilo should contribute towards the cost of building Salem. This was resisted on the grounds that they had left of their own accord when there

Salem Chapel

was room for them in Seilo The leading Methodists of the district were then called to arbitrate on this matter at the monthly meeting and decided that Seilo should pay £1,000 as compensation for the outgoing members' contibution to the £7,000 which it had cost to build Seilo. It is not surprising that Seilo should refuse to pay, not even when the sum was lowered to £500, and the fact that Salem was built so near Seilo strengthened the latter's resolve not to contribute.

The site for the chapel in lower Portland St. was owned by John Parry of Glanpaith and leased to Capt Wemyss. The latter was paid £60 to surrender his lease and Parry received £290 for the land. Money had to be borrowed and the trustees for the loan were Vaughan Davies of Tanybwlch, Mrs. Davies Cwrt Mawr, Llewelyn Edwards proprietor of the first Ardwyn School, Edward Edwards (Pencerdd Ceredigion) David Jenkins Professor of Music at UCW, Principal Owen Prys and David Samuel, the future headmaster of Ardwyn. The church was built by David Lloyd and cost £2,400. 9s. 1d.

By 1896 the membership of Salem was 169 and in the following two years the schoolroom was built and an American organ was bought for £22. 10s from Wheatley. The chapel cleaner was paid £8. 7s. 4d a year. A sale of work held in order to decrease the debt on the chapel yielded £250, a high figure for those days.

In 1899 the membership had risen to 210 and it was decided to have a resident pastor. The church was unanimously in favour of the Rev. D. R. Williams of

Swansea, a native of Aberaeron, who set up home in the newly built Lisburne Terrace. His stipend was £60 per annum, in addition to which Salem paid a total of £100 a year to visiting preachers. This was a characteristic of all the Calvinistic Methodists churches, at Seilo T. E. Roberts often preached on only one Sunday in the month and never more than twice; the same was true of Tabernacl and Salem.

One of the people who moved from Seilo to Salem in 1893 was the Rev. E. Penllyn Jones the librarian at the University College from the beginning, and one who worked extremely hard at collecting money for the College. When he died in 1902 he left Salem an important collection of books and the church appointed Jenkin Humphreys, the auctioneer, as its librarian.

After only four years in Aberystwyth the Rev. D. R. Williams died in 1903. The membership was now 249 and the services were attended by an average of 350 people. Oddly enough, the revival of 1904-06 had little effect on Salem's membership but it did lead to many more attending Sunday School and week-night services.

The new minister, appointed in 1905, was the Rev. D. Treborth Jones but he stayed only a year before leaving for Clifton Road, Cardiff. Despite this, Salem's confidence in its future was now such that it embarked on extensive alterations in the church. Transepts were built on to the chapel, a pipe organ was installed and heating equipment was put in, all at a cost of £1,200. It was noted on the church report at this time that the revival being over, the enthusiasm for week night services

had abated.

To replace D. Treborth Jones, the church invited the Rev. Maurice Griffith to become pastor and he began his duties in 1907. Among the deacons appointed in that year was Professor Edward Edwards, "Teddy Eddie", a most popular man among the students, and active also in the town's public life. He was mayor at the time of the National Eisteddfod of 1916.

The year 1910 saw the appointment as secretary to the Literary Society of Richard Rowlands (Rowlands Pioneer) who not only served his church faithfully and well for the remainder of his life but also figured in almost every movement of note in Aberystwyth, particularly in its musical life.

Maurice Griffith remained minister until 1916. He was followed in October 1917 by the Rev. John Davies who served Salem well for 30 years, a ministry characterised by kindness and helpfulness.

In Salem as in other Welsh chapels it was customary for members of the Sunday School to learn verses from the Bible and to recite these in front of the congregation. It is recorded that in 1905 a total of over 15,000 verses were learned, on average of 97 for every member of the Sunday School.

At the end of the First World War, Salem had a membership of 314, an average congregation of 370 and a Sunday School of 207. The chapel could accommodate 580 and the church debt was down to £300. In 1920 the minister's stipend was raised to £200 per annum.

The pattern of worship in the church was as follows:

Sunday 10.0 a.m. Sermon.
   2.0 p.m. Sunday School.
   6.0 p.m. Sermon followed by a
      church meeting.
   8.0 p.m. Congregational singing.
Tuesday 6.15 p.m. Band of Hope.
   8.0 p.m. Young People's Society.
Wednesday 2.30 p.m. Women's Meeting.
   7.00 p.m. Prayer Meeting.
Thursday 7.0p.m. Church Meeting.
Friday 6.30. p.m. Classes for under 13's
      and under 16's.

On the first Sunday in every month all the Calvinistic Methodists in the town held a Missionary Union Prayer Meeting. An extraordinary collective effort by the Methodists was the Missionary Exhibition of May 1927. It consisted not only of exhibits from all over the world but also a sale of work, a concert, and a collection, and yielded the incredible sum of £5,900 for the missionary cause, equivalent to about £70,000 nowadays.

The women of Salem, like those of most other churches, made a very significant contribution towards the chapel funds and to deserving causes elsewhere. Over the period 1905-31 their efforts produced £1,666.

The Rev. John Davies was succeeded by the Rev. Geraint Thomas from London who returned to the Metropolis in 1952. Then came the Rev. H. R. Davies from Treorchy, and Salem enjoyed over 25 years of his fine ministry. He retired in 1978 and since that time the church has shared with the English Presbyterian church the services of the Rev. J. E. Wynne Davies. Salem is one of the few churches in the town where the congregation has increased in recent years.

The English Presbyterian Church.

By the 1850's the visitors to Aberystwyth in the summer included many Calvinistic Methodists and there were complaints within the Welsh churches that there were no English services for them to attend. In 1863 Seilo decided to remedy this by holding services in English at 11.00 a.m. on Sundays during the holiday season. The first of these was held in June 1863 and the sermon was given by Johanna el Kari, an Arab turned Protestant who had lectured at Seilo in 1861 as a result of meeting the Rev. John Williams in Palestine. Other preachers were the Rev. Kilsby Jones of the Tonbridge Chapel, London, and Alessandro Gavazze, a former Italian Catholic priest who toured the country delivering anti-Papal and anti-Catholic lectures.

The English services were repeated the

The Methodist Missionary Exhibition

following summer when some were held in the newly-built Temperance Hall across the road. There were now morning and evening services as well as English Sunday school classes. But the English-speaking Methodists permanently resident in the town were not satisfied with English services in summer only. In 1865 some serious consideration was given to the establishment of a separate English church. The monthly meeting gave the idea its enthusiastic support and Tabernacl and Seilo committed themselves to supporting the work financially, which they did for ten years. The Temperance Hall was hired and with the Rev. J. Griffith Davies in charge, the English Methodist Church was launched.

After six successful years, the membership had so increased that a proper church became necessary. A plot of land was bought for £200 in Bath St, then called *Newfoundland St.* because the Town Council had just discovered that they owned it, and the present chapel built at a cost of almost £2,500. It held its first services on 18 April 1872 with the Rev. Dr. Lewis Edwards of Bala in the pulpit.

Once established, the church grew steadily stronger, in 30 years the membership grew from 64 to 178. It did, however, have a problem with its ministers. Its policy of appointing ministers for an initial period of three years and then renewing the contract was not liked by the men chosen and during the first thirty years or so, after J. Griffith Davies left for London in 1873, there were a number of relatively short ministries. The Rev. Wil-

English Presbyterian Chapel

liam Evans who came in 1875 from Pembroke Dock returned to his former church in 1881. He was succeeded by the Rev. J. Varteg Jones from Pontypool in 1882 who left three years later for Everton, The Rev. Glyn J. Davies of Betws Garmon became minister in 1887 and accepted a ministry in Newport in 1891. Then came the Rev. Richard Hughes, of St. John's College, Cambridge where he had come under the influence of Lightfoot, Westcott and Hart, and of Heidelberg University, Germany. On leaving Cambridge he became tutor to David Davies, Llandinam before becoming a minister of a chapel in Cardiff. He came to Bath St. in 1892 but stayed only six years before going to a church in Bournemouth in January 1899. The next minister was the Rev. Arthur Wynne Thomas who served from 1900 to 1906. Bath St. seemed doomed to a series of short

ministries until early in 1908 when the Rev. Richard Hughes began his second ministry there, one which lasted until he retired in 1939. He was a man of outstanding ability who returned to Aberystwyth with his reputation as a scholar and preacher even further enhanced. In Bournemouth it was said of him that "his own rare intelligence often made him begin where the rest of us leave off". He had an extremely wide range of knowledge and was completely devoted to his church and to scholarship. He was the author of a standard Welsh commentary on "The Gospel according to St. Mark", and others. He had a natural dignity which was impressive at all times. Despite his poor health and retiring ways he exercised a considerable and beneficial influence over the many servicemen who visited the church during the 1939-45 war.

No successor was appointed until 1943 when the Rev. Stephen G. Griffiths took over, an able and popular preacher who left for Llandinam in 1955. He was followed by the Rev. Howard Williams 1956-1961, and then came the Rev. Dr. D. C. Moir, a medical man who had specialised in psychiatry. He left for the University of St. Andrews in 1965 only to return to Aberystwyth later as medical man to the University College. Since 1966 the church has been ably served by the Rev. J. Ellis Wynne Davies.

The Welsh Baptists

The Baptists had existed in Wales for 150 years before they were recognised in Aberystwyth. The first to visit the district

was Vavasor Powell, who is said to have preached in 1656 at *Y Garreg Fawr* (the Big Stone) in the village square at Llanbadarn Fawr, and was arrested for doing so.

The sect's itinerant preachers of the late 18th century invariably called at Aberystwyth but they were rarely welcome, and if they tried to preach they were generally set upon by the mob and some were driven out of the town and chased to the top of Penglais hill. It became a place to which only special missionary preachers were sent.

One such man was Dafydd Hughes; in 1782 he was chosen to visit north west Wales to win adherents to the Baptist cause. There he must have met John Williams, a Methodist turned Baptist who was related to Mrs Poole, wife of William Poole, the Gogerddan estate agent who, because of Pryse Loveden's absence, was then living at the Gogerddan mansion. A niece of Mrs Poole wished to become a Baptist and with a friend was prepared to go to Harlech to be baptised. But Dafydd Hughes, aware of her connection with Mrs Poole, probably saw an opportunity to become accepted in the Aberystwyth area and decided to perform the ceremony near Gogerddan. Through Mrs Poole they were welcomed at the mansion and guaranteed freedom from persecution "even from the Devil" by the hospitable household. Three of the Baptist preachers then held services there on 8 June 1787. In the afternoon they went into Aberystwyth, probably escorted by a Gogerddan man, and preached in the yard of the Talbot Inn. Their connection with Gogerddan was now sufficient to ensure them a fair hearing. There they announced that baptisms would be held in the river in Bow Street on 12 June 1787 when a crowd assembled to see the two local girls baptised.

Having obtained a footing in the town, the Baptist preachers became frequent visitors and won a number of adherents. More baptisms were held there, in Bow Street and in Penrhyncoch, and early in 1789 a house in Queen St. was rented for use as a meeting-house. On March 18 a travelling schoolmaster named John Williams was ordained minister there, his flock then numbered 34. The chapel was registered as a meeting-house at the Court of Quarter Sessions 15 January 1794.

John Williams was a Llŷn man, a travelling teacher who taught music and was the author of a hymn book—*Caniadau Preswylwyr y Graig*. But he held views which were not acceptable to his flock, and early in 1792 he left for Swansea.

In 1794 another minister was appointed, Thomas Evans, a young man who proved to be a very successful minister indeed. It was he who led his flock to the new chapel in what is now Baker St., the first building to be erected on any part of the commons outside the town walls. The granting of permission to build there was surprising in view of the Court Leet's strong opposition to such building in the past. The clue to this change of policy may lie in the support of Gogerddan and the fact that the town's mayor at this time was a Gogerddan nominee, the William Poole whose wife had earlier welcomed the Baptists to Gogerddan.

The first building was a simple box-like structure and its membership must have increased rapidly, for within a few years of its opening, two galleries were installed in the chapel. Its minister, Thomas Evans, travelled far and wide to preach and to collect money to pay for the building. He probably overworked, for in January 1801 he died of tuberculosis at the early age of 38. During his ministry he had encouraged two young members of the congregation to become preachers and it was to these, Samuel Breeze and John James, that the ministry was then entrusted. Both were popular and hard working preachers, they travelled many miles through the neighbouring counties, each preaching up to four times a day. Such work was hard and often daunting while the remuneration was woefully small. Both opened a school to supplement their earnings and James later became a bookseller and printer. Bethel was spiritually in a poor condition at this time; Breeze left under a cloud in 1811 and died a year later. James carried on until 1817 and then moved to Glamorgan. He was succeeded the following year by William Evans, "God's gift to the Aberystwyth Baptists". He put new life into the cause and Bethel began to thrive.

In 1832-3 a new chapel was built and while this was being done, services were held in the new theatre in North Parade. In 1840 William Evans was succeeded by Edwards Williams of Manchester who stayed for 29 years and saw many changes and much growth, especially during the revival of 1859 when 65 new members were baptized. He was followed in January

1873 by Dr. John Alban Morris from Cefnmawr, an Anglesey man who decided to become a preacher during the revival of 1859. He received at least part of his education from Sir John Rhys in the village school at Rhos-y-bol. It was he who organised the building of the present chapel in 1888 with its main doors facing the main road instead of being at the side. It was opened in October 1889 and the debt was cleared in 20 years. Dr. Morris became an important man in the Baptist cause as counsellor, writer and scholar. He was editor of *Y Greal* (The Grail) from 1878 until his death in 1909, and he published a commentary on the first epistle according to St. Peter. When the Baptist College was moved from Haverfordwest to Loveden House in Bridge St. in 1894, he was appointed one of its professors and it was from his library that the National Library of Wales obtained the valuable collections

The second Bethel Chapel

Bethel Welsh Baptist Chapel

of accounts and books relating to that college. In 1896 the honorary degree of D.D. was conferred on him by the William Jewel College, USA. Dr. Morris retired because of ill-health in 1907.

The day that Dr. Morris died, 17 May 1909, his successor, the Rev. Joseph Edwards was appointed, an effective preacher and a man of considerable charm. He served the church well during the difficult days of 1914-18 and the years that followed, despite failing health. He died in 1936 and was followed by two ministers who served Bethel for short periods only, the Rev. D. Myrddin Davies 1936-37, and the Rev. W. George Evans 1940-45.

In 1946 came the Rev. W. Caradoc Davies a popular man in the church and the town. He left for Llandysul in 1960 and was followed at Bethel by the Rev. T. R. Lewis until he retired in 1977. The present minister is the Rev. J. A. Thomas.

Alfred Place English Baptist Church.

In common with the other Nonconformist sects, the Baptists were concerned about the lack of English services for the Baptist visitors and for English-speaking Baptists who had settled in the town. This became more serious after the railway came in 1864. In September 1863 a deposit of £68 had been paid for a site in Alfred Place on which to build an English Baptist Chapel. It cost £2,300 to erect and was opened for worship in 1870, when 22 members of the Welsh Church were transferred to form a core of membership for the English Church. The first pastor, the Rev. T. E. Williams commenced his ministry in October 1871 and was there for 20 successful years. As in other English Nonconformist churches, it was invariably full in summer and half empty in winter. Among its members were Principal Roberts and Professor Angus of the University College, the latter was a member for 33 years and did a great deal of useful work in the church.

The Rev. T. E. Williams was succeeded in 1893 by the Rev. Thomas Williams who came from Hitchin. His daughter, Grace Williams, was a well-known and influential figure in the town until her death in 1963.

In 1907 Thomas Williams retired and the following year his place was taken by the Rev. Thomas Edmunds, who preached the modern view that knowing God was more important than baptism and creed repeating. During his ministry the membership of the church reached its highest figure, 111. After leaving Alfred Place in 1914, Thomas Edmunds published

a number of books including *The Heart and Mind of Jesus*. He was an uncle of Glyn Daniel, the eminent Professor of Archaeology at Cambridge.

The Rev. D. R. Thomas began his ministry in 1916, a Congregational minister turned Baptist. These were difficult years, there were 10,000 soldiers billeted in the town in December 1914 and the chapel schoolroom was used as a pay office, lecture room, equipment store and later, as a place for band practice. In the evenings, the church organised a recreation room where servicemen could write letters, read periodicals, listen to music and play games. D. R. Thomas coped well with the last two years of war but departed under a cloud in 1922.

The shortest pastorate of all and possibly the most attractive was that of the Rev. J.

Alfred Place English Baptist Chapel

Williams Hughes, 1924-26. Later he joined the staff of the Bangor Baptist College and was its Principal from 1943 to 1959. In 1926 the Rev. Frank Hastings came from Swansea to Alfred Place and remained for eight years. In 1937 there was almost unanimous support for a call to the Rev. Mansel John, a student of Regents Park College, Oxford and a protégé of the Old Testament scholar Dr. Wheeler Robinson, principal of that college. After serving the church well during the trying times of the Second World War, he joined the staff of Coleg Harlech and is now a professor at the Cardiff Baptist College.

The Rev. Russell Jones, one of the founders of the Evangelical Movement of Wales was the next minister (1948-52) and he was followed by the Rev. Mathew Francis, a Llanelli man who had studied at the Moody Bible College of Chicago, Oxford and Cambridge before coming to Aberystwyth. Since leaving in 1957 he has been a minister in Shrewsbury, Tasmania and Perth, Australia.

In 1959 the Rev. Haydn James began his ministry at Alfred Place and six years later, the present minister, the Rev. Geoffrey Thomas, was ordained there.

In 1880 the Bethel deacons formed a mission church in Portland Lane (now Road) where two services a week were held. Much help was given here by Professor Angus.

In the 1890's Wales had three Baptist Colleges, in Cardiff, Bangor and Haverfordwest. The last-named was moved to Loveden House in Bridge St., Aberystwyth in 1894. Soon afterwards the Baptist Union began to wonder if three colleges were necessary and they asked the churches to vote on the issue. The result was the closure of the Aberystwyth College in 1899 after a meeting presided over by the famous Baptist leader, Dr. Gomer Lewis.

Wesleyan Methodism

Between 1739 and 1791 John Wesley visited Wales 46 times but the nearest he ever got to Aberystwyth was in 1768 when he reached Tregaron, where he was not well received. Being unable to speak Welsh he failed to establish a worthwhile contact with the people, a handicap which he much deplored, and left the field to his friend Hywel Harris.

Welsh Wesleyan Methodism began in August 1800 but it hardly touched Aberystwyth until 2 November 1804. On that day four religious men converged on the town in an attempt to establish Wesleyanism there. They were William Parry of Llandegai, Edward Jones of Bathafarn, Owen Davies and John Bryan of Llanidloes and Trefeglwys. They all went, but not together, to the Talbot Inn where Nonconformist preachers were always assured of a welcome. Next day the town crier walked the streets announcing that services would be held in the Talbot yard and a large number of townspeople and others came to listen. Nothing more is heard of Wesleyanism in Aberystwyth until the summer of 1805 when first the Long Room at the Talbot, and then the Nags Head in Bridge St. were used to hold services. But the attendance was so large at the latter that the service had to be moved to a big storehouse in Trefechan.

These meetings proved so successful (and included so many prominent people) that it was resolved to form a society. They first met at the house of a glazier named Davies where they stayed for two years. Growing congregations then forced them to move to the Boat House where fishing vessels were built. But their success led to their being persecuted, particularly by the other Methodist sect. The door of the boat house was daubed with such slogans as "Yma y mae Synagog Satan"

The remains of Salem, the Welsh Wesleyan Chapel in Queen St.

(Here is Satan's Synagogue) and stones were thrown on to the wooden roof during services.

But Wesleyanism continued to grow and by 1806 the boat house was too small. A small, galleried chapel named *Salem* was then built in a court off Barker's Lane (now Queens St.) and opened in 1807. In the following year the Aberystwyth and Llanidloes circuit was formed with a membership of 900, but because of a change of policy by the General Secretariat which considered Welsh Wesleyan Methodism to be too expensive to maintain, the Welsh connections found themselves short of funds and the number of members dwindled. In the 1820's, however, there was a considerable increase in the movement and in 1831 the Aberystwyth circuit was formed and remains to this day. Extensions had to be made to the chapel in 1842 and this was done by incorporating and converting two neighbouring houses.

Welsh Wesleyansism was now thriving in the town and in 1861 the Sunday School teachers in Queen St. opened another school in Moor St., as Cambrian St. was then called. This grew so rapidly that it was decided to build a new chapel there and in December 1869 *Siloam* was opened with accommodation for 300 people. Such was the attraction of Wesleyanism that the new Chapel made no difference to the attendance at Queen St. In fact, in a very few years, the members of the latter found their church so overcrowded, and the Queen St. building so shabby in comparison with Siloam, that they decided to build a bigger and better chapel. The minister at

this time was the Rev. David Evans (Degar) who, in 1875, made Siloam independent of the mother church.

In 1878 £900 was paid for a site in upper Great Darkgate St. on which there were three old houses, one of them in Princess St. This was probably the site previously considered by the Welsh Congregationalists. The design of the new chapel, a handsome structure, was by Walter P. Thomas of Liverpool, and Thomas Jones of Dolau was entrusted with the building, which entailed the demolition of the old houses. On the day that the foundation stone was laid, 31 October 1878, hundreds of promises of financial help were received and all semed to be going well. But soon afterwards, there was a serious misunderstanding between the church trustees

Siloam Welsh Wesleyan Chapel, now a garage

and the builder and the matter was taken to the County Court. The judge, however, sent the case to arbitration and both parties emerged financially the poorer, without having gained anything.

During the building, donations were received from a number of benefactors-- David Davies of Llandinam £110, John Williams of Picton House £108 and T. Hugh Jones £106. A total of £1,000 was collected in this fashion towards the £5,900 which it cost to build *St. Paul's*. The first services were held on 20 June 1880 when six preachers gave sermons, the first being the Revs. John Evans of Eglwysfach and Hugh Jones. It was a beautiful church but it burdened the members with a debt which proved almost impossible to reduce. The interest of £150 a year was as much as the congregation could cope with. The overdraft at the bank rose to £300 and the members became very discouraged. The reason for these problems was largely the economic climate of the time. There was an acute depression which so lowered the value of property that it was felt to be very unwise to dispose of the old chapel and the neighbouring houses owned by the church, at the prices then ruling. Also a considerable number of the cause's old and most liberal supporters died during this period while others were hit so badly by the depression that they had no money to spare. St. Paul's in the 1880's was largely a church of young people.

Despite vigorous efforts, the debt remained at £3,600 for some years. The case was considered by the South Wales

The St. Paul's Welsh Wesleyan Methodist Chapel

district and a committee of ministers and influential laymen met to discuss the matter. At that meeting the sum of £400 was collected for the church. The committee urged the church to make a special effort to raise £1,500 in the next 18 months, apparently promising that if this was done a grant of £500 would be made from the Connexional Fund. It was probably this committee that decided to send the Rev. William Morgan to St. Paul's as its next minister. He was a man well-versed in raising money, having excelled at this at every circuit which he had served. Once installed in Aberystwyth he called a meeting of the church officials of the district and drew up a plan of campaign. With the Rev. Robert Roberts of Tre'r-ddôl he undertook

to tour North and South Wales to collect money and did this so well that he collected hundreds of pounds. He also instructed the members of St. Paul's on how to raise money, his most important suggestion being the holding of a mammoth bazaar of the type then organised by churches in various places.

After months of preparation the bazaar was held in the University College of Wales building from 5-9 August 1889. It was given a great deal of publicity and its importance to the church was made abundantly clear. Among the speakers at the opening were the Mayor, C. M. Williams, and Lord Lisburne. Every denomination in the district assisted and there were many donations of money, some from abroad, especially America. The hall was packed with valuable things—paintings, oriental screens and other objects, silks, woollens, embroidery, Indian cushions, furniture and bric-a-brac of all kinds. The sale was a great sucesss, it yielded £563 which, with the donations, exceeded the £600 needed to complete the required £1500. Tea parties organised during the 18 months yielded £130, donations amounted to £158 and the Rev. William Morgan himself collected over £371. The total receipts, with the grant from the Connexional Fund, were £2,121. 14s. 7d. A debt of £4,040 in March 1884 was reduced in August 1889 to £1,900. As usual, the women members did magnificent work during this period.

All this put new life into St. Paul's and it became a lively church, well known for its soirées, social teas and concerts. The

members became expert at collecting money and the church prospered. In 1890 it was given a fine pipe organ by Theophilus Hall of Oldham. A schoolroom was erected next door to the church in 1904, much of the cost of erection, £1,400, being raised by the sale to the Salvation Army of the old chapel in Alexandra Rd. Five years later the chapel house was built for £250.

St. Paul's began the 20th century solvent and thriving, Despite two great wars and intense economic depression it has continued to flourish. Its present minister, the Rev. Daniel Davies, is also superintendent of the Ceredigion Methodist Circuit. During his eleven years in Aberystwyth he has worked assiduously for the League of Friends of the Aberystwyth Hospital and Homes for the Aged, and has both organised and driven many, many trips for the elderly and the infirm.

St. Paul's schoolroom is well known to summer visitors as the place where the annual exhibition, *Aberystwyth Yesterday*, is held, showing Mrs. Margaret Evans' fine collection of the clothes, pictures, photographs, bric-a-brac and other things used and enjoyed by our forefathers.

Siloam still stands but is now used as a garage while the Queen St. Chapel has become an artisan's workshop and store. Siloam is the only church, as distinct from branch Sunday Schools, that has been closed without replacement in Aberystwyth in modern times, and even it was replaced by the new Penparcau church.

The Queen's Road English Wesleyan Methodist Church.

The Wesleyans were faced with the problem of catering for English-speaking members as early as about 1830 and some preachers began to deliver two sermons on the same text on Sunday evenings, one in Welsh and the other in English. A writer in *Yr Eurgrawn* of 1835 suggested that since the Queen St. church was so full, it should be used for English-speaking members and a new, bigger Welsh chapel be built. By 1840 some of the Sunday School classes were conducted in English. The problem was solved partly as a result of Sir James Graham's Bill to educate factory apprentices, a measure which was successfully opposed because it was believed to favour the Established Church. This started the Wesleyans thinking about education and in the Conference of 1843 circuits were strongly urged to set up schools to educate their children. This was seen by the strong English section in Queen St. to be the solution to their problem and in 1844 a building was erected which was to serve both as a school and a church. It was situated in Lewis Terrace, opposite to the present Welsh Primary School in Alexandra Rd. and it still stands, being now used by the Salvation Army.

The school opened in 1844 with Ellis Griffith Williams, son of Gutyn Peris, a well-known bard, as its headmaster. It proved to be a very good school indeed, and was described by one of the commissioners employed in compiling the *Rcport on the State of Education in Walcs* (1847) as the best school that he had seen up to the time of his visit. Unfortunately, its able headmaster, though a young man, died suddenly in 1848 and the school seems to have been closed soon after.

But the English Wesleyan Church continued there and though it leaned heavily on the Welsh church for support for some years it eventually gathered enough members to stand on its own feet. One of the Welsh members who transferred to the Lewis Terrace church in order to help them was Robert Doughton (Doughton Town Clock), a prominent public figure in the town and a pillar of strength in the church. The 1840's and 50's saw large numbers of Cornishmen coming to work in the lead mines of North Cardiganshire, and outside Aberystwyth, there is no doubt that the establishment of English Wesleyanism was almost entirely the result of the influx of Cornish lead miners. It is recorded that

The former English Wesleyan Chapel and day school

almost every miner was an English Wesleyan. But, with the exception of one man, R. H. Rowse, there is no record of any Cornishman playing a part in the establishment of the Aberystwyth Wesleyan Church. Later however, descendants of the Cornish miners, people who came to live in or near Aberystwyth, and were engaged in work other than mining, did join the Wesleyans as in shown by such names as Trenwith, Williams, Penwill, Kendrick, Collins, Showrings, Northey among the members.

The membership of the English church remained very small until the revival of 1859 when it began to grow. In 1865 there were still only 25 members in winter but there must have been a marked increase in subsequent years for in February 1869 it was reported that the existing chapel was too small and that a site for a new church had been purchased at the Sandmarsh end of Bath St. It cost £2,333 to build, had seating for 450, and was opened for worship on 18 June 1870. A subscription list was opened in 1866 and such was the generosity of the contributors that in 1871 the debt on the new church was only £122.

For the first twenty years the English church did not have a minister of its own but relied on local preachers. One who often occupied the pulpit during this period was the Rev. J. Saunders, the Independent minister. In 1865 the Aberystwyth English Wesleyan Church was recognised and became a Home Mission Station. The Home Mission Department thus became responsible for the appointment and stipend of the minister.

The first minister to be appointed to the newly formed English circuit, the Aberystwyth Home Mission, J. M. Morrell, also served the Goginan and Cwmsymlog areas. In April 1866 Cwmsymlog withheld their contribution to the Aberystwyth circuit because they had not had their usual amount of preaching from the Aberystwyth-based minister, presumably he was unable to travel there because of the weather. As mining declined after 1870, the churches inland gradually closed, those Cornishmen remaining were few in number and probably sufficiently well acquainted with Welsh by that time to be absorbed by the Welsh churches.

In 1879 Aberystwyth ceased to become a Home Mission Station and became a Dependent Circuit until 1911. The Goginan and Lisburne Mines churches were absorbed into this circuit but did not long survive the depression in mining. Borth was included in 1890. Becoming a Dependent Circuit raised serious financial problems, for not only did the payments from the Home Mission Fund cease but the circuit had to pay the rent for the minister's house, and part of his stipend. Strenuous efforts had to be made in the 1880's to keep up with the expenses and pay off part of the church debt. It reflects great credit on the members that by 1894 the church was clear of debt and there were a few shillings in the bank. The new gallery was built in 1898 and Epworth Villa, the minister's house, built in North Rd. in 1900. There were then 96 members of the church with 3 on trial.

The 1904 revival did not affect the English churches as much as the Welsh ones but the Queen's Rd. church gained 10 members. This first decade also saw such an increase in the number of visitors in summer that the Coliseum was engaged for five Sundays in 1906 and extra galleries were built in the chapel.

In 1911 the church was removed from the Dependent Circuits and placed on the University Circuits list, thus receiving a grant from the Home Mission Fund in virtue of work done in connection with the University College

Robert Doughton was still active in the church and proved a great asset until his death in 1918. He was never reactionary, always progressive and far-seeing. When he died he had been a Class Leader for 50 years, a local preacher, a foundation trustee, treasurer and secretary of the trust, chapel steward for 19 years, and pew and

Queen's Rd. English (Wesleyan) Methodist Chapel

society steward. He was on the Town Council for many years and served both as Alderman and Mayor.

Another prominent man for 30 years was Robert Read of the *Cambrian News,* an ardent supporter of the Temperance Movement and one whose work in the Sunday School and Band of Hope brought him into contact with hundreds of young people to whom he set high standards of courage in standing by what he thought to be right. He took a great interest in the Penparcau church.

J. I. Platt a senior lecturer in Geology at the University College was another whose interest in, and labour for the church was matched only by his generosity. He ranks as one of the church's greatest benefactors.

1932 was the year of the Methodist Union but as the Aberystwyth church had voted against union with any other, all that happened was that it was transferred from the Liverpool Union to the Wolverhampton and Shrewsbury District, a relationship which still continues and one which Robert Doughton had long favoured.

Of the numerous ministers who served the church since 1918, one of the best-known in the town was the Rev. Frank Edwards who took an active part in local affairs and is credited with getting for the town its first ambulance.

During the war of 1939-45 Aberystwyth was full of service men and women and on 18 June 1940 a canteen was opened for them in the church schoolroom. It was directed by J. I. Platt and, with the aid of the women of the church, became a large organisation. The canteen was open for

13 hours every day until 30 November 1944 and it was estimated that more than two million separate orders were served. Among the many units for which it catered were men from Dunkirk and for them, as for many many others, the canteen became a refuge. It was closed with a final supper in 1944.

One of the leaders in the move to establish Wesleyanism in Aberystwyth was Lewis Pugh, the saddler with a workshop in Rosemary Lane (Princess St.). He was a very able man with an intense dislike for Calvinism. He loved to catechise children who entered his shop, especially if they were the children of members of Tabernacl. He would ask, "Do you know, my boy, who was the first Calvin?" The child being usually unable to answer, Pugh would then say, "Well, I will tell you, the first Calvin was the Devil." He worked hard to establish Wesleyanism and he was highly respected, but his belief in moderation and dislike of extremism made him leave the sect when the Temperance Revival took place around 1835 and the Wesleyan Church joined the crusade for total abstinence.

He was the grandfather of Lewis Pugh, M.P., who made a large fortune as a result of buying cheaply the lease of Cwmystwyth Mine in the 1830's from a bankrupt firm. There was a great deal of ore lying on the bank which he bought at £5 ton. In a relatively short time the price had almost doubled and Pugh became a rich man. He married into the Lovesgrove family.

The departure of Lewis Pugh the saddler and his family was a serious loss to the Queen St. church.

There were some who believed that Lewis Pugh would have had to leave the Wesleyan Church anyway because of his autocratic ways, for he was what the Welsh called an *uchelwr*, an aristocrat, who was accustomed to be listened to and to be agreed with. By 1835 democratic feelings were more widespread and many young members felt that his age and wealth did not of themselves entitle him to the leadership.

A splinter group of Wesleyans began in Lewis Pugh's house when it was occupied by Gryffydd y Cooper from Rhydypennau. The group formed a sect which they called *Wesle Bach* (the Little Wesleyans) as opposed to Queen St. which was *Wesle Mawr* (the Big Wesleyans). It was also called the *United Free Church*. They first met in a room in the converted windmill in Windmill Court and began to hold public services under the leadership of Stephen Parry, a member of the Llidiarde family. The room in the windmill being too small they moved to other houses and used the town crier to announce the meeting place. A place used on some occasions was the house of William Jones behind the Nag's Head Inn in High St. Later they moved to Lewis Terrace to the old English Wesleyan Chapel. The sect went on meeting until almost the end of the 19th century.

The Welsh Congregationalists or Independents

Until early in the 19th century the only contact which the townspeople had with the Independents was when some of the itinerant preachers of that denomination stayed and preached at Aberystwyth, on their way to and from chapels and congregations in other parts of Wales. The cause was already established in Llanbadarn Fawr and the chapel there, Soar, built in 1804, was attended by a number of people from Aberystwyth who thought nothing of walking or riding the muddy, rut-strewn road that then connected the two places. It was inevitable, however, that an attempt would be made to establish Congregationalism in the town, and in 1810 it was resolved that this should be done.

The moving spirit in this attempt seems to have been Thomas Jones, who had a rope-making business below where North Road now runs. He took over an old storehouse on the wharf below Rheidol Bridge, possibly the one now occupied by McIlquham's, and furnished it roughly as a chapel. It was formally opened by the Rev. T. Jones of Moelfre, Denbighshire, and continued in use for some years with Thomas Jones frequently occupying the pulpit. But it was not a flourishing institution, the congregation was small and consisted largely of a few local members of Soar who divided their chapel-attendance between the town meeting-house and the chapel at Llanbadarn. The members were too few to support the cause and it was kept in being largely through the efforts of

Thomas Jones and the generosity and enthusiasm of Mrs. Edwards, the wife of a former Machynlleth man who had become one of Aberystwyth's leading merchants.

The true founder of Congregationalism in the town of Aberystwyth was a Pembrokeshire man, whose life shows how much could be accomplished by a dedicated man. It also shows how much was expected of the ministers of the period.

Azariah Shadrach was born near Fishguard on the 24 June 1774, and while he was still a young child his family moved to the parish of Borton, where he learnt to speak English by playing with the little children of that district. Later he moved to Trewyddel to live with an aunt for whom he worked as a shepherd. This was where he became deeply interested in religion. He joined the local Congregational chapel and came under the influence of the Rev. John Phillips. Soon he felt the urge to preach and took to practicing while watching his flock, and people became accustomed to hearing this young shepherd declaiming from a distance. Never did a flock of sheep hear more preaching. His urge drove him to learn to read, and even to attend school for a short while. But this was not enough, for he now wanted to become an Independent minister, and felt keenly his lack of education. The problem was to find a way of learning while still earning a living. His solution was typical of his independent spirit. Not far from Trewyddel, in the Trefgarn district, lived the Rev. John Richards, a scholar possessed of what was then regarded as a fine library. Azariah decided that he must have access to that store of knowledge and so he offered to work for John Richards without wages for a year in return for free access to the library in his spare time. The offer was accepted and the minister not only helped him to the best of his ability but also encouraged the young man to preach. At the end of a year, Azariah returned to his aunt, but not before he had preached his first sermon to human beings at Caergowyl near Rhosycaerau.

He was now a preacher without a church and so he and a friend went on a tour of South Wales, holding services whenever and wherever there was a congregation, though there were not many at this time. In 1798 he toured North Wales and preached to every one of the Independent congregations in that part of the country, though these, too, were small in number and had few members. This was probably when he made the acquaintance of Dr. Lewis of Llanuwchllyn, who persuaded Azariah to settle in the north and to combine preaching with the running of a school. He did this for a few years at Llanrhaeadr-ym-Mochnant before moving to do similar work elsewhere, first in Derwen-las, near Machynlleth, and then in the Llanrwst district. There he stayed until 1806 when he was invited to take charge of the newly-built chapel at Tal-y-bont in Cardiganshire as well as the above-mentioned Soar at Llanbadarn Fawr. For this he was to be paid the munificent sum of £8 per annum for Tal-y-bont only, with the promise that if he succeeded in collecting enough money to clear the chapel debt, his stipend would be raised to £3 a quarter. In fact he not only ministered to the needs of these two chapels, but also served every congregation of Independents in Cardiganshire north of the River Ystwyth, work which involved a great deal of work and worry but offered very little worldly wealth in return.

Soon, Azariah Shadrach turned his attention to the establishment, on a firm foundation, of the Congregationalist cause in Aberystwyth. The meetings formerly held in that town must have been discontinued, for there was no longer a place of worship available. With his staunch supporter, Edward Mason, he searched diligently for a suitable building and eventually secured an ideal one for his purpose, the small chapel built by David Jenkins near the lower end of Eastgate. The rent was fixed at £9 per annum, for the payment of which Shadrach took full responsibility. He preached his first sermon in the new chapel (Sion) on Sunday afternoon, 21 January 1816.

But Congregationalism did not thrive in Aberystwyth and the attendance at, and support for, the new chapel was so poor that after two years, when Jenkins doubled the rent, the minister, being unable to afford the new payment, was forced to look for another meeting place. Shadrach and his few followers now moved to an old barn in Queen St. at the back of Brittania Court . But crude as it was, it was this old barn with its earth floor and crude furniture that became the first Independent/Congregational Chapel in Aberystwyth. Until May 1818, those who wished to become members had still to be received at Soar,

Llanbadarn Fawr, but on the 30th of that month a church based on Congregationalist principles was formed at the old building in Queen Street.

But there was very little enthusiasm in Aberystwyth for the new cause and few were prepared to support it. Shadrach had still to pay the rent of six guineas a year himself, to secure and look after the furnishings, and even to see to the repairs that were necessary. Disappointed with the lack of support, some of the members drifted back to the more stimulating atmosphere in Llanbadarn. The chapel's most ardent supporter, Edward Mason, died, another devout and loyal member left the district, and the minister was left without anyone who could even be relied on to have the chapel doors open in time for the service. Congregationalism in Aberystwyth seemed doomed but, fortunately, events were soon to produce a new attitude on the part of many of the townspeople.

What seems to have done most to boost the Independent cause was a big missionary meeting organised by Shadrach and held in tents erected on that part of the Penmaes-glas common that was nearest to the old St. Michael's Church. The preaching of the eminent men who ministered to those gatherings gave the cause new life and attracted many new members to the Queen Street meeting-house. Greatly encouraged by this, Shadrach set about the erection of a new chapel and on the 21st August 1821 the foundations of the new building were laid in Penmaes-glas. The result was that handsome little chapel, also named *Sion*, which still stands in

Vulcan Street and has been converted for the use of the Aberystwyth branch of the Red Cross Society, and St. John Ambulance Brigade.

But however great the enthusiasm for the growing cause, the majority of the members were poor people, quite unable to pay for the erection of the chapel. The financial burden had to be borne almost entirely by Azariah Shadrach, and his efforts on behalf of his church were truly herculean. Not only did he take on the responsibility for supervising the building itself, but he also undertook to pay the workmen their wages. As he had no private fortune, and his salary was barely enough for his own and his family's needs, the money had to be collected bit by bit in the best way possible. He was therefore dependent on the small amounts which were subscribed by friends and on what he could earn by preaching and writing. This meant that sometimes there was no

Sion Welsh Congregational Chapel in Vulcan St.

money with which to pay the workmen building the chapel and work would have to cease until wages were forthcoming. In 1822 Shadrach travelled far and wide in England and Wales to collect money. In January of the following year he rode to London for the same purpose and found himself one of over forty ministers engaged in the same task of collecting for their chapels. He found this almost heart-breaking and one can imagine how hard he must have worked to collect the hundred pounds which he brought back to Aberystwyth a month later. In the same year he rode all the way to Yorkshire to do some more preaching and collecting so that work at Sion might continue. Eventually the building was finished and Aberystwyth had its first purpose-built Congregational chapel, an achievement which was almost entirely due to the efforts of one man, efforts which could only have been made by a person of great strength of will and purpose. Sion was opened 11 May 1823 and Dr. Phillips, Neuaddlwyd, preached the first sermon. The gallery was added later; the space underneath it was without seats until 1830.

Azariah Shadrach continued as minister to the Congregationalists of Aberystwyth and district and was joined in 1830 by his son Eliakin who also made journeys to England to preach and collect money for the church. In 1834 Eleakin went as minister to a church in Dursley, Gloucester. The following year his father retired but continued to preach in different parts of the country until his death in 1844. He was buried in the Old St. Michael's Churchyard at the top of Great Darkgate St. or Castle St. as it was then called. His gravestone can still be seen among those laid out around the flower garden.

Shadrach was followed at Sion by the Rev. John Saunders of Buckley in Flintshire, and it is interesting to note that one of the qualities that appealed to the deacons was his ability to preach eloquently in English as well as in Welsh. John Saunders became well known for his readiness to help weak churches. He remained as minister until his death in 1871.

By this time Sion was bursting at the seams, a much bigger chapel was needed. It was also felt that Penmaes-glas was too far from the centre of the town, for Aberystwyth had expanded considerably to the east and north east. The new minister, Job Miles, then minister at Bethlehem, Merthyr Tydfil, accepted the ministry on condition that a new chapel was built. A block of four houses, nos 15-18 Baker St., was bought from Morris Davies, Ffosrhydgaled for £1,270 and the site cleared for the new Welsh Congregational Chapel. The architect, the designer of many Nonconformist chapels in Wales, was Richard Owen of Liverpool, a relative of Sir Hugh Owen who worked so hard to establish a University College in Wales. The builder was Thomas Jones of Dolau, Rhydypennau.

The chapel was opened on 1 May 1878 to a spate of sermons. This was the day of the noted preacher and the church authorities kept to the rules with sermons from Dr. William Rees (Gwilym Hiraethog). Dr. Thomas of Swansea, Dr. John Thomas and the Rev. D. M. Jenkins of Liverpool

and the Rev. Owen Evans of Llanbryn-mair. According to the *Cambrian News* the chapel interior was the most handsome in the town and its exterior, too, has been admired in recent years. The cost of the building was £4,000 of which £3,000 had already been contributed before it was opened.

Job Miles's ministry lasted until 1907 during which period the membership increased from 239 to 483. For thirty years, "Miles Aberystwyth" was one of the most forceful preachers in Wales, admired and respected by everyone. As E. D. Jones put it, if it was Azariah Shadrach who established a Congregational Church in Aberystwyth, and John Saunders who put it on a sound footing, it was Job Miles who made "Baker St." a household name to the Congregationalists of Wales.

Seion Welsh Congregational Chapel, Baker St.

In 1909 the Rev. John Lewis Williams became minister until 1919. In 1914, the church lost through death not only Job Miles but also Sir Edward Anwyl, a member for many years and the principal-elect of Caerleon Training College, a post which he was never destined to fill. It is believed that the minister found the war years too much of a strain and in 1919 he left the ministry for the Pelman Institute.

From 1920 to 1928 the pulpit was taken by the Rev. Peter Price, well known for his criticisms of some aspects of the Evan Roberts revival of 1904. He was particularly interested in the old Penmaes-glas chapel. It was during his ministry that a memorial stone was placed there to mark its centenary. That stone is now in the vestry in Baker St. He was also instrumental in having £500 spent on restoring the old chapel so that Sunday evening services might again be held there. He was probably hoping to open it as a second church but the attendance did not justify this. Peter Price was able to establish very good relations with young people of all denominations, and Principal J. H. Davies was very appreciative of his work with the college students.

Finding the work a strain and being concerned about the health of his wife, Peter Price resigned in 1928 and was followed by the Rev. Rowland John Pritchard from Liverpool. It was during his ministry that the organ chamber was built and the congregation had to worship at Penmaes-glas for a while. The old chapel also came in for extensive use during the 1939-45 period, first as a school for the Liverpool evacuees, then as a centre for the soldiers from Dunkirk and, for about three years, as a lecture room for budding pilots and aircrews   Throughout this period the Sunday School, which had continued to be held in the Old Sion, had to be moved to Baker St, with the exception of the classes for adults

The strain of the war years probably proved too much for R. J. Pritchard; early in May 1945 he disappeared and his body was found in the sea off Scarborough   A sad ending to a life of devotion.

The Rev. Dr· Tudur Jones was appointed minister in 1948 but left two years later to become vice-principal of the Bala-Bangor Theological College.

In 1951 the Rev. W. B. Griffiths became the minister, from the Priory Church, Carmarthen. It was during this ministry that a Sunday school was opened in Neuadd Goffa, Penparcau. It also saw the sale of the old Penmaes-glas chapel to the Apostolic Church for £1,000, in the hope that it would continue to be used as a place of worship, but it was sold later to the Red Cross Society.   W. B. Griffiths had an exalted sense of propriety in relation to the form of the religious service and, with the co-operation of Professor R. M. Davies, the organist, succeeded in giving a sense of unity to every service.   After several spells in hospital, the minister decided to return to his old church in Carmarthen in 1959.

The next ministry was that of the Rev Dr. Gwilym ap Robert.   He served from 1959 to 1964 when he left to become lecturer in Greek at the University College Cardiff.

Since then the minister has been the Rev. Jonathan Evans Thomas and under his guidance Seion, Baker St. continues to flourish.

Portland Street English Congregational Church (United Reformed Church)

The Rev. John Saunders' ability to preach in English as well as in Welsh probably appealed to the members of Sion because they were already aware of the need to cater for English-speaking people. The method first adopted was a bilingual service, part of which was in English, but it was not a success. Then it became the practice to repeat the Welsh sermon in English every Sunday morning during the holiday season. This, too, was felt to be unsatisfactory because of the strain it imposed on John Saunders and because it did not serve the needs of English-speaking Congregationalists who settled in Aberystwyth. It was then resolved to build a separate chapel.

One of the leading spirits in this move was John Jones, Bridge End, an alderman of the borough, and a prominent Aberystwyth merchant dealing in corn, coal and marine supplies. Later, he also acted as accountant to the well known firm of mining engineers, John Taylor and Sons. He was an ardent Congregationalist and a devout member of the Welsh chapel in Vulcan St. When a building committee was formed to arrange for the erection of the English chapel, he was made co-secretary with Richard Jones of Marine Terrace. He threw himself heart and soul into the work but it was some time before a suitable site was found. There were two large gardens stretching from Portland St. to Newfoundland St. (Bath St). The lease of one of these was bought from Elizabeth Edwards for £200 and that of the other for £150 from Ann Williams. Part of the former garden was later sold to the Co-operative Society for £65.

Plans for the Chapel were drawn, and building began in June 1865. That summer, English services were held on Sundays at 11 a.m. at Sion and at the Town Hall in the evenings. Visiting preachers conducted the services, among them the well known Rev. Kilsby Jones and J. Wild of Nottingham. To enroll as many local members as possible for the new church, English services were held in the Old Assembly Rooms during the following winter and English Sunday School classes were arranged at Sion.

By July 1866 the chapel was finished and on 8 July the first service was held and conducted by the man who had done so much to support the venture, the Rev. John Saunders of Sion. The total cost of building was £2,872. The first minister was the Rev. Arthur K. Griffith of Springhill College, Birmingham, and among the first deacons were John Jones and M. H. Davis. But Arthur Griffith found the work of preaching and collecting money for the church too much for him and in 1871 he moved to London. He was succeeded in 1872 by a man who ministered to the needs of this church until 1918, the Rev. Thomas Arthur Penry who proved not only a successful minister but also an asset to the public life of the town.

By 1875 the church had become very conscious of the need for an extra room where the Sunday school and other meetings could be held. It was resolved, therefore, to build a schoolroom. It also needed a house for the minister and a place to install an organ. In 1876 the members summoned up the courage to go ahead with the building of all three. Despite some delays and second thoughts, the whole programme had been completed by September 1880 at a cost of £2,400. But the debt proved difficult to clear and still amounted to £1,800 in 1888. It was then resolved to hold a mammoth baazar, on the 15-17 August 1888, at the height of the holiday season. An appeal was launched for goods to sell, the response was excellent, articles and donations were received from all over England and Wales.

The baazar was held at the Assembly Rooms, flags were strung across the road and every approach showed "a note of festive gaiety". The opening ceremony was performed by the Mayor, Ald D. C. Roberts, and selling began at what may have been one of the most remarkable baazars that Aberystwyth had ever seen On entering, after paying the required fee, one was confronted first by a fruit, flower, and vegetable stall built in the manner of an old thatched cottage having an open front. Here were sold fruit and flowers from the gardens of Gogerddan, Lovesgrove, Bronpadarn and Reservoir Cottage. There were also large quantitites of vegatables for sale, all the contribution of the villagers of Llanbadarn Fawr. Every item on this stall was given its Welsh name except

tomato, asparagus, apricot, nectarine, which seemed to defy the stallholders' vocabulary. The wool-work stall under Mrs. James Green was decorated with lanterns and curios which included carvings and rare butterflies collected by her husband on his travels to the mines of Spain, South America, and elsewhere. Other stalls sold paintings donated by friends of the church, pottery and other gifts given by the Earl and Countess of Lisburne, 'useful' objects, and unwanted articles which ranged from a baby's cot to a 'smoking-pipe'. Another stall sold jewellery, and part of the room was given to refreshments. One stall, decorated with the photographs of Mr. Gladstone and his family and views of Hawarden, consisted almost entirely of parts of the trunk of a tree felled by the

Portland St. United Reformed Chapel—English Congregational

great man himself, and a pile of wood chips from the felling. That there was a brisk sale of these bits of wood showed the reverence with which the Liberal leader was held in the town.

The most remarkable part of the bazaar, however, was the museum, housed in what was then the billiard room, and commanding an extra entrance fee. It is highly improbable that the room had ever before housed such an interesting collection of objects, and it provided ample evidence of Aberystwyth's connections with the sea and distant ports, and with mining areas all over the world. There were native dresses from China, Korea, New Zealand, New Guinea, and shawls and lacework from India, Persia, Afghanistan, Kashmir, Kirghiz and Brazil. On exhibit, also, were uncut diamonds and rubies from South America, native craftwork, and carvings and curios from every continent. Less attractive, but equally fascinating, was the collection of snakes from Borneo, South Africa and Brazil. The sailor's need for something to do to while away the time on long voyages under sail was shown in a Swiss clock made of 287 pieces of wood by Capt. Rowland Jones, a member of the Portland St. Church. These and many other things—including a fine collection of model ships and antique furniture-made for a very attractive exhibition.

Music was provided in the mornings and afternoons by the Welsh harpist, Telynor Cymru, dressed in his bardic robes and playing on the balcony. The Briton Band played on the terrace in the evening.

One of the outstanding features of this

event was the enthusiastic support it received from people of all classes and religious denominations, a feature of all church bazaars in the latter half of the 19th century. The financial result was a clear profit of over £700, equivalent to well over £9,000 in 1980. But the debt was still over £1,000 and, despite the efforts of the members, it had not been reduced in 1896 when there was a big change.

One of the church members was William Williams, the Chief Inspector of Schools for Wales who lived in St. David's Rd. in a house now called "Morven". He died in 1896 and left a considerable fortune to his son; William Lindsay. William Lindsay Williams graduated in law at Cambridge and entered a solicitors office. He suffered a great deal of ill-health and when his father died, he threw up his work in Swansea and returned to Aberystwyth. Suffering as he did from what was then an incurable disease, and having no friends in Aberystwyth, he was very lonely and the Rev. T. A. Penry set out to befriend the young man, work at which Penry was at his best. The young man's respect and affection for his minister was such that when he died in 1897 at the early age of 26, he left a large legacy to the church.

This bequest was straightforward but the same could not be said of another major legacy in the will. He bequeathed £1,500 to the University College of Wales, Aberystwyth to establish a scholarship in Physics or Chemistry "tenable at the College by a person of Welsh birth who must not be Unitarian or Roman Catholic". This bequest attracted a great deal of

attention and criticism and placed the College in a quandary. While it badly needed the money it could not accept the religious qualification. With the financial support of the Portland St. Church, it tried to have the restrictive clause removed by court order. The attempt failed and the £1,500 went to the church, which then found itself possessed of about £12,000. All the debts of the church were paid, some badly needed improvements were carried out, and it was impressed upon the poorer members that inability to contribute to the fortnightly collections should not keep them from attending their church. There was also a marked increase in the church's contributions to other causes.

T. A. Penry had long been a leading figure and a highly respected man in Aberystwyth when his health began to fail. In 1910 he was forced to give up his work for a while. The strain imposed by the war proved too much for him and he died in September 1918 after 44 years service to his church and the town.

He was succeeded in 1920 by the Rev. George Benton who stayed for only four years. In February 1926 the Rev. Yorwerth Davies became the minister, a very good preacher who served the church well for 25 years. The present minister, the Rev. Alwyn Davies, accepted the ministry in July 1953. During his 27 years in Portland St. Alwyn Davies's has become well known to his church, the town, the students, and to hospital patients for his kindness and good humour. College students have always been welcome at the Manse.

As a result of changes in the way Congre-

gationalism is organised, the church is now known as the United Reformed Church.

Unitarianism, a very strong sect in south east Ceredigion, did not settle in Aberystwyth until late in the 19th century. In the spring of 1895 the Rev. D. W. Griffiths, a convert and therefore full of zeal, came to Aberystwyth to preach Unitarianism in a town where this had never been done before. He was sent by the British and Foreign Unitarian Society on a missionary journey through Mid and North Wales. There were four Unitarian students in the University College at that time from Cribyn, Cwrtnewydd and Cledlyn. Despite his efforts, he achieved very little except that after his departure, the students concerned tried to form a Sunday School

The New Street Meeting House

and met a few times in a house in Pier St.

During the next five years several other attempts were made and the number of Unitarian students did increase. What did make a difference, however, was the coming to Aberystwyth of the Rev. George Eyre Evans, his sister and the "Old Professor" as his father was called. George Eyre Evans called together a few of the Unitarian students to his small library in "Binswood" in Llanbadarn Rd. and together they arranged to hold regular services. The first was held on 23 March 1903, the beginning of Unitarianism in Aberystwyth, and the first sermon was given by George Eyre Evans.

After three Sundays at Binswood the venue was moved first to the Old Assembly Rooms, and later to the new Market Hall which came to be called the Palladium. Then came the change which was to give the cause a permanent home. In New St. there was a converted coach house with an attractive front which was used by Sidney Galloway as a bookshop. As he was moving to new premises in Pier St. in 1906 the Unitarians were urged by their secretary, D. Ivon Jones, to take over the little building. This was agreed to and in order to get possession quickly the members bundled the remainder of Galloway's books and possessions into a cart and took it over to the new premises.

David Ivon Jones was the grandson of a well known Aberystwyth shopkeeper known as Ivon. David suffered from ill health and was believed to have tuberculosis. For this reason, in 1907 he left for South Africa in search of health and there he founded the South African Communist

Party. In 1924, while attending a Communist conference in Moscow, he died and was given a state funeral, a far cry from Tabernacl and New St.

The period 1932-36 was a flourishing one and it was decided to appoint the first minister, the Rev. John Marles Thomas of Talgarreg. One of his successors was the Rev. D. Jacob Davies, whose wit enlivened many a gathering and broadcast programme.

Unitarianism like most other denominations suffered a drop in numbers after 1945, and the congregation became so very small that in 1976 the Unitarians ceased to meet in Aberystwyth.

Also in New St., but near Pier St., is Elim, the Pentecostal Church, once the home of the North and South Wales Bank and still having the appearance of a bank from the outside.

Elim Pentecostal Chapel

Vestry Taverns

For almost a century and a half Nonconformity has disapproved of public houses and the drinking of ale, and has almost always opposed the extension of drinking hours and the erection of new taverns. But before the late 1830's things were very different. The monthly meetings of deacons were often conducted in taverns and a good deal of ale was consumed. Nor did the preachers disapprove of taverns, they welcomed innkeepers as members of their flocks and on occasions even encouraged members to become publicans. That very strict disciplinarian, the Rev. Edward Jones of Tabernacl, advised a member of his congregation to leave his farm in Devil's Bridge and take over a public house in Aberystwyth. A drink of ale (*y dablen*) before the service was a normal thing for a preacher and it was not unknown for him to take a drink in the pulpit before launching on his sermon.

At Aberystwyth almost every denomination had its favourite tavern. The Calvinistic Methodist patronised the *Unicorn*, an old, single-storey, thatch-roofed inn at the corner of New St. and Pier St., owned by Nanteos. Behind the parlour was a smaller room where Methodists congregated for their nightly and Sabbatarian drink. In the 1830's and '40's it was kept by Betty Dafydd Williams, a strict Methodist who, in her younger days, went regularly to Llangeitho for communion Sunday. In the days when the Methodists were persecuted and ridiculed in the town, and had to meet at strange times and places, she was often to be seen going to a service at 6.0 a.m. with a lantern to guide her through the dark streets. After Tabernacl was built the deacons would go after the Sunday service to the Unicorn, but when Mrs. Williams was in charge, they were allowed only one drink each and had to drink it standing up.

The tavern used by the Baptists was the *New Inn* in Great Darkgate St., kept by John Morgan, who, in the early 19th century, was also the postmaster. He was later forced to sell the inn to pay for the cost of a law suit with a man named Herring of London, but recouped his losses by fishing in Cardigan Bay. Afterwards he was fond of saying that he had "been marred by a Herring and made by a herring". The inn was sold to David Rees, a deacon at Bethel Baptist Church and was used regularly by that church's deacons on Sundays.

The Congregationalists' favourite tavern was the *Miners Arms* in Great Darkgate St. kept by Siencyn y Gât (Jenkin of the Gate) a name which suggests that either he or his family may have been connected with some special gate, probably a turnpike gate. The inn was run by his wife, Mal y Gât, for Jenkin was a lead miner and it was he who advised Lewis Pugh the younger to take over the lease of Cwmystwyth Mine in 1830, an act which made Pugh a rich man.

Mal y Gât had a rule that if a customer spent a shilling at the inn on Saturday night he would be eligible for a free glass of ale on Sunday morning. With beer at a penny a quart that would have involved some very heavy drinking indeed. The Miners Arms was much patronised by Azariah Shadrach's strongest supporters when he was struggling to establish Congregationalism in the town. When needing barm or yeast Aberystwyth people usually sent their children to buy it at a public house, and Mal y Gât was a favourite source but, remembering the way the Methodists had opposed Shadrach, she always refused to sell to the child of a Methodist.

The Wesleyans were not known to patronise any one tavern until the Market Tavern was opened in Market St. in 1832. It was kept by a man from Rhydypennau, Griffith James, known locally as Gruffydd the Cooper. When the Wesleyans first went to Queen St. they made some use of the nearby *Lord Hill*, but this seems to have been taken over by the town's cobblers who met there from Monday to Thursday evenings to discuss current affairs, both local and national. They even founded a charity club there to assist the itinerant cobblers who frequently came to work in the town during the holiday season.

Attitudes to drinking and frequenting public houses began to alter in the late 1830's, a change which owed more to Methodism than to any other cause at first. It probably began in Aberystwyth when John Jones, a deacon at Tabernacl and a fervent advocate of total abstinence, raised the matter at a monthly society meeting in 1834. Methodists were very concerned with some social evils of the times and drunkenness was rampant in Aberystwyth. They were also very numerous and influential in the town and when the Rev. Edward Jones and others began to thunder against drunkenness from the pulpit many were converted, albeit unwillingly. Other denominations followed suit and by 1836 the movement had taken the form of a revival, the Temperance Revival. Nor did the movement flag, processions were still being held in the 1840's when a native describes one consisting of about 6,000 teetotallers and others parading the streets "preceded by banners and singing, if not at concert pitch, certainly at the tops of their voices".

Not all the Nonconformists were prepared to follow the path of total abstinence. A number of families left the chapel for the Established Church because they disapproved of what they believed to be extremism. One of these was the Lewis Pugh family, another was one of the Julian brothers. The Julian family came to Aberystwyth from Tywyn and at the beginning

The New Inn, Great Darkgate St.

of the 19th century it was one of the most respected and influential families in the town. They always acted as hosts to Morgan Howell, the famous Methodist preacher when he visited Aberystwyth. There were two branches of the family, both headed by a Capt. Julian. One of these stayed faithful to Tabernacl and total abstinence while the other Capt. Julian disapproved of the temperance revival and left Tabernacl. One of the Julians later kept a shop at the eastern corner of North Parade and Terrace Rd., now a shoe shop.

It says much for the strength of the chapels that they were able to keep Nonconformity firmly tied to the temperance movement for over a century. One institution which helped them to do this was the Band of Hope, another was the local newspaper, for both the *Cambrian News* and the *Welsh Gazette* were strongly opposed to "the drink trade". The temperance campaign remained fierce in Aberystwyth until the outbreak of World War II.

Although there is no record of there having been any gin shops in Aberystwyth bearing the notice "Drunk for a Penny, Dead Drunk for Tuppence", there was a good deal of gin being drunk in the town in the early 19th century, despite the heavy taxes imposed on spirits by the Act of 1851. The following handbill, printed by Esther Williams about 1840, was an attempt to present the economic argument for total abstinence.

"Two glasses of gin every day at $1\frac{1}{2}$d a glass cost £4. 11s 3d. a year." Then it lists what could be bought for that money. "A man's hat, six shillings; pair of men's stockings, 1s 9d.; pair of women's stockings, 1s 6d.; shift and muslin cap, 3s 8d.; printed cotton gown, 5s 6d.; full sized man's cotton shirt 4s.; full size fustian coat, 16s.; pair of large blankets, 12s.; neck-handkerchief, 1s 4d.; pair of men's shoes, 8s 2d.; flannel petticoat, 2s 6d.; coarse cloth coat, 7s.; quilting waistcoat, 4s.; fustian trousers, lined, 7s 6d.; and a pair of large cotton sheets, 6s. Total £4. 11s. 6d."

The Band of Hope

One of the most active and prominent men in Aberystwyth in the middle of the 19th century was the Rev. John Williams, a member of Tabernacl. He was an ardent advocate of total abstinence and had himself signed the pledge in Bethel in the heat of the Temperance Revival in 1837.

In 1851, the year of the Great Exhibition at the Crystal Palace, he went to London at a time when the Temperance Conference was being held there. Being a staunch supporter of temperance he attended an enthusiastic meeting at Exeter Hall where the speaker was the Rev. Dr. John Thomas and the music was provided in part by a Welsh Choir, already in London to sing at the Crystal Palace. The following day he attended an equally enthusiastic gathering at the Y.M.C.A. Hall in Aldersgate. At both of these meetings people spoke in glowing terms of the Band of Hope, especially in the populous towns of the North of England. His interest was kindled, and he made enquiries.

He went to London again the following year to attend the annual Temperance Conference and again heard enthusiastic praise for the new movement and, although meant for juveniles, of how it was helping adults.

He returned home full of the desire to start the movement in Aberystwyth and lost no time in discussing the matter with his friends, including the Rev. Edward Jones of Tabernacl. They all rallied to his cause. David Jones the Bank wanted to call it the *Cold Water Army* as was done in North America but John insisted on using the name by which the movement was known in the remainder of the United Kingdom.

The next step was to contact the well known temperance advocate T. B. Smithies, editor of the Band of Hope Review, and to obtain from him the "Roll" on which to enter the names of the "Band". This was done, the Roll was accepted and the Band of Hope was launched in Aberystwyth.

Each member had to sign a declaration on which were the words "beverages and tobacco" but in deference to the wishes of many of his supporters, John Williams had the words "and tobacco" covered with "of all kinds". The declaration then read

"We agree that we will abstain from all intoxicating beverages of all kinds, and try to induce others to do the same."

The movement began on 14 December 1852 in Tabernacl where lectures and exhortations were held regularly. Enrolment went on for several evenings. The meetings were crowded with juveniles and were often far from orderly, especially when the children were excited by the promise of tea parties and processions.

Copies of the *Band of Hope Review* were distributed monthly, each cost $\frac{1}{2}$d and gave news of different districts and various aspects of temperance. It was illustrated with well-executed wood cuts and engravings, for Smithies was a firm believer in the use of visual aids in teaching.

The pledge card measured 6 ins by 4ins and the ones used in Aberystwyth were in Welsh with slogans surrounded by engravings. The slogans were "Touch not, Taste not, Handle not", and "Wine is a Mocker". Later the Tabernacl Band also used English cards.

The first grand demonstration by the Band of Hope was held in Aberystwyth in July 1855 and it was attended by all the bands within 10 miles of the town. Tabernacl was packed to overflowing and there the children were given lectures and talks. Later, lunch was provided on the field where Seilo was to be built, and in the afternoon the 3,000 children marched in procession through the principal streets of the town.

Processions then became a regular event and it became customary, if possible, to include those who had been cured of drinking alcohol. On one New Year's Day the procession was headed by 50 sailors. There were also competitions, including essays on such topics as "The Relation of the Temperance Movement to the Young" which sounds much too difficult for the children of a town where there was still very little education. There were also debates but the organisers were always

careful to wind up with a convincing argument for total obstinence.

A club was formed, *Clwb Dirwestol* (the Temperance Club) which met in the Town Hall but it lasted only three years.

Tabernacl's example was followed by the other churches who formed their own Bands of Hope. Every attempt was made to enroll young mariners, for sailors were heavy drinkers and special meetings were held for this purpose at Sion, the old Congregational chapel in Penmaes-glas.

September 1864 marked a further advance in the temperance cause with the opening of the Temperance Hall at the corner of North Parade and Queens Rd. Although in existence for only 30 years it was a scene of stirring events. This was the hall where Samuel Wilberforce and Samuel Morley spoke to enthusiastic audiences, where Edward Miall and Carvell Williams pleaded the cause of religious equality, where Henry Austin Bruce, Lewis Dillwyn and George Osborne stirred their hearers almost to mutiny over the plight of those evicted in 1868. This was the hall where Henry Richard, in a magnificent speech, set out the claims of Peace and International Arbitration. This was where the best harpists and singers of Wales could be heard, and the choirs thundered out the "Messiah".

It was formally opened on September 13 and 14, 1864 and the Band of Hope was well to the fore. The hymns sung were specially written for the occasion and while they cannot be described as great music they had a strong temperance flavour. Their titles were "Mae'r Band of Hope yn Codi" (the Band of Hope is

The Temperance Hall

Ellen Davies's Band of Hope Pledge Card, 1892

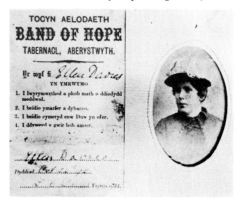

Rising), "Water is the Drink", and "Awn Ymlaen Gyfeillion Sobrwydd" (Let us go Forward, Friends of Sobriety).

The Jubilee of the movement was held in Aberystwyth on 10 November 1897 when there was a procession followed by a children's meeting in Seilo and a tea. At 7 p.m. a public meeting was held at Tabernacl where the chairman was Principal T. F. Roberts of the University College, president of the Union of Bands of Hope.

The Band of Hope continued to thrive in Aberystwyth; shortly before the outbreak of the first World War it had a membership of close on 1,000. It continued to receive support after the war but interest declined and nothing is now heard of it. The Temperance Hall was demolished about 1894.

Our Lady of the Angels and St. Winifride's Catholic Church

Over three centuries after the 'Suppression', Roman Catholicism returned to Cardiganshire. Soon after the Catholic Emancipation Act of 1829 accorded Roman Catholics civic equality, an anonymous benefactor offered them a site on which to build a church in Aberystwyth but they were too few, too poor and not sufficiently well organised to take advantage of the offer. Some services were held in the theatre in Thespian St. but Bishop Brown's plan to convert it into a Catholic Chapel in 1854 proved impracticable. Meanwhile, Mass was occasionally celebrated at William Osborne's cottage in Cambrian Place whenever some Breton or other travelling missionary priest happened to be passing through the town from Carmarthen, Brecon or Shrewsbury.

St. Winifride's Roman Catholic Church

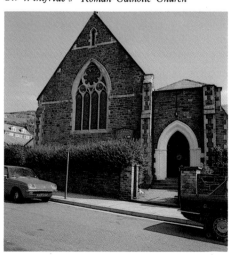

What really established Roman Catholicism in Aberystwyth was the arrival there in 1867 of Bishop Bernard Collier, O.B.E., formerly a missionary in Mauritius. He came for a holiday but when he saw that there was no place of worship for either the Catholic residents or for the much larger number of Catholic visitors, he decided to establish both a chapel and a priest's residence at Queens Square House. He also provided the priest, a Belgian missionary, Fr. Charles Limpens. Queens Square House became the centre of Catholic life in the town from 1867 until 1875 when the new church was opened in Queens Rd. During this period, 67 people were baptised and 43 candidates confirmed.

The building of the new church owed a great deal to the efforts of Welsh-speaking Fr. William Williams from Anglesey, who came to Aberystwyth as resident pastor in 1872. Bishop Collier had already purchased a piece of land in Queen's Rd. from Sir Pryse Pryse, and Fr. Williams launched an appeal for funds in the Catholic magazine *The Tablet* in September 1873. The response was so encouraging that he contracted with James Williams to build the church according to the plans of the architects, George Jones and Son. Building began in 1875 but the unstable ground and rising costs made it much more costly than had been estimated and the 110 foot high bell tower and organ gallery had to be omitted. But the adjoining priest's house was built, for £500. An anonymous benefactor presented the High Altar which was made and installed for £300. Another generous gift was the set of *Stations of the Cross*, described

as the work of a talented Parisian artist, Mons. Aristide Alcan.

The laying of the foundation stone by Bishop Collier in July 1874 was accompanied by a procession of Secular and Regular Clergy, an unfamiliar sight in Calvinist Cardiganshire and not approved of by all who witnessed it. The chapel, an Early Decorated Gothic Building was completed by July 1874 and on the 11 August the dedication took place. The Solemn Opening Ceremony was performed by no less a person than His Eminence Cardinal Manning, Archbishop of Westminster. The famous Cardinal's arrival at the height of the holiday season created considerable interest, and a large crowd gathered in Queen's Rd. before the ceremony was due to begin. Fortunately it was a fine sunny day and His Eminence, magnificent in his purple *Cappa Magna*, assisted by other richly robed high-ranking clergy, was an impressive sight. The special choir consisted of members of the Hallé, Salford Cathedral, and other Manchester choirs.

Fr. Williams was a popular priest and he received a considerable number of converts as well as 96 baptisms and 65 candidates for Confirmation. But his health was deteriorating and in 1883 he died.

The church then entered a difficult period, regular attendance fell to about 40 and there was a rapid turnover of priests, three in one year. After 1888, however, the situation began to improve slowly. The arrival of a group of Breton Teaching Sisters who established a school helped the church but the congregation remained small until after 1918 when the progressive phase began.

In 1923 the house known as Castell Brychan, formerly the home of David Jenkins, Professor of Music at the University College, was opened as St. Mary's College for training priests but it had to be closed in 1934. Two years later the Carmelite Fathers took over the parish and St. Mary's College was reopened. A determined attempt was then made to persuade young ordinands to learn to preach in Welsh and, ultimately, to serve the Catholic Church in Welsh Wales. They also undertook a general survey of the Mission area and since then new churches have been established at Lampeter (1940), Aberaeron (1958), Borth (1969) and Penparcau (1970).

The Salvation Army

About the middle of August 1882, some highly coloured posters appeared in the streets of Aberystwyth. Their contents were as shown.

On Saturday evening August 26th 1882, a large crowd, consisting mostly of children, gathered to meet the train and witness the invasion. Much to their disappointment the "army" consisted of six young city people, three men and three women. As soon as they arrived they began to sell their paper, the *War Cry*, in the streets.

The proceedings on Sunday began at 7.0 a.m. and did not end until 10 p.m. The Temperance Hall was crowded out on three of the day's four meetings and there were 13 converts during the evening service. The beach and Tan-y-cae also

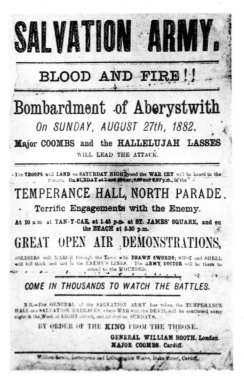

The 1882 poster

saw crowded meetings and there was a great deal of singing at all the services, accompanied by a violin indoors and a brass instrument out of doors.

Inevitably, the coming of the army aroused a great deal of discussion and much controversy in the town. The majority maintained that the Salvation Army movement was more suited to industrial areas, where slums abounded, than to a town like Aberystwyth. Others, a small minority,

disagreed and argued that there were local slums too. As one put it "Let any man go down to Fountain Court, or Windmill Court or Northgate Court and to other places in Aberystwyth and let them ascertain how these people live in the hot days of summer and the cold nights of winter and he will find that these people have no need to go to hell. Their life is hell."

It took Aberystwyth many years to accept the Salvation Army, they annoyed local councillors in the Edwardian days by holding open-air meetings on the Castle grounds at all times. As a result, all religious meetings were banned from this area after 1909, an action which upset those Nonconformists who had been accustomed to holding special services at the castle. The Salvation Army made things worse by continuing to hold unauthorised meetings. They were also accused of being noisy and of making nuisances of themselves on Marine Terrace.

General Booth at the age of 78, visited the town in August 1907 and preached to a crowded audience from the pulpit in Seilo. He was also listened to by thousands in the open air. For many years the movements' headquarters has been in Alexandra Rd, opposite the Welsh Primary School in the little chapel built by the Wesleyans to serve as a school and an English Church in 1844. The Army is now highly respected in the town.

The Port

The Harbour

One of the first descriptions of Aberystwyth, made c.1561 describes it as "a barred Haven of no Valewe, the Mayor of the town claymeth the port . . . from Saynt Davids all along this coaste is no trade of m(er)chandize but all full of Rocks and daungiers." The trade at this time was so small that no ship worthy of the name ever entered it, the only vessels being fishing boats of 4 to 5 tons each. The town had no mariners, only fishermen.

Until the 18th century the sandbar at the entrance to the harbour was of little importance because of the small size of the ships. Before the 1740's they were rarely over 12 tons, any large ships wishing to enter the port had to wait for the big tides.

By the middle of the century, however, the position had changed, there was a considerable amount of lead ore to be exported and much merchandise imported to supply the needs of the industry and a growing town. People became concerned about the sandbar, and the fact that Aberystwyth was still only a creek within the port of Aberdovey which, though a settlement of only a very few houses and a wharf, was the home of the collector of customs.

In 1759 it was resolved by a group called "the Big Fourteen of Aberystwyth" that Parliament be petitioned to move the custom office to their town. and that it would be wise to seek the support of Lord Powis, himself the lessee of Esgair-mwyn mine, by sending him the following plea:

"The trade of late has become greatly increased, and by reason of its proximity to the sea, the same would still become more considerable but for the inconvenience of our having no Customs House within ten miles of the town . . . . But the distance alone from a Customs House is but a small part of the inconvenience we undergo, for we must beg to aquaint your Lordship that the River Dovey is often impassable for a fortnight together by reason of the strong easterly gales that blow down the river . . . . We are thereby retarded in getting despatches, and consequently prevented from sailing on our Intended Voyage when the wind permits it. Inconvenience greatly annoys the Trade of this Place, and such Obstruction very often obliges the Masters of Vessels to discharge their Contract and Protest against the said Passage. We further beg leave to represent to your

A view of the harbour c. 1880

Lordship that the town of Aberystwyth is situated in the centre of the Port, in view of the whole district, having from Thirty to Forty Vessels from Fifteen to Sixty tons burden constantly employed particularly in exporting Lead Ore and Black Jack, and of the former Commodity there is from Three to Four Thousand Tons annually shipped Coastwise from hence—which Trade would still become more considerable if we had a Customs House here . . . We humbly hope for your Lordship's Assistance in getting a Customs House appointed here, or that of Aberdovey removed hither. The latter place having little or no trade besides the exportation of a few Oak Poles sent Coastwise which require no Cocket."

The petition was successful and in 1763 the Customs House was transferred to Aberystwyth, where it has remained ever since. It was first located in Trefechan while a suitable home was being built at the seaward end of Pier Street, behind where the Theological College now stands. From

The Customs House in 1820 was the low building between the two tall houses beneath the hill top

there it was later moved to the bottom of what became Custom House St., and then back to Pier Street.

The transfer proved a great encouragement to trade which, in turn, showed only too clearly the need for improving the harbour.

In 1780 the town secured an Act of Parliament empowering it "to repair, enlarge and preserve their harbour" which "was in danger of being lost or destroyed." It came into force on 21 August 1780 and a body of Harbour Trustees was formed which included the Rev. William Powell of Nanteos, Thomas Johnes of Croft Castle, Roderick Richardes of Penglais, Matthew Davies of Cwmcynfelin, Phillip Pugh of Tyglyn and Thomas Lloyd.

At the first meeting Hugh Hughes was appointed clerk at a salary of £5 per annum

The second Customs House is the building with the balcony

and John Griffith became the harbourmaster at £10 a year. Both had to be sworn in and Griffith had to provide a surety. They also appointed a treasurer. This done, the meeting adjourned until the following morning when, at the Golden Lion, the oath was taken by the harbour master and the collector (as the treasurer was usually called).

John Griffith did not last long, he was dismissed a few months later for failing to collect the dues and rates properly from those using the harbour.

All the meetings were held at inns and taverns—the Golden Lion, Gogerddan Arms, Talbot and others.

The Act gave the trustees borrowing powers and they proceeded to use these "upon the credit of the harbour rates" A notice to this effect was "affixed upon the Town Hall of Aberystwyth and the Church Door of Llanbadarn Fawr". Thomas Fruin was engaged as superintendent of the proposed harbour works at a salary of two guineas a week. He was to contract for machines, tools, implements and other materials needed for the work.

But the trustees were thrifty souls and seeing the approach of winter, when harbour work would be difficult, they dismissed Fruin after a month, paid him £93.16s. and informed Samuel Weston, engineer of Bristol, that they did not propose to do any more work until the return of spring. At their next meeting, however, 23 October 1780, they ordered that "a work to fence in the tide be made and erected immediately or as soon as possible on the south side of the rock called Penhukin".

This was the last resolution of the year. the next three meetings had to be cancelled because too few attended. On New Year's Day, 1781, they met to drink one another's health, and the next day elected new trustees to replace William Powell, Thomas Johnes and Philip Pugh who, it was said, had all died. A new harbourmaster was appointed, William Jolson, and Mathew Davies was asked to purchase a silver badge for the harbour master. He waited seven years before he did this and was not thanked for the badge until 24 years later. It bore the inscription "Rhodd (the gift of) Mathew Davies Ysw., Cwmcynfelin 1788" and is illustrated in G. E. Evans's *Aberystwyth Court Leet*. Unfortunately, it has since been lost.

Jolson proved no better than his predecessor; in 1782 he absconded and, apparently, took with him some of the dues. He was not replaced, but Pierce Evans, one of the trustees, was appointed "collector of the rates and duties at a stipend in accordance with the duties".

Meanwhile, very little work was being done at the harbour because the trustees were so loth to spend money. The reason for this was that though the Act empowered the trustees to borrow £4,000 "on the (harbour) rates" they succeeded in borrowing only £825 until 1834 because the rates and duties were so low and money was scarce.

It was found necessary to clean and widen "a certain place below the Cupola where the vessels usually load and unload". Lewis Evans, appointed harbour master in 1782, was told to "lay out and expend a sum not exceeding 30s on any improvement in the harbour". Even allowing for the great difference in the value of money then and now, he could not have done much with 30s. (The *Cupola* was probably the name of a tavern which stood near where the fire station now stands).

In July 1783 it was pointed out that grain had been very scarce in the county of late and that its import would be encouraged if the duty on corn was reduced. This was done and it was also decided to remit to the masters of the *True Briton*, the *Mayflower* and the *Happy Return* some of the dues paid by them on their cargoes of grain.

Probably because of the difficulties involved in collecting the harbour dues, the trustees "Lett out to the Highest Bidder the rates and duties for one year". The winning bid was £108. The 'letting' was done at the Fountain Inn, Trefechan, while the trustees enjoyed their punch.

Three years after Jolson absconded it was heard that he was with one of the trustees, Jones of Penywern, who was ordered to bring him before the board. Nothing more is heard of him and it is likely that Jolson again made himself scarce.

The main task facing the trustees was clearing away the sand bar and they believed that this could be done by diverting the course of the river Ystwyth. Several attempts were made but all failed, largely because the trustees were loth to embark on what was bound to be an expensive undertaking. The largest sum spent on any one of these attempts was £20 in October 1786, after Sir Thomas Bonsall became a trustee.

During the winter of 1787-88 a sum of £80 was spent on installing mooring posts but only £9.10s. on trying to divert the river.

The following winter saw the river taking things into its own hands and forcing the trustees to act. Early in 1789, soon after the appointment of Edward Humphreys as the new harbour master, it was reported that the rivers Rheidol and Ystwyth had separated, each entering the sea by a different channel. The situation was now worse than before.

A meeting was hurriedly arranged and it was resolved "that the said rivers shall be forthwith joined again in the most effectual manner by such stone work as shall be necessary at....a sum not exceeding ten pounds", which, as usual, was far too little.

For the next few years many small sums were spent on clearing away the sand and shingle which often blocked the harbour mouth. In 1793, £40 was expended on removing a bank which had "lately formed to the great detriment of shipping".

Nor was the sandbank the only obstrucion; in 1795 David Parry was ordered to remove the keel "laid on or near a dock for building a vessel" or the trustees would take possession of it.

About this time, an engineer named Hamilton was engaged to report on the state of the harbour and means of improving it. He surveyed the whole area and reported that both the best and cheapest way to improve the harbour would be to cut a channel for the river through the bank of sand and shingle known as Rofawr. The trustees paid him his fee of thirty guineas and thought no more of his plans.

The end of the 18th century saw a marked increase in the demand for sites for shipbuilding, and in July 1800 the board met to plan the layout of that part of the harbour to be used for building ships. It was ordered that a trench 18 ins. wide and 12 ins. deep be cut at a cost of 4d. a rood to show the boundary of the area. This was the grassy strip to the north of the harbour. It was then divided into lots, one of which was as follows: a stretch of 154 feet extending from the west end of the sawpit built by the late John Jones to the boundary of lot 2. It was let to Isaac Jones for 3 years for a payment of £1.1.0 and 3 guineas a year. Other lots were let at 2 guineas a year. There were also lots on the south side of the harbour.

In 1801 the entrance to the harbour was "so often choked up that the smallest vessels (were) frequently obliged to lie till a land flood set them at liberty". But all the trustees did was to pay £5 to four men "to open the mouth of the Harbour".

This and the increase in shipbuilding brought a demand for more inprovements and early in 1802 a sum not exceeding £120 was ordered to be spent on erecting a wall on the north side of the river and repairing the piles. But no one could be found to do it and two years later the trustees had to send "to Barmouth or elsewhere" for someone to do the work. The result of the sending is unknown but there is an old wall skirting the northern shipbuilding area.

In the same year, probably discouraged by their failure to clear away the sand bar at the harbour mouth, the board decided to do something that had first been mooted and carefully planned in 1755. In that year Lewis Morris, then Superintendent of Crown Mines in Cardiganshire proposed that a stone pier be built out to sea from the end of Weeg (Pier) St., curving to the north so as to provide a shelter for small ships. His plan was as follows: (see p.8). "A Pier Proposed to be Built at Aberystwyth in South Wales For the Advancement of the Fishery and Other Branches of Trade.

Whereas the Bar at the Entrance of the Rivers Rheidol and Ystwyth is so Exeeding bad and Dangerous, and so greatly Obstructive to the Fishery, a most Valuable Branch of the British Trade, which for Several years past hath abounded in this Bay in such Manner that One Boat in Two hours time hath frequently taken Sixty Thousand Herrings.

By the Joynt Advice of the Neighbouring Gentlemen and the Inhabitants of this Place, It is proposed to Build a Stone Peer on the North Side of the Town Extending from the Bank at High-water Mark (along the Rocks on the South Side of a sandy Bight called Y Wîg or Weeg) below Low-water mark, So that a Vessel of Twenty ton may (sail) into Safety at Lowwater on Common Spring Tides. The whole Length of the Pier to be about Two Hundred yards, Containing about Fourteen Thousand Cubic yards. To be Built at the Expense of about Two Thousand Five Hundred Pounds as by the Following Estimate:

	£ s d
1. Two Floats and their Materials to convey the Larger kind of Stones.	200.0.0
2. Casks for Slinging of Midling Stones, Chains, Ropes, Bars, Augers, wedges and repairs of Tools.	200.0.0
3. Gunpowder to Blow Rocks. Capstans. Beams of Wood in the work and Scaffolding Timber.	150.0.0
4. Boathire to Sling Stones and to Tow the Flats and Casks and Freights to carry Materials	200.0.0
5. Cranes, Leavers, Handscrews and other Engines to bring the Stones to their work	150.0.0
6. Workmen's Wages Immediately on the Peer	400.0.0
7. Labourers Wages in Quarrying of Stones for the Peer, attending the Floats, Casks etc.	400.0.0
8. Blowing and Removing a Flat of Rocks that Lie within the Peer Containing about Six Thousand Cubic yards.	300.0.0
9. Paving the top of the Peer at 1600 Super/yards	40.0.0
10. The Breastwork or Battlement to be wrought with Lime and Secured with timber containing about 400 Cubic yards	80.0.0
11. Undertaker and Overseers wages and allowance for clerks and Stewards Supposing the work to be done in three years	380.0.0
	———"
	2500.0.0

But the "Neighbouring Gentlemen" etc. did nothing about it because of the expense, perhaps, or because of Lewis Morris's strong opposition to their working and taking the profits from mines which, in reality, belonged to the Crown.

The trustees asked a Capt. Evans to design "the pier on the Weeg" and in 1802 it was decided to have it erected by a noted builder. But he was too busy and the pier was built by a John Evans. It was built so badly that it was destroyed by the sea in a very few years. An examination of the rocks of Craig y Wîg when the tide is out will reveal traces of the old pier. Pier St. was probably named after it.

From 1794 to 1805 the harbour dues and rates were let to the harbourmaster for £60 a year. After 1835 they were let by auction.

In 1824 it was reported that the harbour was in a deplorable condition and lost to trade for much of the year. The failure of the "Weeg" pier, which was said to have been no more than a dry walled construction in parts, and the growing protests from tradesmen and businessmen eventually forced the trustees to do something worthwhile. In 1834 they employed a well known civil engineer, George Bush, to survey the port and to suggest improvements. He urged the construction of a strong stone pier extending well beyond Tany-bwlch beach on the south side of the harbour. He also advocated the building of a lime wharf, a south wharf extending from the old pier to the Lead Ore House, and a quay along the north side of the harbour at an estimated cost, for the whole works, of £17,394. Similar advice was received from an engineer named Nimmo.

This plan was adopted by the trustees and work began in 1836. A new road was built from Penyrancor to the Ystwyth and a bridge erected over the river. Matthew Davies was paid £200 for the use of his Alltwen quarry for getting stone.

The great problem was still money; in 1836 they secured an Act of Parliament which allowed them to borrow up to £20,000, again on the harbour dues. This was an

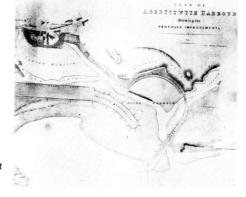

Bush's plan of the new stone pier 1834

The old wooden jetty

act of faith for they could not be sure that the pier would be a success. They borrowed £12,000, the Duke of Newcastle, then at Hafod, gave £1,000 and promised to act as guarantor for another £2,000 (he changed his mind later). But this was not enough.

In October 1837 the trustees were again hard pressed—not only was another £3,600 needed to carry on the work at the pier but the North and South Wales Bank was demanding the return of the money it had loaned. It was then that Joseph Downie of the National Provincial Bank came to the rescue by arranging that £8,000 be borrowed from his customers, enough to repay the bank and to carry on the harbour works. This, with other loans, created an army of "tally holders", all of whom had to be paid interest.

The work on the pier went on for years but it made a tremendous improvement. The scour created by the positioning and long length of the pier prevented sand from collecting so close to the harbour mouth and the sandbar became much less of an obstruction. But it was an expensive undertaking and from 1836 until they ceased to control the harbour, the energies of the trustees were devoted mainly to finding money to pay for the harbour works done by Bush, especially the pier, and paying interest on the money borrowed.

In 1836 new higher rates were substituted for the older ones and because of the improvements the revenue from the ships using the harbour increased from £240 in 1834 to £2,280 in 1858. The trustees were therefore able to meet the expenses and pay the interest to the tally holders.

In November 1847 the limits of the port were extended to include all the creeks and havens from New Quay in the south to the north bank of the river Dysynni, north of Tywyn.

All went fairly well until the 1860's when first, the railway came and took away so much of the port's trade that the dues fell to a little over a £1,000. In 1867 a number of severe storms did considerable damage to the new pier and it became obvious that the slaty stone from the Alltwen quarry was unsuited to the work. It was so easily eroded by the sea that the pier was in danger of being washed away. 12,000 tons of good stone were needed to prevent this happening and a tramline

The stone pier built after 1834

The stone quay which replaced the wooden jetty

was built along Tanybwlch from the pier to a source of good stone under Alltwen. The straight level track along which the line ran can still be seen. A sum of £4,000 was needed to repair the pier properly. According to the Act of 1836 the first charge on the revenue was the payment of interest to the tally holders but, to prevent the pier being destroyed, this could not be paid and the bonds became worthless.

Faced with all this the trustees decided to ask the Corporation to take over the harbour. They rightly maintained that if repair work was not done the harbour would become almost unusable and the railway would be in a position to raise transport rates to a level which would make coal, building materials etc. very expensive. In 1876 an Act of Parliament transferred the harbour into the care of the Corporation who undertook to pay $2\frac{1}{2}$ per cent interest to those who had loaned money.

But the Town Council had much on its plate at that time, especially the water scheme and there was little hope of a revival in sea trade. In 1878 the harbour was said to be still in a very bad state and there were complaints about its condition. The slight revival in fishing caused by the decline in sea trade revealed the serious lack of facilities for fishing boats, probably because such vessels did not pay harbour dues.

In the early 1870's the harbour was connected to the Manchester and Milford Railway by means of a branch line in the hope that this would help the port. It seemed to have little effect and was little used after about 1890. Nor did the exten-

St. David's Wharf, the railway ran in front of the lower buildings. The upper building was the Lead Ore Warehouse. The chute was used to unload lead ore into ships and railway trucks. The tall chimneys were said to be outlets for the smeltery fumes

They even had cows in the harbour

sion of the Vale of Rheidol Railway to the north quay in 1902 have more than a temporary effect, for by this time lead mining in North Cardiganshire was dying and there was little inducement to improve and modernize the harbour. In order to establish its ownership of the narrow gauge line to the harbour, one of the locomotives would puff its way to and from the quay once a year, but loaded trucks were never seen after about 1912. The extension was closed in 1930. The harbour was

Capt. Lloyd, Harbour Master

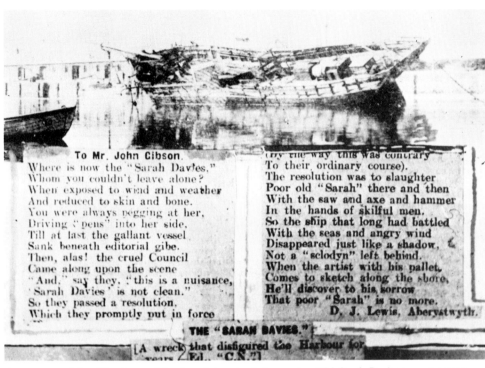

To Mr. John Gibson.

Where is now the "Sarah Davies,"
Whom you couldn't leave alone?
When exposed to wind and weather
And reduced to skin and bone.
You were always pegging at her,
Driving "pens" into her side,
Till at last the gallant vessel
Sank beneath editorial gibe.
Then, alas! the cruel Council
Came along upon the scene
"And," say they, "this is a nuisance,
'Sarah Davies' is not clean."
So they passed a resolution,
Which they promptly put in force

(by the way this was contrary
To their ordinary course).
The resolution was to slaughter
Poor old "Sarah" there and then
With the saw and axe and hammer
In the hands of skilful men.
So the ship that long had battled
With the seas and angry wind
Disappeared just like a shadow,
Not a "sclodyn" left behind.
When the artist with his pallet,
Comes to sketch along the shore,
He'll discover to his sorrow
That poor "Sarah" is no more.
D. J. Lewis, Aberystwyth.

THE "SARAH DAVIES."
[A wreck that disfigured the Harbour for years.—Ed., "C.N."]

An answer to John Gibson's complaint that the wreck of the once-beautiful Sarah Davies was an eyesore

described at this time as a "White Elephant" and "a great burden on the rates for many years."

Attempts at reviving sea trade having failed, it is now accepted that the future of the harbour lies with yachting, pleasure boating, and various forms of fishing, including lobsters. A university college study of the silt problem may be of assistance to the authority in coming to a decision on the future use of the haven. Of the plans discussed, the most promising appears to be the construction of a new quay and a lagoon for sailing boats.

The harbour ferry

The Port— Activities

Ship Building

The building of boats and ships must have been carried on in Aberystwyth for centuries but until the mid 18th century, the great majority were open boats which would carry 10 or 11 tons. They were built for fishing in the months of August, September and October and were used for trade for the remainder of the year. The length of the keel was usually 28ft 6ins and Lewis Morris described them in the 1740's as being very good boats.

Bigger ships became more common later and before 1800 a few vessels of over 300 tons were built; these could have left the harbour only when there was an exceptionally high tide.

The number and tonnage of ships built in Aberystwyth from about 1780 to 1880 was as follows;

	No built	Tonnage		No built	Tonnage
1778-90	33	1349	1830-40	19	1165
1790-1800	20	1110	1840-50	37	2777
1800-1810	31	1921	1850-60	34	3264
1810-1820	44	3089	1860-70	33	4013
1820-1830	12	477	1870-80	15	2537

These vessels consisted of sloops, schooners, brigs, brigantines, and barques. Until well into the 18th century the emphasis was on sloops, single masted vessels needing only 3 or 4 men. As trade increased the sloops gave way to schooners and these formed about 80 per cent of the ships built in Aberystwyth. Over one period of about twenty years, 59 schooners, 11 brigs, 7 brigantines, 6 barques and a slight variation on a brig known as a snow were built. The schooners averaged well under a hundred tons, the barques 300 tons and the brigs were 100-200 tons.

In 1801 the *James* was built, burthen 361 tons, in Aberystwyth; she was owned by Harvey & Co., and traded to Jamaica. All went well on the two first voyages but on the homeward passage on the third, on 26 August 1804, the *James* was captured by a French privateer and taken to Guadeloupe. More typical of Aberystwyth shipbuilding at that time was the *Minerva* (30 tons) built for a Chepstow firm for the coasting trade.

In the 1820's the *Hope* (55 tons) and the *John and Ann* (47 tons) attracted some attention because of their size. Both were still at work in 1885. The largest ship built in Aberystwyth was the well-known *Caroline Spooner* of 1,100 tons, launched in 1877. Other ships which excited comment for some reason or another were the barque *Anne Jenkins* and the brig *Credo*, both of which took emigrants to America, and the beautiful *Sarah Davies*, a schooner of 85 tons launched in 1860 and still going strong fifty years later. (see p.82).

The above table shows that as the century progressed, bigger ships were built, especially after the building of the stone pier when the harbour was much easier to enter and leave, and trade had greatly increased.

The timber traditionally used for building ships was oak, and much of this came from Radnorshire. But as the ships increased in size, timber had to be brought from overseas—Canada and the Baltic countries. Until early in the 19th century it was customary for the master or builder of a

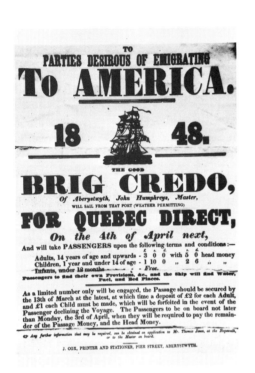

ship to visit Rhayader to inspect the timber available in that district. Auctions of local stands of oak and ash were held in the yard of the Talbot Inn. On 3 April 1829 "All that fine well known grove of wood called Allt Ddu in Cwm Rheidol within eight miles of the seaport of Aberystwyth" was sold. It comprised 1,300 oak trees, 300 ash trees and 900 dozen oak poles.

While small ships were built on the Trefechan side of the harbour, the main yards were on the northern side stretching from the bridge to Rofawr and bordered by what was appropriately called Shipbuilders Row (South Rd.) This was *Tan y Geulan*, a low grassy shelf only just above the high water mark. Until 1800, shipbuilding was carried on wherever there was room but, as stated above, the harbour area was then divided into lots and let to the shipbuilders.

The area now occupied by the castle end of South Rd. in front of the Custom's House, then in Custom House St. was covered with timber yards and a large saw pit. Later, steam saw mills were installed. The timber brought from overseas was unloaded on to Rofawr which was usually covered with large baulks of wood. Within easy reach of the ship building yards were a foundry, sail loft, chain, cable and anchor works, rope yards and a blockmaker.

Of the shipbuilders of the early 19th century the most interesting was known

The shipbuilding yards: note the chimney stack of the saw mills and the Customs House with its veranda

as Williams Fronfraith because he built Fronfraith. His boyhood was spent in Aberystwyth where, being an orphan, he was generally ill-fed and very ragged indeed. He then managed to get away to England where by dint of high intelligence and very hard work he became wealthy. Returning to Aberystwyth he opened a business as a wine and spirit merchant and it was he who built the place long known as Downie's Vaults. After a while he turned to shipbuilding, sailmaking and blockmaking and built himself a place known as *Yr Offis Fach* (the Little Office) at Graig Goch, near what is now the bottom end of Sea View Place.

There were quite a number of shipbuilders living in the town, the best-known being the Evans family. The first was Faulk Evans, he was succeeded by his son John and his grandson John Faulk Evans. This was the firm which built the above *Caroline Spooner, Anne Jenkins,* the barque *Tamerlane* and many others.

The saw mill and timber yard on Rofawr

Baulks of timber on Rofawr

Another well-known builder of ships was Edward James who built the *Sarah Davies.* The most active builders in the second half of the century were Thomas Jones and Thomas Watkins. The former built the *Jane Morgan,* 73 tons, in 1858; *Rheidol Valley,* 90 tons, 1859; *Blue Jacket,* 100 tons, 1860; *Helena,* 88 tons and *Confidence,* 75 tons, 1872; the brig *Sarah Phillips,* 200 tons, 1864; schooners *William and Mary* and *Glad Tidings* 100 tons each, 1866; the brig *M. A. Jones,* 200 tons, 1869; the schooner *Conovium,* 80 tons, 1876; and the *Nerissa,* 117 tons, 1878. Thomas Jones also built the *Lizzie,* the only screw steamer launched in Aberystwyth.

Active also was David Jones who built many ships, among them being *Fanny Fothergill, Jane Llewelyn, Priscilla, Morning Star, Rheidol, Progress, Ann Jones, Sophia and Emily,* and *Native.*

Until about the middle of the 19th century, the ownership of these ships was

A sailing ship nearing completion

shared among a number of people—artisans, clerks, shopkeepers and others. At one time sixteen partners may have been considered correct, for a man's share of a ship was sometimes called an ounce. After 1850, however, the wealthier merchants in the town began to take over from the little men and it was not long before most of the ships were owned by a few men.

There was also a considerable amount of ship repair work, and there were complaints that too much of the best sections of the harbour were devoted to this purpose. One bit of repair work which attracted much attention was that of the *Tamerlane.* John Evans, the builder, sold his quarter share in the ship to Capt. James of the schooner *Susan.* The *Tamerlane,* loaded with salt at Liverpool was on her way to a foreign port when she was driven before a strong gale and stranded under Morfa, south of Aberystwyth. She was brought into harbour and was condemned by

David Jones, Shipbuilder

Lloyd's agent. The ship was then bought by John Evans and repaired, eventually sailing from Aberystwyth for the U.S.A. with emigrants on board, under the command of Capt. James. After returning with a cargo of timber for London, she loaded with coal at a Welsh port and set off for the Mediterranean but was lost in a storm in the Bay of Biscay about 1849; three Aberystwyth men were washed overboard.

The launching of a ship usually attracted a large crowd. When the newly built *Lady Pryse* took to the water in 1875 she was watched by shipowners, shipbuilders, shipwrights, caulkers, smiths, sawyers, coopers, block and spar makers, boat builders, riggers, sailmakers, timber yard staff and sailors as well as many other townsfolk. The launching was watched from *Y Geulan,* the bank near the Sailor's Arms where there was a coalyard. The ship was built on the pebble beach below, an area covered at high tide. It is now the site of the sewage works built in 1924.

The *Wellington* and the *Hope* were regular traders to Quebec, bringing timber to the local timber yards and sawmill. Children loved watching the huge baulks being unloaded with the primitive gear then in use. The *Crusader,* too, was in this trade, carrying slates from Portmadoc to Bremen, then on to Finland for timber for Aberystwyth.

Among other ships remembered by old sailors was the big *Fanny Fothergill* which carried sugar from the West Indies to London, bones, presumably for making fertiliser or glue, from Monte Video to a Scottish port, and then on to Smyrna. The brigantine *Annie Maude* carried salt from Lisbon to St. John and Labrador, returning with salt cod for Genoa and other Mediterranean ports. The *Agenoria* stayed long in people's minds after her crew became fatally stricken with yellow fever in the Bight of Benin in West Africa, the White Man's Grave.

The schooner *John and Edward* was long remembered on account of the fatal accident which killed 21-year old James Williams, Ivon's brother-in-law, and a former pupil of John Evans. On a voyage to the Mediterranean on the *John and Edward* a strong gale sprang up in the Bay of Biscay and the ship ran for shelter to Belle Isle on 24 May 1857. On reaching the port the crew was busy furling the sails and preparing to put up the necessary signal, when the ship was fired on in blank shot by a French warship. This was followed by a live shot which killed James Williams who was aloft at the time.

The French deeply regretted their mistake and tried to make amends by disinterring James's body from his grave in Belle Isle and bringing him back to Aberystwyth in a coffin embedded in ballast on the *Bonne Emile.* His gravestone is among those laid out near the Parish Hall.

With the growth of shipping and shipbuilding in the first half of the century, more use was made of insurance and in 1853 the Mutual Ship Insurance Society opened an office in the town. It then became much easier to insure ships and cargo. It remained in being, with other insurance agencies, until the 1880's.

The coming of the railway and the decline in lead mining and related industries led inevitably to a decline in shipbuilding and by the early 1880's the industry was at its last gasp. The last ship to be built was the *Edith Eleanor* which was launched in 1881. She was built by J. Warrell & Co., for D. C. Roberts, the timber merchant and sold by him to a Wexford firm in 1917. She foundered in 1921.

But boat building continued in the town. Late in the 1880's after mastering his craft, David Williams established a boat building business in a workshop behind St. John's Buildings in Queen's Rd., on what is now part of the car park in Bath St. There, for years, he built fishing boats for use around the coast, and 18 foot skiffs used for taking visitors for trips in the bay in summer, and for herring and other fishing at other times. Each boat could carry from 6 to 7 meise, which would be sold in the town by the fish women, or taken by motor cycles and sidecars or small vans to be sold in surrounding villages. One of the families engaged in the visitor, fishing and fish-selling business, was that of Ben White. These skiffs were made on the whaler principle, pointed at both ends so that they could be pushed off the beach into the sea with the minimum of "wetting" for their occupants. D. Williams also designed the first canoe stern for 45 foot sailing boats in Wales, if not in England.

He was assisted by his three sons Tom, Harry and George, who, in 1937 built a boat building house in Trefechan on the site now occupied in part by Capt. Evans's marine stores, and carried on the work here for over 20 years During the second World War they were extremely busy, they built over 400 life boats for merchant ships and 48 drifter boats for Milford Haven. Under Admiralty Charter they also made 5 motor fishing vessels 50 ft long, 24 smaller motor launches, 36 drifter boats and 2 whaler type boats with small auxiliary engines. Towards the end of the war they were also entrusted with the work of repairing R.A.F. rescue launches. They also did repairs to the only cargo ship to enter Aberystwyth harbour during the war, the Manx coaster *Goldseeker*.

But the end of the war saw the demand for their boats drop sharply and remain low. In 1959 they were forced to close their business, and an industry which had been practiced in the town for centuries came to an end.

St. John's Buildings, Queen's Rd., where David Williams built his boats

Laying the Vale of Rheidol track to the north stone pier in the harbour

Sea Trade

As stated above, Aberystwyth's sea trade remained small until the 18th century. There was an increase in the 17th century following the opening up of the county's mineral resources. Thomas Smythe and Piers Edgcombe set the ball rolling when they took over the Cardiganshire mines from the Mines Royal Society in 1587. Sir Hugh Myddleton increased the scale of operations early in the following century and Thomas Bushell raised the output of the mines even higher. Small quantities of ore and lead began to be exported in the 1590's to France, Bristol and London. In 1614 the Dutch began to visit the port bringing in rye, pilcorn and wheat and returning with lead ore for Magdeburg, Rotterdam, Amsterdam and Hamburg. The Dutch preferred the ore because they believed that they could extract the silver more efficiently than was done in Wales, and continued to buy ore until 1700. Much of the above trade was from the Dovey ports.

In the meantime Bristol became a leading importer of lead while potters' ore was sent to Barnstaple, Bideford, Trevone, London, and Swansea.

But lead and ore were not the only cargoes, small quantities of slates and bark were shipped to Dublin and barrels of fish to other Irish ports. The trade in herrings was probably considerable for there was a great deal of fishing going on in Cardigan Bay in the late 17th century. In return, in 1685, Dublin sent the coopers of Aberystwyth 6,000 barrel staves, 4,000 headings and 2000 hoops. There were also imports of corn from the south of the county. Bushell imported large quantities of this for his miners in 1640.

At the beginning of the 18th century there was a change in the lead trade. The successful use of coal to smelt lead ore virtually put an end to smelting in Cardiganshire and at the instigation of Sir Humphrey Mackworth, who was working some of the lead mines, the ore was sent to be smelted in Neath. But after the failure of Mackworth's Mine Adventurers, Bristol again became the chief recipient with some ore going to the increasingly important smelteries on Deeside in Flintshire. Some also went to Swansea.

The oldest type of sea trade from Aberystwyth was undoubtedly that in herrings, to Ireland, Scotland and the continent of Europe. The earliest reference known is for 180 barrels of herrings to Montrose in Scotland in 1681. The barrel staves etc., mentioned above were probably connected with the salted herring trade.

Before 1670 salt was probably obtained via Ireland but in that year the rich rock salt deposits of Northwich were discovered and Liverpool began to export large quantities of salt. There then developed a regular trade in this commodity to the fishing ports of Cardigan Bay, using for the most part, 10 ton sloops, open boats manned by two or three men. Salt being subject to a duty, this had to be paid before leaving Liverpool, a practice which has provided indirectly some interesting information.

Such small vessels, though noted for their seaworthiness, did not provide much shelter for the cargo and a violent storm might spoil the salt. In very rough weather it might even be necessary to throw barrels of the salt overboard to save the ship. Such losses entailed the master or his deputy appearing before the Court of Quarter Sessions to testify that the loss was due to the elements and not to bad seamanship, so that the salt duty paid might be remitted.

In 1745 John Morgan, master of the 10 ton sloop *Ceres* of Aberystwyth testified that after loading 7 cwt of salt from the works of John Blackburn of Liverpool on 25 August 1744 he left for Aberystwyth and on 9 September was caught in such a violent storm that he was compelled to throw the salt overboard to save his ship. In that year it is recorded that at least seven other Cardiganshire ships suffered the same experience and some were sunk. It also states that such salt was intended "for curing of Fish for Exportation or Forreign Markets". Among these boats were the *Sea Flower* (10 tons) and *Lively* (10 tons) of Aberystwyth.

In 1754 the same fate overcame John Lewis, master of the sloop *The Resurrection*, and his testimony in court was as follows:

"Having on board two hundred and sixty-three bushels of white salt, they sett sail from the said port of Liverpool with a fair wind on Sunday, the seventeenth day of this instant March, and anchored at Beaumaris in the county of Anglesey the same night, the wind being at north-east or thereabouts. That on Monday ye eighteenth of the same instant March, they weighed anchor between the hours of five and six in the morning, came thro the Swiley (i.e., the section of the Menai

Straits lying between the Menai Suspension Bridge and the Britannia Tubular Bridge), and the tide not serving to go over Caernarvon bar they anchored at Carnarvon, and staid there that night. That on Tuesday, the nineteenth day of the same month of March, about six o'clock in the morning, they sett sail from Carnarvon to proceed on their voyage to Aberystwyth, with the wind at south-east of south-south-east, and about seven of the clock that night got thro the Bardsey sound. That about nine of the clock the same night, a most violent gale of wind blew from south-south-east, which obligd them to bear away for Portinllaen harbour to save their lives, and that in the hard gale of wind the cringles of the fforesail and their (?) goss strap broke, which obliged them to drop anchor and bind one cable to another to find ground. But the storm increasing, they were obligd, after eight hours striving in that manner, to lighten the said sloop."

The growth of trade during the 18th and part of the 19th centuries is reflected in the following statistics. In 1701 only 1 ship was registered in Aberystwyth, in 1799 there were 99 with a total tonnage of 3,537, and 157 ships totalling 8,976 tons in 1815. Thirty years later 414 ships with a tonnage of 23,124 left Aberystwyth laden for other ports, and of the total exports of 5,745 tons, just over 5,000 tons were the produce of the lead mines. In 1851 some 13,000 tons left the port of which 10,490 were lead ore.

To revert to the early 18th century, in 1704 the port received coal from Neath, grain of all kinds, malt and iron from Cardigan, and salt from Liverpool and Chester. In 1785-86 Aberystwyth received cargoes from Liverpool, Bideford, Beaumaris, Bristol, Caernarvon, Carmarthen, London, Swansea, Barmouth, Chester, Cardigan and Pwllheli.

Among the goods imported were sound white Spanish wine, cheeses, rum, forge hammers, cast iron, train oil, a printing press, and white salt.

Bideford sent malt, clay tiles, earthenware, tobacco and pipe clay. Old iron was often brought from Swansea, and slates from Caernarvon; deal, English hooks and empty bottles came from Bristol, and cheese from Pwllheli.

From London came Fullers Earth, oil of vitriol, wearing apparel, strong beer, tea, perfumery, British rye and alum. On 17 October 1785 a Chester ship brought 6 tons of fire clay, 8 tons of fire bricks, 3 boxes of tobacco pipes, and 3 dozen pieces of earthenware. The *Ann and Peggy* from "Swanzsey" unloaded 3 tons of "Wrote" (wrought) Iron and one suit of sails for a sloop. In the *Heart of Oak* from Cardigan came a mast, boom and gaff, a suit of new sails, a ton of cordage with ten coils of ropes, and blocks, all for a new sloop being built in Aberystwyth. The *Sally* from Barmouth brought household furniture and apparel, while the *Betty* from Bristol unloaded five bundles of "theatrical machinery" for what must have been one of the early groups of play actors which visited the town.

When Pritchard wrote his *Guide to Aberystwyth* in 1824 mineral produce still dominated the exports with small quantities of wheat, barley, oats, oak bark, timber, slates, butter, eggs and a few manufactured goods. The imports included porter, wines, spirits, groceries, salt, coal, hemp, pitch, tar, ironmongery, dry hides, kips (calf hides) and linen. The local ships sailed to Irish ports, especially Dublin, and Bristol, Newport, Neath, Liverpool and sometimes to London.

In the 1870's the exports were almost identical with those of fifty years before, the only notable addition being a considerable number of poles, mainly oak, reported to be for the iron works of South Wales but more likely to be for the coal pits there. The cargoes were, however, bigger.

The imports included much more timber than in the 1820's, brought from Canada and the Baltic. The other goods were as for previous years except that the local fisheries were no longer adequate and salted fish had to be imported from the Isle of Man and Cornwall.

There was, however, a significant increase in the size of the ships. The new stone pier made it possible for larger ships to enter the port. The first steam ship to enter Aberystwyth was probably the "Fine New Steam Packet" which called there in 1831 from Carmarthen to pick up some passengers for Liverpool. In 1834 the Cardigan Bay Steam Co. was formed to run a steamship service between Aberystwyth and Pwllheli in summer. It was hoped to connect at these places with coaches and other conveyances to and from "all parts of the Kingdom".

A vessel was built for this purpose and enthusiastically received at the ports but the venture was a failure. A steamship called at Aberystwyth in 1842, and two called fairly regularly in the 50's and 60's. In 1856 the Cambrian Steamship Co., was formed to trade between Aberystwyth, Bristol and Liverpool. The following year it changed its name to the Cambrian Packet Co., and raised its capital to £10,000.

In 1864 the railway reached Aberystwyth and the shipping trade soon felt its effect. Port dues dropped from £2,809 in 1863 to £1,036 in 1880. Ten years later, partly because of a reduction in dues in an effort to stop the decline in trade, they were only £583. Another important reason for the decline was the fall in demand for Welsh lead and zinc ores caused by the import of cheap foreign ores. Port dues for these were again reduced from one shilling a ton to 6d on lead ore and from 3d to 2d on zinc ore but it had little effect. The amount of lead ore exported fell from 2,385 tons in 1880 to 700 tons in 1890. There was an increase in the export of zinc ore from 237 tons in 1880 to 953 tons in 1888 but after that the decline was rapid. It was hoped that the building of the Vale of Rheidol Railway to the harbour in 1902 would arrest the decline but it had little effect.

After 1880 general cargo gradually became the dominant import, even coal declined from 126 cargoes (9,943 tons) in 1864 to 12 cargoes in 1890. Timber continued to arrive in sailing ships from the Baltic and Canada until the 1880's but the decline in shipbuilding and repair work put a stop

to the Canadian trade. Cargoes from the Baltic and Scandinavian countries continued to arrive until about 1930.

This timber came direct to Aberystwyth in two big cargoes a year, one in May or June from Norway and the other from Riga in October. The ships were usually moored at the main quay. Rafts made of logs were used to float the timber across to Lloyds saw mills from the ships. Unloading one ship usually took a week. Later, wagons were used.

By the end of the 19th century there was very little trade in lead and zinc ores,

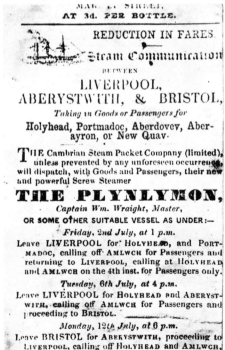

MAIN STREET.
AT 3d. PER BOTTLE.

REDUCTION IN FARES.

Steam Communication

BETWEEN

LIVERPOOL,
ABERYSTWITH, & BRISTOL,

Taking in Goods or Passengers for

Holyhead, Portmadoc, Aberdovey, Aberayron, or New Quay.

THE Cambrian Steam Packet Company (limited), unless prevented by any unforeseen occurrence, will dispatch, with Goods and Passengers, their new and powerful Screw Steamer

THE PLYNLYMON,

Captain Wm. Wraight, Master,

OR SOME OTHER SUITABLE VESSEL AS UNDER:—

Friday, 2nd July, at 1 p.m.
Leave LIVERPOOL for HOLYHEAD, and PORTMADOC, calling off AMLWCH for Passengers and returning to LIVERPOOL, calling at HOLYHEAD and AMLWCH on the 4th inst. for Passengers only.

Tuesday, 6th July, at 4 p.m.
Leave LIVERPOOL for HOLYHEAD and ABERYSTWITH, calling off AMLWCH for Passengers and proceeding to BRISTOL.

Monday, 12th July, at 8 p.m.
Leave BRISTOL for ABERYSTWITH, proceeding to LIVERPOOL, calling off HOLYHEAD and AMLWCH, on the 15th for Passengers only.

Unloading timber

and from that time until the outbreak of the First World War the only regular trade was in general cargo carried by the steamships, *H. E. Taylor, Countess of Lisburne, Grosvenor, Dora* from Liverpool and Bristol. A typical cargo was that carried by the *Countess of Lisburne* on 2 June 1901 from Liverpool. Grain of all kinds, flour, cheese, ham, salmon, sugar, tea, Indian meal, wine, spirits, lard, dried fruit, soap, salt, petroleum, marble, fruit, rice and rice dust, soda, oil, putty, hardware, whisky, bricks, brass goods, margarine, leather, belt shafts, iron joists, china, cement, candles, jam, pickles, bran, glass, granite and iron plates. Even this trade had finished by 1914; the *Dora* was torpedoed and sank during the war of 1914-18.

From the 1920's until 1939 the only regular visits were the biannual ones of the timber ships and of those bringing superphosphates from the Netherlands. By this time the motorship was ousting the steamer. There were also cargoes of road metal from North Wales. The only exports were the occasional cargo of ore

The Countess of Lisburne

The Grosvenor leaving harbour

Fishing

An activity for which Cardigan Bay was renowned for centuries was herring fishing. It was reported in 1206 that at the estuary of the Ystwyth there was "such an abundance of fish that their like was never heard of". By the middle of the 14th century there were twenty fishing boats employed there, probably the only profitable occupation in the town. Fishing requirements such as salt and nets were obtained mostly from Ireland. In the 16th century, before the fishing boats went out, the incumbent of St. Mary's Church would come to offer prayers and when they returned he met them with his basket to collect the fish which were his due. Every boat had to pay a *meise* of herrings at the beginning of the herring season to the local lord. Until the early 18th century this was Pryse of Gogerddan who had by then commuted it to a payment of 30s. Eventually the payment had to be made to Nanteos the owners of which continued to demand it well into the 19th century. A *meise* consisted of 5 long hundreds, each of which contained 126 herrings at Aberystwyth, 123 elsewhere in Wales. The fishermen of Cardiganshire used the *meise* as a unit for counting herrings, and the dozen for all other fish. When counting herring the fisherman took up three herrings in each hand; forty hands made a "hundred", in reality six score, and an extra six fish were thrown in, making 126 fish to every "hundred"; five "hundreds" made a *meise*. The extra six were called *scadan bwrw*, an allowance for error.

Generally, ten per cent of the catch was

and stone dust. One of the ships which carried ore was the *Sutton*, which sank with the loss of all its crew in November 1925, while still in sight of Aberystwyth. The cargo of 400 tons of ore concentrates was valued at only £1,000, a measure of the low prices then ruling in the lead mining industry.

Since 1945 there has been no regular sea trade of any kind in Aberystwyth. In 1950 the county council began to import road chippings in small, easily handled motorships. The last ship to use the port, the *Lady Sophia*, was engaged in this work. Such commercial activity as there is now in the harbour owes more to lobster fishing than anything else. As stated already, the future of the port probably lies with various forms of fishing and pleasure craft.

Finding it increasingly difficult to make a living, some Aberystwyth men began to use their ships for overseas trade. Vessels owned and manned by these men would sail to South Wales and load up with coal for Gibraltar. Then on to Cadiz to load with salt and across to Newfoundland where the salt would be used for salting fish. There, while waiting for the fish harvest

of Labrador they would hope to be chartered to carry coal from Sydney in Cape Breton Island but the competition for this work was such that it was sometimes unobtainable. In September, often in ballast, they sailed to Labrador to pick up fish which was carefully packed into holds which were lined with bark for this purpose. Fish being much in demand in the Mediterranean countries, the packed ships were sailed to such ports as Lisbon, Naples, Gallipoli etc. There they replaced the cargoes of fish with barrels of olive oil for Glasgow, Goole and ports in France and Germany, at rates which were sometimes so low as to yield no profit. Then back to Aberystwyth to lay up their ships for repairs and refitting in preparation for the next voyage overseas.

But as time went on, fewer and fewer men were interested in such work and those that were had to travel to Liverpool, Bristol and other ports to find berths which were almost always in steamers. There are very few mariners in Aberystwyth now.

set aside for the boat, to pay for repairs and refitting. The remainder was divided into equal piles, one to each member of the crew. Then a child who knew the fishermen by name would be asked to turn his back on the piles of fish and, when one of the fishermen out of his sight pointed at a pile and asked for the name of the owner, the child would name one of the men concerned.

In the 16th century the main herring fishing centre was Aberdyfi where there was "grate trade of ffishinge and moche resort yerely at Michelmas for herying". By the end of the 17th century it seems to have moved to Aberystwyth but it lacked organisation. In 1755 the port had about 60 fishing vessels of 10 to 12 tons each carrying 7 men during the fishing season. Many of these were craftsmen, apprentices, shopworkers, labourers etc. who went to sea only for the fishing period. After this the boats were used for the coastal trade with the Bristol Channel ports and Liverpool and each carried a crew of only two or three.

The season began in August or, more frequently, in September and lasted for three or four months. So accustomed were the people to good catches that the very occasional bad season caused near starvation among the poor. The catches were sometimes amazing in size. On 5 October 1745, forty-seven boats, as many as could cross the bar in time, together caught in one night 2,160 meise of herring, i.e., over 1,386,500 fish, a catch worth £1,400. During the season there was also a glut of cod, whiting, pollack, and ray, but little value was placed on these. In November 1788,

cod of thirty to forty pounds were being sold for 3d. and 4d. each. Man-sized monk or angel fish were caught, especially around Sarn Cynfelin. They were regarded as a delicacy and were taken in rope nets of one inch mesh. The local people called this fish a *maelgi* and naturalists of the period maintained that mermaids were in reality angel fish. Lobsters, crabs and oysters were plentiful but fishermen were loth to dredge for oysters lest they break up the spawning beds of the herring. The large shoals of fish also attracted other sea creatures; seals were not rare and porpoises were very common. In 1732 a shoal of one hundred and thirteen bottle-nosed whales was stranded on the coast at Morfa Bach and used to make sperm oil. It was found that one of them had a lead slug in its head which had been fired from some man-of-war, and the others had stranded themselves in chasing the injured one. Blue sharks of fifteen feet length were common and in 1737 a sixty foot sperm whale was stranded on the beach after terrorising the fishermen for years.

Here was an industry which could have brought wealth to the town but there was no one prepared to do the necessary organizing. In 1702, 1,734 barrels of fish were sent to Ireland in English and Irish ships. By the middle of the century the trade was almost entirely in the hands of merchants from Liverpool whose practice it was to send ships from the Isle of Man to Aberystwyth, there to purchase and salt the fish ready for export. In November 1789 there were between 2,000 and 3,000 barrels of herring from Aberystwyth lying on the

quay sides in the Isle of Man awaiting shipment to Mediterranean ports, where they were sold at twenty-five shillings a barrel. Large quantities were also shipped to Ireland and Bristol and it was said that fish from Aberystwyth supplied the needs of the Midlands. But the profit went into the pockets of Liverpool merchants.

Throughout most of the eighteenth century herring were sold at prices ranging from four shillings to five shillings a *meise* of 630 fish. In times of glut the price went down to three shillings but the arrival of the ships from the Isle of Man sometimes raised the price to eight shillings and more. The common people could buy their fish at ninepence to a shilling a hundred, an excellent cheap food much appreciated by a people as poor as that of Cardiganshire at this period.

This continued until late in the century when, in search of plankton, the herring were said to have deserted the waters off Aberystwyth and the townspeople had to pay, at times, 3d. each for fish which had once cost them less than a shilling a hundred. It was a serious loss to the poor.

This led to a marked decline in fishing from Aberystwyth, a state from which it never fully recovered. In 1816, of the 343 householders and tradesmen living in the town, only 1 was listed as a fisherman. This may not have been true but it reveals the attitude of the townspeople to fishing. Among the reasons given for the decline were lead pollution and the movement of the herring shoals elsewhere, but neither was convincing. At the height of the lead mining boom when pollution of the rivers

The catch

Packing the fish into barrels

was at its worst, there was a considerable number of ships from Fleetwood, Hoylake, Liverpool and even Brixham taking good catches off Aberystwyth. In 1878 it was reported that the town had been visited by 27 large fishing boats from elsewhere. On one occasion there were 17 of them at anchor in front of Marine Terrace, and 83 baskets of fish were sent to Liverpool by them on one day, each basket charged as weighing one hundredweight. Fishing boats from Borth, Aberaeron and Newquay were also frequent visitors to the bay during the holiday season and their fish sold readily in the town and inland.

It was a matter of astonishment to many that no attempt was made to utilise the vast stores of fish in Cardigan Bay. Much of the fish eaten in Aberystwyth had been caught there by trawlers from other parts of Britain, taken to Liverpool and sent back from there to Aberystwyth. When herring, mackerel and cod were plentiful a few small boats would put out, take a

Fish women

few fish, and sell them for inflated prices in the streets. There were neither the boats, the tackle nor the enterprise necessary for deep sea fishing. It should have been easy to develop a prosperous fishing industry in Aberystwyth after 1867 for not only was there plenty of fish but there were also excellent transport facilities and connections by rail with the large markets of the country.

Those who studied the situation in 1880 attributed Aberystwyth's failure to organise and develop properly its own fishing fleet to the failure of its Town Council to provide a harbour or refuge into which vessels could run for shelter at all states of the tide. In such hazardous circumstances few could be expected to risk the £400 to £500 needed to purchase a trawling boat and fittings.

More fish carts

It was much easier and less costly to eke out a living taking visitors out in small boats.

There were 77 fishing boats in Aberystwyth in 1883, of these 9 totalled 60 tons and the remainder 258 tons. Their small size was a serious disadvantage, space was so restricted that no attempt was made to take the fish out of the net until the boat returned to port. This meant that the nets could be shot only once on each trip. The catch was landed either on the beach or at the quay, according to the state of the tide. There were always people waiting to receive the fish. Most of it went to Liverpool by rail but some was sold locally.

That there was profit in deep sea fishing was shown by the experience of six Aberystwyth fishermen who stayed at sea for a week. On their return they disposed of the fish and were left with a profit of £10 each, in 1902.

Fish sellers of a later date

Early in the 20th century the fishing was done from the town's 70 rowing boats and other small craft. These were used mainly for taking visitors out fishing in the summer, but at the end of the summer season, before the young men who worked these boats went off looking for winter work on big ships in Liverpool, Bristol etc., there was a brief spell. During this spell they went out fishing for herring and whiting. When they landed their catches they were met by the fish sellers, mostly women in large white aprons trundling white-painted, tray-top hand carts. When plentiful, the herring were sold on the front and in the streets at 1d. each or 13 for 1s., the whiting for 2d. or 3d. each. After 1918 the number of fish carts grad-

The boatmen

ually dwindled but did not entirely disappear until Ernie the Fish retired from his pitch in front of Barclay's Bank in the late 50's.

It is interesting to note that Aberystwyth's fishermen seemed to be less superstitious than most, but they did believe that it was unlucky to burn fish bones and that the reason for the scarcity of fish in the 1840's was a curse put on them for using surplus fish to manure the fields.

Other Industries

Foundries

The growth of lead mining in North Cardiganshire and the introduction of new ore-dressing techniques, created a considerable demand for machinery, and transport being difficult, it was only to be expected that foundries and other industries should develop in a town so well placed for serving these needs as Aberystwyth. These industries also supplied, in part, the needs of the water and sanitation schemes which occupied so much of the attention of the Town Commissioners and the Town Council throughout the 19th century.

According to John Wood's map of Aberystwyth in 1834, the first foundry was in Shipbuilders Row, as South Rd. was then called, opposite the entrance to High St. It was very well placed to serve the needs of the rapidly developing ship-building yards nearby. This was probably the *Providence Foundry* named on a tally in the Ceredigion Museum.

The next foundry was built in the 1840's "opposite to the Old Toll House", i.e. in Northgate St. The first turnpike house was nearer the town than the later one and had only one gate. This was the first Eagle Foundry and consisted of a smithy, a fitter's shop and a moulding shop. Locally it was known as Ellis's Foundry after the owner, the late R. J. Ellis's grandfather, who, after being given a lease by the Corporation in 1840, built a cluster of small single-storey white-washed cottages probably to house some of his workmen. This was the first Poplar Row, named after a line of trees planted nearby.

Remains of the Williams and Metcalfe Central Foundry established 1874

Remains of the Rheidol Foundry, Park Avenue (Ffowndri Fach)

Smithfield Rd. (Park Avenue) had two foundries. The bigger of these—the *Central Foundry*—was almost next door to the Gas Works on the site known as the County Yard. These works began operations in 1874 and were owned by Williams and Metcalfe. Metcalfe, a locomotive engineer of repute later left to work in England and the works became Williams's Foundry.

Metcalfe designed the first of the Vale of Rheidol Railway's locomotives.

At the lower end of Park Avenue, flanking the football field, lay the *Rheidol Foundry* or *Ffowndri Fach* (the Little Foundry) which was probably built about 1870.

Both these foundries benefited much from the lead mining industry in North Cardiganshire. They made castings, jiggers, water wheels and machine parts for these and other mines, and also turned out large numbers of manhole covers and such work as was needed in the town when the water and sanitation systems

were being installed. Many of the town's manhole covers still bear the names of these foundries. With Green's foundry, they also did a great deal of work for the local railways, producing and repairing parts for the locomotives and rolling stock. The remains of the Park Avenue foundries with the tall chimney and arched windows are still to be seen.

The biggest foundry in Aberystwyth was built in Lewis Terrace (Alexandra Rd.) opposite the site of the present railway coal yard, before 1850, and was known as Green's Foundry.

George Green was born in Codsall, Staffs. on 11 January 1824. Soon afterwards the family moved to Manchester where, in time, he began to learn the rudiments of practical engineering from his father, who made machinery and fittings for the water companies of the district. Later, young George worked at various engineering establishments there, especially the Atlas Works.

His grandfather was a contemporary of Boulton & Watt and, like them, made steam engines and boilers but in a small way of business. For many years he was engineer to the Manchester and Salford Water Works and it was he who persuaded them to replace with iron pipes, the stone pipes then used to carry water. He also designed and made the pipes and fittings needed for the change. Another design was an iron ship but he failed to get a Liverpool firm to build it, ten years before such a ship was attempted elsewhere.

As a young man George Green held very radical views in politics. He was a

member of the small group of *Fustian Jackets* which took to the House of Commons a petition signed by almost $3\frac{1}{2}$ million people in favour of the *People's Charter*. He was also a member of the committee created to investigate the questions of piecework and systematic overtime in the factories of the Ancoats division.

His connection with Aberystwyth began in 1848 when he came there to erect a small engine for the Eagle Foundry. About that time he was also involved in gold mining in the Dolgellau area. When the large swing bridge over the Mawddach estuary would not close properly after being opened to allow a ship to pass through, it was George Green who put it right.

There is some doubt as to when he became the owner of Green's Foundry. It is generally believed that it was his from the beginning but written evidence shows that at first he was the manager and not the owner. In 1852 it was apparently the property of J. W. Austen & Co., who sold it to a group of London men for £13,000. These formed a company known as the Cambrian Foundry Co. Ltd., with a capital of £50,000 and Thomas King Stevens of Aberystwyth and Regent St., London, as its chairman.

The prospectus of the Company for 1856 states that until a few years before, there was no adequate provision for the manufacture of machinery—steam engines, castings, water-wheels, etc., for the lead mines of Mid Wales. The Cambrian Foundry was established to fill this gap and despite the depression and shortage of money created by the American Civil War, the venture had been a success. Its average profits for the previous two years had ranged from 15 to 20 per cent. The head office was in Regent St., London but the manager of the works, George Green, had his office in Lewis Terrace.

In time, George Green must have purchased the foundry from the Cambrian Co. His work there showed him to be an outstanding engineer. He designed automatic appliances (jiggers) for separating metallic ores from the worthless stuff in which they were embedded; his improved version of a plant which combined stone breaking, ore-crushing and concentration won him a diploma at the International Exhibition of Mining and Metallurgy at the Crystal Palace, and he produced a steam boiler which was over 20 per cent more efficient than any other on the market. In rock drilling, too, he was a pioneer; as early as 1864 he produced highly efficient drills but, because those concerned in their use were already committed to other producers, the drill was never adopted.

George Green's foundry made everything from garden gates and railings to winding engines but he was best known for jiggers and steam engines.

When the mines began to close in the early 1880's he travelled far and wide in search of orders, and kept his men together, producing machinery for Spain, Italy, Asia Minor, North and South America and Ceylon. In the late 1880's he made machinery for Colombia, Serbia (the Balkans) and the Russian provinces in Asia, and made long journeys to ensure that the equipment was properly installed. It was

in Russia in 1893 that he contracted the recurrent fever from which he eventually died in March 1895. On the day of his funeral all the shops in the town were closed and all the ships in the harbour had their flags at halfmast.

Nor was he the only man to travel abroad, he sent his engineers all over the world to ensure that his products gave satisfaction. In 1891 Henry Miller of Llanbadarn, an engineer at the foundry, was sent out to South America to assemble machinery ordered by the Frias Silver Mines in Hona Tollina, Colombia. It was shipped in the *Affratio*, a part steamer part sailing ship, to a Colombian port, taken up the Magdalena River by boat and then by railway and mule train to the mines. A few years later, probably because of the fire at the foundry, Henry Miller accepted the post of engineer at these mines and accompanied by his wife, Sister Miller of Llanbadarn, went to work in Colombia. Their son, Arthur Miller of Skinner St., was born out there.

Others from the Aberystwyth district who were probably sent by Green's to work at the Frias Mines were two blacksmiths—the late R. J. Ellis's father, Owen Ellis, who had a smithy behind what is now West Wales Garage in North Parade, and John Lewis of St. John's Buildings. Another was John Thomas of Talybont, the mines' assayer, whose daughter Miss Juanita Thomas, still lives at Talybont and is noted there for her love of cats. When she returned to Wales as a small child, she could speak only Welsh and Spanish.

George Green

George Green also played a prominent part in public life. He was a Liberal, a Wesleyan and a staunch supporter of Temperance. He served long terms as a Town Improvement Commissioner and town councillor. His opposition to the Pumlumon water scheme lost him his seat for a few years but he was again in power in the early 1880's and mayor in 1885 and 1886. He was elected to the County Council in 1889.

As a foundryman his last piece of work for Aberystwyth was the casting of the pillars for the new Pier Pavilion opened in 1896, and the reconstruction of the arrival platform at the railway station. He was married twice and had eleven children.

After his death the foundry was carried on by his eldest sons and son-in law. They continued the policy of seeking orders abroad and keeping well in the forefront of progress. Hydraulic mining was just beginning and Green's set about providing suitable equipment. They were soon exporting it, one lot to Malpasse in South America. But on 10 June 1908 the foundry suffered a fire so intense and so disastrous that sailors in the bay thought the town was on fire. This was virtually the end of Green's Foundry; it was later repaired and used by the university college.

It has housed in turn, the first Welsh Plant Breeding Station under Sir George Stapledon, the Geography and Geology Departments, and the Education Department Much of the old building still stands but its future is now uncertain.

The prosperity of these foundries was too dependent on lead mining in Mid Wales for them all to be able to survive the closure of so many mines in the late 19th century, and the only one to continue working after 1908 was Williams's Foundry which lasted into the 1930's. The Rheidol Foundry was worked for a while in the 1870's by Hollier whose wife and daughter kept an interesting haberdashery shop

The Education Buildings, Alexandra Rd.

at the corner of Queen St. and Bridge St. The tiled step of this shop, now an art gallery, still bears the name Hollier. As an examination of the railings surrounding the Alexandra Rd. Welsh Primary School will show, these were cast by Hollier at the Rheidol Foundry. These works were taken over by the Great Western Railway Co. in 1910 largely in order to acquire the site.

Since its closure c. 1900 the Eagle Foundry in Northgate St. has been used as a garage, by Jones Bros., bus proprietors, and then by the Thomas brothers. The old building has now been demolished and the new local office of the Ministry of Health and Social Security erected in its place.

The foundry in South Rd. seems to have had a comparatively short life and was probably replaced by one in Trefechan known as the *Hen Drefechan Foundry*, the name given on an old tally. For a while,

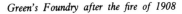

Green's Foundry after the fire of 1908

at least, it was a branch of the Eagle Foundry and served both lead mines and ships. It is possible that the ship's pumps which were then made in Trefechan were made here.

There were also two blacksmiths at work in this part of Aberystwyth; one, Jones y Gof, spent part of his life shoeing horses and repairing farm utensils, and much of the remainder drinking the proceeds at one of the six taverns nearby.

The other smithy was near the bridge and was a much larger affair, having eight hearths. It was in reality a cable, chain and anchor works. The first such works were run by David Jenkins in Vulcan St., the street was probably so named because of the forge. The Trefechan forge was apparently run by one of his descendants, a Mrs. Jenkins who was said to be so strong that she could do the work of any man who might be absent.

Other industries in Trefechan were a wheelwright near the bridge, a firm of carpenters known as Edward Brothers somewhere near Glanrafon Terrace, who not only made jiggers for the local lead mines but also exported them. There was also a cooper and, at the corner of the main road and Spring Gardens on the bridge side, stood George Jones's sail loft. There was also a blockmaker in the area.

The Anchor Smelting Works

In 1786 a serious attempt was made to establish a smelting mill at Aberystwyth by a group of local people. The prime movers in this affair were John Probert,

Robert Wilding, and John Lowe, all partners in mining ventures at Esgairmwyn and elsewhere. Others were Probert's sister, a William Carter, and John Pierce who was the Gogerddan mining agent as well as Customs Officer to the port of Aberystwyth. Each contributed £250 to the venture and with a capital of £1,500 a site was bought at Penyrancor, Trefechan. Building started early in 1787, using local

Green's Foundry Workers

stone, and in June work began on the furnaces, for which special bricks were imported from Chester and special labour brought in. One of these bricklayers, a John Hussey, was lodged in Trefechan for fifteen weeks at a shilling a week. September saw the completion of the furnace and local labour then finished the building, using the product of the local brickworks then in the possession of Mathew Davies, later of Cwmcynfelin. These were demolished c. 1971.

Smelting equipment was obtained from a number of sources. An abandoned smelt-house at Benthall near Broseley, Shropshire, yielded a cast-iron hopper, two cast-iron furnaces, and seven iron door frames. These had to be taken by barge to Gloucester and there shipped to Aberystwyth and took several weeks because of low water in the Severn. A crane to handle the heavy pigs of lead was brought from Liverpool, and Bristol supplied the bellows, cast iron pots, and more iron door frames. An inspection was made of the old Garreg smeltery near Derwen-las and the slag hearth was taken to Aberystwyth. Special iron plates had to be brought overland from Coalbrookdale but other iron requirements were obtained locally or from Jane Lloyd's forge at Machynlleth and Jonathan Kendall's ironworks at Furnace.

Of the raw materials required, only the ore was available locally; large quantities of coal had to be brought in from Swansea and Deeside, and bone ash for refining was obtainable only in London and Liverpool. The process of smelting was quite straightforward but refining, i.e. the extraction of silver, was more complicated and merits some attention. The lead to be refined was melted in a reverberatory furnace the floor of which was covered with a bed or 'test' of finely ground bone ash. The furnace was then heated until the lead was first melted and then changed into the yellow oxide litharge, which in turn itself became molten. The temperature at which litharge melts being lower than

that of silver, the latter remained as a solid while the molten litharge was drawn off from the bottom of the furnace or absorbed by the bone ash. On completion of the process all the lead had been changed into litharge and the silver remained as a solid lump which was then separately melted and cast into small ingots. The litharge was either loaded into casks and sold as such or returned to a reducing furnace and re-smelted into lead. In a good furnace the loss of lead in refining was small. There is no mention of a reducing furnace at Penyrancor as litharge commanded a higher price than the metallic lead at this period.

Bone ash had to be used because litharge corroded most other materials, especially stone and brick. It was unobtainable locally and had to be brought from London or Liverpool where the large meat markets provided sufficient bones to justify setting up a calcining furnace. Its cost was comparatively high, 16s. a ton plus carriage, and as a measure of economy the company later set some men to burn ferns, as fern ash was a well-known if not a very efficient substitute for bone ash.

In January 1788, to facilitate transport, a new road was cut from the harbour to the new smelthouse. In February the works were completed and six weys of coal were brought from Swansea for the preliminary trials. Smelting began in earnest during late April and, satisfied with the product, the partners readily increased their deposits to £400. By September the company claimed to be getting $9\frac{1}{2}$ pigs of lead of a hundredweight and a half each from 18

hundredweight of ore, a very high yield indeed and probably an exaggeration. Unfortunately, the concern now suffered a serious setback; the head smelter, a highly skilled man from Bristol, fell dangerously ill. Unable to get another, a John Thomas was sent to Bristol to inspect the mode of smelting and was promised a house on his return. Thomas could not have been satisfactory for he was soon replaced by a William Hussey who in turn gave way to a Gregory. In February 1789 John Pierce went to Neath and Flintshire to see the smelting processes for himself.

Smelting in Cardiganshire was not easy because of the hard nature of so much of the ore, especially that of Esgairmwyn, the company's chief mine. In October 1788 Lowe bought ore from a mine at Bryntail near Llanidloes to mix with the local ores in the furnace and to act as a flux for the hard ore. Later the Esgairmwyn ore was mixed with the softer product of Grogwynion in an attempt to increase the yield of lead. In Bristol it was found that more lead could be obtained from the bulk of Cardiganshire ores if they were mixed with those of Flintshire. This was tried at Penyrancor but did not prove successful, and at one time Irish ores were imported and used as a flux. It was obvious that the promoters were dissatisfied with the amount of lead obtained; Cardiganshire ores were rich and should have produced about 70% of lead.

Apart from the problem of attracting skilled smelters, labour was plentiful. Men were employed to unload coal, to quarry stones, to work the blowers at the furnaces, and to do general labourers' work at a shilling a day. Carriers of ore, stone, coal, etc., using their own horses and carts received four shillings a day but such work was very irregular. The only difficulty occurred during the herring season when men deserted their posts for the fishing boats, and ships were prevented from sailing with lead and ore and bringing back coal.

At first there was no difficulty in selling the lead produced. The very week that smelting began Messrs. Watts of Bristol offered to take thirty tons a month at £22 10s. a ton. Probert was anxious to get a footing in the East India Company trade. Every autumn that company was in the habit of buying up to 2,000 tons of lead; in 1788 its price was £19 12s. per fodder of 19½ hundredweight. This demand always had a stimulating effect on the market. Prices remained fairly high during the whole of the first year of working and success seemed certain. In March 1789, however, there was a sharp and disastrous drop in price to £11 10s. for the best pig lead produced in Flintshire. In April exports from the country had almost ceased and the only demand was from shotmakers and plumbers. The following month, there were almost a hundred tons of pig lead lying unsold at Penyrancor and 250 tons of ore ready to smelt. In the previous March Probert had received an enquiry from Liverpool for 100 tons to be sent to Venice and so he began to explore the possibilities of export to Southern Europe. The Mediterranean trade was profitable only during certain seasons of the year.

One of these was the fruit season when the availability of return cargoes enabled ship-owners to lower their freight rates from 40s. and 50s. a ton to 25s. Lead was then sent from Aberystwyth and sold for the high price of £23 10s. a ton. Another profitable time for this trade was from October to the end of the year when large quantities of red herrings were sent to Italian ports. At this time lead could be conveyed to Leghorn, Genoa, and Naples at 12s. to 15s. a ton and to Ancona and Venice at 25s. a ton. It could also be sent cheaply during the Naples and Salermo fairs but only as ballast and such lead had always to be on hand at the ports. Much lead was also sent to Marseilles and to the Atlantic ports of France but freight rates were high.

Apart from these sporadic demands the market for lead remained poor and prices low except when the demands of the East India Company made themselves felt as in the autumn of 1789 when the price rose to £17 15s. a ton, it was only £15 13s. a year later. The Anchor Company was now losing money partly because of unwise ore purchases. Large stocks of ore were bought at prices which proved uneconomic soon after the purchase. In an attempt to economise, cheap coal and culm were bought but this proved expensive as it lowered the efficiency of the furnace.

The refinery seems to have been more successful than the smelting furnace. The yield of silver was generally high; in September 1789, over 136 ounces of silver were extracted from 4 tons 14 cwts. of lead. The silver bullion was sent overland to Shrewsbury, as in July 1790 when over 529 ounces were sent to that town to join the London wagon. One of those responsible for the safe conduct of these valuable loads was Thomas Clayton, one-time Master of the House of Correction, who was paid 25s. for taking bullion to Shrewsbury in August 1789.

In 1790 a determined effort was made to prove the venture a success. A new quay was built, a new slag hearth erected, and a new waterwheel installed. But prices remained low and debts accumulated fast. Workmen and tradesmen could not be paid and Job Sheldon, the mine-owner, was owed £290 for ore. By the end of the year the affairs of the company were in a bad state. In December nine tons of ore yielded 6 tons 7 cwts. 3 quarters of lead at a cost of £89 13s. 8½d. The price received for this was only £87 11s. 3d., a loss of over £2. No company could continue at this rate and in March 1791 work ceased.

The failure of the Company owed much to the poor state of the lead trade at this period but another reason was bad management. Control was in the hands of John Pierce, who knew little about smelting and was disliked by the smelters for his unintelligent interference on occasions. Usually, however, he neglected the works, nor is this surprising in view of his other duties as mining agent and Customs Officer. In January 1790 control was transferred to James Lowe, who complained of bad debts. In June, Carter was sent to inspect the smelthouse accounts, which showed a shortage of £1,000 for which Pierce was unable to account. Another reason for the failure was the small size of the works. Smelting furnaces need frequent repair and unless there are a number of furnaces such stoppages involved a large proportion of the men being idle, and marked variation in production. Most important of all, Aberystwyth was not a suitable site for a smelthouse. The only raw material available was lead ore, the bulkiest of all was coal, and this was expensive in Mid Wales. The following is a typical example of a coal bill.

```
8 March 1788. Bot. of Stanley Massey
     Esq. & Co., Ness Colliery
Richard Evans paid for 23 tons of Coal
   at 8s. 6d.    ..     ..     ..        9 15  6
An Allowance for trimming the coal      0  3  0
   Do. to the Colliers       ..         0  3  0
Customs duty being 23 Chaldrons ..      6  7  0
An Allowance for discharging Coal..     0  6  0
Freight to Aberystwyth     ..           7  4  0
                                       ─────────
                                      £23 18  6
                                       ─────────
```

A material which cost about £10 on the coalfield cost over £23 in Aberystwyth. Five weys of culm which cost £8 in Neath cost over £25 in Aberystwyth. Nor were customs duties confined to coal, at times they were heavy on lead too. A cargo of 41 tons sent to Carmarthen had to pay customs duties of £92 11s. 10d., well over £2 a ton. Those lead smelteries in Neath and Deeside could supply a wide industrialised area without having to pay such duties and their coal was always cheap. Aberystwyth was too expensive a site for such an industry and so the venture failed. The following account shows the company's position after work ceased.

Payments

Payments by Mr. Pierce for lead ore, coal, culm, iron, brick, limestone	5,639	1	5½
Workmen's Wages, etc.	3,019	3	9
Keep of the team of horses & payments on that acct. to January 1790	268	14	5½
Payments by Mr. Lowe for ore, coal, culm, wages, team to June 1791	2,062	12	11½
Do. by Mr. Probert	1,787	7	10
Do. by Mr. Lowe for limestone, coal, culm, wages from June 1791 to Sept. 1792	270	2	1½
	13,047	2	7

Money Received

By Mr. Pierce for lead, bullion, litharge, etc.	5,067	4	4
do. for lime	81	14	10½
Do. for labour by team under Mr. Lowe's management to January 1790	390	9	11
By Mr. Probert for lead, wagon, horses, etc.	2,475	3	2
By Mr. Lowe for silver bullion, lead ore, etc. up to June 1791 including coal, team labour etc.	563	0	5
Do. for lime, horses from June 1791 to Sept. 1792	356	5	0
	£8,933	17	8½

There being a deficit of £4,113 4s. 10½d., each of the six partners had to contribute £685 7s. 5¼d. of which £400 had already been subscribed.

On 17 December 1792 John Edwards

and Richard William were paid £6 6s. 0d. for taking down the furnace and cleaning and storing the bricks. Edward Parry and Thos. Edwards took down the slag hearth and the furnace and refinery chimneys. Trefechan was well rid of an industry which poured out smoke and fumes poisonous to man, animals, and plant life alike. The company's own lime kiln, built in June 1789, was worked for many years and the remains of the smeltery were also used for this purpose for a while.

Tanneries. Aberystwyth had long been a port from which oak bark was regularly exported, particularly to Ireland where it was used in the making of leather. But there is no record of tanning being practiced in Aberystwyth until the end of the 18th century, probably because the manufacture of leather was an active industry in the Paith Valley, just beyond Penparcau.

In 1798 John Jones, merchant, was given permission by the Court Leet to "inclose, drain and erect Buildings for a Tan House and Yards" on a piece of ground extending from the North Turnpike Gate to the Mill Leat which then ran as an open stream down from Penglais along what is now Poplar Row and along Alexandra Rd.

Around the middle of the 19th century the Skinner St.-Poplar Row area was inhabited by a collection of bad characters and known locally as Soho. Skinner St. was named after its skin yard where skins were fleeced of their wool and then washed before being taken to the tannery. The skinnery formed one end of a long building which was built end on to the mill stream. The other end was a two-storey structure, on the ground floor of which two donkeys attached to a long upright pole went their circular ways and worked the machinery upstairs. This end was probably the tannery workshop where the oak bark was crushed and the skins put through rollers. Before these works were closed, the donkeys had been replaced by a water-wheel worked by a system of syphon structures. The owner was one Richards who led the singing at the Welsh Wesleyan Chapel.

The second tannery in the town was opened by John Roberts early in the 19th century. He was a member of a Caernarvonshire family which had bought a small mansion on the Derry Ormond estate about 1750. John came to Aberystwyth to learn the craft of tanning and served an apprenticeship with some of the tanners in the Paith Valley. After serving his time he went to London to learn the finer skills of his trade. There he saw some fearsome sights, among them four men hanging from the gallows in Ironmonger Lane, executed for sheep stealing. He also learnt to beware of the press gang, for the war with France was making heavy demands on the nation's armed forces.

After completing his training he returned to Aberystwyth, took a lease of ground opposite Tabernacl and set up a tanyard on the banks of the mill leat.

John Roberts played an active part in the life of Aberystwyth, he became a member of the first town council in 1835 and was made mayor in 1838. He was also a member of the Town Commissioners.

He and his descendants gave the town more than a century of public service. Before he died he retired from the tannery in favour of his eldest son John, who sold the business to Richard James. When tanning ceased the tannery was largely dismantled and the site used for a steam laundry then described as a washing board factory.

The last to be opened in the town was Wattie James's tannery at the bottom of Smithfield Rd. (Park Avenue) where Charles Clark have their showrooms. In 1874 the Corporation built a slaughter house at a cost of £2000 at the extremity of Morfa Road, the first name given to Park Avenue. It was a lofty ornamental structure, lit by large elegant cast iron windows supplied by the "Coalbrooke Dale Co.". The floors were of grooved blue stone Staffordshire bricks and the walls were covered with white glazed Dutch tiles. Wattie James's tan house was therefore well placed and it

The Old Candle Works
(Y Ffatws)

continued working until he died in the late 1930's.

Also in Park Avenue, was what was known locally as the *Ffatws* (the Fat house) where fat from the slaughtered animals, especially oxen and sheep, was melted down and purified to make tallow. This was then made into candles and any surplus sold to other chandlers. The building, which still stands, is next to the freezer centre and carries the inscription *The Old Candle Works*. The stumpy remains of the chimneys of the several fires used to melt the fat can still be seen.

In the 18th century there was a tallow chandler named Scandritt in Great Darkgate St. and around the 1830's there was one in Poplar Row opposite the old skinnery, its source of raw material, Princess St., too, had a chandler.

Breweries.

In the past, ale was considered to be an absolute necessity of life and there was a great deal of home brewing. In 1816 there were 6 malthouses in Aberystwyth and 27 taverns, all of which brewed their own beer using malt supplied by the local maltsters. Large farms and most mansions of any size had their own brewhouses as did the bigger hotels. St. Johns Buildings in Sandmarsh Lane (Queens Rd.) opposite the Life Boat House, originally consisted of a row of small buildings which were used as a brewery. The one tall building was a storehouse for barley. They were owned at first by William

Killan who lived in North Parade, later they were taken over by Jonathan Pell, probably as a brewhouse for his Belle Vue Hotel.

The first brewery established to sell beer to taverns was on the site later occupied by Green's Foundry and it was owned by William Cain Monkhouse who was made a Town Commissioner in 1837. He must have served people on the brewery premises too, for it had both a bowling alley and a skittle alley. Between it and Lewis Terrace (Alexandra Rd.) there was a high wall used by the local boys to play *pos*, a form of fives.

The next brewery developed from a maltster's business in Trefechan. The above-mentioned tanner, John Roberts, had six children, three of them boys. John, the eldest, took over the tannery, Jacob became a doctor and helped to treat patients at the first Aberystwyth Infirmary, and David, who was meant to be a banker, became a brewer instead.

David was born in Aberystwyth in 1820 and was educated at a school run by Miss Morris. There he learnt the 3R's before going to a Bedford school to finish his education. He then returned to Aberystwyth and, at the age of fifteen, began work as a junior clerk in the new branch of the National Provincial Bank of which Joseph Downie was manager. Two years later, his uncle, a vicar in Buckinghamshire, secured him a similar post in a London bank. But there he decided that he did not like banking and in December 1840, with a few friends, he joined a ship bound for Wellington, New Zealand, a voyage that

took 132 days, partly because the ship was becalmed for six weeks south of the equator.

He and his friends found New Zealand disappointing and the party split up. David decided to return home but had to wait some time before he was taken aboard the *Bally,* a ship bound for England laden with whale oil and bone. The voyage home around Cape Horn must have been a hazardous venture and took 110 days.

Having now sailed around the world he was ready to settle in Aberystwyth and, at the age of 23, decided to become a merchant. In Trefechan in the 1830's there was a profitable business run by Morris Davies who died in 1835 and whose gravestone may be seen near the Parish Hall. He owned several limekilns and sold lime to the farmers of North Cardiganshire. He was also a corn merchant, buying large quantities of barley in the Llanrhystud-Llanon district and sending it by sea in small boats to

The Old Malthouse in Trefechan

be sold in North Wales. When he died the business passed to his nephew, James Davies, who lived in one of the two handsome eighteenth century houses known as *The Lawn* and *The Green* in Trefechan. James Davies later moved to Ffosrhydgaled in Chancery, now known as the Conrah Hotel. He then sold the business to David Roberts who not only became a corn and seed merchant but also used some of the barley himself as a maltster, supplying malt to a number of the town's taverns and to private individuals. The maltster business grew rapidly, it was soon busy all the year round using local barley, and some brought from as far afield as Norfolk and Nancy in France. The malthouse, complete with oasthouse, can still be seen on the harbour side of the main street.

Aberystwyth was now growing fast and David Roberts decided to open his own brewery in 1844. Being near the harbour and having two good wells nearby, Trefechan was well suited to the work. John Jones, a local cooper, made him a few barrels for the trial and he began to brew on a small scale. Despite opposition from the town's taverns and the Nonconformists, who were preaching temperance for all their worth, the brewery flourished and grew. Within a few years not only was David Roberts's brewery going well but he had become the owner of several hotels and public houses in Aberystwyth.

Like his father, David Roberts became a public figure in the town; he was an Improvement Commissioner, a town councillor from 1844 to 1908, an active member of the Established Church, a staunch Conservative,

Brewery Workers

and held some progressive ideas on the development of the harbour. He lived at The Green, Trefechan, and was a member of the well known, and sometimes notorious, Smokey Face Club described elsewhere. He carried on the business himself until 1897 when he retired and formed a private company having his two sons, George Fossett and Henry Roberts, as directors, the former as manager and Henry as brewer.

Under the new management the concern did well at first, it came to own three-quarters of the town's public houses, some of them built by the brewery—the Central, Cambrian (formerly the Commercial Hotel) and the Castle Hotel in South Rd. The beer was delivered by horse and cart until 1922 when the first motor lorry was bought, a Leyland with solid tyres. In the same year a water and cooling tower was erected, powered by an electric motor. It was for many years a conspicuous landmark. An ice house was then built, which produced so much ice that there was enough to supply ice cream vendors, local fishermen and others. Sufficient ice was sold to justify the purchase of a 30 cwt lorry for its delivery, its drivers being James Thomas (Jimmy Bridgend of Cor y Castell) and Jack Davies known locally as Jack Ice. The brewery produced a variety of beers, the most popular of which was known as Brown Ale. It also bottled beer from other breweries and imported its Guiness from Dublin.

During the late 20's and much of the 30's, trade was bad because of the depression and the success of the temperance movement in the town. Some public houses were

forced to close, including a few owned by Roberts Brewery. John Gibson having been an ardent advocate of teetotalism, the *Cambrian News* had long supported temperance; an equally strong believer and supporter of the same movement was Robert Read, who in the 20's and 30's waged a ceaseless war on the "drink trade".

The temperance lobby was so strong in Aberystwyth that politicians opposed them at their peril. When George Fossett Roberts stood as parliamentary candidate for the Conservatives in 1910 he suffered the full force of the movement's opposition. In the 1930's he became involved in a much publicised argument with the Liberal M.P., Sir Rhys Hopkin Morris, over brewer's profits in Britain. In fact they were low in Aberystwyth and remained so until the town became flooded with soldiers and airmen after 1939. By that time Sir George had resigned in favour of Henry and soon

David Roberts

afterwards, in 1935, the brewery was sold for a figure said to be £100,000, but Henry remained managing director until he died in 1940.

During the war, it was inevitable that in a town full of servicemen with time on their hands and few places of entertainment, public houses became very popular and the brewery profits soared. Roberts took over Facey's, the Abergavenny brewers together with thirteen public houses, making a hundred tied houses for the Aberystwyth brewers, who were now supplying beer to Tywyn, Newtown, Abergavenny, Llandeilo and Haverfordwest. The manager was bow-tied Mick Williams of Penyrancor and the brewer was Jimmy James.

But the 40's and 50's found the brewery much in need of modernisation and with insufficient capital to do the work. For years no dividend was paid, even on preference shares. About 1955 a new board of directors took over, its chairman being Tom Boardman, Minister for Industry in Edward Heath's government. It proved successful, in 1959 the brewery made a profit of £25,000 after tax, and five years later the company resumed the payment of dividends to its shareholders.

Being now a sound proposition it became the subject of bids by other companies, and in May 1960 David Roberts' brewery was taken over by Hancocks who also bought Emile Evans's mineral water works in Llangawsai. Aberystwyth retained control of the Cardiganshire tied houses only. No worker was made redundant but Hancocks failed to honour their pledge to keep the name *D. Roberts and Sons* for the Aberystwyth section.

Brewing then ceased in Trefechan but the bottling of beer continued. Unfortunately the two old houses adjoining the brewery, The Green and The Lawn, which should have been listed for preservation, were demolished to make way for "improvements". The brewing section was turned into a large wine and spirit department.

In March 1969 there was another change of ownership when Hancocks were taken over by Bass Charrington. Bottling ceased and work began on building a new department designed to improve working conditions and to provide a better service for customers. Many of the tied houses were improved, and the first new public house in living memory was built where there was no public house at all—the *Tollgate* in Penparcau.

Malt-drying kiln in Trefechan

On 28 March 1974, the £105,000 extension was opened complete with temperature controlled beer 'cellars', some 130 years after David Roberts began brewing beer in Trefechan. All that can now be seen of the old building is the office opposite the fire station.

Slate Works. The first slate works in Aberystwyth seems to have been run by Ellis and Owen, the Ellis being, so it is said, a connection of the foundryman of the same name. The works were in being early in the 1860's, and in the 70's they described themselves as being manufacturers of "Plain and ornamental Slate Chimney Pieces, Baths, Cisterns, Milk Coolers, Head Stones, Urinals, Mangers, Cattle Troughs; Dairy, Larder and Wine Cellar Shelves, Window Sills, Door Steps, Hearth Stones, Flooring, Skirting and every discription of Slate Works". They produced "Slate enamelled in imitation of the most costly Marble for Chimney Pieces, Hall Tables, Sideboards, Cheffoniers etc., and Circular Table Tops, Finger Plates for Doors, Paper Weights with Views, Escutcheons, Chess, Flowers Ornamental and Carved". An artist was sent to take Views when required and these were painted on to the article concerned.

They must have had some fine craftsmen for they won first prizes for slate carving at both the Chester Exhibition 1866 and the National Eisteddfod held in Carmarthen in 1867. The location of the works is unknown but as no map shows more than two slate works in the town;

they were probably taken over by either Hoskin and Miller or by Peter Jones.

The Hoskin and Miller Works were situated in Cambrian St. behind Green's Foundry and now form part of the UCW buildings. In addition to being monumental masons they produced large numbers of ornamental mantel or chimney pieces which were stove enamelled and often painted and grained to resemble walnut, mahogany or oak. Some were also decorated with painted panels showing local or traditional scenes such as the "Stag at Bay", "Llanbadarn Church" or "the Harbour" and it is believed that most of these were painted by Worthington, the local artist whose works are now much in demand. Another slate artist was Scott.

The Briton Slate Works, in Cambrian Place next to the Cambrian Chambers, and now used as T. Alun Evans' Garden Centre, probably began work about 1880 and were owned and managed by Peter Jones and John Morris. Its workers were largely engaged in cutting, polishing, enamelling and making mantel pieces from slate brought in from Corris and Dinas Mawddwy.

The slate was cut into thin slabs by machine and then made smooth on a steam-driven revolving turn table. If necessary, it was then enamelled, put into large stoves and heated to a high temperature. When cool they were polished by hand. Many pieces were then painted with land or seascapes, the favourite views at the Briton works being "Devils Bridge," the "Castle Tower" and "Plas Crug". A shortage of artists able to do such paintings and design

others was one of the reasons for Peter Jones's support of the abortive plan to build an art school behind the Town Hall in Queen's Rd.

Peter Jones was born in Marine Terrace in August 1847. He received his education in London and then returned to Aberystwyth where his father articled him to a solicitor. But he soon found that he preferred business to the law and, while still a young man, he established slate works in Cambrian Place in partnership with John Morris.

Peter Jones

They did a considerable trade with Lancashire and the Isle of Man and exported large quantities of slates to South Africa and other distant countries. He was also actively interested in lead mining, and shipped many cargoes of lead ore out of Aberystwyth. In time he became, in addition, a coal merchant and continued in this work until he retired in 1914. There is a reminder of Peter Jones's connection with the quarrying industry in the *Maen Llog*, the Logan Stone in the centre of the Gorsedd Circle in the inner ward of the old castle. It was presented by him to the eisteddfod committee for use in the National Eisteddfod of 1916.

Peter Jones played a very important part in the public life of Aberystwyth and it extended over 60 years. He was elected a member of the Town Improvement Commissioners when only 21 years old and served until their duties were taken over by the town council in 1872. He was then elected a town councillor and but for one short period, served in this capacity until his retirement in 1914. He was chairman of the public works committee for 32 years and Mayor of the town in 1880 and 1881. This was the time when the Pumlumon water scheme was carried out and as mayor he had the honour of cutting the first sod of the two service reservoirs. The silver spade presented to him on that occasion became one of his cherished possessions. Peter Jones also had an eye for the aesthetic and it was he who had the trees planted in Plascrug Avenue.

When the County Council was created in 1888 he was elected a county councillor and became the first chairman. He also filled this office in 1919. Among his many public offices was being a member of the first School Board, a J.P., and one of the small committee charged with the task of finding a site in Aberystwyth for the National Library of Wales. He was for many years a member of the Welsh Baptist Church.

Boot and Shoe Making. As in most other towns there was a large number of shoemakers in Aberystwyth in the past. Some, in answer to the demand for boots from the many lead miners in North Cardiganshire, began to employ others. One of these was John Jones, Boot and Shoemaker of 2, Great Darkgate St. who employed 60 craftsmen in his workshop which extended back to Queen St. In common with many other tradesmen he had great difficulty in getting paid for his goods by some of his customers. One such customer was a mining captain, Mathew Francis of Goginan who managed a number of mines in that district. In January 1858 John Jones sent him the following bill:

Pair of waterproof boots	16s 11d.
Pair of woman's leather boots	8s 6d.
Pair of woman's button boots	7s 6d.
Soling and heeling	2s 11d.
Patent slippers	5s 6d.
Kid leg boots	9s 11d.

It was many months before John Jones received the £7. 8s. 7d. owed to him. He could not afford to go to law, for some of the mine managers, Mathew Francis included, paid part of the miners wages in goods, and boots frequently formed part of the pay. Such was the practice in the Talybont and Darren mines, and in a number of other mines in the 1850's and later.

John Jones was the great grandfather of a former town clerk of Aberystwyth, H. D. P. Bott, whose mother, whenever she wanted a pair of boots, would be sent by her grandfather to the workshop to be measured for her knee-length button boots. All boots were made-to-measure then.

When the Lion Royal Hotel (Padarn Hall) was extended, John Jones's premises became part of the hotel. This probably led to the expansion of D. R. Jones's boot-making business in Bridge St., near the junction with Great Darkgate St., where he employed at least 30 shoemakers. D. R. Jones was known locally as Dai Lad. Periodically, on pay days, he would drive his goods van laden with footwear to the lead mines to sell boots and to collect money owed to him. Such transactions had often to be made in public houses and the settling of a debt was usually followed by a drink. By the end of the day Dai would often be quite incapable of driving home. But this never worried him for once he was securely in the van, he could rely on Lad, his donkey, to take him safely home.

Rope Making

It was in May 1778 that the Court Leet granted John Jones of Wrexham "a certain piece of the Common extending from Bryndiodde leading to the Turnpike Gate for the term of eleven years for the use of a Ropewalk, Two hundred Yards in Length and not exceeding Eight Yards in Breadth", at an annual rent of 10s.; i.e. it extended from a point which is probably now part of the West Wales Garage at Vaenor St., to the car park at the northern end of North road, running in a straight line parallel with what was then Sandmarsh Lane and is now Queens Rd., a little behind the Town Hall. It formed part of the old borough boundary.

It seems to have been owned or managed by Samuel Thomas of Carmarthen for a while, but reverted to the Jones family before the lease expired in 1808. It was then in Thomas Jones's hands, his family later lived at Frongog. The new lease allowed him to extend the ropewalk by 30 yards at an increased rent of three guineas.

With time, the same Thomas Jones developed other interests, tar works were erected at his North Rd. works, and also flag and slate works. He was also a ship-owner and seems to have been involved in some of the timber yards which covered Rofawr and the bottom of Custom House St.

When shipbuilding began to thrive in the early 19th century another ropewalk was set up in Trefechan by Thomas Jones. It ran in a straight line along the eastern part of Dinas Terrace. It is believed that there was another ropewalk in Trefechan running up the lower slopes of Pendinas and owned by the merchant Mathew Davies. The names *Ropos Hill, Banc y Ropos* and *Rhiw Ropos* are reminders of this old industry.

Lime Burning was another Industry which was confined almost entirely to Trefechan. Late in the 18th century there were 8 lime kilns, six in Trefechan and two on the north side of the river between the castle and the bridge. Two of the Trefechan kilns were ordered to be removed c. 1800 in order to improve the approach to the new bridge. Some of these kilns were the property of local landowners.

The use of lime in agriculture greatly increased in the 19th century and by the 1860's there were 15 ships engaged regularly in carrying limestone from Aberthaw, Red Wharf and Milford Haven to Aberystwyth. Other ships brought the culm which was mixed with the lime in the kilns. These vessels generally anchored on the Trefechan side of the harbour. Much coal was also imported to that side and when the tide was out, it was tipped straight into the waiting carts.

The kilns were of the running-lime type which meant that the kiln could be kept burning continuously and that the lime could be carried away without letting the fire out. In the busy season, carts were carrying lime away day and night. In 1860-65 32,000 bushels were sold by one lime merchant alone, at one shilling a bushel.

The lime kilns, being warm, were popular meeting places for the local people, children used them to bake potatoes while their elders clustered round them to exchange gossip and tell stories. In winter, tarpaulins were rigged up to provide shelter for the limeburner, and also made popular meeting places.

One of the limeburners was Billy Penbanc,

noted for his drinking of ale. When anyone tried to reform him he would recite;

Cered y byd i'r sawl a'i caro,
A minnau'n llawen iach,
Llymed nawr ac yn y man,
O'r cwrw, melyn baeh.

Let the world go by for those that love it, while I, hale and hearty, enjoy an occasoinal drink of my beloved golden ale.

Despite their teasing of him, Billy was kind to children and it became the custom at Christmas time for them to meet at Billy's house for a party, the guests providing their own food. When he became ill, they repaid his kindness by running errands for him, especially fetching beer and tobacco. This was one job that the Band of Hope children did in defiance of the protests of their leaders.

Another character was Williams Rodyn (Williams of the Kiln) who lived in a hut above his lime kilns in Trefechan until a few years before he died, when he moved to Vulcan St. He was known locally as *Etifedd Tanycastell* (the heir to Tanycastell) which

A few of Trefechan's lime kilns. The building with a veranda was the Customs House

was a true description for he came of a well-to-do family.

He was born in Penrhiw, Ystumtuen in 1816 with a silver spoon in his mouth, and became heir not only to Tanycastell but also to property in Machynlleth. He was educated at a school in Ponterwyd and later became a schoolmaster at Kingston School. Returning to Wales he opened a school at Mynyddbach Chapel in 1863 where local children were educated for a payment of a penny a day. It proved very succesful, he had from 100 to 150 pupils in his school and he had to engage an assistant. He was then a member of the Wesleyan Church and highly respected. When his father died and he came into his inheritance he gave up the school and went to live in Penlone where he was much in demand for social gatherings and as chairman at local meetings. He even acted as medical adviser and dentist on occasions and gave legal advice on simple matters, even appearing in court at times.

While living at Penlone, he opened a grocery shop and began to build a big house at the side of the Devil's Bridge Rd., but when it was ready to be roofed he abandoned it.

This was the time when he got into trouble over a love affair, and was also charged with an offence against a child in Pembrokeshire. Though found innocent by the court this put him beyond the pale.

He had inherited £1,200 by his father's will and being no longer accepted in his home area he left and went to Aberystwyth where he bought some property, which included lime kilns, from John Roberts,

Aberllolwyn. But the coming of the railway had lessened the trade in lime and Williams lost much of his money on the deal; this made him bitter and he began to go downhill. In time he became very ragged in appearance wearing sacks instead of a coat and trousers, with a large Inverness cape covering everything but his head, which usually bore an old sailor's peaked cap. The cape served not only to protect him from the elements but also to keep him warm at night. He would never sleep in a bed but used a chair or the stairs. For a while he shared his hut with an old grey horse in premises which were not too luxurious even for the horse.

His appearance was such that some people sought to make fun of him. In fact he had remained shrewd, read every bit of newspaper that he could get hold of, and was particulary knowledgeable about Japan and the Far East generally. Some amusing stories were told of the discomfiture of strangers who, misled by his appearance, entered into an argument with him, expecting of an easy victory.

In the last years of his life he became obsessed with the idea that someone was going to kill him and he went around armed with a pistol and a life preserver in the form of a small bag filled with sand. He also kept a double-barrelled gun at home. He once loaded the pistol and threatened to shoot a neighbour and a policeman, but no one believed him and he made no attempt to stop his pistol being unloaded.

Williams Rodyn died, as he had lived for many years, alone. He was found dead at the bottom of a flight of stairs with his cape wound around his head.

Another Aberystwyth lime merchant who also kept a shop in Commerce House, Bridge St., was the prosperous John Evans who married Elizabeth the daughter of Lewis Pugh of Abermad. The Lovesgrove estate was bought either by or for the young couple, who became the first Evans's of Lovesgrove in 1843. One of their grandsons was Brigadier General Lewis Pugh Evans V.C.

The Gas Works

As stated above, William Morley Stears of Stroud was given permission to form a company and to set up gasworks in Aberystwyth in 1838. They were built at the town end of Morfa Rd., the first name given to Park Avenue, on land owned by Job Sheldon. Being on the southern side of the mill leat they were outside the town on the site still occupied by the Wales Gas Offices. Nearby there was a small bridge over the leat, known as Pont Corry.

The works cost £4,000 to build and the money was raised by the issue of £10 shares. For years they were managed by a man who was also the engineer. The company solicitor was William Henry Thomas, clerk to the Town Improvement Commissioners, a strong supporter of the English Congregational Church and town clerk from 1872 to 1880.

While the people of Aberystwyth were proud of the 80 gas lamps which the Town Commissioners had installed in the streets, they were appalled at the price of gas, 7s. a thousand cubic feet, and there were complaints galore from those whose homes were lit by gas, and of the cost of keeping the streets well lit. New types of lamps were installed to cut costs and there was much talk of the Commissioners buying the gas works, but nothing came of it.

The gas was produced and stored in gasometers behind the site of the present showrooms. The coal came by sea until the 1860's when it began to come by rail, and continued to do this except during the 1926 General Strike when ships were again used.

Despite the complaints, the demand for gas went on increasing and in 1870 the gasworks were enlarged. Three years later an Act was passed which made the Gas Company into a statutory body. This meant that it could not use its monopolistic position and raise prices indiscriminately. The law laid down the maximum dividend that could be paid to shareholders and tied the price of gas to that dividend.

When the gasworks were built they were the only buildings in Park Avenue but by 1900 they were surrounded with a school, a foundry and private houses, and it was resolved to move the production section to modern works on the site now occupied by the gasometers etc. near Plascrug playing field. In 1920, to save labour, the vertical retorts were replaced by horizontal ones. This meant the building of the tall chimney which was a landmark for many years. The Llanbadarn site was well suited to the works, near a railway and having its own railway siding where coal trucks could be unloaded with much less labour than in Park Avenue.

The present showrooms were built at the

The Aberystwyth Gas Co. Offices, Park Avenue

time of the move in 1900, and still bear the old name *Aberystwyth Gas Works.*

Until the 1920's most of the houses in the town were lit by gas and gas cooking stoves were making their appearance. The company had about 3000 customers but its staff was surprisingly small, 20 on the production side and 16 engaged in maintenance, distribution and administration. In 1931 a fitter's weekly earnings were £2.10s and the average householder's bill was £4 a year.

The change from gas to electricity owed much to the Town Council's policy of encouraging and even helping people to use the latter. Having bought the electricity works, they wanted to make it pay. Nevertheless, much of the town and its houses was still lit by gas in 1939, and then came the war and gas lighting was soon a thing of the past.

But the post-war period saw the resurgence of gas, as a source of heat for cooking and comfort. The output increased from half a million to a million therms in 20 years. In 1960 the works were linked to the Wales grid and ceased to produce gas. All that was needed at Llanbadarn was reduction equipment and the gasometers. Being already on the grid made the change to North Sea gas, in 1968-70, relatively simple apart from the problems of adjusting household appliances to the new fuel.

It is often said that the 1900 move opened up room *alongside* Park Avenue for the county yard. According to the maps of the period the works were *behind* the position of the present showrooms and the site alongside was already occupied by the foundry.

Electric Lighting

As one might expect, electricity for lighting was first used in Aberystwyth in the physics department of the University College, probably in 1890. The generator was driven by a gas engine which was damaged in transit on the Cambrian Railway and had to be returned for repair.

The next place to use the new form of power was the steam laundry built in Mill St. on the site of John Robert's old tannery. This electricity plant was probably installed by a firm called *Bourne and Grant Ltd.* in 1891. The laundry was then owned by the Aberystwyth Improvement Co. which also owned the pier, the large new Hotel Cambria, the Cliff Railway, and the Luna Park entertainment centre on Constitution Hill.

The laundry generator produced more electricity than was needed and the company began to distribute it to some of its customers. This must have been the source of the electricity used by the Corporation to light a portion of the promenade in October 1892.

In 1895 the Chiswick Electricity Co. made its appearance and eventually took over the laundry plant. The new company's equipment consisted of three steam engines and a vast array of accumulators. In 1910 a Seltzer diesel engine was purchased, and installed by Henry Miller of Llanbadarn, back from his spell as an engineer in Colombia, South America.

Street lighting was at first confined to key positions in the town, and at the north end of the promenade, it consisted of carbon arc lamps. The responsibility for inspecting and renewing the carbons lay with an old "windjammer" sailor known locally as Bill Carbon. He went about his work carrying a ladder with hooks at one end to grip the cross arms of the old type of lamp standard.

The hours of work for the man in charge of the engines were from 9 a.m. until midnight for seven days a week with an hour off for a mid-day meal. Other meals had to be taken while looking after the plant.

The station was shut down at midnight and the load transferred to the accumulators which were recharged during the day.

In 1936 the electricity works were purchased for £46,000 by the Aberystwyth Corporation and, as an inducement to the townspeople to install electricity in their homes, they undertook to put in four lights free of charge. The street lighting system was then changed from gas to electricity. About 1938 the system changed from DC to AC and new plant installed. It was very efficiently run. The works remained a municipal undertaking until it was nationalised in 1945. It is interesting to note that after the national electricity grid was created, the Aberystwyth works were, for a while, entirely isolated from the rest of the country, a situation it shared with no other oil-powered plant in the British Electricity Authority.

The works were first established in Mill St. and remained there until 1978. In 1974 electricity ceased to be generated there, and four years later the remainder of the staff was transferred to new premises at Lluest, overlooking Llanbadarn Fawr. The Mill St., premises are now empty.

Printing

William Caxton set up his printing press in Westminster in 1480; it was another two and a half centuries before Wales had its first press, and well over three centuries to the time when a printer first started work in Aberystwyth.

The first printing press was set up in 1809 by the Rev. John James and Samuel Williams. John James was a Baptist minister at Aberystwyth from 1803 to 1817, having himself been baptised there by the Rev. Thomas Evans in March 1797. In 1802 at the Epiphany Quarter Sessions for Cardiganshire "upon the motion of Mr. Thomas Morgan, it [was] ordered that John James, of the town of Aberystwyth, minister of the Gospel, be licensed to preach according to the Rules established by Law for Protestant Dissenters, he having in open Court taken the several oaths required by the Acts of Parliament in that case made and provided, and he is hereof accordingly licensed".

John James seems to have started printing in 1808, in his own house, at the urgent request of some Aberystwyth business men who also provided financial support.

Samuel Williams, his partner, went into the business with mixed motives. He was a practical man and must have realized that Aberystwyth undoubtedly offered a good opening for a printer at that time. But he was also a very religious man, an ardent Calvinistic Methodist, and his fellow worshippers probably welcomed a press that would advance their cause. In 1812 John James left the town for another ministry, leaving the press entirely in the hands of Williams who was then a leading deacon at Tabernacl.

The first author to take his "copy" to James and Williams was the Rev. Azariah Shadrach, minister of the Independent Chapel in the town. In the spring of 1809 he might have been seen, short of stature and probably clad in the full black cloak that he generally wore, hurrying along Bridge St. with the manuscript of his *Cloriannau Aur* (the Golden Scales), the first book to be printed in the town. Later they also printed his *Goleuni Caersalem* (the Light of Jerusalem) which is named on Shadrach's tombstone near the Parish Hall, the only Aberystwyth printed book to be so named.

The first book to come from the business after the dissolution of the partnership was the second edition of Daniel Rowland's *Deuddeg o Bregethau* (Twelve Sermons) in 1814. Two years later it printed the *Aberystwyth Guide* with its index of house-holders in the town, now a very rare book. In 1817 a most unusual book was printed here, *A Selection of Psalms and Hymns adapted to the Organ in the Chapel of Aberystwyth*. The organ was not what one associates with a chapel these days, but a barrel organ, operated by turning a handle and able to play only a limited number of tunes.

Samuel Williams was a very keen Methodist and he sometimes found it difficult to reconcile his business interests with his religious principles. Aberystwyth in the 1810's was dependent for its theatricals on groups of strolling players who stayed in the town for a few days or several weeks according to the support they received.

They were so very different from the townspeople that they were regarded with much suspicion and were not well received on the whole. It was said of them that they came into the town, engaged rooms, lived extravagantly, ran into debt and often absconded leaving bills and rents unpaid. These actors had to advertise their presence and their plays, and were dependent on the local printer for the long, coloured narrow play bills then used to advertise their performances. Williams consented to produce these at first, but soon his religious principles began to worry him and he stopped printing such bills. It is possible that some pressure had been put on him by his fellow deacons, most of whom regarded theatres as Satanic devices which lured young people away from the stern realities of life and created in them a morbid love for the unnatural and sensational. Williams's refusal left the actors in a very awkward situation, so they bribed a sympathetic young watchmaker named Careswell from Great Darkgate St. to print the bills by stealth while Williams and his wife were attending services at Tabernacl.

After Williams's death in November 1820 at the early age of 38, the business was carried on by his widow Esther, and her scrutiny of what was to go through the press was even more puritanical than that of her former husband. Their son Philip was also a printer, he was taken into partnership by his mother in 1847 but she remained in control until her death in April 1857. Philip enlarged the business and also became a bookseller with a large number of customers for his religious

books. One of the biggest books issued here was Idrisyn's *Welsh Commentary on the New Testament*. Esther Williams began printing a bilingual newspaper in 1836, it was called the *Cambrian Gazette—Y Freinlen Gymroaidd*, and was ultra radical in nature. It was edited by an Englishman named Jefferies who, after the paper ceased publication, opened a school in the town. The Welsh translation was by Adda Fras.

The printing works was first located in Bridge St., next door to Miss Loveden's House now a Ceredigion District Council Office. At some time or another it moved across the road to the corner of Bridge St. and Princess St.

The second printer to set up in business in Aberystwyth was John Cox, son of William Cox who had combined bookselling with being a barber in Great Darkgate St. Like so many others he was apprenticed to a Carmarthen printer before returning to his native town to open a business. He was in Great Darkgate St. when he issued the "*New Aberystwyth Guide*" by Llewelyn Pritchard in 1824 but soon afterwards, he moved to New St. There he began work in 1825 on the same side as the old North and South Wales Bank, now Elim Chapel, but nearer the church. He later moved to bigger premises across the road, a building which became the carpenters and cabinet makers' workshop used by J. Lewis Evans.

John Cox became renowned for the high quality of his work, he would never tolerate even indifferent work and was known to have destroyed a great deal of printed matter because of "one literal or broken type". His printing of the dignified poster announcing the laying of the foundation stone of the second St. Michael's Church in June 1830 shows that he had at least eleven different founts of type available for such work, and the ink used was remarkable for its dense blackness. He also turned out excellent pictorial work such as the framed placard of Humphreys' Medical Hall, Aberystwyth which used to hang in the corridor of the Public Library. John Cox was probably the best printer in Wales at that time, with Rees of Llandovery a close second. His establishment was a very large one for those days and he employed many people. He became the fashionable printer, patronised by the gentry, the Established Church and other important people and institutions. He did a great deal of work for Archdeacon Hughes, printing his *Sermons,* his translation of the Bishop of Norfolk's *Meditation on the Miracles* and others. It was he, too, who printed the excellent T. O. Morgan's *Guide to Aberystwyth,* and lived to print its fifth edition. He died full of honour in 1870 leaving no successor to the business, which then also included a bookshop at the corner of Pier St. and New St., a site which was later occupied by the Emporium.

Samuel Thomas was the nephew of the above-mentioned Samuel Williams. He started his own business in Aberystwyth in 1827 and during the next two years printed a magazine which was edited by a much respected Welshman, the Rev. David Owen, who wrote under the pseudonym 'Brutus'. Despite, or probably because of

his high hopes and his brave efforts to publish what people should read rather than what they liked to read, Samuel Thomas lost a great deal of money and spent three months in a debtors' cell in jail in Aberystwyth.

The printing press used by Thomas had an interesting history, it was once owned by the Rev. Joseph Harris (Gomer) the pioneer in Welsh periodicals. It then passed first to his son John Ryland Harris (Ieuan Ddu) who died young, and then to his successor, J. A. Williams of Swansea, a cousin of the Philip Williams mentioned above. It was then bought, first by Samuel Thomas and then by Philip Williams and, unfortunately, destroyed. A press which had produced the work of "Gomer" should have been preserved for posterity.

Samuel Thomas stopped printing in 1830. He was one of a little fraternity which met informally, but regularly, at the original Coopers Arms. His bosom friends were 'Brutus', Isaac Jones and David Saunders.

His premises were taken over by the above-mentioned Esther Williams, it was situated on the corner of Bridge St. and Princess St.

Certain works printed in the town in 1821 and 1823 bear the imprint *Salters, Printers and Bookbinders, Aberystwyth* but nothing is known of them.

David Jenkins established his press in the town in 1839, he was a native of Llanwenog and was known as "Dewi Wenog", being a poet of some standing. Like most other printers in West Wales he served his

apprenticeship in Carmarthen and like many others he stoutly defended Protestantism. It was once said that this contribution to Protestantism should atone for the iniquitous death of Bishop Ferrars who, because of his religious beliefs, was burnt at the stake in Carmarthen in 1555.

Jenkins served as foreman at Cox's printing works for a number of years before setting up his own press at his home in Great Darkgate St. This was the time when a group of Wesleyans broke away from the main church, which they called *Wesle Mawr* (the Big Wesley) and formed *Wesle Bach* (the Little Wesley) which they regarded as the United Free Church. Soon after their formation the members of the latter published a monthly magazine, printed by David Jenkins, known as *Blaguryn y Diwygiad* (the Young Sprig of the Revival) It was designed to be the great trumpet blast against the main Wesleyan cause. But the latter made use of the similarity between *Blaguryn* and *Blagardyn* and called the magazine *Blagardyn y Diwygiad* (the Bully Boy of the Revival) and made it a laughing stock.

David Jenkins published the first musical periodical to be printed in Wales. It first appeared in July 1852 under the editorship of Ieuan Gwyllt and was called *Blodau Cerdd* (Flowers of Music). It appeared monthly, cost $1\frac{1}{2}$d. and contained lessons in the theory of music in the form of dialogues. It also presented a collection of songs suitable for Sunday Schools. Only seven numbers were published.

The David Jenkins press was first located in a loft in Great Darkgate St, then it moved across the street to bigger premises where it stayed for a few years before being set up in Eastgate. It finally settled back in Great Darkgate St.

A publication which was founded, edited and owned by David Jenkins was the *Aberystwyth Observer*. It was a weekly paper, printed especially for the Established Church but carried on according to Liberal principles. Its first edition appeared in 1858 and it remained in Jenkins's hands until 1872 when it was bought by John Morgan. It was he who took over John Cox's business when the latter died in 1870 which is probably why he was able to publish the *Aberystwyth Guide* of 1874 under his name; it is almost entirely a copy of T. O. Morgan's work. Whether he printed the *Aberystwyth Observer* at Cox's old premises is not known but in its latter years the paper was produced in a building on a site now occupied by the West Wales Garage in Northgate St. John Morgan was an ardent Conservative and the Aberystwyth Observor showed this clearly. It ceased publication in 1915.

Two other printers in the town were William Williams and Richard Samuel. Both had served in the same office but when they started their own businesses, Williams carried on the tradition of the Samuel Williams office, while Samuel kept to the lines established by John Cox.

Cambrian News

In Bala, in October 1860 *the Oswestry Advertiser* published a four-page supplement which was named the *Merioneth Herald*. It was established for the "primary purpose of breathing the new fire of Liberalism into a county which, from time immemorial, had been represented in Parliament by the Tories", and it helped eventually in getting Merionethshire represented by a Liberal. In 1864 it changed its name to *The Merioneth Standard* and in 1869 it became *The Cambrian News*, a year after David Williams of Pwllheli was elected the first Liberal M.P., for Merioneth.

The Cambrian News then began to play an active part in Welsh life. A perusal of its pages will show that its representatives were present at the first official meeting to consider the establishment of a University of Wales, held at a lawyer's office in London, and at the opening of the college in Aberystwyth in 1872. It followed closely and reported regularly the fortunes of the College and the moves to establish others. It played a prominent part in the elections which eventually led to the return of Liberal M.P.'s for Mid and North West Wales, especially that of Stuart Rendel as M.P. for Montgomeryshire. It was the latter's generous gift of land which enabled the National Library of Wales to be built in Aberystwyth on its present site. It reported the first political speech made by Lloyd George at Blaenau Ffestiniog, and gave considerable support to T. E. Ellis.

The newspaper's connection with Aberystwyth really began in 1873 when John Gibson arrived there to organise the paper, to edit, report and manage its publication for the Oswestry firm. He little thought then that he would be still doing this forty years later. His office was at 3 Queen's

Sir John Gibson

Road.

John Gibson was a poor boy who first became interested in newspapers when he began selling them in the streets of his native town, Lancaster. He then formed the ambition to become the editor of a newspaper and set about improving his own English. He did this so well that he eventually became a master of the language.

Some time before 1860 he became apprenticed to a Lancashire printer with

whom he remained until the cotton famine caused by the American Civil War created such a depression in the Lancashire cotton industry that the printer had to discharge some of his men, including John Gibson. He then decided to go to London and on to New Zealand but before doing this he went on the road to Huddersfield, by train to Manchester, by boat on the Manchester Ship Canal to Warrington and on foot to Wrexham. He then walked into Shropshire and, on coming to a fork in the road, decided to take the one which an approaching cart would take, probably hoping for a lift. This led him to Oswestry and a job as a compositor in the *Advertiser*. There he became known as a man of marked ability, soon he was writing for the paper and his articles attracted attention. In 1873 he was asked to go to Aberystwyth to look after the interests of the Cambrian News, which was still printed in Oswestry. Finding the work more than he could manage, he asked for assistance and was sent W. R. Hall on a fortnight's trial. Hall stayed in Aberystwyth for sixty years.

One of the first tasks which Gibson set himself was to get Welshmen to shed their inferiority complexes. Though an Englishman, he believed in Welsh nationality and consistently contended that Welsh people had the right to speak their own language and to develop their own culture. He was also deeply disturbed at the insanitary conditions in the town and waged ceaseless war on those responsible for such conditions, while urging occupiers to improve their living conditions.

Soon after he arrived Gibson stirred up the Burial Board over the untidiness of the cemetery, and upset many householders by objecting to the practice of keeping pigs immediately under house windows, and to the accumulation of rubbish in back gardens and yards.

He exposed the lucrative trade of the lapidaries who sold as being from Aberystwyth, stones which came from Germany. These and other exposures led to his being described by one lawyer as "the Universal Blister".

When an article appeared in the *Lancet* referring to the Cambrian News's description of local insanitary conditions, a public meeting was held in the Town Hall to condemn Gibson for writing the article, which he had not. On one occasion he was followed through the town by a crowd, booing and howling at him.

But the greatest crises in his life in Aberystwyth was in 1879. There existed in the town an exclusive club of professional men known as the "Smokey Face Club" which held its annual meetings, which were festive occasions, at one of the town's hotels. At one of these gatherings, as 11.00 p.m. approached, the order "glasses round" was given; the landlord appeared and apologetically explained that he could not serve the drinks as no extension of hours had been authorized and the police sergeant was at the door. There and then, two magistrates who were present drew up and signed an extension of time, and the company went on drinking till midnight.

This was reported in the Cambrian News with the result that a question was asked about it in Parliament. The magistrates apologised and promised not to do it again. It was too good a tit-bit for English papers to miss and it was widely reported. The following appeared in *Punch*.

Who with law should not make free
If not your J.P. ?
Being Cymru of blood and convivial of habit
The Statute lets shelve
And keep open till twelve
The house where Welsh lions
Wash down their Welsh rabbits.

The magistrates were very annoyed but said nothing, watching for a chance to get even with the editor. It came when a woman was charged with stealing a bottle of wine from a chemist's shop, the case was dismissed and the wine returned to the chemist. This was followed shortly afterwards by a charge against a woman for having stolen pounds of tea, which charge was also dismissed and the tea given back to the owner. These unusual magisterial decisions being humorously critizised by the editor, the magistrates took legal action. The case went before the Lord Chief Justice and Mr. Justice Lush who complained that the case should never have been brought to court. But the justices did decide that the remarks made in the paper tended to throw ridicule on the Bench, and the editor and the paper were ordered to pay all the costs, between £300 and £400.

As a result of this case it was laid down that in the matter of extension of hours, magistrates must hold petty sessions at "appointed places" only, and not wherever they chose.

Scarcely had the Oswestry proprietors of the Cambrian News paid the costs than Gibson wrote an amusing, imaginary report of speeches made at a dinner which included a reference to some of the guests going on to the promenade after dinner to "send" some of their friends, and being then themselves unable to find their way home until day-break. Unfortunately, a slip in one sentence had libellous implications and there was a threat of another action. The Oswestry office then protested to their editor and asked him to apologise for his words and settle the affair as amicably as possible. Gibson's answer was that he would publish a letter of apology but would also insert his letter of resignation.

When the paper appeared with the apology and the letter of resignation, a procession was formed by some councillors, magistrates and some of the principal tradesmen, which marched slowly through the streets escorting a bier on which was a bespectacled effigy of John Gibson. Led by the Militia band playing the Dead March, the procession proceeded to the beach where the effigy was afterwards set alight. The bier also carried a large drawing of the editor lying on a bier with his friends, Robert Bickerstaff, Ald. John James, Ald. Peter Jones, and Dr. R. D. Roberts, as bearers. It was now generally assumed that the editor's goose had been cooked, and that Aberystwyth would be rid of the troublesome John Gibson. But Ald. John James, the owner of the London and Provincial Stores in Terrace Rd., and of a wide strip of land between Portland Rd. and North Parade, had other ideas.

When he heard of the procession and saw the cartoon in which he figured, he decided to go to Oswestry to negotiate with the owners of the Cambrian News for the sale of the paper. They agreed and the paper was sold. His intention was to form a company with his friends and to put Gibson and Hall in charge. But Gibson was not prepared to work at the dictates of others, he suggested that £7,000 be lent to him for three years at 5 per cent interest and that he purchase the paper himself. James and his friends agreed and John Gibson became the owner of the Cambrian News early in 1880.

A former malthouse in Mill St. was leased from one of the magistrates interested in Gibson's expulsion and plant was installed for producing the newspaper. The first copies of the Cambrian News to be printed

The Cambrian News Works in Mill St.

in Aberystwyth appeared in May 1880.

By this time the paper was well known and highly respected by honest men of all parties and denominations. It became the county paper for Cardiganshire and Merionethshire and was once described in *Truth* as "the best Welsh weekly".

After several years of success in the Mill St. premises, John Gibson built a stationer's shop and printing office in Terrace Rd. for some £4,000. There, for over sixty years, the Cambrian News was printed until it was moved to its present premises in Queen St. and Grays Inn Rd.

As owner of the paper, Gibson was free to present his progressive ideas and to criticise mercilessly such things as insanitary conditions, bad housing and injustice. With a Dickensian satire he exposed any form of hypocrisy and cant in the conduct of

The Cambrian News in Terrace Rd.

The Cambrian News in Queen St.

The Welsh Gazette Works in Bridge St.

affairs. His leading articles, "Up and Down the Coast", notes and commentaries on local and national affairs, became widely known and were often quoted in Parliament and the leading journals of the day. When he was knighted in 1915 he received hundreds of congratulatory telegrams from all over Britain.

In the autumn of 1915 the business was sold to a new company with Lord Rhondda as one of its directors and A. E. Harrison of Cardiff as the managing director. The following year Robert Read of the staff of the South Wales Daily Echo, where he had worked with Howard Spring and Percy Cudlipp, was appointed managing editor. In 1926 Harrison was replaced by Robert Read's father, H. Read, who had just retired after forty years as chief of the editorial staff of the South Wales Daily Echo.

In 1916 the National Eisteddfod made a delayed but very welcome appearance in Aberystwyth and the Cambrian News published a unique *Eisteddfod Review*, a souvenir of the great gathering. The following year it opened a London office which proved such a success that representatives were also appointed in Liverpool, Manchester and Cardiff.

Under the management and editorshop of Robert Read, the paper flourished. A succesful bookbinding business was opened in Mill St. in 1920 and was incorporated into the new premises forty years later. In the 1930's Robert Read became the owner of the paper and he intensified his already vigorous campaign for improvements in living conditions in the poorer sections of the town. His agitation and the resulting public meetings led to the erection of the Borough Council's first council house estate in Penparcau. A deeply religious man, he made his views quite plain in the Cambrian News on religious, moral and temperance issues. But managing the firm and editing the paper proved a big strain, especially during the War period, and in 1947, after a long illness, he died. He was succeeded as editor by D. C. Wright and as managing director by his son Henry Read.

The Welsh Gazette.

During the mid 19th-century there was a great deal of agitation in Wales for the reform of the voting system at parliamentary elections. There was no secrecy at the polling booths and voters were subject to threats, abuse and even violence from opposing factions on election day. It was unsafe to vote alone and the small farmers of South Cardiganshire, led by Gwilym Marles, overcame resistance by marching in procession to the polling stations to record their votes, escorted by others on horseback. Farmers and other tenants who were known to have voted against their landlords' wishes frequently became the victims of persecution, were charged extortionate rents, and even evicted.

One of those who supported Gwilym Marles was George Rees of Llanwenog who, as a result, found it expedient to move his home to Llanybydder. It was there that, in 1866, his son, also George Rees, and founder of the Welsh Gazette, was born. Three years later, the elder George moved his family to Lampeter where he started in business as a nurseryman.

George the son attended an elementary school in Lampeter until he was eleven when, like most others of that time, he had to leave and start earning a living. His first job was as a clerk, first in a sawmill and then in a coalyard near the railway station. He took little interest in sport but was active in cultural pursuits, notably the Penny Readings held regularly in the Old Grammar School, at the top of Church St. These seem to have made him conscious of his lack of education and he began to educate himself. He managed to save enough money to buy Cassell's *Popular Educator* and during the winter evenings removed himself to his tiny bedroom to study well into the night by candle light. When warned of the effect of such a poor light on his sight, he replied that the Japanese often read by the light cast by a glow-worm. For years young George Rees spent every penny he could spare on the purchase of text books and he succeeded in getting first class certificates at the science and art examinations. He became one of a group of young Lampeter men who devoted themselves to intensive private study. One of these became famous as Dr. Gwenogvryn Evans, one of the foremost lexicographers of his day; another was an apprentice at Medical Hall, Robert Williams, who became Archdeacon of the Diocese of St Davids, and a third was Dafydd Williams, a cobbler who worked at his last from six in the morning to six at night but still found time to study Latin and Greek.

After years of hard study, Dafydd gained a scholarship at St David's College, graduated and took Holy Orders. He then became a missionary in North America and was eventually made Bishop of Huron and a leader of Canadian religious life. He continued to correspond with George Rees, and entrusted him with the management of his private affairs in Wales.

George Rees's interest in printing was evident when he was only a youth, a large framed engraving of Caxton and his press hung in his bedroom. He once wrote the script for a five minute speech on Caxton for a local eisteddfod competition; it was memorised and delivered by his brother and won the prize.

When he was eighteen, George moved to Aberystwyth where he became in turn a clerk, a book keeper at Griffiths Jones the solicitor's office, and a member of the staff of the Cambrian News, the paper's representative in the counties of Merioneth, Montgomery and Cardigan. Determined to become a good journalist he now embarked on an intensive course of study of English, Welsh and French literature. He also studied botany and in 1896 published *Gwersi mewn Llysieueg* (Lessons in Botany) and wrote numerous articles on botanical subjects for various English and Welsh magazines.

On his travels he met several leading Welshmen and became friendly with Llewelyn Williams, J. H. Davies of Cwrtmawr and T. E. Ellis M.P., all of whom believed that the Cambrian News did not provide an effective platform for the Liberal cause. It was also believed

that the paper did not cater adequately for the people of South Cardiganshire, being primarily the voice of North Cardiganshire and Merionethshire. There was also the argument that it was not sufficiently *local* for the average countryman. As the Rev. J. M. Lloyd Thomas was to write later, "Cardis are neighbourly, gossipy people with a penetrating, if peculiar concern about each other's business. They prefer to learn not what is taking place in Pekin or Moscow but what occurs in Cribyn or Ffair Rhos; who presided at the tea urn at the meeting of the Women's Institute, and who won the challenge solo at the Eisteddfod of the Young Farmers' Club... He wants to read about a 'fair cop' over commercial petrol and food offences, who has been nabbed riding a bicycle without lights, and sometimes, with an unholy satisfaction, who has just died." It is doubtful if John Gibson would have agreed wholeheartedly with this but it is a good argument for a local paper.

Such views fitted in so well with George Rees's aspirations that with the encouragement of J. H. Davies and T. E. Ellis, he determined to bring out a new publication, a truly local paper covering the whole of Cardiganshire. In this he also had the support of many leading Methodists. He resigned his appointment and devoted himself to the many problems which now confronted him, not the least of which was the large capital outlay involved. Determined to be independent, he rejected proposals for the formation of a company and was fortunate enough to have friends prepared to act as guarantors for the cost of

A 19th century Aberystwyth printers' composing room

George Rees died on 22 February 1934, having established his paper on a firm foundation. By his expressed wish he was succeeded by William Lewis, his deputy and close friend for 35 years, and by his youngest brother, Henry Rees of Lampeter. In 1947 William Lewis died and Henry Rees became the managing director with Ben A. Jones as editor. Seven years later the management passed into the hands of George Rees's daughter, Miss Dilys Rees, and his son George Glynne Rees. But running a newspaper in the post-war years was a very expensive undertaking and demanded large reserves of capital which the Welsh Gazette did not have. Rising costs and falling sales eventually proved too much for it, and in December 1964 the Welsh Gazette appeared for the last time, and the plant was sold to the Cambrian News. Miss Loveden's House then became a local government office and still is.

equipment.

The old Miss Loveden's House at the corner of Bridge St. and Grays Inn Rd. having been vacated by the Baptist College, now added to its varied history the housing of George Rees' new venture. When this became known there were many who believed that there was no room for another newspaper and that it would soon fail. The first copy of the Welsh Gazette appeared on 17 April 1899 and was an immediate success, especially in the south of the county and in other rural areas. It exploited local interest to the full; a local historian, George Eyre Evans, roamed the county and wrote numerous articles on local history; David Samuel did the same for Aberystwyth. During its first ten years the paper featured "London Letter" initated and written by W. Llewelyn Davies K.C. and later edited by J. H. Davies, then a barrister in London and, later, the principal of the University College of Wales, Aberystwyth. There is no doubt, too, that the Welsh Gazette benefited from the average countryman's dislike of John Gibsons' merciless, never-ending criticism.

Transport

Until the 1760's Cardiganshire was said to be the most remote county in Wales and strangers were very few and far between. Up to the 1740's, the horse and drag cart were almost the only means of transport and, in some parts, wheeled vehicles did not become common until late in the century. The changes which then occurred were due largely to the improvements in the county's roads, improvements which probably resulted, in part, from the interest taken by wealthy visitors in Aberystwyth.

Cardiganshire had its first Turnpike Act in 1770 when it was reported that all the roads leading to Aberystwyth were in a deplorable condition. These roads were the one to Machynlleth, with a branch to Penrhyn at Ynys-las to connect with the ferry to Aberdyfi; the road to Llangurig and beyond which ran *via* Devil's Bridge, Dyffryn Castell and Eisteddfa Gurig; the Rhayader road which went through Devil's Bridge and Cwmystwyth, and the road to Cardigan. As a result of this Act turnpike gates were set up, the North Gate near the end of what is now Northgate St. and the South Gate at the junction of the five roads at Penparcau or "Piccadilly" as it was then called. From 1783 to 1790 the tolls from these gates averaged £406 *per annum* but

The North Turnpike Gates at the junction of Penglais Rd. and Llanbadarn Rd. c. 1880

this was not enough to keep the roads in good repair and a further sum of £2,900 had to be borrowed. The tolls at this time were as follows: for every passenger vehicle drawn by six horses or mules 1s. 6.; if drawn by 4 horses 1s., 2 horses 9d., 1 horse 3d. For every horse, etc. drawing a wagon, tram or cart etc., 3d. For every horse laden or unladen and not drawing, 1d. Drove of cattle or oxen, 10d. score. Drove of calves hogs, sheep, or lambs, 5d. score. No person was to pay toll at more than two gates in the one district (i.e. the Cardigan district south of the Aeron or the Aberystwyth district north of that river) and even then two payments were not to be made if the gates were less than ten miles apart. Tolls were only to be paid once a day. The Act was renewed in 1791. The yield from the tolls was to be used first to pay for the Act and then to maintain in good repair the roads, gates and tollhouses.

Not all traffic paid tolls; exempt were carriages drawing materials for repairing roads, lime, manure, harvest for storage, or horses drawing agricultural implements or animals for manuring and stocking. Exempt also were passengers on horseback, or coaches or carriages going to or coming from an election, coaches, etc. going to a place of worship or attending funerals, post horses, military men and equipment, cattle going to pasture or water.

Bridges belonging to the county were not included in the Act.

The Act of 1791 made the toll for every horse drawing a passenger vehicle 6d. or 1s. on Sundays unless going to church or chapel. Similarly, that on horses, etc.,

laden or unladen was raised to 2d. on Sundays unless going to a place of worship. Lime and manure, previously free, had to pay half toll, a heavy burden on the farmer who had to travel a long distance for his lime. Twenty-one years later another Act was obtained and there were again additions. It is worth noting that stage coaches had to pay every time of passing, which made long trips expensive.

It was not until 1812 that the road from Aberystwyth to Eisteddfa Gurig via Ponterwyd was first included in the Act. The opposition of Vaughan of Trawscoed to the building of this road was held by some people to be partly responsible for his failure to become the accepted candidate for the Cardigan Boroughs election of that year. The Aberystwyth district roads were well cared for and Lewis stated in 1831 that the turnpike roads leading to the town were among the best in Wales.

Until 1807 the only post-chaises in the whole county were in Aberystwyth and the Hafod Arms. It is not known when the first coach service to Aberystwyth was established but the town was difficult of access from England in 1806. In that year there was a plea for the road from Brecon via Builth, Rhayader, and Cwmystwyth to be opened to carriages so that visitors might see the glories of Hafod and Devil's Bridge on their way to Aberystwyth.

By the 1810's coach services were well established and the *Duke of Wellington* coach left the Gogerddan Arms every Monday and Friday morning at 4 a.m. during the summer but only on Fridays at other times. This coach travelled to

Shrewsbury *via* Machynlleth, Mallwyd, Llanfair Caereinion, and Welshpool. The coach from Shrewsbury arrived at Aberystwyth at 9 p.m. on the same day. The journey took a whole day.

Another Shrewsbury service was run at the same times by the *Princess of Wales* coach from the Old Black Lion every Tuesday, Thursday, and Saturday, *via* Devil's Bridge, Steddfa Gurig, Llanidloes and Newtown. Both these services were designed to connect with the London and other coaches at Shrewsbury.

The *Lord Hill* left the Talbot every Wednesday and Sunday morning at 7 a.m. *via* Devil's Bridge, Cwmystwyth, Rhayader, Kington to Worcester, where it met the London, Bath and Bristol coaches. After the building of the Belle Vue Hotel the first two made it their headquarters. Later, coaches were run to Carmarthen, Hereford, Ludlow, Gloucester, and Swansea. In 1816, the Kington coach took from 5 a.m. to 7 p.m. to travel to Aberystwyth. The single fare was 22s. inside the coach and 16s. outside. On the same day a coach left Aberystwyth at 6 a.m. and arrived at Kington at 8 p.m. The following morning this coach left for London at 4 a.m. and reached its destination on the following morning at 8 a.m. The journey to London from Aberystwyth thus took over 48 hours.

In the 1820's the coaches *Union* and *True Briton* also ran regularly to Shrewsbury whilst the *Leek* ran from the Gogerddan Arms to Ludlow *via* Machynlleth, "the Cock", and Newtown. Later the times of starting became more reasonable, the new *Engineer* coach did not leave for Oswestry until 7.00 a.m. and the *Salop and London Mail* left at the late hour of 11.00 a.m. In 1835 the Post Master General sanctioned a new mail coach to Aberystwyth, and hours before the first one arrived in the town, in May, the streets were crowded ready to cheer when it heard the coachman's horn. The coach left the G.P.O. in London at 8 p.m. and arrived at Aberystwyth at 8.15 the following evening. The return journey began next morning at 5.15. This coach used the newer, Llanidloes, Llangurig and Ponterwyd road, thereby avoiding the old Cwmystwyth road with its dangerous curves and precipices, a route which was said to have deterred many from visiting "a bathing place so improving, and healthful as Aberystwyth". The London Mail coach was a handsome contraption with its black and maroon body, its scarlet wheels, the royal arms on the doors and the top-hatted scarlet-coated coachmen.

In the 1850's there was much rivalry between two of Aberystwyth's coaching inns. The Belle Vue ran the mail coach to Shrewsbury at first but the Gogerddan Arms put a competitor on the same route. Then began the war which eventually lowered the fare to Shrewsbury to the incredible price of half a crown for a journey of 80 miles. The end came when the Belle Vue included a free breakfast in the price; this was too much for the Gogerddan Arms and it withdrew from the fray. Its rival then increased the fare to £1 4s. 6d.

One way of alleviating the boredom of the long tiring journeys was to take and "peruse" *Paterson's Roads* by Edward Mogg which described, sometimes in detail, the features that could be seen, and perhaps examined,

en route. He had nothing to say of Aberystwyth but much that was high-flown about Devil's Bridge.

"The emotion of astonishment, terror and delight produced on the mind by viewing the scene here presented far exceeds the utmost power of language. The yawning chasm beneath these arches is so overhung with woods that the eye with difficulty catches even a partial view of the gloomy depths below; this circumstance however heightens the impression of terror which such a scene is calculated to inspire." He also comments on "the dreadful majesty of the various falls".

Coaches were also run from Aberystwyth to Carmarthen, Hereford, Cardiff, Chester, Holyhead, Milford, sometimes directly and a few indirectly. In the 1850's the *Snowdon* ran from the Belle Vue through Dolgellau to Caernarvon, visiting Llanberis and passing Snowdon *en route*. Coach communication was also established with Cardigan *via* Aberaeron by Messrs. Cummins, Weston and Parker. The *Railway* coach was then running regularly to Swansea *via* Lampeter and Carmarthen.

There were also goods wagon services. In 1816 two wagons ran alternate weeks to meet their counterparts from London and elsewhere in Shrewsbury. A few years later there was also a wagon service to Chester *via* Machynlleth, Dolgellau and Bala, and one to Carmarthen. These wagons were housed either at the Swan Inn kept by the coach driver Enoch Hughes, or at the Hope Inn in Bridge St. The Shrewsbury vehicle, known locally as *Y Wagen*

Fawr (the Big Wagon) usually left on Monday and returned on Saturday.

Until the Shrewsbury service was taken over by some Llanidloes men, all the loading of the wagons was done in a yard, separated from the road by a high wall, on part of the site now occupied by St. Pauls Methodist Church near St. James Square. The Llanidloes men, however, loaded outside the Skinners Arms (Tavern in the Town). Most of the wagons ceased to operate after the railway came, except to Aberaeron and other places not served by the railway.

The Coming of the Railway

Aberystwyth, with its population of 5,000 in the 1850's, its wide network of coach and wagon services, its growing holiday trade and its rich mining hinterland, must have looked an attractive prospect to the freight hungry railway companies of the West Midlands and other areas. The first reference to the new form of transport was in 1845 when solicitors for the North and South Wales Co. wrote to the Aberystwyth Improvement Commissioners asking them whether they would be neutral, agreeable or opposed to a railway passing over their land near Bryn-y-mor reservoir, an expensive undertaking. A similar suggestion was made later by Col. Pryse of Gogerddan when he advocated building the line from Borth to Aberystwyth along the coast instead of through Bow Street. This was considered, but not for long.

The inspiration to build a Shrewsbury-Aberystwyth line came from the L.N.W.R. in 1852, the forging of the final link was done by the Aberystwyth and Welsh Coast Railway Company, formed in 1861 to build a line from Aberystwyth to Machynlleth and along the coast of Merionethshire to Portmadoc and the potentially wonderful harbour of Porthdynlleyn near Nevin.

Among the company's leading members were G. H. Whalley and the Thomas Savin who was later to figure prominently in certain developments in Aberystwyth, notably the building of the Castle Hotel which became the University College.

A public meeting at Aberystwyth with the Mayor, Robert Edwards, in the chair, listened to G. H. Whalley, a noted orator, outlining the scheme which would make it once again the "Brighton of Wales", and gave the plan its enthusiastic support. Within two months the company's Bill received the Royal Assent and Savin, the contractor, began work in January 1862. By the autumn of that year the line from Machynlleth was within two miles of Borth, but then the storms came and the drive across the bog from Ynys-las became so difficult that the navvies rebelled and police had to be brought in to keep the peace. When the line did reach Borth on 17 July the natives greeted it with distrust but they were swamped by the thousands of people from Aberystwyth and elsewhere who came to greet the first train. A 23-coach excursion train brought 600 people from Oswestry, Shrewsbury and Welshpool at 2s. 6d. and 2s. a head. The day being very hot some of the men found the water irresistible and disported themselves in the sea as naked as when they were born. Such was the spirit of the day that further along the beach they were copied by a bevy of females in the same state. According to a Shropshire newspaper reporter even the porpoises took fright.

Work then began on the final stretch of line to Aberystwyth and the Mayor was informed that the railway from Machynlleth would be officially opened on 1 June 1864. On 7 May he called a meeting to discuss how they would celebrate this great event, an event which many thought would bring much wealth to the town. The following arrangements were agreed upon:

1. A procession preceded by a band and consisting of the Corporation and representatives of all the principal bodies in the town.
2. A cold collation for the directors and contractors of the railway line.
3. A dinner for the navvies and other people engaged in the construction of the line between Borth and Aberystwyth.
4. Tea and cake at the Temperance Hall for the pupils of all the schools in the district who were under the age of 14 years.

But it did not come about in that way, Col. Tyler R.E., the Inspector of Railways, examined the line between Borth and Aberystwyth on 26 May and while he found nothing wrong with the line, he found faults in the fencing and gates. This meant postponing the opening until 8 June but the Corporation decided that the navvies' dinner should go ahead. On 1 June a freight train of trucks, drawn by the engine *Borth* arrived at the station opposite Mary St (Terrace Rd.), full of navvies. They marched in procession up to the Assembly Rooms in front of which there was a high pole decorated with a large flag. At 2.0 o'clock, 230 men sat down to a magnificent dinner prepared by the Careswells, with plenty of "cwrw da" (good beer). After ample justice had been done to the food by these "hardy sons of the soil", there were many toasts and several speeches before the event ended at 7.00 p.m.

June 8 arrived but the railway was still officially unopened. In the same year (1861) that the Aberystwyth and Welsh Coast Railway Bill was passed in Parliament, the Manchester and Milford Railway Co's Bill for the construction of a branch line from Devil's Bridge to Aberystwyth received the Royal Assent. The M. & M.R. Co. therefore strenuously opposed the Welsh Coast line Bill and was able to show that they had some cause for complaint. The result was that the Welsh Coast Co. agreed to the inclusion in its Bill of a clause stating that it would not open the line to Aberystwyth until its line to Barmouth was opened, thereby giving the M. & M.R. Co. time to complete its railway first, or so it was thought. A year or so later, however, the two companies were on friendly terms and the Welsh Coast Co. was petitioning to have the clause removed. But the G.W.R. Co., backed by a group of men who had lost their seats on the board of the Welsh Coast Co., opposed the petition. With the support of the Aberystwyth Corporation and town interests, the Coast Co. fought back and took the matter to the House of Lords. There they were granted leave to complete the Aberystwyth line independently of the Barmouth venture as long as the latter was completed within three years.

The line to Aberystwyth having passed its final inspection, it was opened officially on 22 July 1864. It had been in use for goods traffic since 1 July. On the opening day, guns were fired at intervals all day, there were flags, banners and bunting everywhere and all the ships in the harbour, despite all they had to fear from the railway, were rigged with the whole range of their colourful codes of signals. In front of the station was erected an arch "of great artistic merit" surmounted by a model of the engine *Rhydol* and painted with welcoming slogans. The Belle Vue was "Tastefully decorated", and had a superb arch of evergreens at the entrance. Noon saw the arrival of an excursion train of 35 coaches from Oswestry and Newtown bringing 1,800 passengers.

At 2.30 p.m. the procession started off from the Town Hall with three bands in attendance, those of the 1st Cardiganshire Volunteers, the Welshpool Rifle Corps and the Penparcau School. At the railway station the marchers were met by Thomas Savin, the railway contractor, Earl Vane and other directors of the line. The Mayor, Ald. T. O. Morgan, read the message of welcome and thanks, Savin replied and the opening ceremony was performed.

At 7 p.m. all the notables met for dinner at the Belle Vue Hotel and "partook" of a meal the like of which would now cost a small fortune. The menu was as follows:

Soup: Turtle, A la Reine, Printemp
Fish: Salmon, Stewed Trout, Turbot, Fillet of Mackerel
Entre: Sweetbreads, Mushrooms, Compote of Pigeons, Olives, Civet of Rabbit Fenances, Lobster Paté, Lamb Cutlets, Cucumbers, Sauté of Kidney, Vin Madeira, Vol au Vent.
Roast: Saddles of Mutton, Fore Quarters of Lamb, Suckling Pigs, Turkey Poults, Ribs of Beef, Fillets of Veal, Roast Ducks.
Boiled: Legs of Lamb and Spinach, Stewed Rumps of Beef, Calves Head à la Tortue, Raised Pies, Hams, Tongues.
Entreinets: Dantzic Jellies, Maedvine of Fruits, Victoria Jellies, Suidoise of Cherries, Suidoise of Strawberries, Coffee Creams, Carlot à la Parisienne, Canapes of Apricot, Peu d'Amour, Gateux à la Neapolitan, Gateux à la Bohemian, Mayonaisse d' Homward, Aspic of Prawns, Levrets, Green Gesse, Plum Puddings, Ice Pudding, Cheese, Lobster Cheese, Kippered Herrings, Biscuits.

The festivities lasted until 11.00 p.m. when the members of the visiting party were persuaded to take their places in the return train. It was 3 a.m. before they arrived home in Oswestry.

The coming of the railway put paid to the stage coach which was not only slower, more dangerous and more tiring but was also penalised by a government order that made the stage coach pay a duty of one penny a mile for every four passengers it was licenced to carry, whether it had that number of passengers or not. The railway carriage paid a duty of only a halfpenny on every four passengers actually being carried.

As the road traffic decreased so the road tolls had to be lowered but there was no denying the railway and in time it was "the tea kettle with its unmelodious whistle" which triumphed.

Later in the 19th century coaching was revived at Aberystwyth. Capt. Cecil Otway ran a pleasure coach from there to Presteigne in 1876 but it soon stopped.

Aberystwyth not only had its nostalgic memories of the stage coach but also two heroes of those days. One was John Rea, guard on the last official mail coach in the United Kingdom, that from Aberystwyth to Shrewsbury. In retirement with his cherubic countenance, he could be seen imbibing and reminiscing in the bar parlour of the White Horse Inn in Terrace Rd. Even more of a hero was Matthew Marsh, not only a former driver of the Aberystwyth-Hereford coach but also a pensioner of Waterloo.

The Manchester and Milford Railway was first conceived in 1845 during the period of the Railway Mania and was aimed at making Milford Haven, a port abandoned since the closure of the Royal Dockyard in 1811, into a rival to Liverpool for the import of American cotton. The line was planned to run from Manchester to Milford via Crewe, Whitchurch, Oswestry, Newtown, Llanidloes, Lampeter, Pencader and Carmarthen, some of which were already connected by other lines. The scheme was abandoned almost as soon as it was first planned and no more was heard of it until the late 1850's.

In 1859 the Mid Wales Railway began to be planned and interest was re-kindled in the old M. & M.R., but the plan had now dwindled to an absurd route through Llanidloes to meet the Cardigan and Carmarthen

Railway at Pencader. Powers to build this line were granted on 23 July 1860, the main stem was planned to run *via* Devil's Bridge where a branch line would be built to Aberystwyth. Statutory permission was obtained to build the branch line on 11 July 1861. The line from Pencader was extended as far as what came to be called the Strata Florida station at Ystrad Meurig, and the Llanidloes line to just beyond Llangurig. To cross the mountain barrier to Devil's Bridge, it was proposed to build two tunnels totalling one and a half miles in length, connected by a viaduct 280 ft. high. Tunnelling had hardly begun before the company ran out of money and the mountain crossing had to be abandoned. In 1865 another Act was obtained to allow the company to build a line from Strata Florida through the Ystwyth Valley to Aberystwyth, and the Llangurig—Devil's Bridge plan was abandoned. Near Aberystwyth, the line was connected by a branch line with St. David's Wharf at the harbour, which saved the Cambrian Railway having to do this. At Aberystwyth the M. & M.R. had to be content with a short bay platform at the Cambrian Railway station, but it did build its own separate goods station there.

On 12 August 1867, the railway reached Aberystwyth from Carmarthen *via* Lampeter. It took only two and a half years to lay and was so well built that it was passed as fit for use after only one examination by the Government Inspector. A local paper stated that it not only "opened up probably one of the richest mineral countries in the world" but also "a vast district which for agricultural produce (was) unsurpassable", statements which may have pleased its readers but were hardly correct.

Probably because of the financial stringency of the time, there was far less celebration in the town than in 1864. On the opening day, well-fitted saloon coaches were provided for the Town Council and "other gentlemen of position in the town" and all took a trip by train to Strata Florida where they found the station bedecked with flags and evergreens. Some of the passengers expected to see the abbey and were surprised to find that the station was some miles from that ancient edifice.

The party was supposed to return on a train coming from Carmarthen. This was very crowded and was driven by a man who did not know the line. The weight of the train and the gradient on the line were considerable and although he shut off steam and applied the brakes in what he judged to be good time, the train went flying through Strata Florida Station at "express speed", "30 miles an hour", while the intended passengers stared at it in dismay. Eventually the driver managed to stop the train and wisely decided to go on to Llanilar and to return with only two coaches to fetch the "notables".

At the Belle Vue that evening the Town Council gave a banquet for the railway's directors and the contractors, others who came had to pay a guinea each, very different from 1864. The M. & M.R. was never to become a great success and after a long period of financial difficulties it was taken over by the G.W.R. in 1906.

Compared with the stage coach the train was much more comfortable and much faster. By modern standards it was very slow, for a passenger leaving Aberystwyth at 9 a.m. did not get to London until 11.10 that evening. The return journey began at 6.0 a.m. and finished at Aberystwyth at 9.35 p.m.

Aberystwyth's third railway was the Vale of Rheidol line to Devil's Bridge. As stated above, the Manchester and Milford Railway Co. planned to use this route and were granted statutory powers to build in 1861. Nothing came of the plan and in 1888 the company gave up its right to the route. As a result, in 1890 there was again talk of a railway to Devil's Bridge, a narrow gauge line, and seven years later an Act of Parliament was obtained for this purpose. Because of difficulty in raising the necessary money, work did not begin on the line until January 1901.

Opening of Vale of Rheidol Railway Dec. 1902. In front of the engine are bearded Montague Smith, the company chairman, and James Metcalfe, maker of the line's first locomotive.

At the opening of the Vale of Rheidol Railway

One of the line's first locomotives

The driving force behind the construction of the Vale of Rheidol line was George Green of Green's Foundry, then owner of the Rheidol Mines in the valley below Devil's Bridge. It was he who approached Sir James Szlumper and through him was able to get used materials at such a low cost that a start could be made on the building of the line. Another man whose name should always be associated with the Vale of Rheidol Railway was James Rees, father of Don Rees, who left the M. & M.R. to become manager of the new line and to supervise its construction. He served the company well for 14 years.

At first there was difficulty in recruiting labour but this was solved when work at the Elan Valley reservoirs was completed, and hundreds of the Irish navvies then made redundant descended on the quiet Rheidol Valley. In 18 months the rails had been laid to Devil's Bridge from Aberystwyth, but the Board of Trade being dissatisfied

with the work, modifications had to be made and the line did not open until September 1902 when the first goods train used it. Passenger traffic began in the following December. The railway cost £67,900 to build and the route used was the same as that planned by the M. & M.R.

The venture proved an immediate success, the first market day after the line was opened saw Aberystwyth full of country people taking advantage of the new service. Trains were frequent and fares were reasonable, 1s. 6d. return from Aberystwyth to Devil's Bridge. Visitors loved it, for it was far more comfortable and scenically more exciting than the horse-drawn brake, which it soon supplanted. Combined train and charabanc excursions were arranged to enable visitors to climb Pumlumon or to visit other places. During the religious revival of 1904-06, and when preaching meetings were held, evening trains carried large numbers of worshippers to chapels in

the town and the valley. To cope with the carriage of lead ore, aerial ropeways were erected to carry ore from mines in the valley bottom, such as the Rheidol United Mine, up into the trucks on the line. Rails were laid on to the main quay at Aberystwyth to enable the ore to be taken direct to the waiting ships for the voyage to Bristol and the Dee Estuary. Interchange sidings were also built so that ore could be easily transferred to trucks on the standard gauge line for transport to Swansea.

The Vale of Rheidol line was such a resounding success that there was talk of similar lines to Aberaeron, and even to Llandrindod Wells *via* Rhayader. Statutory permission was obtained for the Aberaeron line but nothing came of it. The amount of ore and timber carried on the Vale of Rheidol Railway increased so much that more trucks had to be bought in 1906. In 1912 the traffic was so heavy that an engine was borrowed from the Ffestiniog line. Summer camps near Devil's Bridge for regular and territorial soldiers, and Sunday School trips galore, swelled the summer traffic to record proportions and the profits soared.

In 1913 the line was taken over by the Cambrian Railway Co. when its decline had already set in. Lead mine after lead mine had been closed, and the extension to the harbour had already ceased to be used. The terminus was then moved alongside the main railway station. The First World War made things worse and no trains would be run for months at a time. After 1918 the tourist trade revived but the freight and winter passenger traffic never regained its former proportions. In 1923 the Cambrian

Railway Co., including the Vale of Rheidol line, was taken over by the G.W.R. which did its best to maintain the tourist trade. In 1931 the winter passenger trains ceased to run, country buses had become both cheaper and more convenient to use than the little train.

During the Second World War the line was closed. It reopened in 1945 but trains were few and far between and the service remained poor until 1954 when British Rail, the owners since nationalisation in 1948, made a determined effort by wide-spread advertising to turn the line into a viable concern. The threatened closure in 1963 was averted largely through the efforts of the local Vale of Rheidol Progress Committee. This organisation, formed at the suggestion of the Mayor of Aberystwyth, has contributed a great deal to the success which the line now enjoys.

The Carmarthen line, never a profitable concern, continued to be run by the G.W.R. until 1964 when, as a result of the Governments policy of closing unprofitable railways, it was closed, its track taken up, its bridges dismantled and even the hard core on part of the track was sold.

Horse and Motor Transport

The history of the transition from horse to motor transport in the Aberystwyth area is well illustrated in the work of Jones Brothers, a well-known firm of haulage contractors and omnibus owners in the town.

Thomas Jones was a lead miner who became the miners' agent in the Trisant and

North parade c. 1900

The line of carriages in North Parade

Devil's Bridge area. When a dispute developed between the miners and the mine owners in the 1890's it was Thomas who put the case for his fellow workers. The strike failed and Thomas was dismissed. Being the father of ten children, and there being no unemployment benefit, he moved with his family to Aberystwyth to look for work. There, with two of his sons, Isaac and Hugh Jones, he began to develop a haulage and transport business which seems to have thrived from the start. Soon they owned 35 horses and a considerable number of carts, brakes and carriages of all kinds. One major source of revenue were the visitors. A typical customer was Major Willis of Bristol who took a house on Marine Terrace for his family for a month every summer and contracted with Jones Brothers to take his family for a drive on five half days of every week. There were many who did this in the early part of this century when almost every house in Marine Terrace

was let to visitors in the summer.

Goods traffic, too, occupied much of the firm's attention, carting goods from the railway station to various parts of the district and doing the same for goods brought by the steamers which called regularly at the harbour. They also acted as carriers for local business men. Jones Brothers supplied the horses which drew the M. H. Davis van around the countryside selling Royal Daylight Oil—paraffin. The firm also supplied horses for the Fire Brigade in Park Avenue, and it was their horses which took the life boat from the Queen's Rd. Boat House to be launched from the beach at the end of Terrace Rd. When the sea was too rough for the lifeboat to put into Aberystwyth on its return, Jones Brothers would sent a team of horses to Clarach where it was almost always possible to haul in the boat.

There were also trips for holiday makers. One was known as Panorama Drive through

A brake passing the Phillips Hall in Terrace Road

A trip in a brake

Penparcau to Trawsgoed and back through Llanilar. The cost was 2s. 6d. a head. Another drive was to Devil's Bridge *via* Ponterwyd and back *via* Capel Seion and Penparcau for a charge of 3s. 6d. Such trips were also run by other firms in Aberystwyth, notably Phillips Stables in Terrace Road and J. Hinton Jones, the coachbuilder of North Parade.

The first motor taxi in Aberystwyth appeared in the summer of 1901 and was described as "an unmitigated nuisance", "noisy", "smelly", "a danger to life and limb", and "smothering everything in dust". More taxis appeared in time and, once the horses had become accustomed to them, they took their place in the line of horse-drawn carriages and taxis down the centre of North Parade, which then had a drain down the middle of the street. Aberystwyth remained antagonistic to the car for some years. In 1909 the *Autocar* warned its motorist readers "to rigidly abjure" the

town because of its police traps. When this was brought to the attention of the Town council, some of whom were afraid that it would affect the holiday trade, the police defended their action, stating that the only motorists affected were those who drove at "excessive speeds"—20 to 30 m.p.h. —the legal limit was 20 m.p.h. In the same year Aberystwyth and the county tried to get a speed of 10 m.p.h. imposed in towns and villages. A government inquiry was held, Evan Evans, C. M. Williams and others spoke strongly for the motion, while Dr. Harries and Dr. Bonsall poured scorn on it. Harries maintained that his car could not travel at less than 13 m.p.h. without stalling or boiling. The result of the inquiry was that a speed of 10 m.p.h. was imposed on six streets in Aberystwyth while the others remained at 20.

The first to use motor vehicles for public transport were Jones Brothers, followed by the Primrose Motor Co. The Jones's

began in 1905 when they purchased a Milnes-Daimler charabanc. Two years later they added a Churchill from Sheffield, both were 22-seaters. and were used for holiday trips, Sunday School outings, taking groups of people to preaching meetings, and outings of all kinds. Soon after the first bus was bought in 1905, a Monday bus service was started from Ponterwyd to Aberystwyth.

In 1912 Jones Brothers began to assemble their own vehicles with parts bought in the Midlands, and by 1914 they owned 10 buses and 12 charabancs, including such makes as AEC, Bean, Dennis, Thorneycroft, and the Milnes-Daimler. Each had a special name—"Cymro", "Sais", "Knight of the Road", "Lion", "Tiger", "Barham", "Furious", "Hawke", "His Majesty", "Victory", "Warspite", "Warwick".

Another bus company was the G.W.R. which sent A. C. Willett to the Aberystwyth Aberaeron, Lampeter area in 1906 to open up bus routes, the first being from Aberaeron to Lampeter. On the 4 November of that year he was joined by F.C.A. Coventry who later managed the G.W.R. Road Motor Department for many years. On the day after his arrival, Guy Fawkes Day, with Willett at the wheel, the first G.W.R. bus to operate on the Aberaeron to Aberystwyth route set off. There were two buses a day each way from 1908 to 1910 and three on Mondays. The journey normally took two hours. From 1907 to 1914 in summer, the G.W.R. operated open charabancs on this route, calling them "Observation Car Trips". During the 1914-18 war, because so many of their buses were commandeered by the War Office, the service was curtailed

Off to Devil's Bridge in a Phillips brake

but it did not cease entirely, there were still some buses running in January 1917. One remarkable service run by the G.W.R. before 1914 was a regular summer trip by bus from Devil's Bridge railway station to the top of Pumlumon, using a six-wheeled, double-drive charabanc. The route followed was that leading up the track from Steddfa Gurig.

The curtailment of the G.W.R. bus service during the War period may have been the reason for Jones Brothers starting an Aberystwyth-Aberaeron bus service about 1916, using a 40 h.p. 22 seater Straker-Squire bought at Oswestry. In 1918 they were running a morning and afternoon bus in each direction on Mondays, Wednesdays and Saturdays. A Thursday service was included in 1919 and a six-day service in the summer of 1920. In 1926 they began running a service from Aberaeron to Lampeter in the "Bean", a 14 seater bus.

In November 1919 the New Quay Motor Co. started a service between New Quay and Aberystwyth with two buses. It ceased in 1924/25 and one of the buses, an A.E.C., was bought by Jones Brothers.

The G.W.R. does not seem to have resumed its bus services until 1924 when it began to run between Aberystwyth and Cardigan *via* Aberaeron and New Quay, two services a day in each direction. The bus

depot was in Park Avenue on the site of Gardners' Cash and Carry Stores.

In 1920 Jones Brothers also began operating bus services twice a day to and from Tregaron, and every week day to Ponterwyd. Later a service was instituted to Borth four times a day. The return fare to Borth from Aberystwyth was 1s. 3d. but 2s. 6d. from Borth to Aberystwyth. In its heyday this firm employed about 40 men and had depots in Gwalia Garage, North Parade, now the Aberystwyth Sports Centre; the building which became Nelsons Garage in Castle St.; the Old Talbot Stables, now the garage in Eastgate; the premises of the old Eagle Foundry in Northgate St., which became Thomas's Garage, recently demolished to provide a site for the new N.H.S.S. offices; and the Waterloo Yard, the old name for the Daniels Garage and Chapel of Rest site.

In 1924, at its second application, the Crosville Bus Company, a concern already

A Jones Brothers bus at the Arch, near Hafod

And some went by bicycle

well established in North Wales, secured permission to run a bus service from Aberystwyth to Devil's Bridge. Soon it was competing for other routes and in 1934 Jones Brothers lost both their Aberystwyth-Aberaeron and their Aberaeron-Lampeter routes to this company. As a result they sold out to the Crosville company but continued to run private coaches for some years afterwards. After 1945 T. R. Jones of Jones Brothers became a coal merchant and haulage contractor.

Since the 1930's the bus services in Aberystwyth have been almost entirely the preserve of the Crosville Co., J. James and Son Ltd., Ammanford and the Western Welsh Omnibus Co. Ltd., of Cardiff. In Aberystwyth, the Crosville depot was at Penyrancor Yard, Trefechan until 1934 when the new depot was built on the old railway site in Park Avenue where it still stands. J. James and Sons was taken over by the Western Welsh Co in the early 1960's.

The only private firm operating regular bus services in and out of Aberystwyth in

1980 is that of D. J. Evans of Penrhyncoch who runs a service between Aberystwyth and Penbontrhydybeddau on six days a week. Here until the 1920's and even later in some areas, the only form of transport was the horse drawn vehicle, usually a brake where people sat facing one another on two long seats. From Penrhyncoch on Mondays a regular passenger on one of these brakes, and one who always sat at the drivers' end, was a woman who usually brought with her a basket of live chickens for sale in Aberystwyth market or shops.

On fine days this caused no trouble but when it was cold or wet the brake was covered so that it looked like a prairie-schooner.

The chicken woman then became very concerned lest her charges would suffocate and, to the accompaniment of much squawking, the basket would be passed along from hand to hand to be given an airing at the open back and then returned to their guardian. This would happen several times during the journey. The brakes were then run by William Magor and his son John.

The first motor vehicle to provide this service was a converted coal lorry, where the seating consisted of no more than a number of planks placed across the back of the lorry which was brushed as clean as possible for the journey. Then came John Bumford Morgan, a native of Staylittle in Montgomery

The first GWR Aberystwyth-Aberaeron motor bus

A J. B. Morgan bus

An early Gwalia Garage taxi with David Jones at the wheel

A trip in a charabanc having solid tyres

shire, who like many others, was unable to find work on his native heath and went to work in the coal mines of South Wales. During the strike of 1921 he returned to Mid Wales and decided to become a coal merchant in Penrhyncoch. In that year he bought a Ford T model charabanc, the passenger section of which could be removed so that the vehicle could be used for carrying both coal and passengers. He also ran a taxi service with an Overland car made in the U.S.A. Unfortunately, in 1927/28 his garage, complete with charabanc and car, was destroyed by fire, and not being insured, he lost everything. But John Morgan was not easily defeated; with a borrowed horse and cart he carried bricks from the broken down buildings of the derelict Bronfloyd mine and rebuilt the garage himself. He then bought a second-hand 20-seater Fiat bus for £80 and started carrying passengers again. Unfortunately, this model was prone to half-shaft breakage and while the trouble could be put right in

half an hour, the passengers disliked being kept waiting. This happened once on a Sunday School trip to Aberdyfi and he had to put the children on a train, repair the bus and await their return at Machynlleth, a loss of income and prestige. After this he bought a Reo and then a Chevrolet, the latter being a very good vehicle indeed, and the one which helped to put him on his feet financially. In 1937 he became the owner of a second-hand, 20-seater Morris Commercial bus, his first truly British vehicle, and a very good model. It served him faithfully right through the war and afterwards until 1948 when it was sold for scrap metal. Fortunately, during the war when it was almost impossible to get spare parts, John Morgan had a good friend who worked at the Morris Works in Birmingham and was able to supply him with the parts required. At this time, when Penrhyncoch and the neighbourhood was harbouring many official and unofficial evacuees, the old Morris did sterling work as a bus and as a

transporter of goods, often carrying three times its normal load to Aberystwyth and back.

J. B. Morgan died in 1947 and his two sons J. J. and Bryn Morgan took over the business as Morgan Brothers. After a spell of using Albion and Dennis buses, they took to Bedford coaches and ran a regular service to Aberystwyth, as well as special trips elsewhere, until 1959 when they sold the business to D. J. Evans. Under him the bus and coach service was expanded and now runs a regular scheduled bus service from Penbont-rhydybeddau, Salem and Penrhyncoch to Aberystwyth and back several times a day, and six days a week.

It is interesting to record that the Crosville Co., whose buses are now marked "De Cambria" in the Aberystwyth district, has succeeded in doing what no other transport company has done. It has established a "no-change" bus service running the whole length of Wales using routes not very different from those used by the pilgrims of the Middle Ages. The buses are marked "Traws Cambria".

Outside the railway station c. 1930

Markets and Fairs

When Aberystwyth was created in 1277 it was given the right to hold a Monday Market and has continued to hold it on that day ever since. At that time it had the sole right to trade between the rivers Dyfi and Aeron, a right which proved difficult to establish and eventually disappeared. Where the market was held in the Middle Ages is not known but it was probably somewhere under the walls of the castle, for protection. Until the 19th century there was so much empty space within the town walls that it was never difficult to find room for a market.

The first market of which there is any record was that held round the old Town Hall from time immemorial. But an open market of this kind was unsuitable for grain and a Corn Market was built in Eastgate early in the 18th century. It occupied part of the Talbot Inn yard and faced Eastgate, then called Little Darkgate St.

In 1832 when Market St. first appeared, a new corn market was built on part of the yard of the old Talbot at the corner with Eastgate. Its main door faced the new Talbot Hotel. It was a partly covered building selling corn of all kind, wheat by weight, and all other kinds of grain by imperial measure. This was also the official market for cheese, wool and other agricultural products, some of which were also sold near the old Town Hall. The Corn Market was owned by Nanteos and people using it paid a toll of 1d. to the Powells. At election times, in the days of open voting, this building was usually the town polling station.

By 1870 Aberystwyth was short of entertainment halls and the Corn Market was replaced by another, a two-floored building, the upper floor being used for concerts etc. But this was badly built and in 1895 it was demolished and replaced with a much better building. This had a market on the ground floor and a room upstairs large enough for concerts, dances and even operettas. There were two adjoining rooms, one used as a library, and the other as a grammar school for a while.

Until about the end of the 18th century it was difficult to buy meat in Aberystwyth, for the meat market was in Llanbadarn. In the early years of the 19th century much meat was sold in the open air near the old Town Hall, which was not an ideal arrangement. In 1823 the Court Leet granted a piece of ground on which to build a meat market and this still exists in St. James Square, but it no longer has meat for sale. According to one report this building was formerly partly open.

With the growth of the town, the existence of a market near and around the old Town Hall became a nuisance, and having built the new market in Market St. the Town Commissioners, in 1836, ordered "that the stalls and standing places near to and about the Town Hall used by hawkers, hatters and sellers of fruit, vegetables etc., by reason of their obstruction of the footways, be removed to the new market house in Market Street". But old habits die hard and the resistance to the move was such that, with some reservations, the Commissioners were forced to yield. One change, however, was insisted upon, the fish stalls had all to be set up in the arcaded, open ground floor of the Town Hall. Fish caught locally, salmon from the Teifi, and oysters brought from Milford were sold here. The oysters were brought in by Jack Peel who used to sell them and other fish as far afield as Bala in the first half of the 19th century. Fish was not as plentiful as might be expected, partly because of the state of the harbour and the lack of encouragement given to the fisher-men. From 1836 until the Old Town Hall was demolished, fish, some dairy produce, vegetables, fruit and garden produce were sold there and in upper Pier St. The Corn Market continued to sell corn, dairy produce and, according to visitors, some meat.

Meat prices in the Aberystwyth district in the 1740's were as follows: beef 2½d lb, mutton 1½d, veal and pork 2d or less, but it should be noted that mutton, veal, lamb and kid were never sold by the pound but by the piece. In 1840 prices were, beef 7d to 8d lb, lamb 7d to 8d, mutton 6d to 7d, pork 5d to 6d.

The live stock markets were held out-of-doors and, until the second half of the 19th century, had plenty of room on the town commons. The pig market was held on open land now occupied by Queen St. and Grays Inn Rd. The old Welsh name for Queen St. was *Heol y Moch* (Pig St.). By 1762, however, some dwellings had been built in *Barker's Lane*, as Queen St. was then officially called, and the pig market was presented at the Court Leet as being a nuisance. It was then ordered that it be removed to a "more Commodious" locality, St. James Square. Here pigs were sold by farmers and others from carts ranged round the outside of the Meat Market. In time the carts spilled over into High St. but this was stopped when that, too, became built up.

The monthly cattle market was originally held on the Sand Marsh, between Sand-marsh Cottage, then the only dwelling in this area, and the place now occupied by the Life Boat House in Queens Rd. This continued until 1870 when, again because of the spread of housing, the market was moved to the southern end of Morfa Lane which then became known as *Smithfield*, a name still used by some of the older inhabitants. It is now Park Avenue and still houses the cattle mart.

The demolition of the Old Town Hall left Aberystwyth short of market space. The increasing number of shops compen-

Great Darkgate St., pre 1880, showing market women selling their produce from stalls around the clock. It also shows the Gogerddan Arms (Lion Royal, Padarn Hall)

The second Corn Market on the corner of Market St. and Eastgate

sated for this to some extent and nothing was done until about 1870 when the Aberystwyth Market and Public Hall Co. was formed by John James of the Railway Tea Warehouse in Terrace Rd. They set about erecting a large covered building measuring 125ft by 72ft, designed to serve as a corn and general market for the sale of fish, fruit, vegetables and fancy articles, roughly where W. H. Smith is now located.

Reference is made above to the vain attempt by the Improvement Commissioners to move those using the area surrounding the Old Town Hall as a market place into the new Market Hall in Market St. As the population of the town and the number of visitors increased, so did the traffic, and the increasing number of stalls, boxes, hand-trucks, stationary carts, hawkers and other dealers doing business in the streets became much more of a nuisance. Even the beach was used for nets and clothes. Carts often lined both sides of some streets so that carriages could not pass, and accidents were not uncommon. Church St. (Upper

Great Darkgate St.) was completely blocked every Monday with empty carts and potato carts.

When the John James Market Hall was completed about 1871 the town had three market halls, together enough to house all those who used the streets and pavements to sell their goods. Both from a sanitary and a commercial point of view, it was felt that the streets should be kept free of street-sellers.

In 1872 something between £1,200 and £1,500 was spent by the Town Council on getting a Special Act of Parliament, one of the provisions of which was to enable the authorities to provide markets and to clear the streets of the obstructions which had long been a problem. It became law and no one seriously questioned it at that time. But before the streets could be cleared the Council had to show that it had the necessary market accommodation. It was decided, therefore, that it should first get the markets into its own hands by leasing them from their owners and then sub-leasing them back to their former owners or whoever proposed to control them.

There was a great deal of support for the proposed change among the town's tradesmen and others. Many a shopkeeper who had to pay rent and rates, found the pavements in front of his shop cluttered up with the stalls and goods of dealers who not only paid neither, but also obstructed the way into his premises.

The long-looked for leases arrived at last and at the same time the Council heard that it had been given all the powers formerly wielded by the Improvement

John James's Stores and Market Hall in North Parade and Terrace Rd.

Commissioners, the last obstacle to the clearing of the streets, or so it was thought.

Then the Council did something which seems to have sparked off opposition to the proposed changes. In accordance with its resolutions it auctioned the lease of the meat market in St. James Square and it was taken by John James for £53 per annum. The accounts of the meetings of the period suggested that John James was not popular with all his fellow councillors. He was an active, aggressive businessman who had acquired considerable property in the town and made a good deal of money. It appears that many were jealous of him and resented his success. His support of the new move, and his taking of the meat market lease and that of the John James market hall were probably interpreted by some as an attempt to "take over" the town's markets. He was accused of all kinds of malpractices, such as varying the market tolls to force people into the Terrace

The Meat Market in St. James Square

Rd. market, and refusing to repair the dilapidated meat market for the same season. None of these were true but the opposition liked to believe them.

Placards announcing the market tolls were posted at various parts of the town and announcements were made in the streets by the town crier. The 2 May 1874 was fixed as the day when the streets had to be cleared, and the *Cambrian News* expressed its satisfaction and pleasure at the decision.

But, in fact, despite the new law and the pronouncements in and out of the council, the move had little hope of succeeding. For over thirty years the real power in the town had been in the hands of the Improvement Commissioners, the Town Council had been little more than a "talking shop" notorious for its squabbling. This continued after 1872 and Council meetings were said to be "a source of entertainment" in the town. Too many of the councillors were themselves obstructionists and opposed to the new law.

After a bad accident caused by a carriage trying to get through a street lined with potato carts on both sides, when a small girl barely escaped with her life, John Gibson wrote in the *Cambrian News*:

"We have said so much about tables, and stalls, and carts, and trucks and impedimenta of all sorts, being left in the streets, and on the footpaths, that it seems almost useless to remonstrate further until three or four persons have been killed. Town Councillors block the streets with boxes, Aldermen place trucks on the pavements, and the Mayor defends with all the force he possesses stalls and other obstructions, so there is, we are afraid, little prospect of anything being done."

It was the Mayor who gave permission for clothes to be dried on the beach, after the law relating to obstructions had been obtained. When his attention was drawn to what Gibson had written he said:

"As to the newspaper I look at what it says with disgust and as to Gibson I treat everything he says with the greatest contempt. I look upon him as not fit to be in anybody's company who is respectable."

There was also no cooperation from the magistrates, who were anti-Gibson because he did not hesitate to comment on the gross inconsistencies in their verdicts in court. Whereas a T. H. Jones was fined heavily for obstructing the pavement to the extent of less than three inches, the same magistrates were continually dismissing cases against, or imposing very light fines on people who consistently cluttered up the streets and pavements with their stalls, carts and goods.

Another form of obstruction which was intensely disliked by visitors was the hawking and touting which went on near the railway station whenever a train arrived or departed, but no attempt was made to stop it.

The arguments went on until it was time to appoint a new Mayor, who, it was hoped, would help to clear the streets. But the ruling mayor, although strongly opposed since 1865 to any other mayor being re-elected for a second year, made no objection to his own re-election. With so many councillors, the Mayor and the magistrates opposed to the moving of street sellers into the markets, there was little hope of success for the reformers. This may have been the reason why John James moved his grocery and wine store into the Terrace Rd. market hall in 1886.

At the turn of the century there was much dissatisfaction with the state of the markets at Smithfield. In 1902 the Aberystwyth Ratepayers Association, a body which was intensely disliked by the Town Council, sent out between 200 and 300 letters to the townspeople asking for suggestions for the improvement of the town's markets. Only 15 replies were received and among those was one from Vaughan Davies of Tanybwlch, the M.P. for Cardiganshire, dealing mainly with the cattle market near the slaughter house in Smithfield.

According to him the market had little hope of attracting the first class dealers because of the farmers' habit of selling their best animals to roving dealers and bringing only their second-best to the market.

As for the market itself, he maintained that it did not deserve to be called a market. On market days a barrier was placed across Smithfield Rd. (Park Avenue). Those who kept their animals on the town side of the barrier were prosecuted by the police, while those that paid their pennies or twopences were let through the barrier "into bedlam". There were no pens for the animals, nor was any attempt made to arrange and segregate the animals so that the farmers could show them properly, and buyers could examine them. "The chief occupation of farmers and their sons is rounding up stray bullocks."

"If you want a pig you take it for granted that if something at the bottom of a cart grunts, it's a pig. If you want to see your pig you must turn it out on to the road and then have the pleasure of running after it, probably into some adjoining shop."

"What can be more unfair than taking money from the farmers and giving them nothing in return but a public road to show their animals on."

Poultry and eggs could still be bought only on street corners so there was still obstruction on some streets.

Cattle, sheep and pig pens did not come into use until the skating rink in Bath St. was demolished. The roof of that building was used to cover over part of the open space in front of the slaughter house, pens were erected and auctions took place there. A proper, well organized mart did not appear until 1950.

The hall in Market St. continued to serve as an entertainment centre and a market. In 1910 the first floor was turned into a full-time cinema and proved so popular that it was fitted out properly for that purpose in 1923, and named the Palladium. The ground floor then became known as the Palladium Market and the building continued to serve in these two capacities until it was burnt down in 1934.

St. James Square still has its market hall but it no longer has meat on display. People became accustomed to buying their meat from shops, most of which were more attractive than the old meat market. It is now a place where all manner of things are sold.

The erection of stalls for the sale of dairy and other produce continued in the space between the Town Clock and the

One of the first sales of cattle at the mart in Park Avenue 1954

Skinners Arms and Corfields until the clock tower was demolished in 1956. Then for some unknown reason, the stalls disappeared, the cabbage plant sellers went elsewhere, and a practice which had lasted from time immemorial, came to an end.

Fairs

The Aberystwyth Charter of 1277 allowed the holding of two fairs a year, one on Vigil Day and for two days after the feast of the Pentecost and the other on the Eve, Day and for six days after the feast of St. Michael. These fairs never became important, they were not referred to at all by the 16th century historian, George Owen, nor were they mentioned in the early almanacs.

Until late in the 18th century they appear to have been held on an open field near the castle, but in the early 19th century they were held on Morfa Swnd (Sand Marsh) for the sale of cattle, flannel and other wares, licenced booths being much in evidence. No tolls were levied in the latter place. When the railways came in the 1860's the Llanbadarn Fairs were moved into Aberystwyth, and thereafter two new horse fairs came to be held in Smithfield (Park Avenue), the area used for fairs after the Sand Marsh became built up, one in May and the other in September, displacing Machynlleth which had hitherto been the important fair for horses from North Cardiganshire. Other fairs held during the last two centuries were opened on the Monday before January 5th, the Monday before Easter, Whit Monday and 24 June.

Hiring fairs were held in the town on the first Mondays after May Day and All Saints

Day. They were held in the town itself, those wishing to be hired standing around the Old Town Hall, later the Town Clock, and along Great Darkgate St. As soon as midnight struck the previous night, stall-holders rushed to peg their claims to stall sites and there, next day, they sold fairings, flannel and pedlary.

That Aberystwyth had so few fairs was attributed by John Gibson to the Town Council's lack of interest. Many people would have liked to have had more fairs but nothing was done.

Fair on open ground in front of the Angel Inn and on Cae Bach Judith in 1796

The Banks

The Old Bank House in Bridge St. once housed a bank which may have been the first in Wales. According to tradition, the bank was established in 1762 and was known as *Banc y Llong* (the Ship Bank) set up to help the mercantile and shipping interests in the town, and so named because its notes bore an engraving of a ship. Nothing is known of its founders but according to a local historian of the 19th century, the bank passed into the hands of the Julian family from Tywyn, Merioneth, later in the 18th century.

Whether the partnership was merely changed in 1806 or a new bank was established in that year is not clear. What is known is that an agreement was entered into on 1 June 1806 whereby John Jones of Gracechurch St. London, Thomas Morgan and David Davies, both of Aberystwyth, entered into partnership to carry on for fourteen years the business of bankers under the title of Jones, Morgan and Davies. John Jones was a London-Welsh surgeon and physician; he bought Derry Ormond, north of Lampeter in 1773. Thomas Morgan was a solicitor, the father of the T. O. Morgan who wrote the well known *Aberystwyth Guide* and was Mayor of Aberystwyth when the railway was opened in 1864. David Davies was a native of Machynlleth.

A month after the above agreement was signed, another was made whereby Rice Jones agreed to become a bank clerk to the firm for three years at a salary of £30 *per annum* and free board and lodging at the house of David Davies. At the same time he had to give the firm his guarantee bond of £1,000.

In 1808 Thomas Morgan died and Thomas Williams was made a partner. Williams is believed to have formerly been in partnership with his brother, Evan Williams, in London, in a firm which printed the first edition of Dr. W. O. Pughe's Welsh Dictionary. He was also the son of John Williams, *Yr Hen Syr*, who succeeded Henry Richard as headmaster of Ystrad Meurig School, and brother to the Rev. John Williams who taught Sir Walter Scott's son in the Grammar School, Lampeter, and became headmaster of the Edinburgh Academy.

Whether *Banc y Llong* was closed when the partnership was dissolved or whether Thomas Williams bought out his partners is not known, but later he was a partner in a banking firm at the Old Bank House. His fellow directors were Morris Davies, a merchant who lived at *The Green* in Trefechan and the founder of Ffosrhydgaled (now the Conrah), and David Davies of Cardigan. Rice Jones, the former clerk, was made a partner and so was Henry Benson, a local wine merchant whose business was later taken over by Joseph Downie and became known as Downie's Vaults.

Henry Benson was the son of a prebendary at Canterbury Cathedral. When his father remarried, Henry joined the Navy and was reputed to have been with Nelson at Trafalgar. He was twice mayor of Aberystwyth, 1829 and 1832, and also the coroner. For some extraordinary reason an objection was raised to his becoming Mayor because he was a banker.

On 15 August 1836 the bank was taken over by the newly formed North and South Wales Bank, for £3,000, from the surviving directors, Benson and Rice Jones. The latter was then made manager of the new branch at the magnificent salary of £400 a year out of which he had to pay his clerk's salary. He also had to give security for £2,000 for his clerk's honesty.

Only two bank notes of *Banc y Llong* seem to have survived, one is at St. Fagans in Cardiff, and the other is at the Powysland Museum in Welshpool. There is a photograph of the latter in *Archaeologica Cambrensis* 1935.

The North and South Wales Bank, though based on Merseyside, had a strong Welsh flavour and employed many Welsh-

A Banc y Llong note.

speaking people. Its early history in Aberystwyth was not all plain sailing, for soon after his appointment as manager, Rice Jones died, heavily in debt to the bank. The ensuing dispute between the bank and his family lasted ten years.

Around 1870 the bank moved its office to New St., opposite the post office, to the building which still looks like a bank but is now the Pentecostal Church, *Elim.* It remained here until 1885 when the branch moved to the house in Great Darkgate St, where the confession of faith was formulated in 1823. The manager during most of the bank's stay here was John R. Rees, one of the bank's ablest men. He saw to it that while the branch was there, the room where the articles were drawn up was left exactly as it was in 1823.

In 1907 it was resolved to erect a new bank across the road in Great Darkgate St.

but before it was completed the North and South Wales Bank was absorbed by the London, City, and Midland Bank. The move to what is now called the Midland Bank was made in 1909 and an examination of its facade will reveal carved stone panels of the Prince of Wales's Feathers and the Welsh Dragon, reminders that the building was designed to house a Welsh Bank.

There is an interesting story told of the North and South Wales Bank in 1847 when there was a crisis of some kind in the bank's affairs. Such news could prove disastrous, for it almost always led to a run on the bank. The news was brought to Welshpool by the Aberystwyth coach and the bank immediately closed its doors. Welshpool people having money in the bank and fearing for its safety, hit on a plan which took advantage of the long rest usually taken by the coachman while

The Midland Bank

The site of the North and South Wales Banks in Great Darkgate St. c. 1880

English cattle markets.

The owners of the bank were John Evans of Penygraig, Aberystwyth, Joseph Jones and William Davies. It lasted only from 1810 to 1814 when it failed. Several of its notes, which range in value from £10 to 10s., bear a memorandum across their faces stating that they had been exhibited before G. Bonsall under a commission of bankruptcy against the firm, and that a first dividend of 6s. 8d. in the £ had been paid. There are a number of the bank's notes to be seen in the National Library of Wales, the University College of Wales and the Ceredigion Museum.

This bank's premises too, were in Bridge St. but not at the Old Bank House. The piece of iron bearing a carving of a sheep's head was formerly a door stop and was fixed to the Old Bank House in error by Treborth Jones.

A curious story is told of one or other of the town's two earliest banks. Because of a panic in the local money market, there was a run on the bank. At first, the manager could not think of what to do but eventually he decided to try to restore confidence in his bank by pretending to be able to mint his own money. Taking a large number of new sovereigns into the kitchen he heated them on a shovel over the fire. When they were hot he returned to the bank, paid off the most urgent customers with some hot coins, and told the others to wait while he made some more from the large store of gold he had in his vault. According to this tall story, this so impressed the country folk that they left the bank in peace.

he and his passengers had lunch. The Welshpool people collected as many bank notes as they could find and sent them in the care of a noted athlete to Newtown where he could change them for gold if he arrived before the coach. He just succeeded in doing this; soon after he left the bank the coach arrived and on hearing the news, the Newtown bank closed its doors. In fact the bank did not crash, and the depositors' money was quite safe.

The Aberystwith and Tregaron Bank, Banc y Ddafad Ddu (the Black Sheep Bank) was so named because its notes were engraved with a drawing of one sheep for every pound which the note represented, with a small sheep on the 10s. note. It is believed to have been founded to help the farmers of the county. Like the Black Ox Bank of Llandovery it was probably established to lessen the dangers facing drovers who had formerly to carry large sums of money on their return from the

A bank note issued by the Aberystwyth and Tregaron Bank—Banc y Ddafad Ddu

The National Provincial Bank's first branch was established in Gloucester in 1834, soon afterwards another was opened in Brecon and it was there that we first hear of Joseph Downie who proved such a benefactor to the people of Aberystwyth. He was the accountant at Brecon when he was appointed manager to the first branch of the National Provincial Bank to be opened in Aberystwyth in June 1835.

To assist him, Downie appointed David Jones, a grocer's assistant, as his chief clerk and David Roberts as the junior clerk. As stated elsewhere, all three became important men in the town, Downie for his generosity to the Infirmary, David Jones for his work at the bank and his dedication to the cause of Methodism,

and David Roberts for founding the brewery at Trefechan and for his public service. It is interesting to note that, like so many others of that period, both Downie and Jones had other occupations. The Downie Vaults were purchased and managed by him while he was manager of the bank and David Jones kept on his grocer's shop throughout much of his banking career.

The bank was first situated on the first floor of premises in Great Darkgate St. on the site now occupied by Hodges. After a few years it moved to a large house, owned by Richardes of Penglais, at the corner of Eastgate and Pier St. Downie and his sister lived on these premises, their private entrance being through the handsome doorway still to be seen in Eastgate. (see p. 240).

Joseph Downie was a good business man and was jealous of the reputation of his bank. When confronted with a customer who said that he had been given £10 too much by the clerk when cashing a cheque, the manager maintained that his bank did not make mistakes and the customer had to keep the £10. Downie's efforts to popullarise his bank were not always appreciated by his superiors. The directors raised no objection to his subscribing on their behalf towards lighting the town by gas in 1837, but objected to his giving £10 towards the mail coach service a year later without their permission. When their consent was asked for a subscription towards the new Town Hall in 1841, they agreed after first enquiring how much others were giving. His cashing of a stolen Bank Post Bill earned Downie a reprimand and instructions to be more careful when dealing with strangers.

During the 1847 financial crisis mentioned above, extra gold was sent to the Aberystwyth branch in case it suffered a run. Ten years later Downie wrote to the directors warning them that a few people had already withdrawn their deposits because of a rumour that an earthquake was imminent. The directors sent him £10,000 in notes but nothing unusual happened.

Downie retired from the bank in 1859 and was succeeded by David Jones who remained manager until 1884 by which time the bank was known locally as David Jones's Bank. He was a native of Spite, Llangwyryfon, and was a prominent Calvinistic Methodist in a town where the Methodists were all powerful. He was one of the founder members of Seilo when it was formed in 1863. His brother, John Jones (Ivon) had a grocer's shop at the corner of Queen St. and Bridge St.

David Jones was therefore in a very strong position in a town where most of the leading men were Nonconformists and, as a result, his bank had most of the big accounts.

One of his first big customers was the University College nearby, another was the County Council account when that body was formed in 1889. It was then the practice for the manager of the bank to be chosen to act as the County Treasurer. This was David Jones's successor, J. D. Perrott.

The County Council account was once the cause of a disagreement. After his retirement as manager, Perrott's continued as County Treasurer until 1913, when a number of the councillors wished to move the account to the Midland Bank for reasons of economy. The National Provincial Bank offered better terms than the Midland when there was a credit balance, but the Midland's terms were better when there was a deficit. As the County Council was almost always overdrawn, several members wanted the account moved to the Midland. But largely for sentimental reasons, the majority voted to leave the account where it was. The National Provincial Bank manager, J. W. P. Perry, then became the County Treasurer.

In 1903, during the managership of D. Lloyd Jones, a noted breeder of sheep and horses, the bank moved to new premises at the corner of Baker St. and North Parade

The new bank was designed by W. W. Gwyther, of London and was erected on the site of the very first houses to be built outside the old town wall (*Y Gaer*) and the old Dark Gate in 1797. Among those who attended the opening ceremony in 1903 was David Roberts, born in 1822 and the National Provincial Bank's first junior clerk in Aberystwyth. In the 1960's it merged with the Westminster Bank and is now known as the National Westminster Bank.

Barclays Bank was not established in Aberystwyth until 1875 and was first situated on the site now occupied by the supermarket *Supa Valu* in Terrace Rd. Originally it was a branch of the London and Provincial Bank which may have been why John James gave it room almost

next door to his London and Provincial Stores. It stayed there only two years before moving to the more imposing, purpose-built structure which the bank now occupies at the corner of Terrace Rd. and North Parade.

Once established, the bank thrived and it was not long before branches were opened at Machynlleth, Tregaron and Aberdyfi.

In 1917 the London and Provincial Bank merged with the South Western Bank to form the London Provincial and South Western Bank. A year later this was absorbed into Barclays Bank, itself formed by the merger of twenty private and other banks in England. The Aberystwyth manager at the time of these mergers was G. R. Phillips, and it was he who laid the foundations for Barclays

The National Westminster Bank

Barclays Bank

becoming the "farmers" bank. It is interesting to note that it was one of Barclay's managers, Henry Morgan, who persuaded Seilo to consider Dan Evans as its minister. The two men had been closely acquainted in the Rhondda.

Lloyds Bank as its name implies, has Welsh connections, the link being with the Lloyds of Dolobran, a well-known Quaker family from Meifod, Montgomeryshire. In 1662 Charles Lloyd joined the Quakers and, as a result, he and his wife were put into prison in Welshpool. Both their sons then went to live in Birmingham where the Quakers were strong, and it was the son of one of these, Sampson Lloyd, the grandson of Charles Lloyd, who, with an ironfounder, John Taylor, founded the Lloyds Bank in Birmingham,

Lloyd's Bank

The corner of Terrace Rd. and Cambrian Place in the 1880's. It is now the site of Lloyds Bank.

now one of the Big Four banks of England and Wales.

It was much used in the past by the cattle drovers who drove their herds from Wales into the Midlands. In consequence the bank authorities marked their cheques with an engraving of a Welsh cattle drover's horse, and continue to do so.

The first branch of Lloyds was opened in Aberystwyth in 1912 in the premises which it still occupies at the corner of Terrace Rd. and Cambrian Place.

The Aberystwyth Provident Savings Bank was the first such bank in Aberystwyth and was founded to help ordinary people to save their money. Its founder was a man much given to good works, the Rev. Thomas Richards of Carrog House, Bridge St. It was first established in 1818 in Bridge

St., probably in Carrog House, where it was managed for some years by Thomas Richards and the secretary. Eventually the work was shared with other directors and trustees. The bank was an immediate success, deposits rose from just over £2,300 in the first year to £5,200 in 1822 and to £46,000 fifty years later. The bank was supported by the leading figures in the district; Col. Powell of Nanteos was its president for a while, and Pryse Pryse its vice-president. All the directors and trustees gave their services free.

In the 1850's the bank's books were looked after by Thomas W. Wells, a prominent man in the town. About 1870 the Savings Bank was moved to New St. to the building used as a post office, and the postmaster, Edward L. Cole, was made the bank's secretary.

The establishment of the Post Office Savings Bank in 1881 made the old type of savings bank unnecessary and the trustees closed the Aberystwyth bank in 1884.

The Trustee Savings Bank in Great Darkgate St. was established there by the West Midland Savings Bank in 1954. In 1945 the West Midland Savings Bank, itself an amalgam of a number of savings banks, including Brecon and Welshpool, made a list of those towns without savings facilities of the type provided by the West Midland concern. The T.S.B. was then established in Aberystwyth. It now has about 8,000 depositors and has deposits of over £2,000,000.

The Postal Services

A regular postal service was first set up in Britain in the 1630's when it was resolved to copy the best continental pattern of dividing selected roads into stages, with post boys riding horses from stage to stage until the letter bags were delivered to their destinations—the post towns marked—on the labels. At each stage there was a postmaster, usually an innkeeper, one of whose main duties was to provide the post boy with a good, fresh horse for the next stage. After being delivered to the post town marked, the letters in the bag were then distributed on foot or on horseback to the people concerned.

Before March 1690, letters to Aberystwyth were put in the Welshpool bag, later in the Montgomery bag, and distributed from there. Aberystwyth did not become a post town and a distribution centre until 1763. In 1635 it cost 6d to send a single-sheet letter from London to Aberystwyth, 1660—3d., 1784—6d., 1796 —8d., and 1801—10d.

Stage mail coaches were first used in 1786, they did not arrive in Aberystwyth until after 1800. In 1807 mails came to the town from four different directions, in 1811 there were two rates to London of 10d. and 11d. according to whether the Rhayader or the Machynlleth, Newtown route was used; the former was 30 miles shorter.

The first post house or post office seems to have been opened in the 1810's or earlier in Brittania Court, a cluster of houses behind the present post office in Great Darkgate St. The name was on the entrance to the court until very recently.

The office was kept first by a man named Morgan and later by William Jones the Post House. In 1822 the London mail arrived there at 8.0 a.m. and left at 3 p.m.

Some years later the post office was moved to a little shop at 14 New St., part of a building formerly occupied by the printer, John Cox, opposite what is now Elim, the Pentecostal Church. In the same building was a repository for the storage, sale and hire of pianos. About 1870 letters were delivered three times a day at 9.0 a.m., noon, and 7.0 p.m. There was one midday delivery on Sundays. Letters could be posted in a pillar box on Marine Terrace or in letter boxes at Seilo at the end of North Parade, the railway station, or at the bottom of Bridge St. Letters were collected three times a day and once on Sundays. The post office was open from 8.30 a.m. to 6.0 p.m. from Monday to Friday and till 8.0 p.m. on Saturdays. On Sundays it opened from 9 a.m. to 10 a.m. and from 12.30 p.m. to 1.30 p.m. In 1880, the New St. site having become inconvenient, the post office was provided with a site in Terrace Rd. by John James of the London and Provincial Stores, probably on the spot now occupied by Liptons, next to Barclays Bank. In 1906 it was decided to give it a much more impressive home in Great Darkgate St., the one which it still occupies. It was built under the direction of Daniel Thomas, a draper in Eastgate, and to provide room, two of the last of the old type, low-roofed and single storey houses in Great Darkgate St., were demolished. According to the John Wood map there was also a post

office in Market St. in 1834.

In 1912, most of the letters reached Aberystwyth by the Royal Mail train from Shrewsbury. It was the custom then to send one of the sorting clerks to meet the train at Shrewsbury and for him to sort the letters on the journey back to Aberystwyth, where it arrived at 6.30 a.m. There the bags of letters were transferred into the handcarts and taken by the postmen to the post office. Post for outlying districts was put into the horsedrawn vans from those areas. The van to Capel Bangor and

Goginan was drawn by one horse, that driven by Jenkins the Post to Aberaeron needed two horses.

There were three deliveries of letters a day in Aberystwyth, two in Llanbadarn and Penparcau and one in the other areas served by the Aberystwyth post office. A postman's lot could then involve walking long distances. One round meant walking as far as Capel Seion and returning in time to make the second delivery in Penparcau. The Llanfihangel y Creuddyn round meant walking there via Glan Paith, Nanteos,

Great Darkgate St. in the 1880's. The two low-roofed houses well down the right side were demolished to make way for the present post office

New Cross and Penywern. At his journey's end the postman was provided with a small wooden hut where he could make himself some tea, eat his lunch and have a rest until it was time to collect the letters in the afternoon. On his way back he would alert those with letters to post by blowing a whistle when approaching any dwellings, but he had to call at Nanteos to collect the private bag. Needless to say he carried stamps in his bag.

Another route was to Clarach via Penglais Mansion, Plas Hendre, Cwmcynfelin and other dwellings in the area. After collecting the outgoing letters he returned over Constitution Hill.

One feature of the postal service of that time was the private bag used and paid for by such people as the Pryses of Gogerddan and the Powells of Nanteos. Each bag had two keys, one for the use of the owner and the other in the possession of the head sorting clerk or the subpostmaster or mistress. No one else was allowed to

Aberystwyth's early telephone linesmen on the pole behind the post office

open these handsome brass and leather bags.

The telegraph office was on the first floor of the post office in Great Darkgate St.

and most of the operators were women who used the Morse Code for their work. There were four telegraph boys, one of whom was Arthur Miller, who supplied the information written here. They worked in two shifts, one from 6.50 a.m. to 4 p.m., and the other in two spells, 10 a.m. to 2 p.m. and 4 p.m. to 8 p.m. If the delivery of a telegram involved working overtime there was no extra payment. Each boy was supplied with a uniform, boots and short leggings. There were two bicycles available, a Royal Enfield and a Hudson, both very heavy and one having a fixed back wheel. Delivering telegrams, too, could entail some hard walking or riding. Taking a telegram to Clarach on a dark stormy night could be a frightening experience for a 14-year-old with only the dim light cast by a hand lamp to light his way over Constitution Hill.

In 1912 a postman earned 10s. a week, while a telegraph boy received 5s. plus $2\frac{1}{2}$d for cleaning and oiling the bicycles, a "perk" usually reserved for the senior boy.

The Poor Law and the Workhouse

While pauperism certainly existed in Aberystwyth, it was never regarded as a serious problem until after 1780, when the cost of poor relief increased considerably. In Cardiganshire in 1750 the cost was £307, in 1776 it was £1,085, by 1819 it had risen to £20,418. It then dropped and rose again to £19,566 in 1833. In Aberystwyth itself, the amount paid in poor relief in 1785 was £75, ten years later it was £244, over £450 in 1800, and £766 in 1813.

Relief to the poor was given in a number of ways—the payment of rent, rate exemption, regular money payments, or casual assistance in money or in kind. It sometimes took the form of clothing, as in 1780 when 4 yards of cloth were bought for 1s. 4d. a yard and a tailor paid 3s. to make a suit for an Aberystwyth pauper, possibly to enable him to get work. Or it might be in the form of food as in 1789 when Margaret Jones of Aberystwyth was given a measure of barley. Craftsmen were bought tools to help them to find work and a carter was found a horse for the same reason. On occasions even houses were provided. In the 1780's the Court Leet granted the overseers of the poor a piece of waste ground measuring 34 yards by 12 yards for the erection of poor houses "to be enjoyed for that purpose for ever". Each pauper family was to be given at least one room in these houses. But dire poverty and an absence of supervision soon reduced them to hovels where misery and vice flourished unchecked. Nothing is now known of their location in the town.

Most of the relief was given in the form of money. In the 1790's an old man with no other means of support was given 2s. a week. Ten years later a Mary Jones received 3s. a week for herself and her children. To prevent the money being squandered on alcohol, many overseers gave the aid in the form of food or goods. One pauper, at least, had to do some work for his money, about 1800 he was paid 30s. for winding up the Town Hall clock once a week for two years. To discourage people from seeking poor-relief, paupers had to wear a circular cloth badge with the letter P and a small A (for Aberystwyth) clearly worked on the badge.

The Quarter Sessions records for the late 18th and early 19th centuries show that the authorities were well aware of the high cost of poor relief. There is frequent reference to the removal of paupers, unmarried expectant mothers, and others likely to need relief, back to their native parishes lest they become a burden on the rates of their adopted parish. As the years passed, the effect of the Napoleonic Wars, the agricultural depression, and rising prices made things worse and by the late 1820's the problem of poor relief had become more than the parish officers could handle. A Government Commission was then set up to find a solution and the result was the Poor Law Amendment Act of 1834.

According to this Act the parish was replaced as the unit for Poor Law administration by the union, a group of parishes governed by a partly elected board of guardians, with responsibility for the poor, and charged with the express duty of building a workhouse. Able-bodied persons seeking poor relief were to receive it only if they entered the workhouses, where life was supposed to be less desirable than that of the poorest paid labourer outside.

The Aberystwyth Union consisted of 30 parishes and covered almost the whole of North Cardiganshire; it had a population of 20,026. The Board of Guardians numbered 41, the first chairman being W. C. Gilbertson and the clerk Robert Rathill. Land on Penglais Hill was purchased from Pryse Pryse and in 1840 the workhouse was built, at a cost of £3,000. According to the *Demetian Mirror*, a weekly paper published by John Cox in Aberystwyth for one summer season only, it formed "a very striking feature" on the approach to the town from the north. In style "it was a mixture of simple Gothic of the earlier ages and of the old English, somewhat of the Elizabethan era with a few additions by the architect, apparently of no particular age or class". Its design "evinced a kindly feeling on the part of the architect . . . for the sufferings of the poorer classes". Another writer described the building as being "picturesque, domestic and somewhat collegiate". The architect was W. R. Coulthart, who was then living in Aberystwyth. The house was christened "Bronglais" and it was stipulated that any child born there was to have that name recorded as its birthplace.

Though built to accommodate 200 people the nearest the house ever came to being full was in 1843 when Colonel Love lodged a detachment of infantry there to guard the town's turnpike gates during the Rebecca Riots. In August of that year it lodged only 6 paupers, in March 1847 there were 26 inmates and according to the existing records it seems never to have housed more than about 70 people, omitting vagrants, who were generally very few in number. It may have exceeded this number when it housed evacuees during the Second World War.

Inside the workhouse the inmates were supposed to be separated into seven classes— aged and infirm men, able-bodied men and youths over 15, boys between 7 and 15, aged and infirm women, able-bodied women and girls over 15, girls from 7 to 15, and children under 7 years old. The last class was allowed to mix with the able-bodied women and girls but the others were to be kept apart, they even had separate exercise yards. This segregation aroused much criticism and was described everywhere as being inhuman. Later, married couples over 60 were allowed to live together.

The diet of the inmates was also strictly controlled. It was not supposed to exceed in quantity or quality the diet of the ordinary labourer of the district. In fact the food given to the inmates of the workhouse was equal to that eaten by the better class of

The Bronglais Workhouse

labourers, and small farmers. At Aberystwyth in 1840 it consisted of 8 or 9 ozs. of bread and 1½ pints of gruel for breakfast. Lunch was made up of either meat and potatoes, or bread, cheese, broth and potatoes while supper was bread, cheese, broth and potatoes, or herrings and potatoes or, once a week, cheese and potatoes. The bread was made of barley meal and when potatoes were above 15d. a bushel, rice was given instead. The amounts given were generous and were varied according to the age, sex and health of the inmate. Invalids were given butter, milk, tea, sugar and such foods as the Medical Officer advised. This was all far better food, in quantity and quality than the average working labourer of the time could afford. In 1921 a healthy inmate received, every day, 26 ozs. bread, 1½ozs. of butter, 1 pint of tea, 1 pint of coffee, 1 pint of meat stew as well as milk and potatoes.

The commissioners expected the guardians to reduce the amount of outdoor relief and to increase the number of able-bodied paupers entering the workhouse. This was something that most of the guardians, particularly those representing the rural areas, were not prepared to do. They continued to advocate the payment of outdoor relief to the able-bodied, and to pay the rents of people threatened with eviction.

Writing in the *Cambrian News* in 1874, John Gibson said, "It is useless to expect the guardians to abandon a scheme which makes them donors of the public funds to their friends and workpeople". Many a guardian "comes to the Board at Aberystwith . . . to obtain relief for particular persons in whom he is interested. He is more interested in extending out relief than in encouraging thrift".

In 1873 in the Aberystwyth Union, the sum of £8,055 was paid in out-relief to 1,358 persons. It was frequently given to enable underpaid labourers to eke out an existence, and paid for the maintenance of some people who either made little effort to maintain themselves or could be maintained by their relatives. It was quite common for the farmer who paid his labourer only 9d. a day in the 1870's, to come to the board to plead for increased relief for the same, underpaid labourer. Paupers were often preferred as tenants by landlords because their rents were paid out of the poor rates.

Those advocating greater out-door relief defended it on the grounds of humanity, but Gibson, and such guardians as Pell, Balcombe, John James, Peter Jones and others argued that this policy was cruel. Gibson wrote: "It would be difficult to devise torture more refined than the giving of 1s. or 1s. 6d. a week for a bed-ridden man or woman to live on", and this was done regularly. The out-door relief of many a broken down working man rarely exceeded 3s. a week and there were hundreds in the Aberystwyth Union trying to live on this and starving in the process.

Matters were made worse by the board's inconsistency, its lack of rules, and its refusal to plan things properly. What a person on poor relief received depended on impulse, or the strength of character of his sponsor, or on the mood of the meeting, or on a mixture of these.

These factors and the abuse of the system by paupers and employers of labour who saved themselves money at the expense of the poor rates, strengthened the hands of those who insisted that able-bodied paupers should be made to enter the workhouse, and who believed that out-door relief to those who really deserved it should be more liberal. These people were strong advocates of the friendly societies then becoming popular.

The guardians were often the victims of the policy of their own officers. Relieving officers who had long enjoyed the power and prestige of "the man with the money" were loth to cut down the number of their clients by sending them to the workhouse. They often took matters into their own hands and handed relief to people not strictly entitled to it. Such officers were always sure of support from some of the guardians. One of these, Jenkin Jones, was so strongly opposed to the official policy that he even supported those sons and daughters who refused to support their parents, even when they could well afford it. He and others believed that it was better to pay higher poor rates than to force children to support their parents, for this would lead to many leaving the county to avoid having to pay.

But leaving the county for this reason did not always work, for sometimes the guardians were prepared to send the law after the culprits. Richard and John Evans of Tredegar were the sons of David and Jane Evans, two paupers chargeable to the Aberystwyth Union. On 6 March 1874 they were summoned to appear before a court to show cause why they should not contribute towards the maintenance of their parents. They did not appear, and an order of 2s. a week was made on Richard and 2s. 6d. on John, sums which they could well afford. No payment was received and a second summons was sent which was also ignored. In January 1875 a policeman was sent down to Tredegar to execute the order. He first took possession of the house lived in by Richard who then capitulated and paid up with an extra £4 for costs. But John refused to pay and the policeman made him accompany him back to Aberystwyth. Faced with the prospect of two months in gaol, John gave in when they reached Merthyr and paid up the £2 17s. 6d. arrears and £6 costs.

Public opinion was, on the whole, opposed to the official policy and this became very evident when, in February 1874, an old man of 75 years died, of starvation it was claimed. He lived with his daughters and their illegitimate children in Llanbadarn in a "filthy hovel" and had been refused relief because he repeatedly refused to enter the workhouse, preferring to live in what was described in a "house of ill repute". The guardians were blamed for his death and were subjected to a great deal of criticism especially from the churches and chapels in the town and country. Their only support came from the *Cambrian News*. This event was used by some on the board to try to split the union into two sections, one representing the town and the other the rural areas, but it failed.

In the early 1870's, the Aberystwyth Board set out to bring the problem of pauperism more under control. After three years the cost of poor relief in Aberystwyth was lower than in any union in Cardiganshire. The poor rate, which had been 3s. in the £

for several years, was brought down to 1s. 3d. The cost of out-relief was also reduced and the number of paupers fell from 1,387 in January 1872 to 1,116 two years later. In Aberystwyth itself the cost of pauperism was 9¾d. in the £, in Cardigan it was 1s. 5½d. This decrease was true of all Wales but it was "quite astonishing in Aberystwyth". Expenditure in the latter half of 1874 was £1,000 less than in the first half. To achieve this, new rate collectors had to be appointed to replace the inefficient ones who always had a long list of "arrears" in their books. Relieving officers were issued with strict orders to visit paupers to check on their state, and those people seeking relief had to appear in person before the guardians instead of sending others to plead for them. In the unions' early days some of the paupers went to sea for part of the year and left their poor relief cards for their relatives to use, as a kind of legacy.

According to the law, the guardians had to provide medical attention for the sick poor. They had therefore to appoint a suitably qualified medical officer known as the Parish Doctor. It was the duty of the relieving officer to inform the doctor when anyone needed attention, it was also his duty to see that the doctor's orders were carried out and that the medicines prescribed were supplied and used properly. If the illness was sudden then the officer could make use of the nearest assistance until the parish doctor arrived.

If the sick could not manage at home they were admitted to the workhouse. Those that could afford it went to the voluntary hospital formed for that purpose in Eastgate. Inside the workhouse the nursing was delegated to other paupers. The first attempt to appoint a trained nurse was made on Christmas Day 1887 but it was defeated then and on subsequent occasions until August of that year, when Mary Richards of Gwastad, Llanon was appointed at a salary of £20 *per annum*. When she left, no replacement was appointed until 1910. In time, a close liaison was formed with the Aberystwyth General Hospital and the medical care and attention given to paupers became much more satisfactory.

The first medical officer was Dr. Jacob Roberts, son of David Roberts of Trefechan Brewery. He entertained the inmates of the workhouse to a dinner on the very first "Christmas Day in the workhouse" when they were given roast beef and plum pudding. He served the union for many years. Among others were Dr. Morris Jones, Dr. Rice Williams, and Dr. J. A. Rees who served from 1920 until the workhouse was closed late in the 1940's. The Bow St. and Borth, Upper Rheidol and Lower Rheidol districts of the union had other doctors to serve their paupers. All served also as public vaccinators. They were not only poorly paid but had to supply all the medicines except quinine, cod liver oil and trusses out of their salaries. In the year 1844-45 the nine parish doctors employed in Cardiganshire together earned only £390.

The supervision of the workhouse was in the hands of the Master and Matron who, for many years were paid only £25 to £30 per annum and their keep. All the domestic and menial tasks were done by the resident paupers. The appointments and general administration were in the hands of the Board of Guardians. Their main concern was to provide as good a service as possible for the pauper at the lowest possible price. Whenever a father neglected to look after his family, and it became chargeable to the parish, he was brought to book whenever possible, even if it meant using the police to bring him back. In 1869, Evan Evans, a police constable, was paid the expenses incurred in apprehending and bringing back to Aberystwyth Thomas Bishop, charged with deserting his family and leaving them chargeable to the parish.

There seemed always to be enough children in the workhouse to warrant the employment of a teacher. The first woman teacher was appointed in 1847 and was paid £20 a year to teach the 5 boys and 8 girls there. In the 1870's one of Her Majesty's Inspectors of schools reported very favourably on their standard of education and suggested that the classroom be furnished with a globe of the world and blank maps. The guardians also made provision for the education of the children of those receiving out-relief. In 1869 the trustees of the National School in North Rd, were paid £1 7s. 10½d. for "tuition for pauper children".

The erection of the Board School in Alexandra Rd. in the 1870's presented the guardians with a problem, continuing to educate the workhouse children themselves or sending them to the new school. Opinions were divided but it appears that eventually the children were sent to the Board School, the guardians paying one farthing per child per attendance or 2½d. a week. After 1870, education having become compulsory, this payment had also to be made to the parents receiving outdoor relief, and the relieving officer was obliged to see that the parent spent the extra money on the child's schooling.

It was assumed that most of the workhouse girls would enter domestic service and their training was directed to this end. After the 1870's the boys had an instructor known as the Industrial Trainer, presumably to give them some vocational education. Some were taught how to make nets. Many boys were apprenticed to various craftsmen and some were sent to be trained as seamen to such places as the Clio training ship. On at least one occasion, four children, aged 10 to 12, were allowed to emigrate to Canada. A sum of £40 was voted to pay for their passage and the Master, named Pierce, took them as far as Birmingham in 1882 *en route* for Liverpool.

The guardians were thrifty souls and were careful to spend only the bare minimum whenever possible. When the Machynlleth Guardians asked for their support in a move to supply the Board with free lunches on meeting days, they refused. They condemned publicly those "people of ample means" who "availed themselves of the services of the public vaccinators free of charge" and thus cast a burden on the public funds. When William Jones and his wife were appointed Master and Matron of the workhouse in 1888 they were made to pay 3s. a week each for their children's keep. This was rescinded later.

The inmates had to work hard for their keep. Bronglais had a very large kitchen garden protected by a high stone wall.

All the vegetables needed in the workhouse were grown there, and the surplus was taken to be sold in local shops. All this was done by the male inmates as well as chopping wood, keeping the boiler and other fires going, polishing the extensive area of wooden flooring and, if capable, serving as clerks, book-keepers and handymen.

Vagrants were allowed to stay one night only and had then to tramp to another workhouse at least 10 miles away. Before being given breakfast, each one had to break up stones for use on the roads. This was done before a long grating in the cell and all the

stone had to be broken into pieces small enough to pass through the grating. Some guardians would have preferred them not to work and go without breakfast, to save money.

A vagrant's diet in 1921 was 24 ozs of bread, 2 ozs. cheese, 1½ pints milk, 4 ozs. potatoes, 2 oz. margarine or dripping, 2 pints of shell cocoa, gruel or broth. Female vagrants and children received less bread and cheese.

Aberystwyth had to contend with a large number of vagrants until 1906 when there was a sharp drop. The decrease from 1,078

Some of the inmates of Bronglais Workhouse

in the June quarter of 1905 to 560 in the June quarter of 1906 was attributed to the completion of the new tramps' wards at the Aberystwyth workhouse. Many vagrants had previously been accommodated in the "Common Lodging houses", presumably in Trefechan.

As a result of an Act of Parliament of 1929, the Board of Guardians were abolished in 1930 and Bronglais workhouse became a public assistance institution where the poor and their sick continued to be lodged. In 1948 when the National Health Service Act became law, the workhouse, as such, ceased to exist. The building and the occupants were taken over by the Mid Wales Hospital Board and gradually changed into what is now known as a geriatric unit, becoming very crowded in the process. It remained in use until the new hospital was completed, when the occupants of the old workhouse, none of them able-bodied poor any longer, were moved to the geriatric unit created in the North Rd. hospital. The old Bronglais was then demolished, its place was used for the hospital laundry and its garden turned into the hospital car park. "Bronglais" (Near the Stream) then became the name of the hospital. The stream which still flows alongside Danycoed used to cross the road near this point, it has been covered over for many years.

Among the people who served the institution well was William Jenkins (Will Nell), who, on behalf of Seilo Chapel, organised and conducted religious services in Bronglais for many years.

Dispensaries and Hospitals

In Aberystwyth, as in many other small towns until the 19th century, the medical services were grossly inadequate. What is more, the quality of much of the treatment was poor, for such knowledge as the medical men possessed was often acquired by apprenticeship, and the treatment meted out by others who were regarded as "healers", especially women, savoured strongly of quackery and folklore. Medical relief was given to the sick pauper, but it usually took the form of small sums which the patient used to buy patent medicines or to consult anyone he fancied.

The improvements in medical knowledge and treatment which occurred largely in the big cities in the 18th century did not touch Aberystwyth, but they did show that the best way to deal with the sick poor was by the dispensary.

The first public dispensary was opened in Bridge St., on 18 February 1821 by Dr. Wm. Bonsall or Dr. Richard Williams who was also the official vaccination officer. In its first six months it dealt with 143 patients of whom 53 were discharged as cured (5 of these were vaccinated), 25 were relieved of pain, 3 were discharged for "irregularity", 4 died, 28 did not return to be given a regular discharge, and 30 were still on the books. 120 patients were treated at home. According to one writer the dispensary remained in Bridge St. until 1833 but this is doubtful. John Wood's map shows that there were two dispensaries in Aberystwyth in 1834, both in Great Darkgate St., one being the Medical Hall at the corner of Market St. on the site now occupied by Cecil Jones the optician, and the other in a room at the Heart of Oak Inn opposite the site of the present post office. It seems likely, therefore, that the Bridge St. dispensary was moved to the Heart of Oak Inn, probably when Dr. Richard Williams moved his home from Bridge St. to North Parade. There is also some doubt as to when it was absorbed into the infirmary, for it was claimed that from its opening until 1843 this dispensary had treated 4,433 patients.

The other dispensary, Medical Hall, was probably not set up until 1833 or 4 and is said to have been formed by Dr Henry Bonsall though it was known locally as Humphrey's Medical Hall, Humphrey being the dispenser and the person in charge.

These institutions were entirely dependent on voluntary contributions which were received from a variety of sources. In 1825 the Bridge St. dispensary received two guineas from John Hughes, a solicitor, accompanied by a note which said:

"Moiety (half) of a penalty against Enoch Hughes, part proprietor and driver of the Express Coach between Aberystwyth and Salop for being on the 17th day of September last drunk whilst driving the said coach between Newtown and Llanidloes, and for being abusive to his passengers."

"Moiety of a penalty against John Jones, son of Jenkin Jones of Llwynddinol, for riding on his cart on the turnpike road within the liberties of Aberystwyth."

According to the rules of Bonsall's dispensary, every subscriber of a guinea was classed as a governor and those paying half a guinea were each entitled to recom-

mend and to have continually on the books, one patient. Only poor persons unable to pay for medicine and surgical attention were accepted for treatment, domestic servants were excluded. Outpatients were also treated, and those living within one mile of the town and unable to travel to the dispensary were treated at home. The governors paid six pounds a year rent for the dispensary building and one pound—

Medical Hall, Great Darkgate St.

under 5d. a week—to have it cleaned. With the support of 60 subscribers this served until 1838 when, as a result of the Poor Law Amendment Act of 1834, the dispensary was replaced by an infirmary.

This Act, "a harsh remedy for a terrible disease", was forced on the country by the mounting cost of poor relief and by the pauperisation of even the employed working men, whose wages were kept low by poor relief while ratepayers were being ruined. According to this law the unit for Poor Law administration was to consist of a union of parishes, each union being expected to build a workhouse. The union was to be responsible for the sick and infirm paupers within its boundaries and employed a medical man to attend these people both inside and outside the workhouse. The sick poor, formerly treated at the dispensaries, now became the responsibility of what became known as the parish doctor.

But there was still work for the dispensaries to do and on 6 November 1837 an invitation was sent to all the governors of the dispensaries in Aberystwyth to attend a meeting at Dr. Richard Williams's house in North Parade. There, it was resolved to set up the Aberystwyth Infirmary and Cardiganshire General Hospital and to transfer to it the balance and arrears due to the Aberystwyth Dispensaries on 31 December 1837.

On 18 June 1839, the *Cambrian* reported "with pleasure, the establishment of an Infirmary in the town of Aberystwyth which furnishes a Physician, Surgeon and Apothecary, and medicine, diet and lodging, and suitable attendance to all patients that have been properly recommended". The new hospital was situated in Alfred Place, in the building now used by solicitors, but at some time between 1858 and 1867 it was removed to *Crynfryn* in Eastgate, the handsome Georgian town house of the Bonsall family, recently the office of the Department of Health and Social Security.

Paupers, being now cared for by the parish doctor, were excluded. Women in an advanced stage of pregnancy, children under seven years of age except when in need of an operation, persons of unsound mind or subject to fits, or suspected of having smallpox, the itch, or any infectious distemper or believed to be consumptive or in a dying condition or who were considered to be incurable were not to be admitted to the Infirmary on any account. People suffering from venereal disease were only admitted at the discretion of the Board of Management. These rules were strictly enforced.

An interesting rule stipulated that when patients were discharged, cured or released, they should be persuaded to give thanks to Almighty God at their respective places of worship and, whether cured or not, thank the Governor by whose recommendation they had been admitted.

The infirmary could provide only ten to twelve beds and double this number in an emergency. In the first year 148 patients were admitted and the income was £389, of which £212 was spent in that year. Among items of expenditure were 23s. for a year's supply of candles, 50s. for leeches, £31 for medicine and £15 to the matron, with free quarters.

In 1843, 82 subscribers between them contributed £124 3s.; collections at St. Michael's Chapel after a charity sermon preached by the Rev. John Hughes, Vicar of Llanbadarn, were £11. 7s. 5½d; another such sermon six months later, in September 1843, produced £26. 7s. 1½d. In December the Calvinestic Methodist Chapel (Tabernacl) collected £3. 5s. 6d.; cash found in the poor boxes yielded 1s. 5d., and a load and a half of ashes, presumably from the infirmary fires, were sold for 1s. 6d.

Expenditures for that year were £8. 17s. 6d. for 1217 lbs of flour; £2. 17s. for 69 lbs of butter; £15. 5s. 10½d. for 717 lbs of meat; £1. 10s. for 6 lbs of tea; £1. 16s. 8d. for 72 lbs sugar; £7. 17s. for 235¼ gallons of milk; £1. 12s. 2d. for 54½ lbs of candles and rushlights; 8s. for leeches; 1s. 2d for shaving a patient; £2 for surgical instruments and 2s. 6d. for a pair of crutches.

As time went on, however, waning interest in the infirmary led to smaller subscriptions and the work of the hospital suffered. Nevertheless, the staff did its best and did not deserve the harsh criticism levelled at it by the Cambrian News, which once described it as "the miserable looking premises in Little Darkgate Street".

The infirmary's first officials were: patron—Col. W. E. Powell M.P., treasurer-John James of Maesbangor, consulting surgeon-Sir Astley Cooper F.R.S.,; physician-Dr. Richard Williams; surgeon-William Evans; chaplain-Rev. John Hughes; secretary-Mr. Humphreys; dispensers-Mr. Humphreys & Mr. Cole; matron-Mrs. Elizabeth Owen. Dr. Richard Williams is believed to have extended the invitation to the

Humphrey Roberts's office, Baker St., site of the first infirmary.

Former D.H.S.S. in Eastgate

famous Sir Astley Cooper to act as consulting surgeon. He had a house in Marine Terrace Other medical men who worked there were Dr. G. W. Bonsall and Dr. Gilbertson.

As stated above, the financial affairs of the hospital were far from satisfactory when Joseph Downie died in the town in 1870. Joseph Downie, a Scotsman, came to Aberystwyth from Brecon as the National Provincial Bank's first manager. He became very interested in the affairs of the infirmary and was made its treasurer in 1864. When he died on 8 September 1870 he left the residue of his estate, amounting to £38,000, to be divided between the Aberystwyth District Visiting Society and the Aberystwyth Infirmary.

The will was contested by some of Downie's relatives but Sir James Bacon, the Lord Chancellor decided in favour of the Aberystwyth institutions. He approved of two schemes, one in aid of the Visiting Society and the other in trust for the Infirmary. He also directed that the bequest should be called "the Joseph and Jane Downie Bequest".

The Aberystwyth District Visiting Society's aims were the "relief of the sick and the poor, the encouragement in the poor of habits of cleanliness and frugality and the suppression of mendacity and imposture". It was laid down by the trustees that part of the society's income from the bequest—£300 a year—was to be subscribed to the infirmary in return for the appropriate number of patients' tickets; a ticket entitled the possessor to admit a patient to a hospital bed. There is no longer a need for patients' tickets but the Visiting Society continues

The Aberystwyth Infirmary 1888

to help the sick and the poor to this day.

According to the terms of the second scheme, the infirmary was empowered to hire "in the town of Aberystwyth" extra premises and, if necessary, to spend up to £5,000 on the purchase of land and the erection thereon of new buildings. Being able to pay better salaries than before, it was also able to hire a more adequate and better trained staff. A piece of ground was bought from Sir Pryse Pryse and a new infirmary was built in North Road. The foundation stone was laid on 14 November 1885 by Lady Lisburne, the trowel and mallet used can be seen at the local museum. The ceremony began at 2.0 p.m. when a colourful procession was formed at the Town Hall Square consisting of the Band, Police, Oddfellows and Foresters in all their regalia, the Mayor (George Green of the foundry) in his robes of office, the Corporation, medical men of the town, trustees of the infirmary, and the public. It proceeded to the site via Portland St.,

Terrace Rd., and North Parade.

The new hospital was opened in 1888, it had 20 beds and was considered to be very up-to-date at that time. It was built by David Lloyd at a cost of £3,200. It now forms part of the Geriatric Unit of the hospital but the plaque to Joseph Downie which used to hang in the lobby, now hangs in the Ceredigion Museum.

But Aberystwyth was still growing fast and in 1920 it was found necessary to enlarge the hospital. The British Red Cross offered the governors £3,000 for extensions, provided a similar sum could be collected. Special efforts were made to do this, an extraordinary bazaar at the University College under the chairmanship of Professor Edward Edwards, then Mayor of Aberystwyth, produced the magnificent sum of £3,789 for the hospital. There were collections over a wide area, the stone for the building was quarried behind the hospital and given free by the owner, the Rev. H. J. Morgan; the new operating

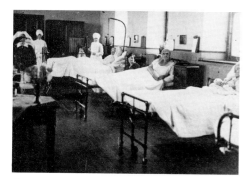

A ward in the first North Rd. Infirmary

The first isolation hospital on Tanybwlch

theatre equipment was paid for by Major L. J. Mathias of Bronpadarn, and £600 was contributed by the Cardiganshire Ex Service men, the whole of their share of the profit made by the Expeditionary Forces' Canteens during the 1914-18 War, known as the "Byng Millions".

The extensions etc. were built by Messrs R. & H. L. Owen and cost £14,907. They were opened on 30 October 1923 by H. R.H. the Prince of Wales and the new male ward was named after him. The number of beds was now more than doubled, but less than fifteen years later there were again complaints of overcrowding in the hospital and yet another extension was planned. In view of the large amount of capital required, over £30,000—it was resolved to make a public appeal—"the Centenary Appeal of the Aberystwyth Infirmary". Its success owed much to the committee of management and, in particular, to its chairman, Sir George Fossett Roberts. The new extensions were opened by D. Owen Evans M.P., on 1 June 1939, they had cost £43,000 and Aberystwyth now had a well equipped hospital containing 66 beds, a number which could be increased to 107 in an emergency. It was known as "The Aberystwyth and Cardiganshire

General Hospital".

By this time the North Rd. hospital was not the only one in the town. In response to pressure from the Ministry of Health, the County Council made arrangements for a Maternity and Child Welfare Department to be set up at the Bronglais institution, i.e. the workhouse, and also agreed to paying the local Cambrian Nursing Home in North Parade for the treatment of difficult maternity cases. In the meantime it built its own Maternity Home in Caradoc Rd., it was opened officially on 28 April 1934.

The first complaint to the Town Council about the lack of provision for the treatment and isolation of fever patients was made in 1890, and the Borough Medical Officer continued to make this complaint every year until about 1911 when a cottage at Penro on Tanybwlch beach was made into a temporary hospital. Eventually an Isolation Hospital was specially built near the bridge over the Ystwyth river at the entrance to Tanybwlch beach. It was never a satisfactory building, the staff accommodation was poor and it was not possible to separate the various diseases for nursing purposes. Nevertheless, it served its purpose, and the man who did most to have it built was Dr. Abraham Thomas who was the Borough

Medical Officer from 1892 to 1940. He was also the very popular medical officer to the local Territorial Battery and accompanied the men on active service throughout most of the 1914-18 war.

In 1937 the County Council decided that there had to be a bigger isolation hospital and planned to acquire Tanybwlch Mansion. But the Ministry of Health had doubts about its suitability. This and the war postponed the purchase until early in 1946. With the assistance of fever hospitals in South Wales, the Tanybwlch hospital proved invaluable during the epidemic of typhoid fever in July 1946.

Bronpadarn in Llanbadarn, the former home of Major Mathias, was also purchased at this time with the intention of making it into a maternity home, but instead it became first a nursing school and later the nucleus of the Cardiganshire College of Librarianship.

Aberystwyth borough also had a small hut on Tanybwlch beach which was used as a smallpox hospital. It was later replaced with an isolated cottage at Alltglais, two and a half miles from the town, between Cwm Woods and Clarach. This ceased to be used in 1948,

A Workmen's Contribution Scheme was started in 1922 when first the employees of the railway, the boatmen and the staff of the National Library agreed to allow a penny a week to be deducted from their earnings. The practice spread rapidly and, with the assistance of volunteer local agents, soon covered much of the county. In 1939 the contribution was raised to 3d. a week, and by 1945 the hospital had received a total of £7,166 from the scheme. It then covered

12,000 members, making with their families, up to 30,000 people eligible for treatment. Largely due to the efforts of W. J. Griffiths, the scheme was a great success and it was decided to abolish the ticket system which had been in use from the time that the first dispensary was established.

Dr. David Ellis.

The outstanding medical man in the history of hospital work in Aberystwyth in the first half of the 20th century was David Ellis M.D., general practitioner and surgeon at the hospital from 1904 to 1948.

He was born in Pencwm, Llanddeiniol, and attended the Old Grammar School in Queen's Square before going to the University College of Wales. From there, after graduating, he went to a London Hospital where, after a brilliant career, he became an M.D. He then held several hospital appointments before returning to Aberystwyth in 1904.

His return was unheralded and unwelcome to some of the town's doctors, they resented his putting up his plate without their permission. But it was not long before the people of Aberystwyth began to appreciate his worth. In a very short while he won the respect and admiration of people in all walks of life. He applied himself assiduously to his work and through his skill and utter devotion played a leading part in overcoming the prejudice and fear associated with entering a hospital. Before long the hospital in North Rd. was looked on not as a place of suffering and despair but where skill and kindness were available to all in need. In those days no one worked harder to

raise the reputation of Aberystwyth Hospital than Dr. Ellis, and it was largely due to his care and control that the hospital soon became the chief centre for surgical work in Mid Wales. He was admired for the high standard of his surgery not only throughout Mid Wales but also at the Royal College of Surgeons. He was spoken of with awe in country areas where it was said that no one in Cardiganshire should be allowed to die without being first seen by Dr. Ellis. His skill as a surgeon coupled with his innate courtesy made him an ideal physician and he was loved not only by his patients but also by nursing staff everywhere in the county. As well as fulfilling the duties of a busy general practitioner he often operated both early and late at the hospital. He was also a deacon at Tabernacl, a J.P., and a member of both the Council and the Court of Governors of the University College of Wales.

During his illness, at a meeting of the Hospital Management Committee, Sir George Fossett Roberts, the President said: "I need hardly say how greatly we miss him. Over a long period of years he has been the main pillar of the Hospital, and it was owing to his skill as a surgeon that the Hospital holds the high position it holds today. Dr. Ellis's reputation spread far and wide and his name is respected in every home in Cardiganshire and, indeed, in very many homes far beyond the boundaries of our county."

Then came the great change. On 5th July 1948 the National Health Service

Act became law and established a comprehensive Health Service for the whole of **Great Britain.** Henceforth, all hospitals not run for profit were vested in the Ministry, and all their endowments went into the Hospital Endowments Fund. Hospital Management Committees were appointed to look after the affairs of groups of hospitals. Aberystwyth Hospital became the area hospital covering Newtown, Llanidloes, Machynlleth, Tywyn, Lampeter, Tregaron and Aberaeron, providing services for the smaller hospitals in these towns when required. In 1974 the number of dependent hospitals was reduced, Machynlleth and Tywyn were transferred to the Powys area authority, but the principal of a good-sized general hospital providing services for smaller hospitals remained.

A much bigger hospital was needed at Aberystwyth to serve the needs of the Welfare State and in 1966 it was built in Caradoc Rd. with beds for 194 patients. The old North Road Hospital then became a Geriatric Unit with accommodation for 82 patients.

During the first World War (1914-18) the large building facing the entrance to the pier at the end of Pier St. was used as a Red Cross Hospital for wounded soldiers. It had been built for visitors and named Hotel Cambria but it proved a failure. In March 1906 it was bought for use as the Presbyterian Theological College and began admitting students in November of that year. It was reopened as a college after 1918.

Some Schools and Schoolmasters

Until late in the 19th century the provision of primary and secondary education in Aberystwyth was grossly inadequate. There were no Tudor foundations as in Bangor, Brecon and Carmarthen, only private adventure schools conducted by individuals for private profit, and there were many of them.

One of the earliest of the schoolmasters was *Hugh Hughes* who lived about 1780 in Bridge St. near the bridge, in a very old house on a site later occupied by the Freemasons Inn, and now a shop, probably the one at the upper corner with South Rd. He held his school in the old Town Hall and, in addition to giving a general education, he gave instruction in surveying and mathematics. In time he gave up the school and became the land agent to Nanteos.

His sons formed the firm of Hughes Brothers, Solicitors. One of them, James, became the proprietor of Glan Rheidol, a mansion near Capel Bangor. He was the mayor of Aberystwyth when the new Municipal Corporations Act came into force on 1 January 1836. A holiday had been declared for that day and the mayor was carried shoulder high through the main streets. In the afternoon another procession, preceded by a brass band was held, when Hughes in his mayoral robes was drawn in a phaeton by a team of men through streets decorated with flags and bunting and having almost every window lit with candles.

One of Hugh Hughes's pupils walked to and from school every day from Tyllwyd, Llanfarian, he was Owen Morris who later kept a good school at Bethel, Mynyddbach. Another Aberystwyth schoolmaster of the same period was Evan Evans, *Ieuan Brydydd Hir*, but the location of his school is unknown. He usually lodged in a tavern in Bridge St. and, like his old schoolmaster at Ystrad Meurig, was a classical scholar. In teaching as in almost everything he tried, he was a failure.

The most successful school of all the old establishments was that of *John Evans* (1796-1861) born at Blaenplwyf, the son of a humble weaver. For a while he worked at his father's trade, but at the age of 17 he decided to walk to London in search of an education. There he entered the service of a bookseller and was brought before the court for selling books without a licence, but the magistrate, realising that John had committed the offence in ignorance, set him free. Through the kindness of another London Welshman he was later sent to a school kept in the capital by Griffith Davies, a well-known Welsh mathematician, where he stayed for some years. John Evans then returned to Wales and taught for short periods at schools in Welshpool and Llanfair Caereinion before settling in Aberystwyth at the age of 21. There, for nearly 50 years he kept his *Ysgol Drafnidiol a Meintonol* (Commercial and Mathematical School) at a house, now demolished, at the corner of Chalybeate St. and Alexandra Rd.

His pupils were of two kinds, the younger section, being of secondary school age, were taught the traditional grammar school subjects. Among these were some who became well-known in adult life, Dr. Lewis Edwards, Principal of Bala Theological College; Henry Richard M.P., of the *Peace Society*; the Rev. Principal David Charles

John Evans's School

Davies of Trefecca; Rev. Wm. Ellis of Dolgellau Grammar School; Edward Jones of Aberystwyth Grammar School and John Evans's own son who had a brilliant career at Edinburgh University.

Another section consisted of adults, especially sailors who wished to become more proficient in such subjects as Navigation, Astronomy and the theoretical side of seamanship. Many of these aspired to be masters of their ships. The younger section was taught in an upstairs room while the adult class was immediately below this. A hole in the floor enabled the master not only to keep an eye on those below and to answer questions, but also to detect any smoking, a habit which was strictly prohibited.

To teach navigational astronomy he made his own telescope and a large sundial. (The sundial at **Llangorwen Church** was of his making.) He also used magic-lanterns in his teaching, one of these was an extra-ordinary device worked by the rays of the sun. To aid him in teaching astronomy he used a large umbrella which had the constellations painted inside it. His clock, which faced the gasworks, consisted of an outside face worked from the kitchen, it was an eight day affair and "regulated by astronomical observations". Its accuracy was a source of wonder to everyone. In his observatory in the tower alongside the house, he had a camera obscura with which he often amused his pupils and friends by showing them living pictures of people crossing the small Corry Bridge opposite his house.

Many of Aberystwyth's sea captains had cause to thank John Evans for his excellent teaching. He was also a good musician, a student of Divinity and a dedicated worker for temperance. The children of Tabernacl C.M. Church always enjoyed his talks.

Jeffreys school was established by a man of that name who settled in Aberystwyth about 1835. He was English speaking and always described as a "gentleman". Before coming to Aberystwyth he had been a journalist and with the support of a local printer, Esther Williams, he published a newspaper in the town—the Cambrian Gazette—which was bilingual and radical in its views. He believed strongly in the coming of the "Golden Age" and thought that it was near. The paper failed and he opened a school in a house in Alfred Place, the house which was used as an infirmary before it moved to "Crynfryn" in Eastgate. Jeffreys was a good classical scholar and taught many who planned to enter the Established Church. He was the son-in-law of W. C. Monkhouse who had a brewery in Alexandra Rd.

Old St. John's Buildings, opposite the Life Boat House formerly consisted of a row of small houses with one tall building in their midst. In the loft of this, a former barley storehouse, was where the Rev. *Thomas Richards* had a day school in the 1840's. It was known as *Ysgol y Morfa* (the Marsh School) and was largely a secondary school. Richards was a Methodist minister who had been a pupil of Robert Roberts at Llangeitho. His school was much used by private pupils from the Nanteos estate, the Powell children as well as those of some of their tenants. He also taught Robert J. Davies of Cwrtmwr and pupils from as far away as Amlwch in Anglesey. He gave up teaching in 1851.

William Jones's school was in being in the town about 1820, if not before, and was held in the loft of a house at the corner of St. James Square. William Jones was born in Ystrad Meurig and may have been a pupil of Edward Richard and certainly of the Rev. John Williams. Nothing is known of his school but it is known that he was called "William Jones the Post House". His daughter, who later lived in Portland St., earned her living by writing and reading letters for people who could do neither.

Skinner Street Day School. This school was opened in the same building as that used as a Sunday School by the Methodists, largely due to the efforts of Griffith Thomas and David Jones the Bank. It was strongly supported by Tabernacl people but was open to all denominations. One of its teachers was the well-known Ieuan Gwyllt, an excellent teacher who taught singing very well indeed. He was followed first by the Rev. Robert Thomas and then by Thomas Lloyd, a leading member of Tabernacl. Then came J. Jenkins of Llangeitho but he soon gave way to the man whose name was most associated with the Skinner St. school —the Rev. William Jones. He took over the school about 1840 and stayed there for ten years. He always insisted on calling it a "British School", the name then given to Nonconformist schools. William Jones made his reputation on his very first day at Skinner St. A mill leat then ran open in front of the school and because of heavy rain, was running deep and fast. One of the pupils fell into the stream and was in danger of drown-

ing when William Jones dived in and saved the child. After he left, the school was taught by a man named Edwards but he soon gave up and the school was closed.

Another schoolmaster, *John Williams* of Trefechan, was an amusing fellow, noted for his story-telling. His school was in Trefechan, in or opposite the room once used by the Tabernacl Sunday School, and was approached by a flight of stone steps. He was the son of a Lledrod bellringer and had himself been a bellringer on his travels, in Ludlow and later in Leominster. His whole family, including his sisters, were bellringers.

By trade he was a hatmaker and was

known locally as *Jac yr Hetiwr*. This was his trade when he lived in Ludlow. But he made a poor schoolmaster for he regularly fell into a deep sleep in the classroom. He also fell asleep in Tabernacl during the sermon and while waiting to be served in shops. This may well have been the result of his having been a hatmaker, a user of mercury.

At one period in his life he was made supervisor of a group of reapers who went regularly to the Marches to work on the harvests. Being fluent in English it was his responsibility to arrange the terms of work and payment. For doing this he received a shilling for every reaper in his group on top of what he earned himself. During the hay and corn harvests, excursions were run by coach from Aberystwyth to Worcester and Shrewsbury at a fare of half a crown to the latter, when the normal fare was a pound. But even that was too expensive for many, and they walked or travelled in carts via Devils Bridge, Cwmystwyth and Rhayader. These travels provided Jac with information and experience which made him much in demand at social gatherings, he could weave a fascinating tale out of the most meagre material.

John Lewis kept a number of small schools in the town and found the business most unrewarding. Each pupil paid him twopence a week and he usually had from a dozen to fifteen in his school. His first was in Mill St. near Mill Court and Tabernacl, and he became noted for his use of the cane but not for his scholarship. In his classroom there was an upright post to which any boy who misbehaved was tied and thrashed. His second school was in Lewis Terrace, next to

The tower of John Evans's School and, on the right, the Wesleyan day school (1844-48) described under Nonconformity

John Evans's school, his third was in High St. behind the Old Bank House in Bridge St., and his last school was at the old skinnery in Poplar Row known in Welsh as *Yr Hen Glwferdy* (the Old Glove House).

Griffith Edward's first school was at the corner of South Rd. and Bridge St. near the old Freemason's Inn. He was there in 1822/23 and then moved to a loft in High St. in a house kept by Nellie Cupola who had previously lived in a house in Trefechan known as the Cupola.

Griffith Edward generally took a nap in the afternoon while his school was in session, and after waking would give a half penny to one of his pupils to keep order while he visited the Miners Arms in Great Darkgate St. He had some strange ways; periodically, when the sun shone brightly into the classroom, he would mark or re-mark the times of closing school—12.0 noon and 5.0 p.m.—on the wall by means of lines coinciding with the shadows cast at those times. In dull weather, having no watch or clock he would send a pupil out to enquire the time. He had little scholarship and was able to teach only a little reading, writing and arithmetic.

After a few years of teaching, he became a chandler in Llanbadan Fawr and in time became a well-known figure there.

In 1836 there was a schoolmaster named *Craig* who kept a school at his house in New St., no one knew his Christian name. He was classed as a gentleman and attracted pupils from a higher social class than most of the other schools. He competed with John Evans whom he regarded as catering for an inferior social class. But he was a good teacher, and insisted on good behaviour among his 40 pupils. Craig laid great stress on good handwriting, something which John Evans thought unimportant because it did nothing to make a pupil think for himself. Handwriting was taught in the New St. school by John Rowlands, a former pupil of John Evans and the son of Rowland Rowlands who kept the Raven Inn. John was also a clerk at the Customs House. The school was half way along the sea side of New St.

The *Rev. John Jenkins* M.A. was an Aberystwyth man, born in Bridge St. opposite the Old Bank. The family later moved to Lewis Terrace where he opened his school. He was a keen member of Tabernacl and, like Henry Richard, took advantage of the church's custom of giving young men an opportunity to develop their powers of oratory by speaking in public. After keeping a school and preaching for a short period he went to Edinburgh University where he took his M.A. He then returned to Aberystwyth and reopened his school. But the monetary rewards were too small and he went to Chester where he opened a school in Abbey Square which did well. It was he who gave Seilo its baptism cup.

Monsieur du Tarraux's school was in upper Portland St. opposite Bethel, and possibly the same house as that used by Jeffreys. The general belief was that "Tarraux" was an adopted name and that he was in reality an Englishman. Whatever the truth of this he knew France and its language very well and had beautiful handwriting. His arithmetic, however, was poor and he was much given to using "cribs" instead of working things out on the blackboard.

Dr. Lewis Edwards was born on 27 October 1809 at Pwllcenawon, Penllwyn, about four miles from Aberystwyth. He was educated at the Llanfihangel Genau'r Glyn Grammar School and John Evans' Mathematical School. He opened a school in 1827 in a room at the back of the White Lion Inn in Great Darkgate St. The room above was used by John Cox as his first printing works. (The White Lion was almost opposite the place now occupied by the Co-operative Stores.) But Lewis Edwards was not a good teacher, he was more concerned with adding to his own knowledge than to that of his pupils and the school had a short life. It then became a carpenters shop. Dr. Edwards became Principal of the Bala Theological College.

The *Rev. Richard Lumley* was born in Aberystwyth in 1810 and was educated at John Evans' school and Llanfihangel Genau'r Glyn. After leaving school he became a tutor to the children of one of the local gentry. He then opened a school in a good building which his father, a builder, erected for him at the bottom of Queen St. But Richard Lumley was not a good schoolmaster and his school was too near that of John Evans, with whom he could not hope to compete successfully. In 1831 he stopped teaching in Aberystwyth and went to Llandeilo where he opened another school which was much more successful.

The Queen St. school then became a storehouse.

Ysgol Penparcau (Penparcau School) was built in 1846 through the efforts of Elizabeth

Penparcau School

and Martha Pritchard, maiden ladies from Shrewsbury who settled in Aberystwyth. For a short time the school was run by a man who had once been a teacher at one of Madam Bevan's schools. Then came George Hunt Thomas, who became known as Thomas Penparcau, and made the school into a very good one. He had previously been a mariner and this was reflected in his teaching. Though supposed to provide an elementary education only, the schooling went well beyond the 3 R's. He taught Trigonometry, Geometry, Surveying and Navigation. He also formed a most successful drum and fife band among the pupils which took part in town celebrations.

The Nanteos family took a great deal of interest in Penparcau school. Whenever Major Powell (known locally as the "General") had to wear his very colourful dress uniform for some special occasion, he would call at the school to "give the children a treat". The school prize-giving ceremony was always at Nanteos and all the children

were then entertained to tea with the General at the head of the table, flanked by the prize winners. Treats were also provided for the children at Glan Paith and Tanybwlch mansions. The Board of Education reports on the school were always excellent. George Hunt Thomas retired in 1884 and died two years later.

Ysgol y Morwyr (the Sailors' School) was opened in North Parade in the 1850's by Lewis Roderick. It was for mariners only, young men who, after a number of years at sea, wished to improve their chances of promotion by studying the subjects involved in seamanship. After the death of the famous John Evans, Roderick's school became highly regarded and men came there not only from all parts of Cardiganshire but also from further afield.

The town also had a number of "dame schools" run by women and concentrating on primary education. There must have been a large number of these over the years but the only ones of which the author has any knowledge are the following;

Eliza Pirs had a girls school for at least 20 years after 1821. Her first was at Tanydref, as Chalybeate St. was first called. Later she moved to Sydenham House in Great Darkgate St. where she also kept a toy shop. When young she was a very beautiful woman but the drudgery of the work and the poor reward told on her health and her beauty. Her method of teaching English, like that of most mistresses of that time, was to set her pupils tasks involving the use of a small dictionary. Another book used was the well-known *Reading Made Easy* which the Welsh pupils always pronounced as

"Reedimaresi".

Mrs. Shelby's school was in a small low-roofed house at the junction of Terrace Rd. and Portland Rd.

Miss Morris, who died in 1860, kept a school for 50 years, first in Windmill Court off Eastgate, where one of her pupils was the David Roberts who founded the brewery in Trefechan. For most of her teaching life, however, she taught in Portland St. where her house, though near Terrace Rd., was then the last in the street.

Mrs. Jones—Gwraig Mr. Jones y Dansin, (the wife of Mr. Jones the Dancing Master) kept a school in the 1810's but its whereabouts are unknown.

Mrs. Margaret Rees (Mal Rees) had a school in a small, single-storey, thatch-roofed house in upper Great Darkgate which had once been a prison and, possibly, the town's House of Correction for a short period.

A Ladies Boarding School of "a very genteel description" was kept by a *Miss Owen* in Queen St. in 1824, and a similar one was run by *Miss Margaret Rees* twenty years later. Another such school was *Miss Babington's* "Lady's Boarding School" in North Parade in 1835, and five years later a *Mrs. Ann Lloyd* had a girls' school somewhere in the town.

Until the beginning of the 19th century the Established Church took little interest in education but then, largely in response to demands made by leading churchgoers, some clergymen became interested in setting up a school, and in 1809 began to ask for contributions for this purpose. But it was another three years before anything definite was done. A public meeting was then held and it was resolved to open a school. But progress was very slow and in the meantime Pryse Pryse of Gogerddan, Matthew Davies of Cwmcynfelin, George Bonsall of Glanrheidol, Richard Evans Vicar of Llanbadarn, and Richard Morgan Minister of St. Michaels, were granted a piece of land by the Court Leet on Penmaes-glas as "Trustees of a certain charitable institution for the education of Youth according to the established principles of the Church of England". The rent was one penny *per annum*.

The school was then built on this site at a cost of £366 7s. 8d. and opened its doors on 8 November 1813. It occupied a piece of ground measuring 150 yds by 50 yds where the Parish Hall now stands and, when built, had Penmaes-glas Common to itself. It was known as the Grammar School. The first master was Lewis Jones who gave his pupils a classical education combined with arithmetic and reading. After twelve years at the school he married the daughter of John Jones, a well-to-do merchant and grocer in the town, and left teaching for his father-in-law's business. In time he became prominent in local affairs and mayor in 1845.

The assistant at the school was William Owen, a cripple who lived in a dilapidated old house in Bridge St. which had stone steps leading up to the front door and housed all manner of people—vagrants, drunkards and others. It was probably the old Nanteos house. Owen eventually hanged himself and was buried in unhallowed ground in Llanbadarn.

An attempt was made to have the school

The Grammar School

recognised as a National School but for some unknown reason this was not done.

Lewis Jones was followed by others but the school did not thrive and was closed in 1835-36. In 1845 it was reopened under a woman teacher for the education of primary school children but in time it again became a grammar school.

Aberystwyth's leading school in the mid 19th century was run by *Edward (Jasper) Jones*, a first class honours graduate of London University. It was held in Jasper House which still stands opposite the Old Assembly Rooms in upper Great Darkgate St. In 1862 or 1868 he moved his school to the old grammar school building on Penmaes-glas and stayed there until 1892. He himself taught science while his assistant handled the classical and modern side. By the time he retired many of his former pupils occupied important positions in the Church, in the medical profession and in banking. His pupils came from all over Britain, and

even from India and the U.S.A., and many won scholarships to the older universities. He used his own home, Jasper House, for the boarders. In 1886 he was persuaded to open a junior department for boys aged 7 to 10 years and he put this class under the control of a trained teacher.

His successor was R. A. Pope M. A. scholar of Sidney Sussex College and a former assistant master of Shrewsbury School. With his assistant he prepared his pupils for the professions and the universities, paying particular attention to modern languages, commercial subjects and outdoor recreation. The boarders were housed at 7, Laura Place. The school thrived until the County School was opened in 1897, then it lost a considerable number of its pupils and was eventually closed.

Having become a private affair since being taken over by "Jasper" Jones, no objections were raised when the old school building was demolished c. 1910 to make room for the Parish Hall. R. A. Pope became a member of the U.C.W. staff and taught classics there.

In 1874 a boys' school was opened in North Parade by the *Rev. Llewelyn Edwards* formerly of Lincoln College, Oxford. After a short stay there it was moved to Bridge St. and a year or so later to Ardwyn, a fairly large house off Llanbadarn Rd., where he ran his school for 20 years. As a result of the Intermediate Education Act of 1889 it was decided to set up a county intermediate school in Aberystwyth. In 1896, soon after this decision was taken, Llewelyn Edwards died, his school was bought by the County Council and Ardwyn became the town's county school. The first headmaster was David Samuel.

David Samuel was born in Aberystwyth in 1856 and began his secondary education in "Jasper" Jones's grammar school. He then went to Llandovery College for a year where he seems to have made a special study of Welsh. In 1873 he entered the University College and two years later moved to Clare College, Cambridge, where, having been placed in the first class of the mathematical tripos, he became a wrangler in 1879. He then became mathematics master at Appleby under the man who became Bishop Owen of St. Davids. After a brief period at Ashburn Grammar School in Derbyshire he returned to Aberystwyth and opened his own school in January 1887 in the Old Bank House in Bridge St. Seven years later he was made headmaster of *Ardwyn County School*.

His first assistant there was Thomas Owen who also had a private school in the town, first in the Market Hall in Market St. and later in Queens Square.

When Ardwyn opened, it took boys only, 65 of them. In January 1898 girls were admitted and the school numbered 110. When David Samuel died in 1921 there were 365 pupils and the accommodation was so inadequate that entry had become difficult.

David Samuel was a man of outstanding ability. His interest in mathematics was first aroused by Chancellor Silvan Evans, and that became his main interest. But he was also an able Welsh scholar, for years he was an examiner for the degree of ovate at the National Esteddfod and his knowledge of

Ardwyn, Aberystwyth County School c. 1920. Llewelyn Edwards had his private school in the older building on the left

David Samuel and his staff at Ardwyn

the original version of the *Mabinogion* was extensive. His lectures on Welsh syntax were most instructive. In Eisteddfodic circles he was known as Dewi o **Geredigion**.

No one had a more extensive knowledge of old Aberystwyth, and his essays on that and other topics run into hundreds. He was

a life-long Calvinistic Methodist and, at the time of his death, the only survivor of the original diaconate at Salem. He was also a very successful Sunday School teacher. As a member of the town's Public Library Committee he did very useful work indeed.

The National School. Just as Pryse Pryse had actively supported the establishment of the Penmaes-glas school so he was again active in the setting up of the first National (Church) School in the town. First he made a handsome donation of £200 to the Charity responsible for National Schools and then he was instrumental in securing a suitable site. In 1813, he had acquired from the Corporation a grant of land near the north turnpike gate for his own use. But on hearing that this site was well suited for a school for poor children he surrendered the property and in 1819 the first National School was built there, in what is now Northgate St.

After it was built Pryse Pryse continued to be interested in the school but the man who did most to keep it going was the Rev. Thomas Richards of Carrog and Bridge St. But for his generous financial aid and moral support the school could not have continued. In 1828 it contained 85 boys and 75 girls who each paid one penny a week for their education. The salary of the headmaster in 1845 was £30 while the mistress received £20. A house was provided for the headmaster. The money needed to run the school was obtained by contributions, private collections and collections made in the Established Church after special sermons. More often than not, any deficit was borne by Thomas Richards.

A report on the school in 1846 stated that

The first National School, in Northgate St.

The second National School, in North Rd.

while the standard of religious knowledge was high, the pupils were very ignorant of Geography, they read well but were poor in Arithmetic. Nevertheless it was a better report than that received by many other schools. A surprising comment was that nearly all those attending the school were the children of Dissenters, a reflection of the strength of Nonconformity in the town. It was therefore impossible to require all the children to attend at least one Sunday service in the local Anglican Church as was done in most other National Schools.

By the 1850's the condition of the school buildings had deteriorated considerably, there were also problems of accommodation, the employment and payment of trained teachers, and the repairs and maintenance of the fabric. The school's income was far too small to cope with these, in 1857 the annual income of the boys school was £34 9s. 5d. made up of £13. 11s. from subscriptions and £8. 18s. 5d. from children's fees. In December 1861, after inspecting the school, one of

H.M. Inspectors concerned informed the managers that the school would be given a Capitation Grant on condition that new buildings were erected without delay.

Faced with the need for a new school the Noncomformists wanted to erect a British School, while the Rev. E. O. Phillips, the newly-elected vicar of St. Michaels, argued for another National School. A committee was appointed in 1861 to set up a British School but did nothing but talk. The Established Church authorities did more than talk, in 1866 the new National School was opened on a site above the old school in North Rd. where it can still be seen but is no longer a day school. There was now accommodation for 600 children. It was resolved to demolish the old school and to use the site to build houses, the rents of which would help to maintain the school. The total cost of school and houses was £5,739, all secured by voluntary subscriptions.

During the remainder of the century, the

history of the school was one of satisfactory, and often very good academic attainment, but difficult financial problems. Despite the grant, it was still dependent on voluntary contributions and, as interest in the school waned, these tended to fall. On one occasion the teachers had to suffer a cut in salary, loans had to be raised and some of the houses in Northgate St. had to be sold to pay the interest on the debt and to keep the school going. This state of affairs lasted until 1902 when an Education Act passed in that year declared that, henceforth, the National Schools be called Non-Provided Public Elementary Schools and be financially assisted from the rates.

The headmaster of the North Rd. school from 1892 to 1925 was the greatly respected T. Ainsleigh Jones, a fine Shakespearean actor.

While the Noncomformists made full use of the Church schools they did not approve of them. Most of the people in Wales were in favour of free, secular and undenominational education and Aberystwyth's Nonconformists strongly supported this view. The case for and against such schools was thoroughly debated and a number of public meetings held, the most important of which was that held in January 1870 attended by ministers of religion, mayors of towns and others interested in education from all over Wales. It resulted in the formation of the Welsh Education Alliance which became the spearhead of the Welsh attack on Forsters Education Bill.

Further meetings were held and all decided in favour of amalgamating all denominational schools into one national system of sectarian education. Consequently, when the new Act came into force in August 1870 and it was realised that Church schools would be allowed to retain their independence, there was much disappointment in the town.

It was then resolved to press the town Council to exercise its right to appeal to the Department of Education for permission to elect a school Board to be responsible for providing elementary education in the area. The council agreed to do this and permission was granted. Aberystwyth became the first town in Wales, if not in England and Wales, to elect such a Board.

The Board had now to be elected, it was to consist of seven members, three of them to be churchmen. The election was conducted in a far from amicable atmosphere. Canvassing was rife, election meetings were noisy and sometimes very rough. On the day of the election, some voters were roughly handled and the police had to interfere. The ballot was not secret and there were allegations of bribery—gifts of tea and blankets—and of much irregularity in the conduct of the election. The result of the ballot was a shock to the Nonconformists, the three Church candidates headed the poll.

The first of several meetings of the School Board was held on 15 December 1870 and it was eventually decided to build an undenominational school next to the railway station, the school now used as a Welsh primary school. It had accommodation for 600 pupils, 200 boys, 200 girls and 200 infants. The architects were Szlumper and Aldwinkle. Because of the unstable nature of the ground and the rising costs of materi-

The passive resistance sale at Old Bank House in Bridge St.

als, the estimated cost proved too low and there had to be more borrowing. On 4 August 1874, the school, built in the early English domestic Gothic style, was opened with a large crowd watching the proceedings.

The Nonconformist opposition to Church schools was revived at the turn of the century when the Education Act of 1902 was passed. This not only allowed the National Schools to remain in the hands of the Established Church but also "put them on the rates". In 1904 both the Board School in Alexandra Rd. and the National School in North Rd. became the financial responsibility of the Cardiganshire Education Committee. Many Nonconformists objected to paying for the upkeep of Church schools and refused to pay the "Church rate". As a result, some 60,000 people were prosecuted in England and Wales and among them was a man who came to live in Aberystwyth and had some of his goods distrained there.

On 4 October 1905 the Old Bank House

was the scene of a "passive resistance sale". It was then inhabited by a descendant of the famous Rev. John Jones of Talsarn, a staunch Nonconformist. The descendant, the Rev. Treborth Jones, for a year the minister of Salem Methodist Church, and previously at Chesterton, Cambridge, had refused to pay the church rate of 3s. 4d. levied on him at the latter place. He was then summoned to appear before the court but before this could be done he had moved to Aberystwyth. There, at his home in Bridge St., he was served with a distress warrant which had suffered "a monstrous increase" to 18s. 10d., a sum to be recovered by means of a sale of the minister's goods.

The sale was conducted by A. C. Lloyd Williams with Superintendent Richard Jones and Sergeant Phillips in attendance to keep the peace. When the sale began Treborth Jones came out and handed the auctioneer a set of silver plated fish carvers. The first bid, made by Prof. Edward Edwards, was 3d., gradually the offers increased to 35s. when the carvers were sold to David Lloyd, the timber merchant. This being more than enough to pay the fine, the sale then ended.

T. J. Samuel, the Town Clerk and a staunch Methodist, then mounted the steps fronting the house and addressed the crowd, thanking and congratulating Treborth Jones for "making a stand" and resisting the oppression of the Church rate. He described Jones's action as the Nonconformist's resistance to the Education Act of 1902. Others to speak in the same vein were Prof. Edwards, the Rev. T. A. Levi and the Rev. T. A. Penry. In his reply Treborth Jones made his beliefs clear and revealed that it was the second time that the fish carvers had been distrained.

From the date of its opening to 1948 the organisation of the Alexandra Rd. school remained unchanged with three departments—boys, girls and infants—each having its own head teacher. Outstanding among the headmistresses were Miss M. A. Nicklin of the girls' department, and the Misses Ann Morris and C. A. Samuel who, by the 1920's, had made the infants' department into a model of its kind. For 33 years the boys benefited from the services of D. J. Saer, a headmaster who was a fine teacher, a local historian and a psychologist who did some research work of standing in bilingualism, in association with Frank Smith and John Hughes (Montreal).

The 1944 Act led to changes at Alexandra Rd. which took over three years to establish. In September 1948 all the infants aged 4 to 7 years in the town were housed in Alexandra Rd. under Miss E. G. Morgan, the headmistress since 1929. The 202 infants enrolled were grouped into 8 classes, 3 Welsh speaking and the others English. Welsh had been taught to primary children at this school since 1895 and to senior pupils since 1890. The infants occupied only one part of the school, the remainder housed the 11+ pupils and was classed after 1948 as a secondary modern school under its new headmaster, Hywel Watkins. All primary pupils between the ages of 7 and 11 who wanted a free education were placed in the North Rd. school under Griffith Davies, one time Mayor of the town.

Then came another change. The movement for educating children in Welsh had led in 1939 to the formation, with only 7 pupils, of a small Welsh language school under Miss Norah Isaac at the headquarters of the *Urdd Gobaith Cymru* (Welsh League of Youth) in Llanbadarn Rd. This grew rapidly and in May 1946 it was moved to Lluest Gwilym, a mansion on the Waun, where in 1949 it came under the headmastership of Hywel D. Roberts, now Warden of the Guild of Graduates in the University of Wales. By January 1951 the school had 118 pupils and a staff of 6.

There was then a strong move in the town in favour of forming a Welsh school under the Local Education Authority, incorporating the Lluest venture, and in 1951 the education authority agreed to establish such an institution. In September of that year the North Rd. school was made into an English primary school for children aged 5 to 11 years, and the infants section of Alexandra Rd. turned into a primary school where, in two years, Welsh would be the first language for all pupils. The Lluest children were placed in a Welsh stream here. In September 1952, with the permission of their parents, all the Welsh-speaking children aged 5-11 in the North Rd. school were transferred to the primary section in Alexandra Rd. and *Yr Ysgol Gymraeg* (the Welsh School) came into existence. The first head was Miss Morgan and on her retirement in 1953, Hywel D. Roberts became the headmaster, followed by J. Hywel Jones three years later.

In the meantime a new secondary modern school, Dinas, was being built at Cefn-llan on the Waun, and in September 1955 the senior section at Alexandra Rd. moved up there. The North Rd. pupils were then moved to the vacated section at Alexandra Rd. and their old school fell vacant until it became part of the College of Further Education. For the first time since 1874, all the town's primary school pupils not in private schools were housed in the same building. This continued until 1969 when, under its headmaster, Ceiriog Evans, Griffith Davies's successor, the English section at Alexandra Rd. moved into a new school. Since that time the whole of the Alexandra Rd. building, apart from a small section set aside for a Teachers' Centre and a Remedial Unit, has been occupied by *Yr Ysgol Gymraeg*.

When the Welsh school was first opened in September 1952 it had 164 pupils, in 1967 it had 249 pupils of whom 68 came from English-speaking homes. In 1980 it has 212. In 1966 Huw J. Evans, formerly of Llancynfelyn, became its headmaster until his untimely death in 1973. A sculpture of Pinocchio, by Jonah Jones, was presented to the school by the Parent-Teachers Association in memory of Huw Evans. He was succeeded by the present headmaster, T. I. Thomas.

Ardwyn, the local grammar school, was not seriously affected by any of these changes until it was proposed to establish a comprehensive school in the town. David Samuel was succeeded in 1922 by Major Charles Lloyd Morgan who, on his appointment as headmaster of Judd's School Tonbridge, was succeeded in 1928 by D. C. Lewis of Swansea. He served until his retirement in 1954 when A. D. Lewis became headmaster. In response to the needs of children coming from the Welsh School, and in keeping with the mood of the time, A. D. Lewis introduced more Welsh into the school. It was towards the end of his period of office that it was finally decided to make a comprehensive school of Ardwyn and Dinas. The task of organising the change fell to his successor C. G. Suff, appointed headmaster in 1971

The change came in 1973 and for two years, while extensions were being made to the Cefn-llan school, Penglais Comprehensive School, as it came to be called, had to be housed in two buildings almost a mile apart. It was a difficult period, there was a considerable movement of teachers between the two buildings, and, in some subjects, some movement of pupils. Time-tables had to be planned to allow for travel time, and buses had to be used to take pupils from one building to the other. A late bus could cause chaos while insufficient room in a bus meant having to provide extra transport at short notice. One, at least, of the school caretakers spent much of his time driving a car, taking teachers and some pupils to and from one or other of the school buildings. It was a great relief to all concerned when Penglais School was eventually housed in the one building on the Waun in 1975. Its maximum pupil population to date was just over 1,260 in 1978, and in 1980 the first A-level pupils to be educated only in a comprehensive secondary school have been taking their examinations.

In the same year that Penglais school was formed, the first all-Welsh secondary school in the county was founded. For two years

(1973-75) this school shared the Ardwyn premises with the English medium school, and there were two headmasters on the premises, C. G. Suff and Gerald Morgan. When the English pupils left for the Waun the whole of the old Ardwyn premises became an all-Welsh comprehensive school named *Penweddig* after an ancient geographical division of North Cardiganshire. This school now numbers some 500 pupils.

A private school which earned much respect in the town was that established by Miss Dorothy Trotter in Meithrinfa in North Rd. in 1915. It catered not only for day pupils but also for boarders, some of whom were the children of parents serving

Alexandra Rd. School, now Ysgol Gymraeg

abroad. It was a good school and continued to give its pupils a sound education until Miss Trotter retired in 1949. Her brother, Wilfred Trotter, was an eminent London surgeon who operated on Edward VII.

Another school which was once private and still flourishes, is St. Padarns Primary Catholic School in the Old Vicarage in Llanbadarn Rd. In 1898 Bishop Mostyn visited Aberystwyth at a time when the Catholic Church in the town was going through a difficult period. To strengthen the church he advocated the setting up of a Roman Catholic school. Very soon afterwards this was made possible by the unexpected arrival in Aberystwyth of a group of Breton Sisters. Their first home was in 2, Penglais Terrace and then they bought Salisbury House, formerly a vicarage, and turned it into a school. It was a move of which Methodist Aberystwyth strongly disapproved, but gradually the St. Padarn Convent School overcame local prejudice and by 1908 was beginning to expand. The First World War accelerated this growth and by 1922 a bigger building was needed. At that time another Vicarage, that formerly occupied by the Vicar of Llanbadarn, also in Llanbadarn Rd., became vacant, it was bought by the Catholics and the school moved there, a building which it still occupies. During the inter-war years it drew its pupils from far and near, catering for boarders as well as for day pupils. Until 1965 it was an all-age school, but in that year it closed its senior department and three years later was recognised by the Ministry of Education as a voluntary aided primary school for about 120 Catholic pupils.

Plas Crug English Primary School

Penglais Comprehensive School

The University College of Wales

Castle House and Castle Hotel

As stated already, until the late 1780's the town authorities had been very loth to allow any building on the town commons but in 1788 Sir Uvedale Pryce of Foxley in Hereford applied for leave to enclose a piece of ground "from a certain Ground in Castle St. called Mrs. Jenkins' Garden to a Road leading down to a certain well called Funnon (Ffynnon) Twlc yr Hwch, being 132 yards in Length and bounded upon the North side by the Sea Rock". Permission was granted provided the house was built in two years, the garden laid out and a road made on the south side.

Sir Uvedale Pryce, a friend of Thomas Johnes of Hafod, and the author of an *Essay on the Picturesque*, gave the work of designing the house to the famous John Nash. The result was a triangular building with an octagonal tower at each corner and having a balcony overlooking a private promenade on the sea side. The drive to the house led roughly along the line of the present promenade from a gate a little to the south of what is now the Theological College. Castle House was built to serve as a summer residence for Lady Caroline, Sir Uvedale's wife, who became "very partial to the place". After her death it was modernised and in 1824 was used by the proprietor of the Talbot Inn as a superior lodging house. It was later let to yearly tenants and in 1848 was furnished and let in apartments. The house had changed hands more than once before it was bought by John Taylor the eminent mining engineer who did so much to develop lead mining in North Cardiganshire. After using it for some years he sold it to A. H. Novelli who extended the building but was careful to keep to the same style. The house continued to be occupied until the 1860's when it became vacant and was again for sale.

In the 1860's the prospect of Aberystwyth being connected to large centres of population by railway led many to anticipate a rapid expansion in the holiday trade. The Hafod Co. was busy building the Queen's Hotel, the Marine Terrace was being widened and the promenade built, and the iron pier was under construction. One who saw the possibilities of profit in such a situation was Thomas Savin, a man of extraordinary enterprise and wide knowledge of railways. It was he who had built the line from Machynlleth to Aberystwyth. He produced a scheme, probably the first package holiday deal, whereby tickets purchased at various railway station in parts of England would entitle the buyer not only to a train journey to and from Aberystwyth, but also to board and lodging at the resort. Castle House being for sale, Savin bought it and expressed his intention of turning it into a huge hotel "of which there would not be another like it in the kingdom". Had it been built to the original design this would have been true.

One morning in the spring of 1864, Savin sent for J. P. Seddon, a well-known architect, to survey the hotel and to suggest how it could be enlarged. Seddon went on to the roof of Castle House and sketched out a design for the southern wing. That night Savin approved the plans and immediately

Building the northern wing of Castle Hotel c. 1865. A part of Castle House, an octagonal tower, is on the right

Men at work on the main entrance to Castle Hotel 1864

The University College of Wales

The inadequacies of education in Wales were made abundantly clear by the *Report on the State of Education in Wales* 1847 and one of the reasons why it bothered thinking Welshmen was the dismal problem which the report highlighted. There was a pressing need for educated adults in every walk of Welsh life and there was no institution large enough to cope with it. The first serious discussion of the problem took place in 1854 when a meeting was convened in London by Hugh Owen at the house of Dr. Thomas Charles, grandson of Thomas Charles of Bala, and attended by eminent Welshmen from London and Wales. Little was achieved then, but it was made clear that the aim should be a University for Wales. In 1863, Hugh Owen revived the project but there was little interest among the majority of Welshmen until late in the 1860's, when the working men in the Principality, responding to pressure from the ministers and leaders of their Nonconformist chapels, began to wake up to the need for more education. Such a project demanded a great deal of money and among the first to respond to the appeal for funds were the quarrymen of North Wales. By the middle of 1865 more "pennies from the people" of Wales and some very hard canvassing had resulted in a fund of £5,000. Several sites for a college were offered to the sponsors, among them one at Menai Bridge and another at Llantwit Major. Conscious of the impatience of some of their supporters, Hugh Owen and his committee, confronted with a chance to buy a magnificent building cheaply in Aberystwyth, took the plunge and bought

gave orders for thirty men to make a start the following morning, as he wanted the new wing to be ready for visitors the following year. The result was that the work often proceeded faster than the plans could be prepared. Plans for another wing were ordered and five hundred men engaged to await the architect's instructions. Seddon, unable to keep up with the work, made a wooden model which enabled the army of draughtsmen on the spot to prepare plans. On one occasion it was observed that a group of workmen had no work to do, plans were hurriedly drawn and within an hour or so the men were busily engaged in building the main staircase. Even the handsome triangular porch at the main entrance was largely the result of the builders using their own initiative, for there were no plans available at first. Inside the building, a mixture of carved and uncarved stone in the

same arch still bears witness to Savin's desire to get the hotel built quickly and he did succeed in having part of it open in time. In June 1865 the Castle Hotel, as it was called, though incomplete, was opened to the public "well lighted by gas and replete with every convenience for the accommodation of families and private individuals".

But there was serious trouble ahead. Savin was engaged in a number of enterprises involving a total of about a million and a half pounds. The money-market panic of 1865-66 and a bank rate of ten per cent forced him to curtail some of his activities, and work on the Castle Hotel had to cease, after £80,000 had been spent on it. Efforts were then made to sell it, but at the auction the only bid was for £5,000. The hotel was widely regarded as a white elephant and remained unsold until March 1867.

Sir Hugh Owen

the Castle Hotel for the very low price of £10,000 in March 1867.

There was a good deal to be done and more money collected before the College could be opened but by October 1872 it was ready to receive at least some students. The first Principal was the Rev. Thomas Charles Edwards, 35 years old, already a leading Calvinistic Methodist minister in Liverpool, and a scholar of distinction, the protégé of Pattison and Jowett of Oxford. His staff consisted at first of only three members, Professor Hoskins Abrahall to take Classics, Professor H. M. Grimley for Mathematics and some Natural Science, and the Rev. Penllyn Jones as Registrar and Librarian. The opening day, 16 October 1872, was declared a public holiday in Aberystwyth.

There were 26 students ranging from boys of 14 to men in their mid 20's, all had to lodge in the town, paying 15s. to 16s. a week for full board. All the staff had heavy teaching loads, the Principal being responsible at first for the teaching of Greek, English Language and Literature, Logic and Philosophy as well as running the College. Yet he still found time to publish standard commentaries on *I Corinthians* and *Hebrews*.

The first years were very difficult, not only on account of the shortage of money but also because the eyes of every public and religious body in Wales was on the College, ready to find fault. Some of the criticisms levelled at the Principal were absurd, rabid Calvinists professed to be horrified because he had attended an athletics match "in broad daylight".

Gradually, the number of staff and students increased, but the load on the Principal and staff remained very heavy. Money was still a major problem and the future of the College was far from secure.

Two views of the first College building

Small sums trickled in from various bodies, eisteddfodau, groups of working men and a few benefactors but it was becoming clear that if the College was to survive there had to be government aid. Appeals were made to the Treasury but all were rejected despite the fact that help was being given freely to Scottish Universities and to the Queen's Colleges in Ireland. The common folk of Wales were still contributing, but it was not enough. However, these appeals did eventually have an effect, in 1881 the *Report on Intermediate and Higher Education in Wales* was published. The Government agreed that there should be a College in Cardiff or Swansea for South Wales and that the Aberystwyth institution, whether removed elsewhere or not, should be the College for North Wales. Aberystwyth then received a grant of £4,000 for 1882, but a conference held later in Chester to decide on the site of the College for North Wales, voted against Aberystwyth and chose Bangor. The Government grant thus went to Bangor and

The triangular portico and part of the southern wing of the College

The College on fire, 1885

Aberystwyth was again in danger. This was when the M.P.s Stuart Rendel and David Davies, Llandinam, both generous benefactors of the College, began to press Parliament over the matter. Rendel initiated a debate in the Commons and as a result, the Government agreed to give Aberystwyth a grant of £2,500 a year. But Rendel remained unsatisfied and continued the fight until, in 1885, the College was given the same as the other Welsh Colleges—£4,000 a year.

In the meantime, in July 1885, the College buildings were gutted by fire, doing damage worth £20,000. The art treasures donated to the College by G. E. J. Powell in 1879 and some valuable books were saved, but three workmen lost their lives fighting the blaze. Aberystwyth seemed finished, but a great wave of sympathy swept the country, and Welshmen everywhere, of all sects, rallied to the support of the College. This may have been noted by the Tory Government of the day when they yielded to the appeal and gave Aberystwyth parity of grant with the other Welsh Colleges.

The fire raised the problem of whether to rebuild or to erect a new college on another site. The former was much cheaper and the work of restoration began. The next session saw the student numbers up to 132 with 24 from England. To provide accommodation during the rebuilding, the Queen's Hotel was hired and all sorts of rooms in the town used as classrooms. Women students were first admitted in 1884, the following year *Abergeldie House* became the first Women's Hall of Residence, and the legendary Miss E. A. Carpenter appointed as Lady Principal to look after the female students. Carpenter Hall, converted from three large houses on Marine Terrace and made into a women's hostel in 1919, was named after her.

In 1889, the University College of Wales, Aberystwyth, was incorporated by Royal Charter, just in time for one of its greatest benefactors, David Davies, Llandinam, to see the College firmly rooted in Aberystwyth before he died in 1890. In the latter year Principal Edwards returned from what was partly a fund-raising visit to America with £1,050 to equip and furnish the College Library, which then became the College's most handsome room.

At about the same time, W. T. Jones of Melbourne, Australia, provided enough money for an ornamental roof to be built over the "College Corridor" thus forming the Quadrangle, a focus of student life for about 60 years, until the various departments began to move up to the Penglais campus. For many years, however, there was strict segregation of the sexes there, helped by a long line of museum cases down the middle of the "Quad" floor.

Having shepherded his college through the initial period of doubts, fears and frantic endeavour to a position where its existence was no longer threatened by extinction, Principal Edwards resigned in 1891 to become Principal of Bala College. He was succeeded by the son of an Aberdyfi police sergeant, Thomas Francis Roberts who, after a brilliant career at Aberystwyth and Oxford, had become a much-praised professor of Greek at the Cardiff University College.

T. F. Roberts, an ardent Baptist and a faithful member of Bethel Chapel, was fired by an intense desire to serve Wales and was utterly devoted to his new charge. Soon after taking office he set about creating in the College a Day Training Department for elementary school teachers. This was in 1892, two years later a secondary school training course was added. In that year student numbers reached 200 and the Old Student's Association was formed with

Principal T. F. Roberts

T. E. Ellis as its president.

In 1893 the University of Wales was incorporated by Royal Charter and it was decided that its Chancellor should always be a member of the Royal Family, the first being the Prince of Wales. Both Aberystwyth and Cardiff claimed the right to stage the installation ceremony and there were some sharp exchanges before the University Court, by a small majority, decided for Aberystwyth, much to Cardiff's annoyance.

When news of the impending Royal Visit was received in Aberystwyth, probably the first since that of Prince Henry in the early 15th century, there was much rejoicing in the town. Some special illuminations were put up and a torchlight procession held.

The date for the ceremony was fixed for 26 June 1896 and preparations began. It was also agreed that on the same day, the Princess of Wales should open the new hall of residence for women students for the College, and the new Pier Pavilion for the town. The fact that all those who were to receive honorary degrees were Liberals bothered Sir Francis Knollys, who was in charge of the Royal side of the arrangements, but as no Conservative who had done anything worthwhile for Welsh education could be found, no further objections were made. Once the news of the visit became public there was a rush to rent houses in the town and, inevitably, the cost of all kinds of accommodation became "truly astronomical".

The great day dawned bright and warm "with the slopes of the hoary crags purple with the lovely blossom of the heather, their margins lined with the golden flowers of the broom". From all parts of the Principality and across the border, thousands of "good men and true foregathered to participate in the Coronation of the Educational System of their country". In addition to the normal railway services, there were special trains from Newtown, Welshpool, Whitchurch, Ellesmere, Oswestry, Builth, Bangor, Caernarvon, Dolgallau and the coast, Taff Vale, Cardiff, Neath, Milford, Pembroke and Tenby, and Hereford. By mid morning there were from 25,000 to 30,000 people in the town.

The town decorations, carried out for the Town Council by a London firm, were described as the finest ever seen. Near the railway station was erected a light arch consisting of two royal groups of Venetian masts each surmounted by a crown and standing in bases upholstered in royal blue. Suspended between the masts was a banner bearing the words "Welcome to Aberystwyth". The arch was further enriched with heraldic shields and national banners. Venetian masts lined the route along Terrace Rd. and Marine Terrace, each surmounted with spearheads and hung with banners and heraldic devices, the masts being linked one to another by festoons of streamers of different colours. North Parade was lined with a series of royal lances couched, each bearing the Prince of Wales's emblem, the three feathers, and decorated with artificial flowers. At the junction of North Parade and Great Darkgate St. a royal canopy, 60 feet in diameter, was erected, and the latter street was festooned with artificial flowers suspended between, and hanging from houses, with baskets of varicoloured flowers lining the street. Each corner of the clock tower was connected to neighbouring buildings by lines of bunting and Queen St., Bridge St., Pier St. and Laura Place were all elaborately decorated with Venetian Masts joined by streamers. Portland St. too was decorated in the same way and at its junction with Terrace Rd. was erected a large floral canopy with masts.

Almost every house in the town bore some kind of decoration—flags, shields, trophies, bunting or bannerettes. Plynlimon House had flags galore and in the main doorway there was a 200-year-old spinning wheel worked by a buxom Welsh damsel in Welsh homespun and tall hat. Special lamps were erected along all the main streets.

The great W. E. Gladstone, despite his age, had arrived at the Queen's Hotel the previous evening and had expressed a wish to hear the singing of some Welsh songs. At 11.0 a.m. next morning the Rheidol Choir, dressed in Welsh costume, under their conductor J. B. Edwards, went to the hotel to sing to Gladstone, who later in the day had the degree of LL.D. of the University of Wales conferred on him by the Prince of Wales.

At 12.10 p.m. the Royal Party arrived at the station from Machynlleth where they had been staying with Earl Vane at Plas Machynlleth. The train was drawn by an engine decorated with evergreens, and carried in front a large circular device bearing the royal feathers. The platform, lined with carpet for the occasion, was guarded by a Company of the 1st Volunteer Battalion of the Welsh Regiment. The Royal Party was welcomed by Lord Rendel, President of the University College, and other dignitaries while a choir sang outside the station. At 12.30 the warships in the bay boomed their welcome by firing the Royal Salute.

The procession to the Installation Pavilion, a large marquee erected in front of the Town Hall in Queen's Square, was a grand affair made colourful by the soldiers uniforms, the academic dress of the University officials and the robes worn by the town councillors, the churchmen, and visiting dignitaries. At intervals during the ceremony of installation, music was provided by the Treorchy Male Voice Choir. After the Prince had been made Chancellor of the University of Wales, there was another procession to the College Hall where honorary degrees were conferred on Mr. Gladstone and others. Luncheon was held

The Installation Ceremony, 1896.

in the new Pier Pavilion opened that day by Princess Alexandra, and at 4.0 p.m. there was yet another procession, to the new women students' hostel at the northern end of Marine Terrace where, on a specially constructed wooden platform on the promenade, 700 children, conducted by the well-known J. T. Rees, sang to the Royal Party. Princess Alexandra then performed the opening ceremony for the hall which bears her name, and the party was entertained to tea there before returning along the Marine Terrace and Terrace Rd. to the railway station for the journey back to Machynlleth.

But for the ordinary people there was still much to do, to wander round the town examining the decorations, watching the giant warships in the bay and, after dark, being entertained by a fine display of fireworks from the pier head and the Castle grounds. By that time the lighting of the hundreds of fairy lights, the Chinese and Japanese lanterns and the Vauxhall lamps,

had turned Aberystwyth into a fairyland, while the powerful searchlights of the ships played on the town, castle and Constitution Hill.

The ceremony was a great success and went off without a hitch. The 184 policemen drafted into the area from a number of counties had little to do except to arrest the 3 or 4 pick pockets caught stealing. Even the *Western Mail* conceded, five months later, that it was the "most brilliant pageant witnessed in Wales in modern times", times which represented the climax of the "happy and glorious days" of the great Queen's reign.

The last decade of the century was marked by the growth and consolidation of work of University standard at Aberystwyth, and by a vigour and independence which were the outcome of the years of struggle against almost insuperable odds. The result was seen in the strong corporate life within the College amongst the students and staff, and in the constant and practical support given to the College by its Old Students Association. It had been customary from the 70's onwards for old students to visit their old college, especially on St. Davids Day, and to take part in its social life while there. After 1892 the Easter Reunion became an institution and continues to this day, it has proved a rallying ground for the support of the College in its many crises. There always has been a strong corporate life in the Aberystwyth College, its remoteness from large centres of population has strengthened this, by forcing the students to rely on their own resources.

Much thought was given during this

period to the acquisition of land for extensions, and in 1897 Lord Rendel bought 14 acres of Grogyddan land for £2,000 to provide a site for the proposed National Library and for new College buildings. Always a good friend to the College, he leased this to them for only a peppercorn rent and, later, when student numbers reached 400 and money was again in short supply, he undertook to contribute £750 a year during his lifetime towards the College for its maintenance, and £250 a year for scholarships. In 1898 Sir William Harcourt opened the Central Block devoted mainly to the Natural History Sciences. It was he who, as Chancellor of the Exchequer in 1894, had made the grant of £10,000 towards the scheme. The building of this block involved the demolition of the last remnants of the old Castle House.

The need for research facilities and accommodation, especially in the Chemistry department, made extension imperative, and a new temporary laboratory was opened in the Old Assembly Rooms. This problem was solved in 1907 by the generosity, once again, of the Llandinam family. David Davies and his sisters, the Misses Davies of Gregynog, bought land on Buarth Mawr and built the fine Edward Davies Laboratories in memory of their father, who had succeeded his father, the first David Davies of Llandinam, as one of the College treasurers.

Yet another gift was one of £1,000 given by Penry Vaughan Thomas and his family towards providing a College Gymnasium. The Old Students Association gave another £450 and Vaughan Thomas also paid the

Lord Davies of Llandinam

remainder. The Vicarage Field was then bought and levelled by David Davies and leased to the College for use as a sports ground on the understanding that the rent should be used to maintain a Professorship of Colonial History, to be built around Stanley Roberts, a Pembrokeshire man who had been Davies's tutor at Oxford. He occupied the chair from 1915 to 1934.

The number of departments increased rapidly during the principalship of T. F. Roberts. From 1891 to 1919 the following were formed—Agriculture, Education, Law, German, Music, Dairying, Geography and Anthropology, Pure Mathematics, Applied Mathematics, Political Science and Agricultural Botany. There was also a lectureship in Welsh History. This expansion

owed much to the generosity of the Misses Davies of Gregynog, who gave the College £100,000 over five years. This enabled the eminent H. J. Fleure to become Professor of Geography and Anthropology instead of Professor of Zoology. These ladies also wished to launch an ambitious Music scheme and, as a result, the well-known Dr. (later Sir) Walford Davies, organist and director of the choir at the Temple Church in London, was appointed Director of Music for the University of Wales and Professor at Aberystwyth in 1919. His enthusiasm and great energy made a tremendous impact on the musical life of the University and of Wales in general, not least because of his contribution to the musical side of broadcasting.

The re-establishment of a Music Chair was a reminder of Dr. Joseph Parry's brief period as professor (1874-80). His students, and the audiences which heard his choir, were delighted with him but the College Governors disliked his showman attitude to his work and he was forced to resign. When he left Aberystwyth, the townspeople turned out *en masse* to see him off.

It was generally difficult to establish a chair in those penurious days but in January 1901 it was resolved to set up a Faculty of Law and two appointments were made, one being the brilliant T. A. Levi son of the great Methodist leader, Thomas Levi, minister of Tabernacl. But money was short and Levi and his new colleague, Dr. Jethro Brown, had to travel the country giving lectures to articled clerks and others in Swansea and elsewhere in return for contributions to the upkeep of the Law Depart-

The plaque on Sir Walford Davies's former house in Brynymor Terrace

Dr. Joseph Parry

ment. Brown hated it but Levi seems to have revelled in it and did it extremely well. He produced a Law School at Aberystwyth which became the leading school for the teaching of Law in all the Universities of England and Wales, not excepting Oxford and Cambridge.

Another important institution which appeared at this time was the Students Representative Council, of which H. J. Fleure, then a student, was one of the founders. It was an attempt to secure, and to develop further, a greater degree of student control over their own affairs and a more democratic form of government in the College. A few years later the college magazine, the *Dragon*, began to be published.

By 1914 Principal Roberts was a sick man and very dependent on his registrar, John Humphreys Davies of Cwrt Mawr, a descendant of eminent Methodists on both sides of his family. He was an excellent administrator who knew the College, its inmates and Aberystwyth very well indeed. T. F. Roberts died in 1919, and despite the strong support for Dr. Thomas Jones, the Deputy Secretary of the Cabinet, J. H. Davies, who was himself a well-known Welsh scholar, was appointed principal. The College Staff respected Davies and welcomed the appointment, for the change could be made smoothly and without any "running-in" period. It was he who drew the Old Students Association's attention to the need for a larger Student's Union with the result that they bought the Old Assembly Rooms for that purpose. He supported David Evans's plan for a Student's Medical Service—one of the first in Britain—and in general created an invigorating atmosphere which promised well for the future of the College.

A venture which came into being at this time and was strongly supported by J. H. Davies, was the Welsh Plant Breeding Station. R. G. Stapledon had been on the staff since 1912; he firmly believed that Britain could, and should grow much more of its own food. In 1919 as a result of overtures made by the Professor of Agriculture, C. Bryner Jones, to Laurence Philipps (later Lord Milford), the latter endowed the College with £10,000 and £1,000 a year for ten years to establish a Welsh Plant Breeding Station (P.B.S.), modelled on that at Cambridge, and designed to improve hill farming. Stapledon was made Director and Professor of Agricultural Botany and, with his staff, took over the Old Greens Foundry in Alexandra Rd., bought for £3,700, and adapted for the work involved. Starting with 100 acres of farmland for experimental purposes, in 20 years the P.B.S. made tremendous and valuable contributions to land improvement, and made the name of Aberystwyth known all

Principal J. H. Davies

over the world. But the endowment was for 10 years only and the future of the P.B.S. seemed in jeopardy when, as a result of a letter written by the College Principal to the *Times*, Sir Julien Cahn gave £3,000 a year for seven years and the work was able to continue. After the Second World War it was said by a former Minister of Agriculture that without the improvements made by the P.B.S. under Stapledon "the country would have been starved of food" and would not have survived war-time conditions so successfully.

Unfortunately, when in London in 1923, J. H. Davies was struck by a falling tree and was so injured that he died a premature death in 1926. In the same year the College lost its aged President and generous benefactor, Sir John Williams. The latter was promptly succeeded by David Davies, Llandinam. The student numbers were now over 1,000.

One of Aberystwyth's professors during the 1920's was R. D. Laurie who took over the Zoology department when Professor Fleure vacated this for the Chair of Geography and Anthropology. When Laurie took over, the Zoology department was poorly housed and very short of accommodation, and there was no money for any alterations or extensions. Behind Green's Foundry and not used by the P.B.S., were the buildings of the Old Slate Works, and in 1924 Laurie, assisted by his staff and some students, started a programme of "do-it-yourself" alteration which produced a useful, if far from beautiful extension for his department. Professor Laurie was founder, first President, and honorary General

Secretary of the Association of University Teachers, and for 33 years he ran the association from his home in Caradog Rd. at an incredibly low cost.

J. H. Davies was succeeded in 1927 by Sir Henry Stuart Jones, Camden Professor of Ancient History at Oxford. Though not a Welshman, he mastered the language in a surprisingly short time. His principalship saw the establishment of the departments of Welsh History and Agricultural Economics. This was when the decision was made to concentrate future building on the Penglais site, and the following year (1929) 87 acres on Penglais were purchased and presented to the College by Joseph Davies Bryan, an old student who had built up a large and prosperous business in Egypt and bought a house in Aberystwyth against his retirement. Hopes of another large donation of money from another source, enough to start building on the new site, were not realised.

The year 1933 saw the College Hall off Queen's Rd. destroyed by fire after only eleven year's use. This was where, on occasions, public lectures given by C. K. Webster, Professor of International Politics,

The College Hall in Queen's Rd.

and others, attracted journalists from all over Britain, and were reported in all the world's free newspapers. No attempt was made to rebuild the hall and the College was without a large auditorium until the Great Hall was built in the 1970's. The following year (1934) Sir Henry Stuart Jones resigned. He was the only Anglican Principal to serve the Aberystwyth College.

In 1934 came the appointment as Principal of an extremely able young man, Ifor Leslie Evans, Fellow and Bursar of St John's College, Cambridge, and an economist of the first rank. His "reign" can be divided into three parts. The first five years were full of promise, he seemed prepared to reorganise and revitalize every department in the College. Departmental surveys were undertaken, an extensive review of Funds and Trusts was prepared and the office of Registrar, vacant since 1919, was revived. He was very taken by the possibilities of the Penglais site and by 1936 had completed, with a firm of architects, a provisional layout of the proposed College buildings. A year later building began on the handsome Rural Science Block. Principal Evans was inten-

The College Hall on fire 1933

sely interested in the future of the College, which he believed would develop into a fine institution. During this period, because of the economic recession, student numbers fell, but the financial state of the College improved, partly because of the Principal's wise policy, higher fees, and by the improved administration of the College's affairs which followed the appointment of J. Morgan Jones as registrar.

Then came the 1939-45 war and the situation changed. Leslie Evans found this period very frustrating, personally and administratively, for although he had much to offer the war effort, he was never given a chance to serve. During the war the College began to receive its substantial share of the assets of the disestablished Church of Wales, and the Principal was for many years the chairman of the University Estates Committee which handled these and other funds. He proved an able steward of the University and College finances.

When peace was declared Principal Evans found himself out of sympathy with the government policy for more and larger universities. He saw no connection between the needs of Aberystwyth and the large scale development of pure and applied science. His Penglais plan envisaged a harmonious collection of attractive buildings built of traditional materials and including a Great Hall, Students Union and a Hall of Residence for Women, the whole catering for not more than 1,200 students. It would have been a handsome campus. As a result of the changes in policy he lost interest in much of the College's future development, and immersed himself in such matters as

the College farms and estates, the P.B.S., and the University of Wales estates. He died in 1952 leaving the College in a sound financial state for future development.

After a period during which Professor Lily Newton proved a worthy Acting Principal, Morgan Goronwy Rees, the son of yet another minister of Tabernacl Chapel, Fellow and Bursar of All Souls, author, journalist and having a distinguished war record, was appointed Principal in 1953. But Goronwy Rees and Aberystwyth College did not see eye to eye with one another and in 1957 he resigned.

Then came a period of relative stability and steady growth under the Principalship of Dr. (later Sir) Thomas Parry, an eminent Welsh scholar, the National Librarian and a former Professor of Welsh at Bangor. This is when the post-war layout of the Penglais site was finally settled and large scale building began. During Dr. Parry's term of office several new chairs were established and in 1960 there were 1,500 students in College. The expansion in numbers again led to the fear that the Welsh character of the College was being seriously threatened. The proportion of students coming from Wales fell from 66% in 1960 to 47% in 1965 and to 37% in 1969 when there were 2,000 students. Early in the 1960's it was made clear that there were many who felt that the College could, and should do more to foster the Welsh language. In 1963 the Council approved in principle that Welsh be given equal status with English in the College. This was not fully implemented but it was recommended that all College literature, signs etc. be bilingual. The academic staff

was deeply divided on this issue. The teaching of subjects through the medium of Welsh, long practiced in the Education department, became more common, and, despite much opposition, two of the hostels became Welsh Halls, Pantycelyn for men and Neuadd Davies for women. It was at the former that Prince Charles spent a term in 1969 learning to speak Welsh in preparation for his Investiture.

Dr. Parry's Principalship was one of wise leadership resulting in planned growth in every direction. It was not an easy term of office, for this was a period of protest when many of the traditional features of life, university life especially, were under fierce attack from the young. The Principal's easy, democratic way of dealing with students and staff suited Aberystwyth admirably, and most people regretted his going.

The unanimous choice of his successor in 1969 was Sir Goronwy Hopkin Daniel, an old student, a former university teacher and the first Permanent Secretary to the Welsh Office. Under him the College continued to run smoothly. In 1970 the superb Great Hall and the first stage of the fine new Students' Union building were opened on Penglais. In October 1972 Theatr y Werin (the People's Theatre) opened its doors. This with the Great Hall, a small studio theatre and the Exhibition Gallery form the Arts Centre, a million pound complex well equipped for use by professional and amateur companies for drama, dance and musical performances.

Principal Sir Goronwy Daniel retired in 1979 and was succeeded by Dr. Gareth Owen, formerly Professor of Zoology at

Queen's University, Belfast. The move up Penglais is proceeding apace, almost all the departments housed in the Old College are now on the new site, which includes a handsome College Library. A number of buildings in the town will have to be put to new use, the old Green's Foundry, a reminder of the town's industrial past, will probably be demolished.

The College by the Sea, a listed building, and an excellent example of Victorian architecture, established largely with the help of the ordinary people of Wales, will remain a monument to the successful endeavours of a poor nation to help itself to higher education.

The Physical Sciences Block on the Penglais Campus

The Great Hall and the new College Library

Literary Societies and the Public Library

At the beginning of the 19th century, at the top of Bridge St. between Princess St. and Upper Great Darkgate St. there was a tavern known as the *Shades*. It was then kept by Thomas Jones a native of Llangwyryfon who had prospered in a milk business in London. But Thomas found that inn-keeping was not as lucrative as selling milk and went back to Blaennant, Llangwyryfon. He was succeeded at the *Shades* by David Davies, also of Llangwyryfon and he, too, failed to make a success of the inn. No tavern had ever thrived in Llangwyryfon and apparently, its natives made poor innkeepers.

The inn then came into the hands of **Margaret Morris, sister to Dafydd Phillips,** deacon and precentor at Tabernacl Church. Peggy Philips, as Margaret Morris was known in Aberystwyth, was a well known character with a good strong voice. She was the wife of Jenkin Morris, a carrier of Trefechan and son of one of the founders of Methodism at Rhydyfelin. Having been converted to temperance, Peggy turned the Shades into a Temperance House where she became famous for her elderberry wine, probably as potent as anything that came from the brewhouse. The house then became the rendezvous for certain young men of a literary turn who wished to form a literary society. They met in the back parlour once a week.

About 1820 a wave of nationalism swept Wales and numerous Welsh societies were set up to study Welsh and things Welsh. One such society was formed in Aberystwyth in 1823 and that, too, first met at the Shades. It lasted about a year. The old inn later became a storehouse for Doughton the Chemist whose business was one shop away from the corner of Bridge St. and Great Darkgate St.. The corner shop was formerly kept by Robert Doughton, a ship's chandler and an ironmonger. He was the chemist's father.

Another Welsh society which may have developed out of the above was the *Cymreigyddion*. An account in *Seren Gomer* tells of this society's annual meeting in March 1825. The members met at 10.30 a.m. at the Gogerddan Arms, their regular meeting place, and from there marched in procession to the Old Assembly Rooms headed by a military band. There they were awaited by a number of ladies and gentlemen of the town and district who had been specially invited. The object of the meeting was to present prizes to the winners of literary competitions held by the society. Every prizewinner was expected to make a speech or recite a poem on his special subject. Among the subjects were *Y Mor* (the Sea), *Heddwch* (Peace) and *Cywydd ar Gastell Aberystwyth*, a peculiarly Welsh kind of poem on Aberystwyth Castle.

Frank Careswell, a local harpist and the winner of a prize of two guineas, played some Welsh airs, and all sat down to a feast accompanied by *penillion* singing.

None of the above societies appears to have been long lived and the same was true of the Literary, Scientific and Mechanics Institute formed in 1850 and aimed at giving shopworkers and working people in general a chance to enrich their minds by studying the arts and sciences. Its chairman was Dr. Henry Bell, a local physician who lived in Marine Terrace and ran Penbryn House, the Bath House established by Dr. Rice Williams at the north end of the sea front. The secretary was the Rev. John Williams of Band of Hope fame, and a leading member of the work committee was *Ivon*. But the venture was not a success probably because of the existence of the much more stimulating Radical Club.

The Radical Club was formed in 1832 to discuss current affairs in general and the town's affairs in particular. They did not have to wait long for burning topics to arise. The actions of the Town Improvement Commissioners provided plenty of topics for debate—the so-called extravagant demands of the Commissioners, the high water rate, the supply of water, the price of gas, and sanitation in the town, led to lively debate and frequent protests. The members of the club were greatly animated and generated much heat, and their protests did produce economies. The leader of the Radicals was Joseph Roberts, a man of considerable ability who was more interested in the affairs of others than in his own. He lived at London House. The club met at the Talbot Hotel until it ceased to exist in 1852.

About 1850, a Welsh Literary Society was started by Ivon Jones, John Matthews, Ieuan Gwyllt and others, to promote an interest in Welsh language and literature. It held an eisteddfod every year; in 1853 a prize of 20 guineas was offered for the best poem on Ieuan Gwynedd, Ioan Tegid, Rhys Stephens and Morgan Howell, four eminent Welshmen who had died in 1852.

Such a prize attracted exceptional entries, Caledfryn took a whole afternoon (3 hours) to deliver his adjudication, reading through every poem in the process. The winner was the Rev. W. Ambrose of Portmadoc.

The Junior Radical Club was founded in 1882-83 under the presidency of W. H. Palmer, later the Mayor of the borough. It moved to the Liberal Club in St. James Square in 1901. Unlike its predecessor it devoted almost all its meetings to discussing national rather than local affairs—the "Duties and Rights of Minorities", the "Nationalisation of Railways and Land" etc. and the occasional literary topic such as "A Night with the Poets". It horrified the older members of the town by ending its meetings with *Hen Wlad fy Nhadau* instead of *God Save the Queen*. There were about 200 members.

A movement which led to a much more permanent institution was the formation of the Literary Institute. Its chief promoters were Canon Phillips and T. B. O'Halloran, editor of the *Aberystwyth Observer*. They held their meetings in the building now occupied by the solicitors Roberts and Evans, in upper Great Darkgate St. The institute later moved to premises owned by John James in North Parade on a site now occupied by the Barclays Bank. Over the years the members collected quite a number of books and it was these that formed the nucleus of the first free library in the town.

Another Literary Society which was glad of the library was that formed at the Assembly Rooms in 1880 by the Rev. T. A. Penry. There were both lectures and debat-

es and the number of members reached 300.

The Public Library and Museums Act was passed in 1871 and Aberystwyth was among the first to adopt it. The library was first opened in Compton House in Pier St. and most of its first books were those presented to it by the Literary Institute. The first librarian was Edward Hughes. Initially it was a poor affair and there were many complaints about the foul atmosphere of the small gas-lit room and the shortage of books. Its annual income was only £80, the yield from a penny rate. Of this, £20 was paid to the librarian, £15 was spent on newspapers, and from £10 to £20 on bookbinding. In 1874 only £4. 8s. 6d. was available for purchasing books. Largely because of these complaints and the comments of John Gibson in the *Cambrian News*, other premises were sought and the library was moved to the Assembly Rooms. There, surroundings were much more congenial, and gradually, mainly because of the generosity of local people, especially Col. Powell of Nanteos, the library had accumulated about 3,000 books by the time it was again moved back to Pier St. in 1903, to the premises vacated by the National Provincial Bank at the corner with Eastgate.

A gift of £3,000 from the Andrew Carnegie Trust enabled the Corporation to build the present Public Library on its present site. The foundation stone was laid by David Davies Llandinam on a fine day in July 1905 when a procession was held and flags and bunting decorated the streets. The new building was opened the following April by Mrs. Vaughan Davies of Tanybwlch,

These premises were demolished to make room for the Carnegie Library in Alfred Place

members of which read set books and meet to discuss them under the direction of college tutors. Alun Edwards has done a great deal for education and the Welsh language in Ceredigion.

The Aberystwyth library produced a valuable *Bibliography of Cardiganshire* prepared by John Lewis Jones who is also responsible for the collection and arrangement of a first class collection of photographic negatives, over 10,000 in number, illustrating life in Ceredigion past and present. A most useful local history library is now being formed.

The building in Alfred Place was designed by Paynton, a well known architect of the period. It contains some interesting examples of *Art Nouveau,* especially the attractive green tiles in the lobby.

The Public Library

wife of the M.P. for Cardiganshire.

Until 1947 there were two free libraries in the town, the Borough Library in Alfred Place and the County Library in Queen's Square. In that year they were united as the Cardiganshire Joint Library and Ivor Davies, a London Welshman, was appointed librarian. He soon saw the need to make it easier for the country people to borrow books, and tried to get the County Council to purchase a van for this purpose. But there was no money available and an approach was then made to another former London Welshman, Dr. Alban Davies of Llanrhystud whose generosity had helped many a cause in Cardiganshire. He, too, refused, but his wife offered to help and as a result the first circulating library van

appeared in the county, the first in Wales if not in England and Wales.

Ivor Davies died in 1949 and was succeeded by Alun Edwards who greatly expanded the circulating library scheme, which now covers the whole of Ceredigion, visiting remote villages and even farms. He has also played a leading part in the establishment of the Welsh College of Librarians at Llanbadarn Fawr, the publication of Welsh books and books for children, and the compilation of a good collection of cassettes containing recordings of music, talks on Welsh life-styles past and present, and aids to learning languages. In conjunction with the University College's Department of Extra Mural Studies he has also launched book-discussion groups, the

The National Library of Wales

The National Library of Wales

While the British Museum was being formed in the mid 18th century, a group of Welshmen in London were establishing the first *Society* of *Cymmrodorion* to cultivate the Welsh language and to search into the antiquities of Britain. The constitution of the society provided for a library at the Welsh School in Clerkenwell Green, maintained by the *Society of Antient Britons*. The librarian was to procure a copy of every book printed, or to be printed, in Welsh, and as many manuscripts as could be acquired, in any language, which would help to promote the aims of that society. When the first society was dissolved the books etc. were left in the care of the Welsh School, then in Grays Inn Rd. The first mention of a National Library of Wales may have been when Edward Williams (Iolo Morgannwg) made a will, leaving his manuscripts and books to such a library provided it was formed before 1820. But in 1843 the prospects of establishing such a place seemed so remote that the manuscripts at the school, and those belonging to the second Society of Cymmrodorion were presented to the British Museum. In 1850 Sir Thomas Phillipps's magnificent collection was offered to the nation if a central place could be found to house them, but no place could be found.

In 1858, at the National Eisteddfod in Llangollen, G. H. Whalley of the Cambrian Railway proposed that a museum and records office for Welsh manuscripts and books should be established. This set people thinking, but again nothing was done.

The first definite steps made towards the creation of the library were taken at the National Eisteddfod in Mold in 1873. There, largely through the efforts of Sir Hugh Owen and Stephen Evans, a committee was formed to consider the matter. It was taken for granted that the library would be housed at the University College in Aberystwyth and it was Principal Edwards who first gave practical form to the idea. He was himself the possesor of a fine library of Welsh books and manuscripts and it was he who succeeded in negotiating the purchase of the collection of *Gwrnant*, a well-known Welsh solicitor in London. These were the nucleus of the national library collection. The museum at the college was already fairly well stocked, largely due to the efforts of Professor Rudler and others.

Unfortunately, the calamitous fire of 1885 put a stop to all this, the ensuing financial straits allowed no thought to be given to national libraries and museums. But the idea was not forgotten and a conversation between Principal Edwards and Gwenogvryn Evans in 1895 put new life into the movement. In the meantime, in 1893, [Sir] John Herbert Lewis, M.P., began his campaign in the House of Commons for a share for Wales of the Museums Grant. In 1904 the Chancellor of the Exchequer indicated that support would probably be forthcoming in the next budget.

By that time Sir John Williams, T. E. Ellis, Dr. Henry Owen, J. H. Davies and others had been busy putting new life into, and reorganizing, the movement for a national library; preferably in Aberystwyth. Rough catalogues were compiled and circulated to people asking for contributions to the collection. A committee covering the whole of Wales was formed and went to work on the business of getting the library.

From the beginning Sir John Williams saw the need to acquire a site near the town of Aberystwyth and, with the help of the town's civic leaders, Peter Jones, C. M. Williams and D. C. Roberts, the present Grogyddan site was chosen. It was T. E. Ellis who persuaded Lord Rendel to purchase it for the proposed library.

Next came the business of acquiring a collection of books and manuscripts worthy of a national library, and funds were low, but again Sir John Willims, T. E. Ellis,

Lord Rendel

J. H. Davies, Sir Henry Owen and others came to the rescue, they not only promised to bequeath to the library their own collections but also set about adding to them. The result was a very fine collection indeed. The superb Peniarth-Hengwrt MSS acquired through the generosity of Sir John Williams, represents the labours of Robert Vaughan of Hengwrt and his friend John Jones of Gellilyfdy in the 17th century, both experts in their day, and fine Welsh scholars. The Shirburn collection contained the pick of that gathered by Edward Lhuyd, the father of modern philology, born at Glanfread near Aberystwyth, as well as the manuscripts of the Revs. Samuel and Moses Williams of Llangynllo. Another collection promised to the library was that of *Gwallter Mechain*, the Rev. Walter Davies, the finest Welsh literateur of his day. Together they constituted a collection made by some of the greatest experts in this field in Wales, from the 16th to the 19th centuries.

In addition, the printed books promised by Sir John Willimas (16th and 17th centuries) and J. H. Davies (18th century) were of the top rank.

But Aberystwyth was not the only town wanting to house the new library. Cardiff set about strengthening its claim by forming as fine a collection of books and manuscripts as it could, and it soon became clear that the struggle was between Aberystwyth and Cardiff. Sir John Williams and others went around the country seeking support for Aberystwyth and succeeded in getting this from eight of the thirteen counties.

On behalf of Aberystwyth it was claimed

that it was much more truly Welsh than Cardiff, where there was "not much that was Welsh in spirit". Aberystwyth was also more centrally placed in Wales, had a much finer collection of books and manuscripts than Cardiff, was able to provide free a 14-acre site, and had already collected £20,000 towards the cost of the building.

A large number of small boys had been recruited to address and send out letters of appeal for contributions to the library in Aberystwyth. They did the work at the Old Assembly Rooms and were paid 1s. a hundred letters.

Cardiff, too, claimed a fine collection but this proved to be less valuable than was claimed. The city authorities also made much of the size and progressive nature of its population and hinterland, and of the remoteness and supposed lack of vitality of Aberystwyth.

In June 1905, the Privy Council announced that Aberystwyth was to have the

Preparing the site for the National Library C. 1910

National Library and Cardiff the Museum. The *Western Mail* stated that the decision would remain "a permanent reminder of the inability of Wales to agree on any question of national importance . . . because of the rival jealousies which had been the greatest enemies of Welsh nationalism in the past". It was also argued that the National Library of Wales could never become a national institution in the true sense since it was isolated from the main currents of Welsh life and out of touch with the vitalizing influences at work inside and outside the Principality. There were even accusations of Aberystwyth supporters having made *ex parte* statements to the Privy Council, and threats of re-opening the whole business, but nothing was done. Almost all the other parts of Wales welcomed the choice of venue.

It seems clear from some of Sir John Williams's statements that had the Privy Council supported Cardiff, he would have worked to build a magnificent library to

Sir John Williams and the foundation stone

house his, and the other collections promised, in Aberystwyth. The Privy Council must have known this.

The news of the Privy Council's decision was received with enthusiasm by the town and college and it was resolved to hold a torchlight procession as a celebration. Unfortunately it proved a fiasco. The college students were invited to attend and asked to put on a tableaux but they failed to do this and turned up looking like "a half disorderly crowd of gownless and capless boys". Very few of the college staff attended and none wore academic dress. The Town Council, too, made a poor show, few attended and not one wore his robes. The lifeboat and its crew, always a popular part of a procession, failed to appear.

The procession was timed to start at 9.0 p.m. from Smithfield, where a large crowd of townspeople and visitors was assembled. A band was engaged but because of a disagreement over whether it should march before or after the motor cars the big drum went off in a huff and without it the band "sounded like playing Hamlet with Hamlet left out".

Matters were made worse by the fact that the procession was very closely followed by the rotary road brush (it being Saturday night) and three watering carts minus any decoration of any kind, making a ludicrous anticlimax. As the *Cambrian News* reported "Altogether it was the poorest procession Aberystwyth has ever seen".

The Library received its Charter of Incorpation from King Edward VII in 1907.

About two years later the first Librarian, John Ballinger, began work at the Old Assembly Rooms in Aberystwyth where the library's collections were housed until the new buildings were erected. He was a native of Pontnewydd in Gwent, and formerly the librarian of Cardiff Library, which he had made into a very good institution.

When building began, it was resolved that the foundation stone should be laid by their Majesties King George V and Queen Mary when visiting Wales for the investiture of the Prince of Wales in Caernarvon. The date fixed for the visit to Aberystwyth was 15 July 1911. As in 1896, the Royal Party stayed at Plas Machynlleth with the Marquess of Vane and Tempest. The town was profusely decorated for the visit, but instead of the streets being lined with the Venetian masts so dominant in 1896, they were lined with garlands of green leaves and clusters of purple flowers. A large number of policemen were drafted into the town.

The Royal Party was met at the railway

Building the central block

The decorations for the Royal Visit

The Royal Party at the railway station

King George V and Queen Mary at the library site

station by the civic dignitaries and a guard of honour mounted by the 1st Battalion of the South Wales Borderers in their scarlet tunics. They were greeted with singing by the Moelwyn Male Voice Choir accompanied by a Royal Navy band. The Royal Carriage was escorted to the National Library site by a travelling escort of Household Cavalry in full dress uniform. Many thousands of people, most of whom had travelled to Aberystwyth by special trains, lined the route. At the entrance to the National Library drive, the procession paused to listen to the singing of 4,000 school children from every part of the county.

After the King had laid the foundation stone the eight warships in the bay fired their 21 gun salute. Beneath the stone were embedded copper caskets containing a set of George V coins, a copy of the charter of the National Library of Wales, certain reports, photographs of the Library's president, chairman and chairman of the building committee, a newspaper account of the investiture at Caernarvon and an investiture medal.

After laying the stones, the King conferred the Grand Cross of the Victorian Order on the President of the Library, Sir John Williams, and the Order of St. Andrew on the Librarian, John Ballinger. The Royal Party returned to the town and visited the University College before returning to Machynlleth.

No fewer than 107 trains entered Aberystwyth station that day, some from as far afield as Bristol, the East Midlands and the North of England. Over 20,000 people came to Aberystwyth to see the Royal Party. A banquet was held in the Pier Pavilion that evening. A year later the library received its first books under the Copyright Act of 1911, and the occupation of the new building, on a commanding position overlooking Cardigan Bay, began in 1916.

The National Library was again the recipient of a Royal Visit on 16 July 1937 when King George VI and Queen Elizabeth came to open the new Central Block at the institution. On this occasion the Royal Party spent the night on the Royal Train somewhere between Aberystwyth and Carmarthen. It was a brief visit with far less ceremony than on previous occasions. But the town was again profusely decorated with red, white and blue streamers, flags, banners and heraldic devices. The guard of honour at the station was a group of ex-service men led by Colonel Taylor Lloyd, some 2000 policemen from all part of Wales lined the route, reinforced in places by soldiers from the various Welsh regiments, complete with bands and a regimental goat. One feature which reflected the Kings special interest was the large number of youth organisations lining the route including the Welsh League of Youth (Yr Urdd).

The Library received its third visit from a reigning monarch on 8 August 1955 when the Queen and the Duke of Edinburgh came to open the final section of the library, according to the original plan. On the appointed day the summer population of 20,000 was swollen to 60,000 and people began to line the Royal route at 7.00 a.m. The town was decorated with what was said to be the biggest floral display that Aberystwyth had ever seen. After spending the night in the Royal Train, the Queen was met at the station by local dignitaries and a guard of honour composed of the Welsh Guards in their scarlet uniforms. At the National Library the Royal Party was entertained by the Aberystwyth Madrigal Choir under Charles Clements.

After the ceremony at the Library the Queen and the Duke proceeded to Gogerddan to open the new headquarters of the U.C.W. Plant Breeding Station and the experimental gardens.

The object of the Library is to collect, preserve, and make available for use by research workers and others, all books, manuscripts, documents, etc., in Welsh or any other Celtic language, or which deal with the Welsh and other Celtic peoples; and further, works on all subjects and in all languages which help to attain the purposes for which the University of Wales and other educational institutions in Wales were founded.

The collection of Welsh printed books and manuscripts, the most valuable portion of which, as stated above, was brought together by the munificence of Sir John Williams, Bart., G.C.V.O., is the finest in the world. These he presented to the library on January 1, 1909. Many other well known collections of books, manuscripts and historical records have since been acquired by gift, purchase, bequest or on deposit.

Included in the Library's collection of manuscripts are THE BLACK BOOK OF CARMARTHEN, the oldest manuscript in the Welsh language, written at Carmarthen at the end of the 12th century; many of the oldest manuscripts of Welsh poetry, such as the Henregadredd MS., which contains poems of the bards of the period of the independent Welsh princes; the oldest manuscript of the Mabinogion; the Laws of Hywel Dda, and the Bruts of Chronicles; and a valuable manuscript of CHAUCER'S CANTERBURY TALES (The Hengwrt Chaucer).

The Library has also received notable accessions in general literature. For example, it has a superb collection of early French romances, printed and in manuscript, while its collection of early editions and manuscripts of LE ROMAN DE LA ROSE and of early editions of Euclid are among the finest in the world. Since July, 1912, the Library, under the Copyright Act of 1911, has been entitled to claim a copy of all books, pamphlets, maps, volume and sheet music, etc., published within the British Isles, a privilege it enjoys in common with five other principal libraries in Great Britain and Ireland. This alone means growth at the rate of about 45,000 items annually, and has assisted materially towards realising the second purpose defined by the Charter, namely, the formation of a general reference library where students and workers may obtain material for their work.

The number of printed volumes is approximately 2,000,000 and of manuscripts 30,000, whilst deeds, documents and records number over 3,500,000. There is also a large collection of maps, portraits, topographical prints and drawings

King George VI and Queen Elizabeth at the Library 1937

Queen Elizabeth II and Prince Philip at the Library 1955

dealing with Wales and the four border counties.

The Library is the national storehouse for printed, manuscript and graphic material relating to Wales. But, and especially since the passing of the Copyright Act of 1911, it has become something more than a general reference library for Wales; it is a 'national' library in the widest sense of that term, catering for the needs of all, irrespective of the language which they speak or of the subject in which they are interested. By means of its photostat and microfilm apparatus, the library is able to supply facsimile copies of books, manuscripts and documents of all kinds for the use of research workers who are unable to visit Aberystwyth. The library is available for use, without charge, by any responsible person who obtains a ticket of admission as a reader.

The first librarian, Sir John Ballinger, served from 1909 to 1930, his successors have been Sir William Llewelyn Davies, Sir Thomas Parry 1953-58, Dr. Evan David Jones 1958-69, Dr. David Jenkins 1969-80, and Dr. Robert Geraint Gruffydd 1980- .

Politics

For over three centuries, Cardiganshire county and its boroughs were represented in Parliament by members of the gentry or their nominees. It was hoped that the passing of the Reform Act of 1832 and the Municipal Corporations Act of 1835 would lead to more democratic forms of government. This did happen to some extent in local government in Aberystwyth but the Acts had very little effect on parliamentary representation in Cardiganshire and, until well into the second half of the 19th century, Aberystwyth's parliamentary politics continued to be of the deferential type. The Gogerddan family held one of the county's parliamentary seats continuously from 1818 to 1855. The town was too dependent on the gentry-dominated countryside, and too accustomed to defer to the wishes of the Pryses and the Powells, who owned large sections of the town and its immediate surroundings, for it to be politically independent. Every candidate for a parliamentary election was expected to seek the approval of the ruling house, Gogerddan. Henry Richards's withdrawal from the Cardiganshire election of 1865 was due largely to the failure of the county's Nonconformists to show any spirit of independence.

The Reform Act of 1867 did extend the franchise and this may have helped to secure the first Liberal victory in 1868, but even then the candidate, Evan Matthew Richards, had to travel to Gogerddan to be approved by the head of the house before he delivered his address to the electors. During the campaign he continually stressed the fact that his candidature was approved by Gogerddan. His election HQ was the old Gogerddan town house in Bridge St. The next election was won by the Tories.

But attitudes were changing, and by the 80's the situation was very different. A new urban middle class was emerging in Aberystwyth, shopkeepers, tradesmen, bankers, doctors, solicitors and ministers of religion, natural leaders who were becoming impatient with the politics of deference. Such were John James, Peter Jones, D. C. Roberts, C. M. Williams Job Miles and T. A. Levi, all Liberal Nonconformists. Their voice was that of the dynamic, vitriolic John Gibson of the *Cambrian News,* no regular chapel goer but a powerful critic of the Establishment and tradition for almost half a century. This force was emerging at a time when the squirearchy was becoming economically less able to resist the change. The deep agricultural depression and the closure of lead mines had seriously reduced their revenues. Nor did the county's gentry have a leader of any note at this period.

The result was seen in the election of 1885. Unlike his Liberal predecessor in 1868, David Davies of Llandinam ignored the landed gentry when he decided to become a candidate in Cardiganshire, his appeal was to the Methodists. He defeated Vaughan Davies, the Tory candidate, by over 2,000 votes. Probably because of his wealth he did have the support of some of the squirearchy, but his appeal was to the chapels. There were over 13,000 Methodists in the county in 1885.

This was the beginning of the Liberal ascendency in Cardiganshire but there was soon a crisis. David Davies proved to be less radical then was hoped, and too interested in becoming a landowner himself to please his constituents. For all his Methodism and humble origins he was in reality a social conservative. He even joined the "Loyalist Patriotic Union", a body dedicated to opposing Celtic separatism, and became thereby a Liberal Unionist.

Davies had been greatly assisted in the 1885 election by the formation of a Liberal Association in the county, which, under the guidance of H. C. Fryer, an Aberystwyth solicitor, organised the campaign so efficiently that hardly a vote was lost. This association created an organised body of opinion which was not slow to voice its dissatisfaction with Davies. The result was that at the next election, after only a year in the seat, and despite the support given him by almost all the squirearchy, David Davies was defeated by Bowen Rowlands by a narrow majority, after a fierce campaign. Furious at being rejected, he withdrew his financial support for the College at Aberystwyth and roundly denounced the Methodists for what he called their treachery. The Liberal Club was formed in 1891 and Cardiganshire's Liberals were now firmly tied to the values of Nonconformist Liberalism, and remained so until the end of the First World War.

Rowlands was "no great shakes" as the county's representative and was an odd choice for a Welsh Nonconformist county. He could not speak Welsh and was a High Anglican in religion, but he was against patronage and for Gladstone, and that was what the Cardiganshire Liberals wanted. The *Aberystwyth Observer* rightly attributed his success to the influence of the Nonconformist ministers over their congregations. The great mass of "Cardis" remained true to W. E. Gladstone, for despite his being a devout Anglican, he was to them the symbol of their claim to civil and national equality.

The period from the mid 1880's to the early 1920's was one of consolidation of Liberalism in the county. Bowen Rowlands rarely visited his constituency but since he voted according to his elector's wishes in Parliament, he continued to be re-elected until 1895 when he gave up his seat to become a county court judge. His successor as Liberal candidate was a surprising choice, none other than Mathew Vaughan Davies of Tanybwlch, the Conservative candidate who opposed David Davies in 1885.

After being a staunch Tory for many years this small, fox-hunting squire made it known that he would like the Liberal nomination. The reason for the change

The Memorial Service to Gladstone at Castle 1898.

seems to have been his marriage to a wealthy Swansea widow who was such an ardent Liberal that Davies found it paid to adopt Liberalism. Though 'ill educated..., uncultured and ill informed" he was adopted as Liberal candidate in 1889 and duly elected.

There seems little doubt that Vaughan Davies's election and his inactivity in Parliament, "a silent backbencher", was bad for the morale of the true Liberals in the county but they held their peace, and went on re-electing him until 1918. In that year the formation of a coalition government aroused considerable dissatisfaction and an even greater dislike of Vaughan Davies, who supported the coalition. This dislike was strong among those who had been involved in the war. There was no longer the same support for Nonconformist Liberalism, and the electorate was more critical than the pre-war age of what they saw around them. All this came to a head in 1921 when there was another crisis.

In June of that year it was suddenly announced that Vaughan Davies had been given a peerage. The title he chose was Lord Ceredigion, but this was refused and he became Baron Ystwyth. "He sought a county but had to be content with a river." It soon became clear that Lloyd George had arranged this in order to provide a seat for his young private secretary, Ernest Evans, a member of a well-known Aberystwyth family of solicitors, Roberts and Evans. This greatly upset the local Liberal party who strongly objected to being used to support a govern-

ment consisting mainly of Unionists already tainted with the atrocities committed by the Black and Tans in Ireland. At a stormy meeting, Ernest Evans's candidature was rejected and the Liberal Association chose, instead, Llewelyn Williams, the Recorder of Cardiff, a supporter of Asquith and bitterly opposed to Lloyd George since the introduction of conscription in 1916.

Williams's interest was largely in the past and his appeal was nostalgic. Evans was of the younger generation, a barrister and a member of Tabernacl Church in Aberystwyth. The Liberal party split, both men were adopted and the result was a bitterly fought by-election, and some very rowdy meetings in the Coliseum. It was a shrewd move on the part of Evans's supporters to bring Mrs Lloyd George into the fray for there were over 14,000 women voters in

The Liberal Club in North Parade.

Cardiganshire in 1921. She delivered 48 speeches and undoubtedly assisted in getting Evans elected with a majority of over 3,500 votes. He won, it was said, with the aid of Tory voters and of over 250 Tory-owned motor cars. For the Independent Liberals, so Lilian Winstanley wrote in the *Welsh Gazette* "it was a victory for material power over spiritual power".

The true Liberals felt that they had been betrayed and refused to use the official Liberal Headquarters erected in St. James Square in 1901. Instead, they set up their own H.Q. in North Parade.

In 1923 when Baldwin advocated a return to Protection, Asquith and Lloyd George were reunited. Liberals all over Britain forgot their differences and agreed on common candidates, except in two constituencies—Camborne in Cornwall, and Cardiganshire. The latter was totally opposed to the reunion, and to Ernest Evans as their candidate. Seeing the rift, the Tories saw their chance and the Earl of Lisburne decided to fight the election, thus robbing Ernest Evans of much of his support. As a result, he was soundly beaten by Hopkin Morris, Llewelyn Williams's successor. For this, Evans blamed the "Mussolinis of North Parade". Henceforth the house in North Parade was the Liberal H.Q., and the building in St. James Square lingered on as a Liberal Club until the early 1950's when a meeting was called which was attended only by the few officials. It was then resolved to close the club and it became part-dwelling and part-auction room run by R. J. Morgan.

Hopkin Morris represented the county

until 1932 when he resigned his seat to become a stipendiary magistrate in London. His successor was another Nonconformist barrister, D. O. Evans, who was also an industrialist. He retained the seat until his death in 1945.

The next M.P. for the county, also a Nonconformist barrister, was Roderic Bowen, a Cardiganshire man who served his constituency well in Westminster. Prevented from doing much in Parliament by the numerical weakness of the Liberals, he was a very good constituency member. He went to endless trouble to help any of his constituents. In 1966, when he had been their MP for 21 years, he was presented by the Liberal Association with a handsome desk.

For just over 80 years the majority of "Cardis" had voted Liberal. While Labour had become strong in other rural constituencies in Wales, no Labour candidate appeared in Cardiganshire until 1931 when John Lloyd-Jones opposed Hopkin Morris and was heavily defeated by 13,000 voters. Labour was not regarded as a serious threat until 1964 when Bowen's majority was alarmingly small.

In the 1966 election he was opposed by another lawyer, also a Nonconformist, Elystan Morgan, a member of a well-known and much repected family in North Cardiganshire, and a previous vice-president of Plaid Cymru. Not only was he a good speaker but he was also known to have a strong, emotional feeling for both the Welsh language and for Cardiganshire. He won the election by a 3 per cent swing. In the House of Commons Elystan Morgan continued to take a strongly nationalistic line on some Welsh issues, notably the language and the council for Wales. He was an able politician, was re-elected to Parliament and became a minister in Wilson's Government. There is little doubt that he would have been the Secretary of State for Wales had he won the second 1966 election. But this was not to be, he lost to Geraint Howells, who has represented the Liberals of Ceredigion at Westminster ever since.

The Brighton of Wales

Life for the well to do in the latter part of the 18th century had become over civilized. Men began to react from this artificial state of affairs and inevitably there was a revival of interest in nature. The formal Dutch garden was replaced by the landscape garden but this was not enough, the desire was for nature in the raw. This meant travel, for the populated lowlands of England had long been tamed to a pattern of field, path and hedgerow. The less wealthy visited the mountainous areas of their own county while the rich went abroad. Late in the 18th century, however, foreign travel became impossible because of the Napoleonic Wars, and Wales began to receive the attention of the wealthy. In addition to a liking for mountains, the "quality" had a craze for sea bathing and for the taking of chalybeate waters whenever possible. It was this combination of mountains, sea, and chalybeate spring that first drew visitors to Aberystwyth.

It is difficult to state exactly when the town first became a watering-place, it was already fashionable when visited by Wigstead in 1797 and it was he who first called it the *Brighton of Wales*. Until well into the 19th century the visitors had to be content with the natural attractions, for the town itself had little to commend it except that accommodation, food and service were then cheap. Visitors were loud in their praise of its bathing facilities and they also enjoyed the castle walks which had been laid out by John Probert, formerly steward to Lord Powis. These walks had been planned "with some taste and ingenuity" round the castle ruins; stone seats were placed at vantage points where the promenaders could admire the view, especially seawards where "the occasional arrival and sailing of ships [gave] some degree of animation to the scene". The popularity of these walks among the visitors was such that some at least spent a third of their time there where they could see "all the beauty and fashion of the place".

Another feature which excited interest was Castle House but the comments were often uncomplimentary to the house and to its owner-designer, Sir Uvedale Pryce, who was said to be very critical of the tastes of others.

At first visitors "must have been contented with very moderate accommodation". There were only three hotels worthy of attention, the best being the Talbot, with the Gogerddan Arms a close second and the Old Black Lion a noisy third. None of these was elegant but they were cheap and commodious. By 1807 there was much more accommodation. South of the Customs House were built two large houses called

Aberystwyth beach 1790's showing the old windmill

The Black Lion

Mount Pleasant, now part of the College

inland. A report of 1806 suggests that they had no qualms about mixed bathing.

"Natives of both sexes among the mountains are much addicted to sea bathing during the summer nights. They assemble together by blowing horns the whole way through which they travel to the shore. On reaching the beach they strip and take a promiscuous plunge without any ceremony. This kind of ablution is generally taken on Saturdays in order that they may rest on the following day."

Apart from bathing and promenading round the castle there was little to entertain the visitors at first. Some hotels employed Welsh harpists at meal times, and an occasional ball was held at the Talbot or the Gogerddan Arms. Demonstrations of marching and manoeuvring given by the local Militia served to attract some attention, but the spectacle of dirty unshaven men in dirty uniforms evoked more criticism than praise. One "amusement" open to visitors was to attend the meetings of the local Methodists, who were known as "jumpers" by those who were ill-disposed towards them.

Another of the town's attractions was the chalybeate spring discovered in 1779 near the present entrance to Plas Crug. Little notice was taken of the discovery until its possibilities as an attraction for visitors were realised. An attempt was then made to put it in the same category as the waters of Bath and Tunbridge Wells. A local resident, Richard Williams, "Honorary Member of the Physical Society, London, and of the London Vaccine Association", was asked to

"Mount Pleasant" which housed visitors. These must have been the first houses in Marine Terrace and adjoining them was an arched gateway which led to a walk in front of the nearby Castle House. The building of Marine Terrace greatly increased first-class lodging accommodation and by 1825 complaints about the quantity and quality of accommodation seemed to have ceased.

The most popular portion of the beach for bathing was that which now stretches from the pier to the bandstand. In 1807 it had four bathing machines for women near the end of Pier St. and two for men at some distance to the north. In 1826 there were 21 such machines but there were complaints that there was no awning to protect the bathers from the public gaze. This beach was also used on occasions by country people from the more mountainous districts

perform an analysis. By "minute investigation and repeated experiments" he claimed to have established that the water 'exhale[d] a chalybeate smell," "was not unpalatable", and when allowed to stand in the air in a vessel, the mineral properties of the water were deposited as a brown precipitate. The analyst found that "it much resembled the Tunbridge waters" and believed that it would be "found very salutary in all relaxations of the stomach and intestinal canal as well as general debility, stimulating the action of the heart and arteries and increasing the florid colour of the blood". He was firmly of the opinion that "by perseverance in its use the appetite becomes excited and the spirits improved".

No watering place of the period could do without its bath house and Aberystwyth was no exception. John Probert proposed to supply this need in 1800 and this may have

Marine Terrace c. 1850

been the one referred to in 1824 as being rather a humble affair of wooden baths somewhere in Marine Terrace.

A much better bath house was that built by Dr. Rice Williams at Bryndiodde at the northern end of the above-mentioned beach and described elsewhere.

When visitors first came to Aberystwyth one of its attractions was the cheapness of food and accommodation. This did not last long, complaints of extortion were being made as early as 1807. A house on Marine Terrace in the 1830's cost nine guineas a week, a very high price. There were also complaints of the high cost of meals at the hotels.

The high cost of travel and such high charges for accommodation suggest that the majority of these visitors were wealthy. Even in 1801 a visitor noted that though there were more visitors in Tenby, they were "not so fashionable a set" as those he saw in Aberystwyth. In 1808 *The Cambrian*

began to publish the lists of visitors to Aberystwyth and these show the high social position of the vast majority and the marked popularity of the resort. In the 1808-1812 lists are the names of such people as Sir Robert Peel, M.P., Lord Lanesborough, Lord and Lady Grey, Lord Dundonald, Lord and Lady Grosvenor, the Earl of Forsham, the Duchess of Newcastle, Lord and Lady Bolingbroke, the Duke and Duchess of Dorset, etc. Staying together at the Belle Vue in 1824 were Lord Warwick and family, Lord Caernarvon and his daughter, the Duke of Gloucester was expected, and there were "Barts seven in Number". The visitors were undoubtedly wealthy and as early as 1817 they were said to have left £30,000 in the town and its environs.

The exaggerated fashions and manners of the period must have presented a very marked contrast to those of the local Welsh inhabitants. One visitor who arrived a little too early in the season found the people very dull until the town began to fill and he was once again "able to move among civilised beings". The following description of the appearance of one of these "civilised beings" might be of some interest.

"In going to church we were preceded by a handsome young man walking mincingly along, in the very height . . . of the fashion. He was dressed in a short coat, with such narrow skirts that they seemed neither adapted to answer, or even to be meant to answer, any of the purposes for which the skirts of coats were ever intended. They were so narrow that he was obliged to carry his small prayer-book in his hand, as the pocket-less ladies were

lately wont to carry theirs. The collar of his coat was low, but surmounted by an enormous cravat; and this again was overtopped by a wide and stiff shirt collar cut into the form of the outward edge of a scimitar, indeed it almost seemed able to perform the duty of one, and stood up so high that we were in some pain lest it should cut off his ears . . . The points of his shirt collar projected two inches beyond his face, and, when viewed *en profile,* completely concealed it, from his nose downwards. The sleeves of his coat were very short; but then his shirt wrists stiff as its collar and having, like it, a worked border) were continued two and a half inches over his hands. His pantaloons were white of an enormous bulk."

During the service at St. Michael's another "blood of the same order", similarly dressed, stood up during the whole of the service, presumably so that people could admire him at their leisure.

All the "fashionables" of both sexes attended morning service and their dress must have astonished the Welsh, whose costume was so very different. In one pew sat an English woman with a high Leghorn bonnet and brightly coloured trimming, a green veil, and a muslin dress; by her side a fat Welsh woman dressed in a grey stuff gown, a large shawl, a long thick blue cloth coat,—her head dress consisting of a mob cap, a black silk handkerchief tied under the chin, and a low black beaver hat. Such contrasts were part of everyday life during the holiday season.

A fashion which started in Aberystwyth in 1823 was that of the "Welsh Trowsers".

These were first worn by "a gentleman of fortune" on the promenade of Marine Terrace and were made of a dark blue cloth with narrow red stripes, i.e., the identical material used for making ladies' gowns in Wales. In a few days the tailors were over-run with orders. Even the local inhabitants adopted this fashion and on St. David's Day the town was full of men parading in their "Welsh Trowsers".

The presence of the "quality" in Aberystwyth led to a demand for a meeting place fit for such distinguished company. A subscription list had been opened in 1805 to erect rooms on the castle walks but nothing came of it until September 1810, when W. E. Powell of Nanteos leased a piece of land, part of Castle field, to James Phelps of Coston, Leicestershire, his daughter Laura, John Lewes of Llanaeron, and John James Bedinfield of Ditchingham Hall, Norfolk. According to the agreement, the lessees were to build Assembly Rooms and Powell was to lay out the land between the Rooms and Castle House as a shrubbery and pleasure ground for the use of members of the Rooms, i.e., the ground now occupied by St. Michael's Church. Powell eventually married Laura Phelps, the gardens were named Laura Gardens and the houses which skirted the gardens became known as Laura Place.

Nothing was done for some years but in time the work of designing the structure was given to Repton, an eminent London architect. In July 1820 the Assembly Rooms were formally opened, having cost £2,000 to build, a cost borne by subscriptions of £10 each. The control was no longer in the hands of Phelps and company, it had been transferred to Pryse Pryse of Gogerddan, John Jones Derry Ormond, J. N. Williams Castle Hill, John Lewis Llanaeron, and George Bonsall, Glanrheidol. The building consisted of a "Ball and Promenade Room" (also used as a reading room) a card room, a billiards room, and a "Refreshment House" having a bar for the use of the guests. Balls were held every Tuesday from 9 p.m. to 1 a.m. from July to September, country dances alternating with quadrilles. A season ticket cost 30s. for a man and 20s. for a woman. Strict rules ensured :

"That no servant be admitted.

That no gentleman (military excepted) be admitted in boots.

That all ladies who go down a dance do continue in their places till the rest have done the same.

That ladies will draw Tickets for places as they come into the Room which will be entered in a book, and by no means allowed to change them.

That ladies take their place at the bottom after a dance is begun.

That the Master of Ceremonies shall be supported in the execution of his office by the subscribers at large; and any misbehaviour towards him shall be considered as an offence to the company."

The programme then adds "The Master of Ceremonies entreats those Ladies and Gentlemen whom he has not the honour of knowing personally, to afford him an opportunity of being introduced to them, that he may not be charged with want of attention if he should happen to omit visiting persons whom he may not be informed of, for want of that step being taken; as it will not only be the means of preventing improper company entering the Rooms, but enable him to pay that attention and respect which he is ambitious and studious to show to every individual resorting to this place." It was important that everything should be done correctly, as was done in Bath.

"Promenades" were held in the large room on Wednesday and Friday afternoons throughout the season. On Wednesdays music was provided by a Welsh harper and on Fridays a small military band alternated with the harper. These musical evenings were later held every evening except Sunday.

Card playing, too, was strictly controlled and rules ensured:

"That all persons playing Whist, Quadrille Commerce or Loo do pay 12s. for two packs of cards; 6s. for a single pack.

No games of Hazard to be allowed.

No Cards to be played after 12 o'clock at nights, except on Ball nights, when they will be permitted to as long as the dancing continues.

No person to play with cards left by another party."

The charge for playing cards seems exorbitant but the Assembly Rooms did much to increase further the popularity of Aberystwyth with the "fashionables".

When Ayton first visited the town in 1814 an old inhabitant informed him that of all the amazing changes that had taken place in Aberystwyth in the previous twenty years, the most wonderful was the coming of the theatre.

The first reference to theatricals was in 1786 when some "Theatrical Machinery" was unloaded from a Bristol ship at Aberystwyth. Three years later it was said that "players" regularly visited the town in September. It was inevitable that the growing importance of the town as a watering place should attract "strolling players". In April 1806 at the Quarter Sessions it was "Ordered that Henry Baker Comedian be Licensed for himself and Company to perform Plays and Entertainments in the Town of Aberystwyth . . . for Sixty Days". Later came Messrs. Gloster & Dunn who must have caused some trouble for their 50s. deposit for possible damages was later raised to ten guineas. These were followed in 1815 by Messrs. Saunders & Deproze.

A handbill of 1789 gives us some idea of the nature of these performances.

By Desire of Thomas Powell Esq.
For the Benefit of Mrs. Pearson and Mrs. Feriger
At the Theatre in Aberystwyth
On Monday evening September 14th 1789
will be performed the
Celebrated Comedy called
Duplicity
or
The Generous Gamester
Caste . . . .
To Conclude with Gray's Elegy by Mr. Feriger
Pits 2s.   Gallery 1s.
Tickets to be had at the Principal Inns.

Another playbill of a much later date (1818) was as follows:

On Monday evening September 14th will be presented an entirely new musical drama, now performing at the Theatre Royal, Covent Garden with unbounded applause
Rob Roy
or Auld Lang Syne.
Caste . . . .
End of play, song by Mr. Maitland, a hornpipe in the character of a British sailor by Mrs. Deproze. To conclude with a Comic Entertainment of
Modern Antiquities
or
The Merry Mourners
Boxes 3s.   Pit 2s.   Gallery 1s.
Half prices to the Boxes and the Pit but not the gallery.
Tickets at Inns and Mr. Cox's Library.

At first the plays were performed in the Town Hall at the top of Great Darkgate Street but there was a demand for a more elegant structure. A proposal to build 'a new and elegant theatre on a very large scale' was mooted in 1805 but nothing came of it and it was not till about 1813 that Aberystwyth had its first theatre. This was in a building originally built by Matthew Davies of Cwmcynfelin as a storehouse for corn. The grain was unloaded from incoming ships into boats which took it right into the storehouse through an arch. This was built up in 1860 but its outline can still be seen. The cargo was then hauled up through trap doors to the storage loft above. It was this loft which was converted into a playhouse in 1813 and served this purpose until 1825. The building still stands at the Aberystwyth end of Trefechan Bridge and

is now occupied by McIlquham's china store. It was certainly not elegant and there was much dissatisfaction with the "lowly beams and rude rafters" on which many a noble crown was cracked. In 1824 a local resident published his protest in the form of some verses entitled:

Drama's Petition to the Ladies and Gentlemen of Aberystwyth.

At present I occupy a frightful hole
In gloomy Bridge Street on the banks of the Rheidol.
I, too, a lady of lofty soul,
Fashion's darling and Improvements Idol.
: : : : :
Not that I seek a lodging on the Terrace,
But fix me somewhere west of the market
For me and mine though ambition fire us
Would quite content us in the street of the Dark Gate.

The second theatre was built to serve as a playhouse, but not "west of the market" nor "in the street of the Dark Gate". In 1824 in the *New Aberystwyth Guide* it was announced that Mrs. Coutts "with that princely spirit of liberality for which she is eminently and deservedly distinguished" had offered a handsome contribution towards the building of a theatre. The story behind this was that some years before the offer was made, a young actress, member of a theatrical company which failed to win support, was stranded at Aberystwyth, penniless and homeless. She was given food and shelter by a well-known and warm-hearted character known as Mali Rees who lived in an old house which was demolished when the present post office was built in Great Darkgate St. The young actress, named Harriet Mellon, then returned to London and became very popular. Some years later a fine carriage drew up outside Mali's cottage and from it descended a richly-dressed woman who embraced Mali and gave her a fistful of sovereigns. The former Harriet Mellon had become Mrs. Coutts, the wife of the very rich banker. She later became the Duchess of St. Albans.

On hearing of the proposal to build a theatre, Mrs. Coutts made her offer but it is doubtful if it was ever accepted for it was several years before the theatre was started.

The man responsible for building the second theatre was a Robert Stephenson who had lived in Aberystwyth for eighteen years. Largely as a result of his generosity, a play-house was erected at the junction of North Parade and Thespian St. in 1828. At that time the site was part of a green field used for pasture and known as Cae Dafydd Lewis (David Lewis's Field). Dd. Lewis was the son of a pious Methodist deacon in Llangwyryfon who begged his son not to do anything so sinful as selling land for building a theatre. But David preferred the money to the field, and the new play-house was built with its main door facing what is now North Parade and surrounded by a low wall. It was a crude box-like structure having a gallery facing the stage but, despite its unplastered walls, it was a lot better than the storehouse.

The first company to perform at the theatre made a poor impression on one holiday-maker. When he visited it in August 1831, the building was unfinished and the audience so small that he was able to enter at half price. The play billed was

She Stoops to Conquer and both scenery and acting were poor; the players paid no regard to the text and said just what came to their minds with frequent repetitions and hesitations. His comment was "Nothing could have been more wretched than the performance".

By 1832 the congregation at the Tabernacl Methodist Chapel had so increased that it had to be enlarged, and while this was being done the new theatre was used for religious services and the Sunday School. As one put it "the stage was turned into a pulpit and the House of Belial into a temple of the living God". Despite this, the Methodists continued to preach against theatre-going and they were much to blame for the theatre being demolished c. 1857. The site was later occupied by Fox's Vaults and private houses.

After 1857 a stage was built at one end of the ballroom of the Assembly Rooms and such popular plays as *Ticket of Leave Man*, *Uncle Tom's Cabin* and *Lady Audley's Secret* were presented there regularly until well into the 1890s.

There is a tradition that Sarah Siddons once played in the town. If this is true, then it must have been early in her career and since she was born in Brecon this is not so unlikely as it sounds.

A famous actor who did come to Aberystwyth but not to practice his art was Henry Irving. He came in 1834 in search of health and stayed in the house of Mr. Brown. There he became very interested in the work of a fellow lodger named Carre. In a letter to his daughter, Irving said of him:

"he goes out preaching every evening at five o'clock and I go out and stand beside him. Since my coming Mr. Brown has opened his house for morning and evening worship to those who are godly disposed where I have had an opportunity of instructing and counselling many of the Lord's people. Dear Carre preaches in the open air at the head of the North Parade where the main street of this ancient town descends into the noble crescent which hath been builded of late years for the accommodation of the Company who chiefly resort from the West of England for the sea bathing and the sea air, and he was wont to open the scriptures further, at seven, to those who came to Mr. Brown".

Irving's 'North Parade' was probably somewhere near the sea end of Pier St. Later he left for North Wales and Liverpool *en route* to Scotland where he died. Incidentally Mr. Brown, who lived in Aberystwyth, sought for his cure elsewhere, at Maddington.

Among the many painters who visited Aberystwyth during the early part of the 19th century were Rowlandson, J. M. W. Turner, who was probably attracted by the magnificent sunsets, and David Cox. Turner's famous painting of an Aberystwyth sunset was shown in a recent exhibition of his works, in London.

In the late 1850s' Aberystwyth became increasingly aware of the possible effects of being connected by rail with other parts of Britain. In anticipation of the large number of visitors which would then visit the town, one of the railway contractors began to

The old Queen's Hotel, now a Local Government Office

The Coliseum

until a new company took it over in 1872. Then it was repaired and a new gallery and refreshment room added at the sea end where, in the summer, a band played every morning and, weather permitting, in the evenings.

It had long been customary for the Corporation to hire bands to play in the town in the mornings and afternoons and on the unpaved promenade in the evenings. One of these was a local band, Walters and Adie who, with singers "discoursed music" where required.

The 1870's saw the erection of three places of entertainment, the John James Hall, Market Hall and Temperance Hall. The John James Hall in Terrace Rd. was built as a large covered market with an access to Baker St. but it was later divided into a wine store and an entertainment hall. This is where Joshua Dyson presented his indoor shows which, on one occasion, included a gypsy choir, a diorama, comic songs and a lecture on the Sudan. The diorama (miriorama, panorama) consisted of scenes painted on huge canvas screens which were wound on giant spools across the stage. The scenes were usually of foreign countries or pictures of incidents in the Boer War and the Russo-Japanese War. Concerts and operettas by local people were also presented here. The hall was twice the scene of a disastrous fire, c. 1880 and 1890. The latter not only destroyed the hall but also Williams and White's ironmongery store in Baker St. It was believed that the fire was started by children who had been rehearsing an operetta, the *Village Children*, by David Jenkins, the night before.

build a mammoth hotel and even to plan 'package deal' holidays. His financial failure robbed Aberystwyth of what might have been the best hotel in Wales at that time but gave it instead a college which proved, in time, a major source of revenue. Another large and very fine hotel, the Queen's, was built on Marine Terrace and opened in 1866. This had its own Assembly Rooms where concerts, dances, etc. could be held. This is now a local government building but the 'Rooms' (Cambrian Hall) remains intact.

Easter 1865 saw the opening of the pier and 7,000 people paid for the privilege of walking on it the first day. But the builders had not heeded the warning of a local editor and the following year it was badly damaged by a storm and left in that state

This disaster proved a set back to John James for it was partly responsible for the success of a rival enterprise owned by David Phillips further along Terrace Rd. David Phillips had earlier acquired the Belle Vue posting stables and turned the upper floors into the *Phillips Hall* where he staged nigger minstrels, comic operas, comedies and variety. In 1897 an evening's show included the *Queen of the Royal Epping Forest Gypsies*, a *Scientific Palmist* and *Fletchers Waxworks*. The shows proving profitable, and the hall being badly built, Phillips replaced it in 1904 with the ornate *Coliseum*, still one of the town's features and now being converted for use as the Ceredigion Museum. The ground floor consisted at first of offices, an arcade and *Phillips Stables* while the remainder of the building was an entertainment hall with red plush seating for 1,000, partly in the form of two circles.

Despite having as its first manager a man whose only qualification was that he had been a corporation workman, the Coliseum was a success. F. R. Benson's Shakespearean Company paid it regular visits, and there were plays, musicals, variety, eisteddfodau and public meetings. It was also used for college plays, degree ceremonies and examinations. This was also where the P.S.N.'s (Pleasant Saturday Nights) were held, entertainments organised by the Free Church Council. Admission was one penny, and one could get a bun and coffee for twopence during the interval.

In the meantime, in Market St., the second Market Hall, built in 1870, was staging vaudeville, diorama and musical comedy in the holiday season, and local shows in winter. But the authorities were not satisfied with the building and in 1898 a

Some of the ladies who served refreshments at the Coliseum on Saturday nights

third Market Hall was built, and it was here that the first regular moving picture shows were presented, though the cinematograph was not new to Aberystwyth. Here, in 1900, Arthur Cheetham began his regular cinema shows, combined with live turns, until 1910 when *Cheetham's Picture Palace*, Aberystwyth's first cinema, opened its doors at the Eastgate end of Market St. It was modernised in 1923, renamed the *Palladium* and continued in use until it was destroyed by fire in 1934, leaving a site which remained empty until 1967, when, appropriately enough, a trust set up by a London cinema magnate, Sir David James, the philanthropist, acquired it for the offices of the Pantyfedwen Trust which opened its doors in 1970.

Another place of entertainment to appear in the 1880's was a roller skating rink in Portland St.; it extended through to Portland Rd. A decade later it became a playhouse featuring melodrama and a

The Palladium after the fire

The Pantyfedwen Trust Building

concert hall first named the *Rink Theatre* and then the *Bijou*, but known locally as the *Pareezer Hall* after its manager Benjamin Pareezer. It could not have been profitable for it later became, in turn, a livery and posting stables, a bicycle store, reverted to being a rink for a year during which it proved a noisy and unwelcome neighbour to the Salem Calvanistic Chapel, and finally, in 1913, a cinema—the *Rink Picture Theatre*. In 1918 it was reopened as a cinema by E. J. Evans of Llanelli who was then christened and remained 'Evans y Rink'. He proved a challenge to Cheethams who was forced by the competition to show better films.

Other innovations of the 1880's were the public baths in Newfoundland St. which then changed its name to Bath St. There were two separate baths, one for 'Gents' and the other for 'Ladies'. They contained a number of brine and freshwater slipper baths. The town also contained establishments where Turkish baths were available. A show which greatly attracted children was *Simms Marionettes* held in a marquee near the lifeboat house in

The Roller Skating Rink, Portland St.

The audience at an Elysian Grove concert

Some of the audience sat on the stage
One of the concert parties at Aberystwyth

Queen's Rd.

Until 1896 the pier had only a small pavilion. In that year the Prince and Princess of Wales visited the town, the former to be installed as the Chancellor of the University of Wales, and Princess Alexandra to open the college women's hostel at the north end of Marine Terrace and the new Pier Pavilion at the town end of the pier. This pavilion had seating accommodation for 2,000 and proved an immediate success. It provided a wide variety of entertainment ranging from the Russian Imperial Ballet, Paderewski, Kubelik and Mark Hamburgh to Carl Rosa operas, musical comedies and variety. The famous Adeler and Sutton pierrot troupes also appeared here. Among those who featured in the more 'popular' shows were Arthur Roberts, George Robey, Albert Chevalier, George Grossmith, Maud Allan and, later, Jack Hylton and Mrs Mopp (of ITMA fame). Its Sunday evening sacred concerts became an institution in the town.

After 1918, indoor entertainment was increasingly dominated by the cinema. In the 1920's the Pier Pavilion began to show films, Evans y Rink closed the Rink and opened the *Imperial Cinema* which replaced the men's public baths in Bath St. This was later named the *Forum Cinema*. The ladies' bath was made into a concert hall and was used by the BBC in the early days of broadcasting. The coming of the "talkies" in 1928 proved too much for the Coliseum and it, too, became a cinema in 1931.

Out-of-doors the most ambitious, and probably the most misguided attempt at entertainment was that which followed the building of the Cliff Railway on Constitution Hill in 1897. The top of the hill was developed as an entertainment centre known as Luna Park. Walks, terraces and gardens were laid out, there was a pavilion for bands and pierrots, a large open-air dance-floor and a handsome band-stand. There were also kiosks, a camera obscura, a scenic railway and shelters. At night the park was lit with Japanese lanterns and there were firework shows and fair ground amusements. But the venture was never a real success, the heavy rain and strong winds which beset Aberystwyth sometimes, even in summer, made the park less popular than was hoped and all that now remains are traces of the walks, a wooden building where refreshments are still sometimes served in summer, and the concrete foundations of other attractions.

A much better-placed concern was that set up at Elysian Grove in the woods near the bottom of Penglais hill. A large stage stood alongside the stream and on it the nigger minstrels and the pierrots gave their shows to an audience seated either on chairs on the sides of the wide stage or on the tree-covered slopes. Bottled lights hung from the branches and there was a "Lovers Walk" laid out in the woods nearby. There were gala nights, usually including a competition for singing while holding a pig. When the weather was unfavourable the shows were held in a specially built, large, wooden hut known as the Sylvan Palace and now demolished.

Pierrot and similar shows were also given on the bandstand on the promenade and, after 1904, in what was called the Castle Pavilion, a marquee on the stretch of ground created when the castle moat was filled in, now used as a putting course.

And there were always bands, one of which was the Briton Band. In the 1880's and 90's when the band performed near the pier, Harry Collins' entertainers were at the other end of the promenade, the

following evening they changed positions. The band had its own bandstand, a platform on wheels which could be drawn around from place to place. It was fitted with equipment which could be attached to the public gas lamps so that the players could read their music in the evenings.

The Edwardian period was one of considerable growth and prosperity in Aberystwyth but the war of 1914-18 put an end to much of this, even the National Eisteddfod planned for 1915 had to be postponed for a year. Once the war was over, a deter-

The Pier Pavilion and the Pier after 1896

The interior of the Pier Pavilion

203

An entertainment in the Castle Grounds

Pierrots on the beach

The life boat "Elizabeth Lloyd" on the beach in the 1870's

An Edwardian beach scene

Ladies bathing huts, those for men were well to the north

May Queen Festival, the Music Festival, the Cardiganshire Eisteddfod, the Bowling Tournament, Sheep Dog Trials, the Agricultural Show, the Chrysanthemum Show, the Horse Show, Lifeboat Demonstrations, the Golf Championship and the Swimming Gala.

The charabanc and the motor car, together with the railway, increased tremendously the number of day trippers to the town, and the promenade and beach on a fine day were packed with people. This benefited the shopkeepers, the caterer and some forms of light entertainment but did nothing to help the theatre companies and concert artistes in their struggle against the moving pictures. The cinema was fast becoming the most popular form of entertainment, and being well patronised by visitors and others in the summer, and by students and the townspeople in the winter, survived without difficulty. Other forms of entertainment were fighting a losing battle. Luna Park failed to survive the immediate post-1918 period and the Elysian Grove shows finished in 1926. An attempt begun in 1920 by the Quarryettes Costume Concert Party to perform at the Quarry Concert Pavilion at the north end of Queen's Rd., behind Plynlimon Hall, also failed in 1926. Later this theatre was taken over for live theatre shows by Caradog Evans's widow, the Countess Barczinska and her son, Nicholas Sandys. With a good repertory company they also played in nearby towns and villages but the venture had failed before 1939 and the building became a skating rink for a short period. The site is now used by the Post Office telephone

mined attempt was made by the Town Council, private individuals and the railway company to recreate the former prosperity. Housing was improved, the railway station was rebuilt in 1925, the Marine Terrace was extended to the wooden pier at Rofawr and motor transport facilities, mainly in the form of charabancs, were improved considerably. A number of attractive events were organised annually for visitors—the

Bathing huts on the beach

The horse drawn lifeboat

Boat trips from the pier head

department.

Largely because of the efforts of Sir Walford Davies, Professor of Music at the University College, good music flourished during much of the inter-war period. The open area between Queen's Rd. and North Rd. had been turned in the early 1920's into tennis courts and a bowling green. To these in 1922 was added a concert hall which could seat up to 3,000 people and had excellent acoustic properties. Here famous orchestras, singers and instrumentalists performed under such conductors as

Edward Elgar, Adrian Boult and, of course, Sir Walford Davies. But the building, a converted aeroplane hangar and made of wood, was completely destroyed by fire in 1933. For various reasons the college used the insurance money for other purposes, one reason being that the town council was building a new municipal hall on the derelict site of the old Waterloo Hotel burnt down in 1919.

This became the *King's Hall* and served as concert hall, dance hall, college examination hall, as well as providing a setting for

Some pleasure boats c. 1928

A concert at the College Hall c. 1930

Two scenes from the Peace Pageant 1935

The Hydro—Waterloo Hotel, Aberystwyth's largest hotel. Destroyed by fire 1919, replaced by the King's Hall

school eisteddfodau, operettas, lectures and the annual college degree ceremony. The basement, originally designed to be a Palm Court where the promenade orchestra could play in bad weather, became an amusement centre.

The considerable use made of this hall by local people was a measure of the extent to which local people provided their own entertainment during the inter-war years. One outstanding event was the Peace Pageant of 1935, staged in the castle grounds with a cast of a thousand students and school children.

During this period the Pier Pavilion, now equipped with a great Wurlitzer organ, continued to provide for dances and concerts; the Parish Hall and the various other church halls went on being used by amateur actors and townspeople generally. In summer, the pierrots and negro minstrels went on performing on the bandstand and the castle grounds, and that enduring weekly event—Côr y Castell—met every Sunday evening in the castle shelter to sing hymns.

During the 1939-45 war most of the large hotels, parts of the college and some church halls were taken over by the armed forces. The Queen's Hotel became the headquarters of the R.A.F. in Aberystwyth and the Old Assembly Rooms were used for the instruction of budding pilots and navigators. Among other changes, the Forum became a NAAFI and the English Wesleyan Church Hall was

The Aberystwyth front in holiday time

some of the time rehearsing plays which were presented to appreciative audiences at regular intervals.

The post-1945 period saw the post-1918 change in holiday habits carried even further. Once petrol rationing was over and cars became plentiful, the touring holiday with one-night stops became very common, bed and breakfast was all that was needed. Catering for coach trippers increased but the demand for entertainment decreased, especially when the television set became an integral part of every hotel and boarding house. The touring caravan holiday made even less demand on any form of entertainment, except that provided at caravan parks. The stationary caravan has replaced the boarding house for thousands of holiday makers and appears to have come to stay. The larger of these residential caravans parks provide their own entertainment, even cabaret shows.

The attempt to revive the live theatre at the *Little Theatre* in Bath St. in the 1950's did not last long and ended in 1958. Aberystwyth now has only one cinema, the Pier Pavilion was badly damaged by fire in 1961 and ceased to show films. The Coliseum has closed, and the Celtic/Conway Cinema has been demolished, but a new, purpose-built cinema, the *Commodore*, has been erected and appears to be flourishing.

Since 1970, however, the decline has been arrested to some extent. The opening of the new Arts Centre on the college campus on Penglais has put new life into certain forms of entertainment in Aberystwyth. First class concerts by world-famous artistes are given in the Great Hall,

turned into a canteen.

But there was a crying need for entertainment and this was provided largely by the cinemas and at the King's Hall, where Evered Davies and his Band played for dances and presented Sunday night concerts to crowded audiences. Ardwyn County School continued to hold its annual eisteddfod and to present its yearly Gilbert and Sullivan opera at the King's Hall, and the

Charles Clements Madrigal Choir was much in demand there and elsewhere. As accompanist, solo pianist, organist, member of the college quartet of instrumentalists, and conductor both of the madrigal choir and the town choral society, Charles Clements made a considerable contribution to the musical life of Aberystwyth, both during and after the war. There being little for the air-raid wardens to do, they spent

and the neighbouring Theatr y Werin (The Folk Theatre) presents plays, ballet, puppet shows, pantomime, performed in Welsh and in English by companies of players from all over Wales and parts of England, including the Old Vic company.

One form of entertainment which has never ceased over the years has been the weekly college concert presented by the department of music.

The new type of holiday combined with the growth of Aberystwyth as an administrarive and educational centre has had a marked effect on the type of accommodation available for visitors. The Marine Terrace bears mute evidence of the change; the Queen's Hotel is now a local government office and many of the boarding houses there have become government offices, college departments, students' hostels and an old people's home. The large hotels rely more on commercial bookings than on visitors and the many small boarding houses cater mostly for the bed and breakfast trade or have been turned into flats.

A view of the pier from the sea

Marine Terrace and the Promenade

The building of this terrace must have begun very early in the 19th century, for according to the accounts of the overseers of the poor, there were 5 houses there in 1809, one of these being the home of Thomas Jones the ropemaker, and another owned by Dr. Rice Williams. The first two to be built were known as Mount Pleasant, they are now between the Theological College and the University College and are part of the latter. Thomas Jones, and his son after him, lived in number I. Dr. Gilbertson lived in the third house which was demolished towards the end of the 19th century to provide a site, with the Customs House garden, for the large Hotel Cambria. The latter proved so unsuccessful that it was bought by Lord Davies in 1905 and presented to the Calvinistic Methodists to form a Theological College.

The first to live in Rock House was Captain John Jones, formerly landlord of the Ship and Castle Inn. He was said to be the last man in Aberystwyth to wear silver buckles on his shoes.

Soon after building began on the main terrace it became clear that the houses would need some protection from the sea, for at high tide the water came to within a few yards of their doors. A subscription list was opened in the town and in 1822 work began on the promenade. By that time building had about reached the Belle Vue Hotel and by 1834 the terrace was almost up to the Bath House where it seems to have stopped until the 1860's. In 1848 there was "a range of nearly sixty modern built houses" all except 5 or 6 of which were let for lodgings during the

Marine Terrace, pre-1850.

Alderman Palmer who also ran the Belle Vue. After the disastrous fire at the college in 1885, the Queen's Hotel was used for academic purposes for a while. In 1892 the hotel was again put at the disposal of the college for an experiment in hostel life for students.

Among those who stayed "at an inn" on the Terrace, probably the Belle Vue, in 1839, was Lord Tennyson. Of Aberystwyth he wrote,

"This place, the Cambrian Brighton, pleases me not --- a sea certainly today of a most lovely blue, but with scarce a ripple. Anything more unlike the old Homeric 'much sounding' sea I never saw. Yet the bay is said to be tempestious---"

Had he seen it during a winter storm he would have found it frightening.

Another visitor of note was Sir Astley Cooper, the famous surgeon. He, too, stayed on Marine Terrace in 1827 when he began to learn to speak Welsh. While there he agreed to act as honorary consulting surgeon to the Aberystwyth dispensaries.

The coves below the castle before the promenade was built.

summer season.

As illustrations of the terrace in the 1850's show, while the great majority of the houses were of four storeys above ground level, a little to the north of Rock House there were four of five houses of only two storeys. These were raised to the level of the others after 1850, but still show some differences.

In 1866 the magnificent Queen's Hotel, designed by Hayward, "in an exuberant French style" was opened. It was described in the *Times* as "the noblest of its kind" and had 83 bedrooms. It made special provision for disabled, infirm and aged people by having bedrooms on the ground floor. It was given some interesting recessed panels beneath the windows, made up of fragments of ore and quartz from local lead mines, and other geological specimens. John Balcombe, the moving spirit in the building of the hotel, was also actively involved in the lead mining industry in North Cardiganshire. Once the hotel was built, J. P. Seddon set about building the Victoria Terrace. Unfortunately some attractive decorative work on these houses has been painted over though some may be seen on the chimneys from the rear. By 1874 the whole crescent was complete except for Alexandra Hall which was opened by Alexandra, Princess of Wales, in 1896. The promenade with its "excellently constructed wall" was complete by 1874.

The first Queens Hotel Co., did not succeed and the hotel was taken over by

The new pier c. 1870

Extending the promenade to the south

A view of the pier head through the unfinished sea wall

Laying the foundation stone for the extension

Building the extension of the promenade in front of the castle

In 1855 Prince Louis Lucien Bonaparte stayed on the Terrace and professed to be very taken with Aberystwyth. Within a few doors of Alexandra Hall is *Blaen-llynant* where, as recorded on a plaque, Sir John Williams the Queen's surgeon and one of the founders of the National Library of Wales lived early in this century.

Until the beginning of the 20th century the promenade did not extend further south than the northern end of the College. The extension past that institution and round Castle Point was made in 1901-03 at a cost of £16,000. The remainder, to the wooden pier, was built in 1929-31 at a cost of £12,000.

The Bath House

At about the time that accommodation began to be provided for visitors and others on the town's sea front, facilities of another kind began to be provided towards the northern end. In 1808 the Court Leet leased to Dr. Rice Williams a piece of land of about three acres stretching roughly from just north of the present Marine Hotel to Constitution Hill. Such was the abundance of open land then, that the rent was only 5s. per annum. At that time there was only a cart track leading from Pier St. along the sea front to Constitution Hill or "Craiglais" as it was called then.

In 1810 Dr. Rice began to build Penbryn House but he never lived there himself. It was built to serve mainly as marine baths, well away from the town, on an outcrop of rock which projected some distance into the sea, where the most northerly shelter on the promenade now stands.

The Bath House

The building was protected from the waves by a very strong wall reinforced with big boulders of hard black and blue stone which acted as a breakwater.

The baths, of which there were several kinds, were constructed "on scientific principles". Water was conveyed to the house by pipes from a sand-free, clean, rocky portion of the bay and pumped into a 500 gallon boiler from which it was fed to the tiled bathrooms or shower rooms upstairs. The pump was first worked by horse power but a steam engine was used later.

In addition, the house had a handsome sitting room with large windows facing south towards the terrace and the castle. There was also a dining room and some bedrooms. Every room was very well furnished and contained some fine paintings and engravings. The Bath House, as it was called, proved very popular with the visitors and the more prosperous inhabitants

of the town.

The name "Penbryn House" was derived from the old Welsh name for a small tumulus nearby, known as Penbryndioddef (the Hill of Suffering). This low sandy hill was the site of a whipping post and gallows in former times. The rock forming the mound was slaty, and countless children came here to look for slivers of rock to use on their slates. When the houses near Albert Place were built, the mound was removed and yielded portions of two women's skeletons and several other human bones.

Dr. Rice had built a handsome stone arch spanning the road approaching Penbryn House, it contained a gate which was locked every night. The arch remained there until 1836 when the authorities began to extend Marine Terrace northwards. The Improvement Commissioners wanted the arch removed but Dr. Rice refused and so the "improvers" resorted to guile. A "great dinner" was arranged at the Belle Vue and there was much feasting and drinking. At the right moment, when the diners were well into their cups, a toast was proposed to the future of Aberystwyth and was enthusiastically received. Every man present was then asked to pledge himself there and then, on a document which each signed, to do what was in his power to bring about the designed changes. Following the example of the others, Dr. Rice signed. Next day the arch to Penbryn House was demolished.

After the death of Dr. Rice Williams, the house was leased to another physician, Dr. Bell who was responsible for establish-

Part of the destruction of January 1938

Rebuilding the sea wall

The damage caused to the reconstruction works by a subsequent storm

ing the town's Literary Society. Later, in 1874, the house was again under the supervision of a Dr. Rice Williams and was called the "Sanatorium and Public Baths".

In time, the Marine Terrace was extended beyond Bath House and, because of its position, the latter became known as Black View House and there was agitation for its removal, but this wasn't done until 1892.

A street so exposed to the sea and the south westerlies as Marine Terrace must have experienced many severe storms during its history; the ones of which most is known were those of 1927 and 1938, the latter being the worse. It came so suddenly that there was talk of a tornado and a tidal wave, a belief reinforced by a statement made by an officer of an oil tanker in the Irish Sea that his ship had been struck by a tidal wave. The Castle Rocks and South Marine Terrace escaped the full force of the storm but from Bath Rocks northwards, the force of the gale was tremendous.

From about 4.30 a.m. on Saturday 15 January 1938 to midday on the following Wednesday the residents watched with grave concern the enormous seas battering Victoria Terrace. The velocity of the wind was estimated to be 90 m.p.h. and the tide, which in normal conditions would have been 29 feet high, was driven by the wind to a tremendous height, well above the height of the houses.

The promenade first gave way in front of Lenten House (now the Sea Bank Hotel) and the sea soon began to gouge out the area immediately in front of the house.

The front door was smashed in and some people in the hall were swept along the long passage by the rush of water. Every window on the house's first three floors were smashed, and the basement flooded to the depth of several feet. Soon, other sections of the promenade gave way and, in a relatively short time, the basements and the foundations of most of Victoria Terrace were exposed to the elements. Every house from the Marine Hotel northwards was damaged, some losing only front door steps and railings and others with their basements so battered that they appeared to be on the verge of collapsing. Viewed from the bandstand the scene resembled a street under heavy gunfire, with gaping holes in the road, the area littered with promenade seats, smashed doors and windows, with stretches of promenade railing twisted, torn and hanging crookedly over empty spaces. All the basements were flooded, and some people sleeping in them had narrow escapes from drowning.

The worst experience was probably that suffered by an elderly woman and her two daughters at a cottage built in the shelter of the pebble beach on Tanybwlch. Mrs Linett and her daughters were staying there, trying to sleep, when the storm broke. In a remarkably short time most of the bungalow was razed to the ground, with the three women pinned to the floor under heavy furniture and fallen timber. With waves washing over them at intervals they lay there until their plight was seen by the driver of a passing train. At Llanilar he phoned the police but by the time

The Tanybwlch cottage after the storm

they arrived the women had been extricated by some local men.

When the tide receded, rescue parties of council workmen and hundreds of volunteers, many of them students, began to build barricades with timber, stones and sandbags at Victoria Terrace, and attempts were made to strengthen the basements of houses in danger of falling. The storm raged for five days but appeared to be over on Wednesday. That night, however, there was another severe storm and such was the volume of water blown over the Terrace that its weight battered down a wall behind Abergeldie House. The Queens Hotel was at one period completely surrounded with water and its cat was found swimming around the kitchen.

The work of restoration was put in hand by the council as soon as possbile. The cost was estimated as near £30,000 to the Corporation alone, no more than the price of a small house nowadays, but a great deal of money in 1938. In fact, the total cost of the damage caused by the storm was £60,000 and repairs had to be put in hand immediately. In the 1960's there was again concern over Victoria Terrace and shale from Constitution Hill was spread in large quantities on the beach in front of the terrace.

The Militia and Volunteers

Until early in 1980, one of Aberystwyth's interesting features was the old barracks on Penglais Rd, formerly the headquarters of the Cardiganshire Militia. The only reminder left in the town now is the name "North *Parade*" given to one of the main streets.

The raising of militia seems to have become well established in the Middle Ages when there was hardly a village that was not able to provide some soldiers, properly equipped, in times of danger. The Cardiganshire Militia can be traced back to the time of Henry VIII, to the Great Muster initiated by an Act of 1539 which required returns of "All Harnessed and Furnished men and others fitt for warre". According to the Cardiganshire return there were 2,858 men in the county, ready to serve their king.

In 1557 the Lord Lieutenant replaced the Sheriff as the commander and organiser of the militia in each shire and the following year, when Queen Elizabeth came to the throne, an Act was passed making it compulsory to recruit and train a body of men in every county.

During the Civil War, in 1644, Col. John Jones of Nanteos raised a Regiment of Foot to fight for the King but it is not known whether these could be called Militia. It will be remembered that although he was an ardent Royalist, and was later fined heavily by Cromwell for his beliefs, the colonel, because of a private quarrel, used this regiment to help the Roundheads capture Aberystwyth Castle.

In 1648 the Militia was disbanded by a county committee at Lampeter and nothing more is known of them until 1762 when a new Regiment of Infantry Militia was raised in the county under the Militia Act of 1757. It was styled the *Cardiganshire Militia* and had its headquarters in Aberystwyth. In 1764 at the Tregaron Quarter Sessions, it was ordered that £5 be paid to Thomas Lloyd Esq., adjutant to the Militia, in repayment of "money spent by him to the men of the Militia for their maintenance for four days in saving the goods of a ship stranded on the coast in the parish of Llanrhystud". Those were the days of the wreckers and the smugglers.

More is heard at the Epiphany Quarter Sessions of 1766, where an order was made to pay Lewis Gwynne Esq, "the sum of four pounds for the carriage of arms, ammunition etc., belonging to the Militia from Cardigan to Aberystwyth". A similar order was made in 1769 when "cloathing" was mentioned, the first reference to uniform. Eight years later the men's annual training was held in Carmarthen and the order to move the arms etc. from there to Cardigan again mentions clothing. The following year it was stated officially that the Cardiganshire Militia was embodied for service under its C.O., Major Lord Vaughan of Trawsgoed, and that the colour of the new uniform was red with blue facings.

In 1783 the regiment was again disembodied but ten years later, following the outbreak of war with France, it was embodied once more. When Barber wrote of his tour of South West Wales in 1803, he referred to "the late descent of 1,400 French invaders who, after a few days possession of the neighbourhood, surrendered to the

Welsh peasantry". The Cardiganshire Militia, under the command of Lord Cawdor, were part of that "peasantry" which in 1797 defeated, or at least tricked the French into surrender at Fishguard. Four years later they were disembodied only to be embodied again in 1803 under Lt. Col. John Brooke. The following year, after receiving Royal permission to "bear the appellation" of a Royal Regiment, it became the *Royal Cardigan Militia*. They now wore the gorget and high stock. The drum major's staff belongs to this period.

Six years later it was renamed the *Royal Cardigan Light Infantry* and in 1811 commenced a period of service in Ireland under the command of Lt. Col. J. P. Chichester, of Barnstaple, Devon, a member of a family which once owned the tithes of 15 parishes in Cardiganshire. Major W. E. Powell M.P., was second in command, and later became the C.O. While in Ireland the regiment was quartered at Loughrea, where in 1812 it was redesignated as the *Royal Cardigan Rifles Militia*. Its uniform then became green in colour with scarlet facings. and it had 14 officers and 280 men.

Its history for the next half century was as follows:

1814, July, the regiment disembodied.

1823 Lt. Col. W. E. Powell succeeded J. P. Chichester as the C.O.

1824 Redesignated as the *Royal Cardigan Riflemen Militia*.

1825 Redesignated as the *Royal Cardigan Rifle Corps*.

1861 United with the Militia Regiments of Radnor and Brecknock under the title *Royal Cardigan Brecknock and Radnor Rifle Corps*. Regular training restarted under Col. Powell.

1867 Regained its independence and resumed its old title, the *Royal Cardigan Rifle Corps*. Two years later its C.O. was Lt. Col. Edward Lewis Pryse of Gogerddan.

1877 The regiment then commanded by Col. John Phillips of Mabws, was converted into an Artillery Militia Regiment of three batteries and styled the *Royal Cardigan Artillery Militia*. Its uniform became blue with scarlet facings, like that of the Royal Artillery except that the Cardiganshire men had white lace and silver buttons instead of the customery yellow lace and brass buttons. A fourth battery was added in 1887 and the establishment increased to 414. The following year saw yet another change of name to the *5th Brigade Welsh Division Royal Artillery Militia* and the uniform became identical with that of other artillery regiments.

1884 Officer commanding—Lt. Col. G. G. Williams of Wallog.

1887 Officer commanding—Lt. Col. Thos. Lloyd of Plas y Brydell.

1889 A sixth battery was added and the strength raised to 20 officers and 600 men.

1892 Regiment redesignated the *Cardigan Royal Garrison Artillery Militia*.

1900 The above regiment was embodied on 2 May and after a period of service at Milford Haven was disembodied at Aberystwyth in October.

1908 Redesignated as the *Cardigan Royal Field Reserve Artillery*.

1909 The regiment was disbanded.

After becoming an artillery regiment, most of the annual training sessions were held at one of the Milford Haven forts but Aberystwyth was selected in 1891, 1892 and 1895. In the last year the Town Council was so impressed with the behaviour and smartness of the men that it presented the regiment with a silver cup for competition.

Storage space for the militia's arms and equipment had long been a problem. Mention has already been made of the use for this purpose of David Jenkins's little chapel in Baker St. At some time before this the old school in Trefechan had been used for storage. In 1809 the Court Leet gave permission for the equipment etc., to be stored at the old Town Hall, and this continued until that place was demolished in 1855. The depot then became Loveden House, the Gogerddan property in Bridge St. and it was here that Sergeant Major Stott and his family lived until 1867.

During the Fenian riots of the 1860's the Court of Quarter Sessions sought and obtained the approval of the Secretary of State for the erection of barracks in Aberystwyth to accommodate the permanent staff. The "Barracks" were built above the North Turnpike in 1867 to a design by J. W. Szlumper at a cost of £4,000. Szlumper was the engineer of the Manchester and Milford Railway and later the designer of the new Trefechan Bridge. The barracks then became the Militia's H.Q. Here the Sergeant major, the sergeant, the regimental bandsmen and their families were "most comfortably quartered". The buildings were surrounded on three sides by a high wall, at each of the four corners of which there was a low tower carrying a gun em-

The Militia Barracks

The Militia Band

A group of Militia officers

placement. A church parade was held every Sunday morning when the men marched from the barracks to St. Michael's Church complete with the regimental mascot, a goat. One of the services which the Militia provided for the town was to send a bugler up Great Darkgate St. to the town clock every morning, sounding the reveille at intervals. In summer this was done at 6.00 a.m. and one wonders if it was always appreciated. It should be remembered, however, that clocks were expensive things and there were many, very poor people living in the town.

Parades were held on various parts of the town commons. One part was known as South Parade, a part of Penmaes-glas, another which could only be used in summer because of the marshy nature of the ground, was North Parade, the name now given to a street in the town.

The Barracks remained the headquarters of the Militia in Aberystwyth until 1909 when the regiment was disbanded. The following year the War Office informed the County Council that the building was no longer required. The Aberystwyth Town Council, well aware of the shortage of houses in the town, applied for, and was granted a Government loan to purchase the Barracks and convert them into dwelling houses. This was done and in 1912 the first civilian families moved in.

In the late 1970's it was decided that the Barracks were no longer fit to live in and a demolition order was applied for. Despite much opposition from conservationists, this was granted and the bulldozers moved in late in 1979.

The Volunteers

The Volunteers were completely separate from the Militia and were first formed in Cardiganshire in 1860. They were known as the *Cardiganshire Volunteer Rifle Corps* and were commanded by Major Richardes of Bryneithin. Two companies were formed, one in Talybont and the other in Aberystwyth. The former's drill ground was the village green in front of the Black Lion and its commander was Lieut. (later Col.) G. C. Williams of Cwmcynfelin. The Aberystwyth company drilled on the Sand Marsh, moving northwards as the common became built up. The new Town Hall served as their armoury. The company soon produced its own band, drum and fife at first and brass later. Their shooting range was at the bottom of Craiglais (Constitution Hill) and manoeuvres were carried out on the beach nearby.

The treat of the year was a visit to Nanteos to fight a mock battle with the Nanteos "army", composed of household staff, gamekeepers and selected tenants, when Col. Powell posted some of his men on the mansion's flat roof to guard against an attack by the invading force—the Volunteers. The Colonel, in his wheel chair, acted as umpire. The battle was usually followed by target shooting on the lawn and refreshments. In 1900 the Volunteers numbered 141 men.

For some unknown reason, the volunteers were formed as the 1st *Cardiganshire Artillery Volunteers* in 1901, and redesignated the *Cardiganshire Royal Garrison Artillery Volunteers* the following year.

During 1901 the Volunteers had a strength of 194, nine years later it was 289, all the officers and men being recruited from Aberystwyth town. About 1903 the unit was rearmed with modern guns and the following year it was given what it badly needed, adequate headquarters. In January 1904 the new Drill Hall in Glyndwr Rd, off Park Avenue, built for £2,000, was opened by Lord Stanley. The C.O. was then Capt. George Fossett Roberts.

In April 1908 the R.G.A. Volunteers were transferred into the new Territorial Force, the members of the former being given three months to decide whether to transfer into the Territorials or not, most of them did transfer.

The new force was known as the *Cardiganshire Battery, 2nd Welsh Brigade, Royal Field Artillery*. In 1914 they were still so styled, their H.Q. was at the Drill Hall in Aberystwyth and the unit was commanded by Major J. C. Rea. In December 1915 the battery left for France.

It is worth noting that the *5th Volunteer Battalion of the South Wales Borderers* also had a connection with Aberystwyth. In 1900 a company consisting of volunteers from Aberdovey and the University College of Wales was formed. By 1901 the U.C.W. supported "E" Company in its own right with a strength of 92 rank and file. With the formation of the Territorial Army in 1908 the "E" company was transferred to the Aberystwyth College Officers Training Corps.

In August 1939 the 146 *Field Regiment Royal Artillery* was formed from 407 and 408 Batteries and the 102 Field Regiment (Pembroke Yeomanry) Royal Artillery. Regimental H.Q. and 408 Battery were based upon Aberystwyth, 407 Battery at Cardigan. The regiment was present at El Alamein and later fought in Italy and N.W. Europe. It was disbanded in Germany in December 1945.

A feature of the Militia which created much trouble and expense to the various parishes was the choosing of the recruits. In 1802, while Britain was at war with France, an Act was passed amending the old laws relating to recruitment. According to the new law it was the Deputy Lieutenant of each county who decided what number of men should serve. He then instructed the chief constable or chief borough/parish officer to give notice to each borough or parish concerned, stating how many men would be required from that borough or parish. The militiamen were then elected by ballot and the chosen had to serve for five years or find a substitute "able and fit for service" and having "not more than one child born in wedlock".

This led to the formation of "Substitution Clubs" consisting of men who were prepared to serve in place of the balloted men *for a price*. Such instances are often mentioned in the Quarter Sessions records and the magistrates fully approved of them.

A parish which gave much thought to this problem of substitution was Llanfihangel y Creuddyn. In the Vestry Book of the parish is the entry "Agreed to pay towards Morgan Jones's substitute in the Army of Reserve £25". Behind this lies the story of an energetic curate's work in establishing a sensible scheme for providing the Militia with recruits who wanted to serve, and ensuring that the recruits' families did not suffer thereby.

In January 1808 the parishoners of Llanfihangel y Creuddyn met and discussed the following: "Messers William Wickham, Edward Morgan and James Evans have engaged to find two substitutes to serve for this parish and to have them enrolled before the 20th January for the sum of £15 15s. 0d. (besides the £40 fine for each substitute) to be paid such time as the substitutes are sworn." The three men named also bound themselves to these conditions under a penalty of £120. But the substitutes proved unsuitable and on the 8th February the Vestry again met and it was "agreed that James Evans and Edward Morgan must find single men as Substitutions to serve in the Militia for this Township on paying them the Expenses".

It was clear that the chosen recruits were finding it difficult to find substitutes, and in November 1810, after much thought by the curate, and much discussion with the parishioners, the Vestry passed the following resolutions:

1. "That a Society be formed that all persons liable to be balloted should become members thereof at a fee of one guinea, the money to be in the hands of the Treasurer appointed by the Society.
2. That balloted men (who are members of the above Society) should pay £20 each to the Overseers of the Poor of the ... parish and they be vested with authority to find substitutes for them, at the Expense of the Parish.
3. If a balloted man should wish to serve in the Militia rather than pay £20 to the Overseers of the Parish and a Substitute be provided for him, he will be entitled to £20 on the above terms, and an additional Relief be given him from the Parish, as the Overseers of the Poor, and the Inhabitants thereof deem reasonable.
4. That a rate be assessed and levied by the Overseers of the Poor, on the Parish, in order to defray the expenses incurred and providing and paying for Substitutes.
5. If any balloted man should abscond five Guineas of Reward be given for apprehending him.
6. These Resolutions are to be held valid DURING THE PRESENT WAR. The Overseers are invested with Authority to advance immediately, at the Bank, as much money as will be necessary towards paying the Substitute."

An entry dated 3 March, 1813, states: "It was agreed to allow William Morgan, Dolmadog, 6s. for his trouble to go a day around the Parish, with John Morris the Constable, in order to get a correct list of the names fit to serve on the local Militia. . . . Ale at John Evans 3s."

It is obvious that the parishioners of Llanfihangel y Creuddyn went about the business sensibly under the guidance of their curate. But three shillings for ale was enormous at 1d. a quart, and either William Morgan had a Falstaffian capacity or he had been forced to treat many others to get the necessary information.

The Town Halls

The Old Town Hall

Under the names Town Hall, Guildhall, Shire Hall, this building seems to have existed in Great Darkgate St. since at least the 17th century and probably before that. In September 1657 the following complaint was made:

> "We doe present ye wante of a Shire Hall in ye towne of Aberystwyth in ye said county to be a greate greevance and think fitt that it should be erected upon ye charge of ye said county."

Whether this means that there was no hall there before or that the old one was unusable is not known. In 1690 the Court Leet had to be held in the house of John Lewis, probably an innkeeper, while the Town Hall was either being rebuilt or repaired. Three years later it was in use for both county and town purposes—Quarter Sessions and Court Leet. Since that time there are a number of references to its needing attention—a new lock and staple for the Hall door and other repairs in 1744, some more repairs, plastering and a new coat of paint in 1749, and a thorough cleaning in 1764 when it was so dirty that Stephen James, the Hall keeper was threatened with a fine of 5s.

George Eyre Evans thinks that the need for frequent repairs meant that the building may have been of timber construction with lath and plaster walls. In 1770, probably tired of having to be continually repairing the structure, it was decided by the Quarter Sessions that the Rev. W. E. Powell, Roderick Richardes and others "be desired to agree with proper workmen to rebuild the Guildhall of Aberystwyth, the same

being ruinous". This was done at a cost of £321 15s. 6d. and paid for out of the "County Stock". The new hall was fit for use in October 1771. Nine years later it again needed repair.

The Old Town Hall was in front of the Skinners Arms (Tavern in the Town) facing Bridge St. In 1797 Thomas Morgan father of T. O. Morgan author of the *Aberystwyth Guide,* was allowed "to erect a building to rest on the west pine end of the Town Hall, to extend over the County ground so far as to adjoin his own dwelling house, at a rent of 6d. a year". In 1821, however, as part of the town's attempt to improve its appearance and to cater for increased traffic, the permission of W. E. Powell was obtained to pull down the sheds attached to the end of the wall so as to widen the road between Pier St. and Great Dark-

The Old Town Hall, demolished 1856

gate St. By this time there were again several references in the records to the need for repairing the Town Hall.

The hall was built largely for the use of the Court of Quarter Sessions and the Court Leet, but over the years it had many other uses. In 1807, and later, it was used for theatricals by visiting players, and in 1809 the militia began to use it for the storage of their arms, clothes and other equipment. The space around the hall had been used as a market from time immemorial and attempts by the Town Commissioners and the Town Council to clear it failed. From 1836 onwards the open, arcaded ground floor of the hall was used primarily as a fish market, though other produce was also sold there.

The Town Hall in Queen's Road

By 1840, the County Magistrates were dissatisfied with the accommodation at the Old Hall and the following year it was described as being "unfit, insufficient, and inconvenient for the holding of sessions". It was resolved to pull it down and to erect a better building. After confirming that the new site belonged to the county, the magistrates offered £800 to the Corporation of Aberystwyth towards the cost of the new building, provided it was erected according to one of the plans then submitted to the Court of Quarter Sessions.

Contributions towards the building were invited and by 4 December 1841 a total of over £2,387 had been received. Evidently this was not enough and a week later a special appeal was made to the "Mercantile Houses" in the town by Richard James,

TOWN HALL, ABERYSTWYTH.

The Town Hall in Queen's Rd.

The present Town Hall. This is a reconstruction of the above hall which was seriously damaged by fire in 1967.

John Cole, David Lewis and John Cox. In June 1843, "in consequence of the depressed state of agriculture" the Quarter Sessions instructed their clerk to ask the Corporation to postpone its application for the £800 until conditions improved.

At the same meeting they were shown Coulthart's (the architect) model of the new Hall and approved of it, calling it the County Hall.

The name 'County Hall' implied that it would be used only for county business, something which the Corporation of Aberystwyth refused to contemplate. John Parry, the Town Clerk, was ordered to write to every magistrate residing in the north of the county requesting their attendance at the next meeting of the Quarter Sessions to support the Corporation's demand that the new building should be used partly as a County Hall and partly as a Town Hall. Largely because of the support given by John Lloyd Davies, Alltyrodyn, the magistrates agreed and henceforth it was known as the Town Hall. Some Corporation land was sold to Gogerddan and J. J. Atwood to pay for the new building. Opinions differ as to when the hall was built, the date on the hall itself is 1842 but this is incorrect, the foundation stone was laid in 1844 and the building was completed two or three years later. The foundation stone was to be laid by W. E. Powell M.P., of Nanteos but, because he had voted for the removal of the Quarter Sessions to Lampeter, the Corporation refused to allow him to do this, and the stone was laid by the Mayor, Alderman Lewis Jones. The hold of the great landowners on Aberystwyth was weakening.

The Town Clock

Aberystwyth's only town clock seems to have been the one on the old Town Hall and that stopped working before 1840. This led to many complaints and John Evans the schoolmaster of Chalybeate Terrace (St.) decided to provide a substitute. His house at the corner with Lewis Terrace had a small tower and on this, facing the gasworks at the top of Morfa Lane (Park Avenue) he fixed an eight day clock, "regulated by astronomical observation". But it did not entirely satisfy the townspeople for it did not strike the hours, and the demand for a town clock persisted. Eventually it was resolved to erect one on the site of the old Town Hall.

Using material from the old hall and money from the sale of surplus materials, a column 62 ft. high was erected in 1856 at the junction of Pier St. and Bow Street,

i.e. part of Upper Great Darkgate. It cost £1,250 to build and had a small gallery at the top reached by a winding staircase which, for a small charge, people were allowed to mount to see the view. The clock was presented by Sir Pryse Pryse of Gogerddan and it first began to strike the hours at 9 o'clock on the evening of Tuesday 4 September 1859.

The Town Clock c. 1880

The Town clock became a focus of interests in the town. It was the scene of many a notable St. David's Day gathering, and in the days when teenagers of both sexes liked to congregate to talk and make eyes at one another, the clock was the starting point for the customary walk round the block—Pier St., Eastgate, Market St., Great Darkgate St. and back to the clock. It also became a symbol of home for the town's many mariners who, when they happened to meet in some distant port, would usually end their conversation with the words "See you at the Town Clock".

The drinking fountain at the base of the clock was given by the Rev. John Williams, founder of the Band of Hope and a fervent advocate of total abstinence. He hoped that the fountain would make it less necessary for the people visiting and working at the nearby market to visit the Taverns to quench their thirsts.

Much to the regret of the vast majority of the townspeople the clock was demolished in 1956 because it needed some expensive repairs.

Our Lady's Mill

In Mill St. when approaching Trefechan Bridge, the last building on the left was once the corn mill, and it is believed by some that part, at least, of the existing building was built in the Middle Ages, as old perhaps as the 1280's when the mill was first erected. Nothing further is known of it until the 16th century when the question arose as to whether the inhabitants of the town had the right to grind corn without the consent of the Crown and the payment of a toll. In 1573 an important trial, involving the Queen and the burgesses of Aberystwyth, was held in Shrewsbury, in which the Crown succeeded in establishing its right to the mill and the tolls therefrom, one sixteenth of the corn ground. In 1586 the Crown leased the mill to the Pryses of Gogerddan for 40 years at a rent of £3 *per annum*. Later it was leased to them *in perpetua* for the same payment. As stated already, the profits from the mill were to be used to provide religious services at the ancient St. Mary's Chapel which collapsed into the sea in the early 18th century.

In 1743 there was again trouble because the inhabitants were taking their corn to be ground outside the town. A legal action

An artist's impression of Our Lady's Mill in the past

This ancient building is all that remains of Our Lady's Mill

down the south side of Alexandra Rd. and Mill St. to the corn mills and, as stated already, was crossed by two small bridges, Waterloo Bridge opposite the entrance to Terrace Rd, and Corry Bridge at the entrance to Park Avenue.

The name "Our Lady's Mill" is said to have referred to Queen Elizabeth but it is more likely that the mill was so named after the Virgin Mary, to whom the chapel concerned was dedicated.

was begun but the Corporation resolved the problem by granting the Pryses a piece of land between the mill and the bridge, to enable them to enlarge the mill sufficiently to cope with all the grinding required. This seems to have been done by building another mill. Both are shown in the view of Aberystwyth c. 1790.

In time, as the town grew and the commons were built upon, the agricultural activities of its inhabitants declined, there was less demand for grinding corn, and the extension was turned into some kind of factory with its own watercourse and waterwheel.

At some time, a large building was erected between the corn mills and the bridge. Its original function is unknown but at the end of the 18th century it was a lodging house reached by a flight of steps descending from Mill Lane. It was much used by vagrants and was said to lodge an incredible number for its size.

The mills were served by the Mill Leat which was formed by the meeting of the Penglais and Plas Crug streams. It flowed

Trefechan Bridge

The view of Aberystwyth c. 1790 shows the old six-arched bridge which crossed the Rheidol at that time. It was described as being an ancient structure and could well have been built in medieval times. The first written reference to it was made in 1747 when, at the Court Leet, Morgan Jones was presented "for digging and building ye part of a Storehouse or Cellar below and to ye west side of ye Bridge belonging to this town and liberty, it being a Nusance". Six months later the "nusance" was still there. The bridge was even then in poor condition for there are many references in the Quarter Sessions records to payments being made for its repair.

In 1792 it was described as being in a ruinous condition and there were again orders that it be inspected by certain gentlemen of the district and that they employ "John Nash of Carmarthen, architect," or any other fit person to prepare plans for a new bridge. In the meantime, £20 was paid to Richard Lloyd J.P., to employ someone to repair the bridge. No sooner had the repairs been effected than the county suffered an extremely cold winter and the spring thaw of 1796 so swelled the river Rheidol that the old bridge collapsed under the pressure of water. A William Morgan was then paid £28 6s. in full "for planks and other Materials for erecting the Temporary Bridge at Aberystwyth". This was probably the one seen and drawn by the artist Rowlandson when he visited the town with Henry Wigstead in 1797.

The rebuilding of the bridge was advertised in the Hereford and Shrewsbury papers and tenders were invited. Nash was paid £10 18s. "for journies and attendance at Aberystwyth on account of Aberystwyth Bridge". At the Epiphany Sessions in 1797 a contract was made with Lewis Davies, mason, to build the bridge. Six months after the contract was ratified, Lewis Davies was paid the first instalment of £200. The rebuilding took three years and in 1800 the new stone bridge was open to traffic, having cost £1,467 19s. 11d. to build. No sooner was it opened than the Quarter Sessions ordered that the approaches to it be improved and certain limekilns which obstructed the way on the Trefechan side were ordered to be removed.

At that time the town had three pounds for stray animals, one was in Great Darkgate St. roughly where the Midland Bank now stands, the other was in Pound Place, entering Trinity Rd., and the third was at the town end of Trefechan Bridge.

The new structure, described by visitors in 1817 as a "long handsome bridge" with five arches, lasted until 1886 when the town

Fairholt's drawing of the temporary bridge 1797. It is almost exactly the same as that drawn by Rowlandson

The bridge built by John Nash c. 1880

Building the new bridge 1887.

The broken bridge 1886, showing part of the aerial ropeway

again suffered a disastrous flood.

Thursday, 14 Oct. 1886, was a fine day but early next morning, very dark clouds began to gather and soon it was raining very heavily. By 5.00 p.m. the rivers Rheidol. Ystwyth and Teifi had burst their banks. Then came the gale from the south-west which raised the level of the water in the rivers even higher, and pounded the sea front. Spray was blown right over Victoria Terrace and such was the effect of the wind and the rain that there were floods behind the Queen's Hotel.

The first intimation that anything was seriously wrong was observed at the railway station where 200 to 300 people were waiting to go on an excursion to London at 12.30 a.m. They were told that there would be a delay in getting away because the engine shed was flooded. The spaces between the platforms were seen to be filling with water and the place began to look more like a dock than a station. Some of the excursionists then went home but others, determined to get their money's worth, climbed into the train and had to stay there all night.

Suddenly, because of the collapse of the embankments near Penybont bridge, the town was invaded by a wall of water which advanced so rapidly that people had to run upstairs to get out of its way. By midnight the whole of North Parade, Queen's Rd. as far as the Town Hall, Thespian St., Moor (Cambrian) St. and Alexandra Rd. were inundated to a depth of several feet in places. The water reached a depth of six feet in some streets. The railway and the Flats were covered with water, and the wall dividing the station from Smithfield (Park Avenue) had given way in places. Between 2.00 and 3.00 a.m. Trefechan Bridge collapsed, leaving a yawning gulf of about 100 feet between the town and Trefechan. Penybont Bridge in Llanbadarn and six others within a few miles of Aberystwyth were swept away.

In the town, the gas works were flooded and there was no gas for lighting. Williams and Metcalfe's foundry was badly affected, Garner's bakery in Portland Rd. was knee deep in water, telegraph wires were down and no telegraph message could be sent anyway because the batteries in the Post Office telegraph department were flooded.

Long before dawn, rescue parties led by Superintendent Lloyd, C. M. Williams, D. C. Roberts, A. J. Hughes, John Jones, John James, John Evans the solicitor, the Rev. T. A. Penry and others set about helping people. John Gibson and Penry provided and distributed straw mattresses for the homeless, food was obtained and funds were provided by the Downie Trust.

Next day the town was in a pitiful state, 300 houses were affected and people who could ill-afford it had lost many of their possessions, or had them damaged. Those who had stayed in the train were rescued by boat and trolley. The state of some streets was indescribable; the sewage pipes, unable to cope with the flood water, had burst, discharging their undesirable contents all over the lower parts of the town. Gibson of the *Cambrian News* was quick to point out to the councillors that the proper disposal of sewage was a serious matter and not a joke as some of them thought.

Something had to be done to help people to cross the swollen river to Trefechan and the south. Boats were used and a novel aerial railway was constructed consisting of a small carriage suspended from two wheels running along a stout wire rope stretched across the river, and wound back and fore by means of an endless rope worked by hand. Its construction led to a certain amount of unpleasantness because of the erection of a rival enterprise. The town surveyor erected a swing bridge and made a profit out of it, much to the annoyance of the townspeople.

As a temporary replacement C. Williams, a local carpenter, undertook to erect a suitable bridge for £200, and to guarantee it for 12 months, an offer which the Council was quick to accept. No time was then lost in clearing away the remains of the old Nash bridge and building the present structure in its place, a handsome three-arched affair designed by Sir James Szlumper and built by David Lloyd of Aberystwyth.

The staff of Garner's Bakery in Portland Rd.

Trefechan and Penparcau

South of the bridge over the Rheidol is the little community of Trefechan (the Little Town) a bridge settlement which developed around the south side of the harbour. It has long played an important part in the economy of Aberystwyth and may originally have been a trading settlement used by people acting as entrepreneurs between the people of the castle and the town, and the Welsh in the surrounding area. Over the years it has housed many limekilns, a lead smeltery, ship and boat building sheds, timber yards and sawmills, brickworks, brewery, cable and anchor works, blacksmiths, coopers, ropeyards, sail lofts, foundry and makers of lead mining machinery.

Some light is thrown on life there in the past in accounts kept by a merchant in the 1830's and 40's. In November 1840, Hugh Roberts, a merchant who lived in Bridge St., and owned a timber yard and woodworking business in Trefechan, took an apprentice whose name is not known. Recorded in the accounts are the payments made to, or on behalf of the apprentice. The boy was allowed 2s. 6d. a week, which was well above average, and must have lived with his master for it was the latter who saw to "mending his (the apprentice's) shoes 1s. 6d." "making him a shirt 1s. and calico for the making thereof 6d." "making his trousers 2s." and "for drawers, tape and making 2s. 2½d." The boy evidently came from, or had relatives or friends in Tywyn for he was given 5s. "to go to Towin" at Christmas. Beer was not considered unsuitable for a boy in the late 1830's, and we read "paid for his ale to Mrs. Jones 10d", "for his ale off G. Rees 1s." A stock for

his neck cost 1s. On Easter Monday the boy was given 2s. which was very generous indeed. Buttons for his clothes cost 2d., a pair of shoes 10s, which was expensive, and a great moment in his life, he was given "cash to buy razor, 1s."

The craft for which the boy was being trained was cooperage and general woodworking. John Jones the cooper, who seems to have worked for Hugh Roberts, not only made barrels but also wooden barrows with wide wheels for Nanteos. Lord Lisburne ordered two wooden buckets for his kennels, to be painted blue with LL on them in large white letters. What is more, they had to be got ready immediately, so John the cooper must have had some in stock.

Included in this chronicle of Trefechan is a reference to a bidding, "An account of Donations at the Bidding of John and Mary, Spinster" at the White Horse Inn, 29 January 1835. The contributions were— Mrs. Drew, White Horse Inn 5s; Evan Jones, Sailor, Trefechan 1s. 6d; Mrs. Warrington, Kings Arms 2s; Mrs. Killing, Feathers Inn 2s; Mrs. Anne Griffiths, Brewerswoman, Trefechan 1s; Mary Thomas, Ship Aground 1s. More than £5 was collected to help launch John and Mary on their wedded life.

Among the above papers are a number of billheads of old business houses which make interesting reading: John Cole, Pier St., Chemist and Tea Dealer; Richard Lewis, 2 Pier St. (from Redmayne's, Bond St., London) Silk Mercer; William Edwards and Son, established 1750, Draper; David Lloyd, 36 and 37 Great Darkgate St., Dealer in Foreign and British Shawls; David

Jenkins, Never Despair, 10 Market St., Linen Draper; John Evans, Successor to Lewis Pugh, Linen and Wool Draper, Grocer etc., Commerce House; J. Jones, 8 Pier St., Silk Mercer, Dealer in Merinoes, Orleans and Lama Cloths; David Jones, 18 Bridge St., Grocer, Dipt and Mould Candles; J. R. Jones, Hats for the Million, Successor to Robert Pugh, Kersey-meres; and David Williams, Mercer, Corner of Market St.

It may have been the above J. R. Jones who, in 1857, from his draper's shop in Pier St. sent out a handbill stating that he "could give satisfactory reasons for relinquishing his business" and offered his hats for sale "no less than 700 in number, at great sacrifice", some at half price and some even less. Hugh Roberts was also a building merchant and bought his slates at Derwen-las, presumably from Corris. In September 1852, the *Union* was loading there with a cargo of slates and ready "to leave with the first wind for Aberystwyth".

But John Jones, the cooper, "honest" and "ever paying his way", "kind to widows and orphans" and minding his own affairs, was informed in August 1855 that his name was being "objected to being retained on the List of persons entitled to vote in any election". True democracy was still to come.

Around 1800, Trefechan was a hotchpotch of buildings of all kinds from the handsome 18th century structures of *The Green* and *The Lawn* to the narrow, crowded little streets and courts of which some were later described as "unfit for human habitation." The road line was far from even, lime kilns obstructed the way to the bridge, buildings projected into the pavements and

the stone steps which rose to the many lofts obstructed the footways. One large loft which, over the years, served as a day school, a brewery store, a place for band practice, a depot for the militia, a meeting place for the Church Army, a warehouse and a carpenter's shop, was served by a double set of stone steps, one set pointing to the bridge and the other in the opposite direction.

It was built about 1810 and was known locally as *Y Star Fawr* (the Big Steps) and formed a considerable obstruction, pedestrians had to leave the pavement to pass them.

In 1795, grain was in such short supply throughout much of the country that soldiers were used to guard the wagons bringing it to market. But Aberystwyth was more fortunate than most places for on 23 July,

it was said that:

"a Ship laden with Rye and Barley has arrived at Aberystwyth and today the High Sheriff has a meeting here to regulate the price. They are able to sell it to the poor at 6s. per strike, Winchester measure. Such has been the plenty of corn in the county (Cardiganshire) that till now they have not imported any, but have supplied the neighbouring counties with large quantities, particularly with Barley and Oats, and they expect to reap new Corn either next week or the week following. The price has not been above 10s. in this county."

The weather must have been extraordinary for it to be possible to harvest corn in West Wales in early August. Most of the barley

A view of Trefechan and the harbour c. 1880

probably came from the lowland tract south of Llanrhystud.

Then, and on other occasions when grain was in short supply, the country people came to Aberystwyth to buy barley for making bread at 10s. a bushel. It was doled out to a clamouring crowd by a man who stood at the top of the Big Steps. People threw their sacks to him with money in them.

Two views of Old Trefechan c. 1880

Each then received a quantity matching the money and the size of his or her family. The steps became such a hindrance to traffic that they were demolished about 1900.

At the beginning of the 19th century there were seven taverns in Trefechan, *Bridgend Inn, Black Horse, Plough and Harrow, Fountain, Three Tuns, Beehive* and the *Cupola*. The Beehive was connected with Deio Coes Bren (David of the Wooden Leg). When a young man he was fond of playing tricks on people and lost his leg because of it. One version of what happened is that he was courting a girl at Pantybarwn, then in the possession of an old clergyman. One evening Deio climbed on to the roof of an outhouse, stood on his head and waved his legs in the air to amuse the maids. The old clergyman, named Lewis, looked out of the window, saw what he thought was an apparition, took his gun and shot the boy in the leg. Another version is that Deio went courting a girl named Jane at Crugiau. Captain Davies, who lived there, objected to his coming, as did the old clergyman in the other version, probably because of the prevailing Welsh custom of courting in bed, and warned Deio to stay away. But the latter persisted in coming and seeing him about one day, the Captain, who had a gun under his arm, pretended to shoot him. Seeing this Deio threw a somersault which so startled Capt. Davies that the gun went off accidentally and Deio was shot in the leg. According to the stories, after losing his leg, he married the girl concerned and kept the Beehive Inn at Trefechan.

Deio was a good musician and led the

singing at the Calvinistic Methodist Sunday School. It was he who built the houses known as Beehive Terrace near the demolished railway bridge. By trade he was a shoemaker. But he was not always law-abiding and spent more than one spell in gaol. On one occasion, when serving a three-month sentence, he shared a cell with Tom White. Behind the prison was an orchard containing some heavily laden apple trees. Tom White cast envious eyes on the apples and, eventually, was able to steal some without incurring the wrath of the gaoler by tying Deio's wooden leg to his own, and stealing the apples while Deio was asleep. Deio was blamed and suffered an extension of a month on the original sentence. On his release he returned to the Beehive but after a short while reverted to shoemaking and also keeping a lodging house.

Trefechan was notorious for its lodging houses, of which there were four during the 19th century. The oldest was the *Cupola* or "Cupillo", which had once been a tavern. Its name suggests that it either had a rounded roof or was once part of a smeltery, and tradition says that it was connected underground with the two tall chimneys that used to stand on the hill to the south of Trefechan. Such underground passages were the method used to lead poisonous fumes released during lead smelting away from the built up areas. But there is a difficulty here, for the name "Cupola" predates by several years the date when the smeltery was built—1788. Since tradition is notoriously unreliable, the passages may have been from the later works

or the so-called chimneys may have been navigation aids for ships. There were certainly ships being loaded and unloaded near the Cupola in 1782. Early in the 19th century the Cupola was a lodging house for the many vagrants, many of them ex-soldiers from the French wars, who tramped the country. These "receptacles of profligacy, called lodging houses," were very unpopular with the authorities and the police were continually being asked to keep an eye on them. In 1840 the most notorious house was kept by Mary Evans, who was often in trouble, not only because of the lawlessness of some of her lodgers but also because of her own vicious behaviour. She was far too ready to use a knife during her many quarrels with her neighbours and others. The last lodging house in Trefechan was kept by Dai Lavin who, in the 1920's, charged 4d. for a night's lodging provided the lodger took off his shirt before going to bed. His lodging house, which is believed to have been the Cupola, was attached to the fire station end of the row of cottages lining the Penyrancor road. Remains of it are still visible.

Begging was a fine art in the 19th century. The "Queen of the Beggars" in 1840 was Gwen Jones who was often fined for being drunk and disorderly. Even a 5s. fine failed to stop her from drinking too much, and fighting. Also in Trefechan at that time was an old woman named Mary Jones who kept a large stock of old clothing which she hired out to those who went begging, one of her best customers was Gwen Jones. Even "respectable" women were not above begging during the summer season and they

The approach to Trefechan Bridge in 1880 and c. 1930

One of Trefechan's old houses c. 1930

went to Mary Jones to be disguised beforehand. She also supplied beggars with borrowed children "the more to excite the pity of the charitable".

Trefechan also had its sorcerers, one of whom was John Miles who called himself *Agrippa Cornelius*. After preying on the credulous for some time he fell foul of the law over his treatment of John Morris, a mender of umbrellas in Trefechan. Morris was stricken by an illness and was visited by Miles who told him that a local witch had put a spell on him. According to Miles, all Morris had to do was to confront the woman after taking some preliminary precautions. For advice on the nature of these precautions Miles wanted 7s. but Morris possessed only 6d. which the former took on account. Morris was then given a piece of paper on which were certain signs, which he was to pin to his clothing as near to his heart as possible. Then he was told to cut his finger nails and part of his hair, mix them with two spoonfuls of salt and reduce the mixture to a powder by heating it between two hot flat irons. The resulting powder was then to be sprinkled over the floor near the door that the witch would enter. All this was supposed to make her unable to rest until she had seen Morris and confessed her iniquity. Miles then gave John Morris eight different kinds of weed to boil in water which he then had to drink every three hours. In fact the concoction made him ill, and Miles who had promised to call on him the next day, did not appear. The police were then informed, Miles was arrested and put in gaol for three months.

Trefechan too, had its court—Fountain Court, known in Welsh as *Cwrt y Ffwlbart* (the Polecat's Court). Whether this referred to an animal or a resident is not known but there were times when law-abiding people stayed away from Fountain Court.

Part of the Trefechan side of the harbour was a quay known as *Turkey Shore*. One story is that a ship laden with Turkish carpets was forced to put into the harbour for shelter and because of bad weather and the sandbar, was there for several weeks. The crew, being short of money and needing food, sold the carpets to buy provisions. Another explanation is that Turkey is a corruption of *Twr Cae* (the Tower Field), probably a reference to the two tall chimneys or erections which used to stand on the grassy slope overlooking that part of the harbour. In April 1838, over 200 emigrants for North America were taken from the Turkey Shore in boats to a fair sized steamer waiting in the bay. Griffith Jones built his timber store on this quay.

Penhukin, the steep bank over which the road from Trefechan to Tanybwlch runs, is believed to have been named after a half-witted boy known locally as Huwcyn, who used to spend most of his time here in a shallow cave overlooking the harbour. It was said that the hundreds of sand martins that nested in the bank were so accustomed to him that he did not disturb them. The name Penhukin has been in use since at least the early 18th century.

The road from Trefechan to Penparcau was avoided by most people after dark. Until well into the 19th century it was the

Ship repairing near the malt-drying kiln

resort of footpads who were not averse to attacking and robbing passers-by. What frightened people most, however, were the stories of ghosts, mysterious lights and eerie sounds seen and heard in the space between two trees, one of which was a landmark in the area and known as *Y Goeden Fawr* (the Big Tree). One traveller claimed to have seen corpse candles there, another talked of having seen a coffin sailing through the air above the trees, before plunging into the harbour. Two or three days later, it was said, the dead body of a person was found floating at the spot where the coffin was seen to disappear under the water. When the original Goeden Fawr was blown down in a storm, the name was given to the other tree until 1916 when that, too, was blown down.

On the south side of Penparcau on the steep hill down to Rhydyfelin was a tree bearing a large discoloured knob and known locally as *Coeden y Gwaed* (the Tree of the

Spring Gardens c. 1890

The main road to Penparcau

Blood). The popular belief was that a man had been murdered there and that his blood had spurted on to the tree, marking it for ever. What really happened was that a young woman from Lledrod was walking home from one of the November fairs when she was run down and killed by a cart driven by some drunken men returning from the fair. The tree was marked to record this tragedy.

Penparcau itself remained a small old-world community, with white washed low-roofed houses, until late in the 19th century. As stated already, its only tavern, the *Piccadilly,* was closed when the owner went to live in Marine Terrace in the 1850's. Piercefield was the home of Pierce Evans who, in the late 18th century was a member of the Harbour Trustees, and a collector of the Customs. His son of the same name was active in the town's affairs in the first half of the 19th century.

A Pierce Pierce of Penparcau was the first working bookbinder in Aberystwyth and was employed in 1816 by Samuel Williams the printer.

Five roads met at Piccadilly, and in the centre was not Eros, but the tollgate house. It was built c. 1770 by the Nanteos estate and remained there until 1959 when it was demolished carefully by men from the Folk Museum at St. Fagans where it has been re-erected. For the last 40 years of its existence in Penparcau it was the home of Mrs. Kate Hopkins. While the Turnpike Act was in force this tollhouse covered four very busy roads.

The South Gate Tollhouse

The National Eisteddfod

The first eisteddfod recorded in Wales was held at Cardigan not long after the castle was built in 1176. It was proclaimed a year in advance and competitions were held in deeds of arms, poetry and music.

The modern eisteddfod dates only from 1789 when a meeting was arranged in Corwen which was followed later by one in Bala. Soon afterwards, Iolo Morgannwg devised a ritual which he claimed had been used by the druids in ancient times, and in June 1792 he held the first *gorsedd*, a meeting of bards, on Primrose Hill in London. This gorsedd ceremony became accepted in Wales, was used at a Carmarthen eisteddfod in 1879, and has become an integral part of the national eisteddfod ever since. From this time on, eisteddfodau were held regularly in the country and gradually they have come to reflect the growing national sentiment of Wales. In 1858, at an eisteddfod in Llangollen, it was decided to hold a National Eisteddfod every year, and from that time onwards, despite many difficulties, usually financial, this has been done. The eisteddfod has acted as a great formative influence in Wales. It has centred the recreation of the Welsh people on literary and musical competitions and it has stimulated literary production. Above all, it has contributed to national consciousness. It is no exaggeration to say that wherever the National Eisteddfod is held, that place is, during the festival, the capital of Welsh Wales.

The national eisteddfod has been held in Aberystwyth on three occasions—1865, 1916, 1952. For the first of these the executive committee had as its chairman T. O. Morgan a barrister, antiquarian and local historian, and as its general secretary the indefatigable John Jones, "Ivon". The president elect was Prince Louis Lucien Bonaparte who had spent a holiday in Aberystwyth in 1855 and had shown great interest in the town and its cultural pursuits.

Among the adjudicators were Brinley Richards the eminent pianist, a professor at the Royal College of Music and the composer of the popular "God Bless the Prince of Wales", Edith Wynne, the soprano, then at the height of her vocal powers, Lewis Thomas the well-known baritone, and Llew Llwyfo the versatile singer, poet and entertainer, a great favourite with eisteddfod audiences. They all also performed at the evening concerts.

The eisteddfod was held for five days in September 1865 in a marquee with accommodation for 6,000, erected on what is now Queen's Square in front of the Town Hall. Unfortunately, Prince Lucien was unable to leave his home in Torquay because of illness and his place was taken by the vice presidents, one of whom was E. L. Pryse M.P. of Gogerddan, Lord Lieutenant of the County.

Much to the disappointment of the crowded audience, there was no chairing ceremony. The subject set for the bardic chair was *St. Paul*; "Caledfryn" announced that not one of the entries deserved the prize and, using his great powers of speech, powers which could make or mar a piece of prose or poetry, he soon convinced the rebellious audience of the justice of the adjudication. The bardic chair was therefore left empty on the stage and the great sword remained in its sheath.

Another disappointment, perhaps, was the failure of anyone to win the chief essay competition. A prize of £100, the gift of the Prince, had been offered for the best essay on "The Origins of the English Nation", a topic which was hardly to the taste of Welshmen attending a peculiarly Welsh festival. The Prince, himself said to be a scholar, wrote, "I have perused with considerable attention the essays received, but I find that neither of them come up to the modern linguistic science, and I decline to recommend the prize to any competitor."

To everyone's surprise, the best poem on "The Wedding Ring" was by a spinster, "Cranogwen", Sarah Jane Rees the school-mistress at Pontgarreg near New Quay, who not only taught children, but also gave instruction in navigation and astronomy to sailors studying for their masters' certificates. The prize for the poem on "Dafydd" was won by Llew Llwyfo, while the second prize went to Ivon.

The Aberystwyth National Eisteddfod was one of the first to pay as much attention to music as to literature. This attracted more people to the festival, for the choral items, in particular, were very popular. The chief choral was won by Cor Dewi of Llandysul. One of the outstanding performances was in the under 15 class where the boy prodigy, Richard Samuel Hughes, played "Home Sweet Home" on the piano. He won despite having had some fingers bitten by a monkey at a travelling zoo, only a short while before the competition. David Davies, Llandinam, was so taken with the boy's playing that he added two guineas to the prize and said that the boy could almost

Richard Samuel Hughes

make the piano sing. R. S. Hughes lived at the upper corner of Bridge St. and upper Great Darkgate St. and became a famous Welsh composer in his day. Unfortunately, he died comparatively young.

No one succeeded in winning the £20 prize for composing a cantata, but the eisteddfod choir under its conductor Edward Edwards, "Pencerdd Ceredigion", who kept a bookshop in Great Darkgate St., gave a stirring performance of the cantata *Llewelyn* by John Thomas at one of the evening concerts.

Among the visitors were Hugh Owen who explained his scheme for establishing day schools in Wales for the advancement of popular education. Another was the above-mentioned David Davies, Llandinam, attending his first eisteddfod and apparently enjoying it. The theme of his speech was "Learn to speak English or stay where you are and eat brown bread", by which he probably meant barley bread.

A greatly disappointed visitor was Joseph Parry, who had emigrated from Merthyr to North America where he worked at a factory while studying and writing music. With nine others he came to Aberystwyth only to find that some compositions which he had forwarded to the eisteddfod committee had not arrived, and were never recovered. One of his motets was sung at the eisteddfod. He was introduced to the audience as one showing great promise, a prophecy which he fulfilled. He became famous as a composer, was Professor of Music at the University College at Aberystwyth, and, for a while, was organist at the English Congregational Church in Portland St. He was the composer of the well-known hymn-tune *Aberystwyth*.

The 1865 eisteddfod drew large crowds, many of whom travelled on the newly-built railway from Newtown and Machynlleth. It being September, the town also contained a considerable number of visitors, and was so crowded that the price of a night's lodging went up to a pound, an extortionate price, and it was very difficult to get a meal. One of the bards present, "Taliesin of Eifion", bought himself a piece of beef for eightpence and called at a number of houses to have it cooked. Everyone was so busy catering for visitors that he failed to get this done and, in verse, he much bewailed the loss of his meal and his eightpence.

Financially, the eisteddfod was a success, the proceeds amounted to £1,700 while the costs were only £1,300, yielding a profit of £400 which was sufficient to wipe out the losses incurred on previous festivals.

The National Eisteddfod 1916

The 1914 National Eisteddfod was supposed to be held in Bangor but because of the war it was postponed to the following year. The Aberystwyth event had, therefore to be postponed from 1915 to 1916. At Bangor a strong plea was made for the National Festival to be continued to be held throughout the war, and Aberystwyth was asked to set an example. Inevitably there was much disagreement on the issue, the *Welsh Gazette* was strongly opposed to the venture, arguing that "to hold a National Festival during the present terrible struggle is as impolitic as it is unseemly" and "Indulgence in every form of costly and ostentatious pleasure should disappear in the face of a common task and a common danger."

When Lloyd George, then Minister for War, was asked for his opinion, he expressed his firm support for continuing to hold the National Eisteddfod during the war, but advised that in view of food and other shortages, and the curtailment of railway services, it would be wiser to keep the event smaller than usual. And so, after the guarantors had expressed their willingness to renew their bonds despite the prospect of loss, it was resolved that the Eisteddfod be

held. Had "Hedd Wyn", the Welsh bard, been killed early in 1915 instead of in 1917 the decision might have been different.

In the circumstances, the festival was a small, simple and economical one, lasting only three days. Considerable modifications were made in the programme, particularly in the number of musical items, several popular features being omitted.

The president of the executive committee was Sir John Williams who had done so

Gorsedd Ceremony at the Castle 1916

much for the National Library of Wales, and the general secretary was S. Gwilly Davies, a local banker. The marquee was erected on the College playing field (Vicarage Field) in Llanbadarn Rd., and the Arts and Crafts Exhibition was held at the Alexandra Rd. Council School.

The Gorsedd Ceremony was held in the circle of stones erected in the inner ward of the ancient castle. There are 13 stones in the circle, one from each of the Welsh counties, and one, the Maen Llog (Logan Stone), in the centre. The last was the gift of Peter Jones and was brought from Hafan, about halfway between Brogynin, Penrhyncoch, believed to be the birthplace of Dafydd ap Gwilym, the 14th century Welsh poet, and Bedd Taliesin, according to tradition the burial place of Taliesin, the 5th century poet.

When Lloyd George addressed the audience in the pavilion, he was given a rapturous welcome, partly because his presence and support helped to dispel the

The Rheidol United Choir

feelings of guilt which troubled some of those present. He strongly defended the holding of the festival and "his melodious, impressive eloquence roused the audience to the highest pitch of enthusiasm". He ended his oration with the following words: The Cymro "sings in joy, he sings in sorrow. He sings in prosperity, he sings in adversity. He sings at play, he sings at work. He sings in sunshine, he sings in the storm. He sings in peace, *why should not he sing in war?*".

The audience was made to feel happier when a telegram of good wishes from the 38th Welch Regiment in the trenches in France was read out, and cheered to the echo. The presence of eight M.P.s stressed Westminster's support for the festival.

This time the bardic chair did not remain empty, it was won by the Rev. J. Ellis Williams who happened to be in Aberystwyth on his honeymoon. The winner of the chief choral competition was the local Rheidol United Choir.

At one of the evening concerts a performance was given of Professor David Jenkins' *Scenes from the Life of Moses*, and one of the soloist, in this and other performances, was Sophie Rowlands, a professional singer from Aberystwyth. David Jenkins himself had died the previous year.

A special *Gymanfa Ganu* (Singing Festival) was arranged on Sunday evening for people who, because they could not take time off, were unable to attend the eisteddfod on week days. It was conducted by J. T. Rees of Rhydypennau, father of a future H.M. Ambassador to Brazil.

Despite the restrictions, the festival was a financial success. The total receipts were £2,550 and the profit was between £1,100 and £1,200. The decision of the Customs and Excise authorities to levy an amusement tax on the proceeds from the concerts was not well received.

The National Eisteddfod of 1952

The third National Eisteddfod in Aberystwyth was held on the Plas Crug playing fields in August 1952. The task of preparing for the festival, work which usually took two years, was entrusted as usual, to the executive committee—Ald. David Thomas (chairman), Canon Gwilym Owen, Jenkin Alban Davies, Emlyn Evans, and Dafydd Morris Jones, the general secretary. It did its work so well that it was said to have excelled not only in the organisation of the festival, but also in what *Y Faner* called the things that mattered most—courtesy and kindness. Dafydd Morris Jones, at 26 the youngest secretary ever, was much praised for his work and manner by the Archdruid, Cynan.

The problem of finding extra accommodation in a seaside resort in August was very difficult but it was overcome with the cooperation of the residents and the use of empty buildings, such as schools, to house the younger visitors.

Despite much criticism, it was resolved to adhere to the "Welsh only" policy. This meant the translation of 16 musical pieces into Welsh, among them translations of *Carmen* by Prof. T. H. Parry Williams, Haydn's *Creation* by T. Gerallt Jones and the *Hymn of Praise* by Enid Parry, wife of the National Librarian.

The weather was bad, extremely wet, and the Gorsedd ceremony had to be held in the College instead of among the circle of stones in the Castle, much to the disappointment of the hundreds who waited to see the procession.

Among the "sensations" was the adjudicators' decision to withhold the bardic crown on the grounds that no competitor was worthy of it. As usual, this aroused much controversy from the unofficial adjudicators, and provided food for comment in the correspondence columns of some newspapers for several weeks. On the positive side, there was high praise for John Evans, headmaster of Llanegryn school, whose ode won him his eighth eisteddfod chair, enough to give one to each member of his family. He is reputed to have said that his next aim was to win a stool for his wife; when he arrived home after his victory he was given one by an admirer.

The chair was presented to the eisteddfod committee by Miss Myfanwy Mayers on behalf of the Cape Town Cambrian Society, of which she was president. Miss Mayers was herself a professional pianist and before going to South Africa had been the official accompanist of the Royal Welsh Ladies Choir.

There was very high praise indeed for the work of E. O. Roberts of Liverpool who won the Prose Medal. Among the outstanding musical performances was the singing of the Treorchy Male Voice Choir, a performance so moving that the adjudicators laid down their pens and just listened. The audience also greatly enjoyed the playing of the Welsh National Youth Orchestra, the fine performance of the Mozart's Requiem by the eisteddfod choir under Charles Clements, and the performance of Carmen by the Welsh National Opera Co. on Saturday night. Professor Ian Parrot's composition *Luxor* aroused a great deal of interest.

Despite the weather, the festival was a great success, it was attended by some 160,000 people. Among these were people from 13 countries, the largest contingent being from North America, led by Professor John Hughes from Montreal, formerly a member of the staff of the University College in Aberystwyth. He acted as president of the eisteddfod meetings arranged for Welsh people from overseas.

The eisteddfod had some novel features, the chief choral competition was held on the first day. This being a popular item, it attracted the crowds earlier than usual and also enabled people who had a holiday only on that day, a bank holiday, to take part without losing a day's work. Also, the field being large, it was possible to set up the Arts and Crafts Exhibition near the main marquee instead of in another part of the town, the result was a greater interest in this aspect of the festival.

Financially, too, the event was a success, the costs amounted to about £44,000 while the expenses were just over £40,000 and Aberystwyth has still to stage a National Eisteddfod which has made a loss.

Urdd Gobaith Cymru

The Welsh League of Youth

Ifan ab Owen Edwards was the son of Owen M. Edwards, a man who, as Chief Inspector of Schools for Wales, almost revolutionised the curriculum of the schools in the Principality by getting Welsh taught in the classrooms. Ifan, after graduating in the University College, Aberystwyth, went into the army and served three years in France before returning to complete his studies in Oxford. On returning to Wales he became much more aware of the decline of interest in Welsh and in things Welsh. At Oxford he found that the Society of Dafydd ap Gwilym no longer conducted their meetings in Welsh, but he soon changed that. Like his father he became very much concerned with the preservation and encouragement of what was good in the Welsh way of life.

When he left college his first appointment was as history and physical education master at Dolgellau Grammar School, but soon afterwards he was invited by Principal J. H. Davies of Aberystwyth to join the staff of the University Extra Mural Department. One of his classes was at Llanarth where he used to lodge for the night at a house named Pandy, and it was there, late at night, by the light of an oil lamp, that he wrote the article for a children's magazine which he edited, *Cymru'r Plant,* appealing to the children of Wales to join together to create the Welsh League of Youth, known to Welshmen everywhere as the "Urdd", in order to preserve the Welsh language and to prevent Wales from losing its identity. The appeal evoked an enthusiastic response, *Cymru'r Plant* began to include a supplement,

Cronicl yr Urdd, dealing with the new movement. Within a few months the circulation of the magazine had increased from 5,000 to 10,000 copies, and a few years later to 30,000.

The 'Pandy' appeal was written in January 1922; in July of that year Ifan was married and went to live in Neuadd Wen, Llanuwchlyn and it was there that the Urdd had its first headquarters, with Mrs Edwards as its first secretary. The movement increased so rapidly that extra staff had to be employed at the Llanuwchlyn village post office, to cope with the mail. It soon became necessary to deal with the movement in a different fashion, there had to be some decentralisation. Branches were set up in different parts of the country. To enable the members to meet, summer camps were arranged, the first at Llanuwchlyn in 1928. The following year the first Urdd National Eisteddfod was held. The country was then divided into regions, and the movement launched such enterprises as a Welsh cinema to tour the country, athletics meetings, and the never-to-be forgotten pleasure cruises to countries in Europe.

By the 1930's the movement had become too big for two people to handle in their spare time, and a new method of administration was sought. At about this time Sir Ifan and Lady Edwards, as they became later, moved to Aberystwyth where their new clerk, Miss Elsie Williams joined them. Soon afterwards, in 1932, the Urdd was formed into a company to administer and control the movement. Salisbury House in Llanbadarn Rd. was acquired as its headquarters, the Edwards's moved into part of it to help pay the running expenses, and lived there until the movement had so grown that it needed the whole building to itself. It is still the Urdd's HQ, including several extensions. In time a national organiser was appointed, R. E. Griffith, who later became its director and gave a lifetime of devoted service to the Urdd.

Its principal aim has always been to foster Welsh citizenship among the nation's young people. Any one up to the age of 25 years may join if he or she is prepared to accept the movement's three-fold pledge of service to Wales, to one's fellow man, and to Christ. Much stress is laid on the preservation of the nation's culture, its language, and service to the community.

Varied and interesting activities are arranged at local, regional, county and national level—games, athletics, folk dancing, eisteddfodau etc. Summer camp and training centres are held at Llangrannog, Glanllyn near Bala, and at Blaencwm in the Croesor Valley. Together they offer activities ranging from sailing and canoeing, mountaineering, and table tennis, to local studies, drama and public speaking with experts to guide and train when necessary. The annual eisteddfod has become a national institution and the formation of a Youth Drama Company promises another type of national event. Not far from Llangrannog is the Urdd farm where, on 250 acres, food is grown for the movements' summer camps.

The movement's appeal to the young people of Wales remains strong, it now has 1,200 branches and 62,000 members. The staff numbers 50.

All this costs a great deal of money, about £450,000 a year. The annual grant is £60,000; it says much for the affection which the people of Wales have for the Urdd, that they are prepared to contribute the remainder. Sir Ifan ab Owen Edwards died in 1970, he will never be forgotten while the Urdd lives.

An Urdd procession, headed by Sir Ifan and Lady Edwards, during the Peace Pageant 1935

Social Clubs

The first social club in Aberystwyth is reputed to have been formed as a result of a suggestion made by one of the Pryses of Gogerddan, possibly Lewis Pryse. On 14 March 1780, a group met to discuss the matter and it was resolved to form a *Society of Gentlemen, Inhabitants of the Town and Neighbourhood of Aberystwith*. Articles to be observed were drawn up stating that the membership should be limited to 21 men, all resident within 5 miles of the town. Meetings were to be held on Tuesday evenings at a "House that produces good Ale." Every member was expected to act as chairman in turn and anyone failing to do this, unless through illness, was to be fined 1s. 6d. over and above the normal weekly contribution of 6d., 4d. of which was for his club, i.e. evening's entertainment, and 2d. for the box, a strong wooden affair kept locked up by the treasurer. Each absentee from a meeting, unless ill, was expected to pay 6d. into the box for every absence. The box money was to be devoted to giving the members a grand feast and also, upon the death of a member of at least 3 years, to paying his widow the sum of 5 guineas. Later this sum was changed to 5 sovereigns for every 5 years of membership. The only gift of charity recorded was one of £5 towards enlarging and repairing the church organ in 1860, probably at St. Michaels.

The meetings were convivial affairs with a good deal of drinking, and among the club articles or rules, was one which stated that "if the acting Chairman for the Night, through intoxication or any other cause be judged incapable of supporting the Dignity of the Chair, he is to resign the same to the next present Member in Rotation." Guests were allowed as long as they were paid for at 4d. a head per visit. The articles imply that there was at least some discussion at these meetings, but most of the time was spent in drinking and smoking, while some had lobsters, grog (diluted rum) and cigars. Not many years after the club was formed it became known as the *Social Club*.

The meetings were held in the Gogerddan Arms (later the Lion and now Padarn Hall) until the Belle Vue Hotel was built c. 1820 when these two houses were used in alternate years. The members consisted of merchants, well-to-do tradesmen, businessmen and such professional men as solicitors, doctors and bankers. It was also used by the local gentry, the Pryses, Powells, Richardes, Bonsalls, Vaughans of Crosswood, Pughs of Abermad and Vaughan Davies of Tany-bwlch, but their attendance was far from regular.

The great event of the year was the annual feast held on the first Tuesday in the year. In 1866 it was held at the Belle Vue and attended by 39 men of whom well over half were guests. The total cost of the "dinner" (which seems to have meant the main course only) was £38 14s. 9d.; dessert and wines were £21 9s. 6d.; 28 bottles of wine at 6s. each cost £8 8s.; brandy £1 13s. grog £1 5s. 6d. and cigars £1 0s. 3d. Not content with all this, 28 suppers were later served at 1s. 6d. a head.

During the 1870's the club may have been known for some strange reason, as the "Smokey Face Club". Its quarrel with John Gibson is described in the section on the Cambrian News in "Printing in Aberystwyth".

Financially the club was a success, for in 1872 its assets were £276, including shares worth £50 in the Aberystwyth Gas Co. But all was not well, some of the leading members were dissatisfied with the poor attendance and general lack of interest shown by the majority of the members, some of whom were heavily in arrears with their fees and fines. There were also signs of disagreement among the members, and on 21 November, 1888, the Social Club held a meeting to consider the future. It was then resolved to dissolve the club and to divide its assets among the members at the rate of 8s. 6d. per year of membership. A club which had met regularly for over a century thus ceased to exist.

Among the club property was a much-prized Queen Anne snuff box believed to have been given to the members by Lewis Pryse in 1798. What happened to it at the dissolution is not known but it was back in the hands of a Gogerddan man, Sir Edward Pryse, in 1913.

Another social club in the town was the *Society of Gentlemen, Merchants and Tradesmen* formed on 29 March, 1838, and called the *St. David's Club*. It was limited to 25 members, all of whom had to be at least of the standing of a merchant or master tradesman, and resident within 10 miles of Aberystwyth. They met at the Gogerddan Arms every Friday evening from 8 o'clock to 10 o'clock or longer if the club money for that evening had not run out. The entrance fee was 10s, and an evening's entertainment cost 1s. of which 6d. went into the box. The chair was occupied by each

member in rotation as in the other club.

This club held its annual feast on St. David's Day whenever possible. The dinner was supposed to be on the table at 5 p.m. and the coffee had to be served promptly at 9.0 p.m. The cost of the dinner was paid "out of the box" and cost 10s. a head. The number of diners varied from 40 to 50, guests had to be paid for. They were grand affairs, full of pomp and ceremony, it is recorded that 16 toasts were drunk at one feast, the most important being that drunk to St. David "in solemn Silence."

Most of the rules were similar to those of the Social Club, widows of members were paid the same amount but the St. David's Club paid more attention to charitable causes. On 20 April 1839 it launched a fund to purchase a lifeboat for the town. It also loaned £10 to a J. C. Rowlands to enable him to continue his studies in London.

Exactly when this club ceased to exist is unknown but John Cox printed fresh copies of its rules and regulations in 1855.

A club which existed for less than two years was the *Queen's Club* formed in October 1888 just before the Social Club was dissolved. It met at the Queen's Hotel and had the use of the billiards and smoking rooms. It was defunct in 1890.

On 8 December 1890 the present *St. David's Club* was formed by a mixture of members of the old Social Club and of the Masonic Lodge. The latter were probably interested because the new club's rooms were to be in part of the Masonic Hall in Market St. It was much more of a club than the others were, for it had its own premises, with facilities for billiards, reading, dining

and drinking, and was open every day.

Its original members were of the same type as those of the Social Club with the addition of some of the College staff. It also admitted country members. The first Committee of Management consisted of the new Liberal M.P., Vaughan Davies (later Lord Ystwyth), David Roberts the brewer, R. Geddes Smith the solicitor, John Morgan —probably the proprietor of the *Aberystwyth Observer* and J. R. Rees the bank manager. W. P. Powell of Nanteos and Hughes Bonsall were also members. The entrance fee was 10s. 6d. and the annual subscription £2. 2s. 0d.

The club began by holding social evenings, and guests were invited to smoking concerts and musical at-homes. But these were far from popular with the members and it was then decided to allow ladies to join the club. Some did join but the disapproval of the male members was such that the ladies soon left. The club members were much criticised in February 1902 when they decided by 23 votes to 6 to open on Sundays.

Possibly because of the increase in membership, in 1903, when there were 100 members, the club moved to the place previously occupied by the National Provincial Bank, at the seaward corner of Little Darkgate St. (Eastgate) and Pier St., a large building owned by the City Brewery, Lichfield. The facilities there were as in Market St. These premises, with a handsome entrance in Eastgate, the home of the St. David's Club ever since, were opened with a smoking concert on 17 October 1903.

The most eventful year since the move was 1915, when fire broke out on the

239

premises at 2.0 a.m. and completely gutted the inside. The only occupant at that time was the caretaker, who barely escaped with his life by climbing down a clothes line from a bedroom window. Though insured for £350 this did not compensate for the loss of valuable furniture, mementoes, records and the damage done to a billard table on which Peel, the champion, had once made a record break. The inside of the building having to be completely rebuilt, the club met at the Old Post Office next to Barclays Bank in Terrace Rd. until they were able to return to Eastgate on 27 January 1916. The cost of refurnishing being more than the insurance cover, the members had to bear the extra expense.

In the 1950's an attempt was made by Professor Ellison and W. J. Jones, the Chief Constable, to change the nature of the club, talks were given by experts on varied topics and discussions were held, but the change was not popular and St. David's reverted to being a purely social club.

It is interesting to note the extent of inflation during this century. The price of a tot of whisky at the St. David's Club in 1907 was 3d., in 1936 it was 8d., it reached 1s. 2d. in 1943 and is now, 1980, 38p., over 7s. 6d. in the old money.

The Cliff Railway

When the promenade was built it had to end in the north at Constitution Hill though its extension along the foot of the cliff was seriously considered for a while. Climbing "Consti", as the hill is called locally, became very popular, and the name "Constitution" is said to have been adopted because so many considered the climb to be good for their "constitutions" i.e. general health.

The view from the top is magnificent, not only is there a fine view of the town but also of a very large part of Wales. On a clear day, seawards, the view extends from the Llyn Peninsula in the north to Strumble Head in the south, while inland, Snowdon, Cadair Idris, Pumlumon and the Preseli range can be seen. A panorama of over 1,000 square miles, more than 100 miles of coast line, and 26 mountain peaks.

But Constitution Hill is 400 feet high, its sides are steep, and many visitors found the climb daunting in the extreme. In 1896 the Aberystwyth Improvement Co., decided to build the cliff railway, using the water balance principle. Two carriages were connected by thick steel ropes *via* a pulley at the top end of the railway. On each carriage there was a tank which was filled with water when it reached the top station and emptied at the bottom station. As it descended, the heavy top carriage was therefore able to haul the much lighter lower carriage up the steep incline. This method was abandoned in 1922 when the railway was converted to electric power. Much has since been done in the interests of safety but the carriages have retained their 1896 design. For walkers, the new zig-zag path makes the climb less arduous.

Some Aberystwyth Worthies

Over the years, Aberystwyth has been well served by many worthy people of whom little or nothing is known. Of those of whom something is known, a number deserve special mention. Some have been described in this book in connection with their work— Peter Jones (Industries—Slate Works), David Roberts (Industries—Breweries), Sir John Gibson (Printing—Cambrian News), George Rees (Printing—Welsh Gazette), John Evans and David Samuel (Schools and Schoolmasters), Dr. David Ellis (Dispensaries and Hospitals). Eminent ministers of religion have been described in the sections on their churches, while there are others of whom accounts are given below.

Job Sheldon was a native of Staley in Derbyshire and well-versed in lead mining before coming to Wales where he was first heard of at the Llanfyrnach mine in Pembrokeshire. In 1780 he was manager for a mining company in Cardiganshire, working Esgairmwyn and other mines. Sheldon was probably the most able mine manager in Mid Wales from about 1780 to 1820. He acted as mining agent for both a local and a Flintshire Co. working in Cardiganshire, while operating mines on his own account at Cwmsymlog and the Llanfair Clydogau mine near Lampeter. His treatment of his miners was a model to others. To keep an adequate labour force together he not only kept his mines working when the price of ore was low, but also ensured that there was an adequate supply of corn for them during the Napoleonic Wars, when the cereal was in very short supply. When the demand for lead ore was small, he urged the increased production of "black jack", a zinc ore which

was then in demand, and he was always sufficiently aware of the state of the market to sell at the right time and in the right place. In the early 19th century potters were paying almost £5 a ton more than smelters for certain kinds of ore, but few if any of the mineowners of Cardiganshire took advantage of this except Sheldon. He sent cargoes of ore direct from Aberystwyth to Bridgewater, Bideford and Barnstaple, instead of letting the ore merchants of Bristol pocket the profit. As a result of all this, Job Sheldon became a wealthy man.

He was equally dynamic in public life. He became a burgess of Aberystwyth in 1787 and lived first in Trefechan, then in Bridge St. and later in Sea View Place. He was Mayor of the town at least 12 times between 1804 and 1833. This was the period when the borough began to develop its commons, and Sheldon took· advantage of this. Like others he secured for himself leases of large slices of land which he then sublet at a substantial profit. But he did prevent the borough representatives from selling land cheaply, as their predecessors had done, and persuaded them to grant leases instead, a policy which brought the Corporation a considerable income in later years. Sheldon's policy was "Never sell, always lease."

He remained a leading figure in the town until 1833 when the malpractices over the purchase of land led to a government inquiry, and eventually to the passing of the Municipal Corporations Act which created the Town Council. In the report on the inquiry, doubt was cast on the propriety of Sheldon's behaviour in leasing Corporation land at a low price. He then seems to have retired from public life but still remained a strong supporter of the Established Church. He was one of those who strongly advocated the building of the second St. Michael's. He died in 1844 at the age of 84 years.

Ivon. One of Aberystwyth's most active residents in the second half of the 19th century was John Jones, generally known as "Ivon". He had an extensive knowledge of local antiquities, an excellent memory and a lively sense of humour, all of which made him a most interesting and amusing companion.

John Jones was born on 10 May 1820 in Mynydd Bach and was the brother of David Jones, manager of the National Provincial Bank in Aberystwyth for many years. But whereas the latter was very much a public figure, Ivon shunned publicity.

Both were educated by Owen Morris in Bethel, one of Ystrad Meurig's old pupils who, after leaving school, became an excise officer in Ireland for a while. He was an expert surveyor, a good mathematician and "wrote a beautiful hand", an art much appreciated in those days.

When 15 years old, Ivon came to Aberystwyth as an apprentice to Lewis Jones of Canton House, one of the town's merchants, the owner of at least two shops and the Mayor of Aberystwyth in 1843. Ivon began his training in a shop in Great Darkgate St. near the Old Town Hall. Soon afterwards he began a life-long study of the art of writing Welsh poetry, and in time became good enough to win the second prize at the National Eisteddfod of 1865.

In 1836 the Temperance Revival began and Ivon, who then lived in Canton House, signed the pledge at the house of John Matthews, where the Temperance Book was kept. Henry Richard, the future M.P., lived there.

Early in the 1840's, Edward Edwards, the choral conductor, formed a choir but was handicapped by the cost of the music. Ivon helped by copying out hundreds of pages of music in old notation, and the extent of his help over the years was such that the choir was able to perform the Messiah, Creation, and Mozart's Twelfth Mass. He also wrote temperance hymns, and translated others into Welsh to be sung to familiar tunes at the many temperance meetings which he attended in various parts of Mid Wales.

In February 1848 he married Mary the daughter of John Williams, mercer, of Bridge St., and in the same year opened up his own business, probably in partnership with his brother, in a former tavern in Princess St. Twelve years later he moved his business to the well-known Commerce House, now the Gallery, at the corner of Queen St. and Bridge St., where he stayed to within a few months of his death in 1898.

During much of the second half of the century he had a hand in starting or helping every important movement in the town. He was a member of the group which met in the *Shades* to study Welsh grammar and the writing of poetry, he helped to run the Literary Scientific and Mechanics Institute, did what he could for the library, and became general secretary to the executive committee of the National Eisteddfod held in Aberystwyth in 1865. He then became a

bard, "Ioan Ivon", and was given a gold medal for his work for the festival. Ivon also did a great deal towards the erection of a statue of Daniel Rowland in Llangeitho.

Ivon had a strong sense of humour and was well-known for the stories he told. One was of a man named Thomas Jenkins who, though very devoted to the Baptist cause, had not been baptised. When well on in age he fell mortally ill and expressed a desire to be baptised in proper Baptist fashion—total immersion. Being too ill to be taken to a river or a pond, and baths being unknown in his neighbourhood, it was decided to use what the Welsh call a *noe*, a large wooden trough used to make dough for bread. This was filled with water and the old man laid down on his back, but the trough was too short and the water didn't cover his knees. When the Welsh bard known as "Tegid" heard of this, he wrote the following:

Bedyddiwyd Tomos Siencyn,
Gwr egwan fel fy hun,
Mewn noe a dwr i'w guddio:
Heblaw ei ddwy benglin.

Bydd ryfedd gweled Tomos
Yn y Gaersalem fry,
Ei gorff yn wyn fel eira
A'i ddwy benglin yn ddu.

It tells of poor Thomas, not having been totally immersed, arriving in Heaven with a snow white body, except for two black knees.

Another amusing story involving Ivon is of a militia bugler in 1844. At that time, though the excitement occasioned by the Rebecca Riots was beginning to subside, a company of regular soldiers was brought from Llanidloes to Aberystwyth to keep the peace, and was billeted in the workhouse on Penglais. It so happened that there was then a movement on foot in Aberystwyth for the early closing of shops. Young men in the town banded together to stage a demonstration which was to start at a given signal. The man entrusted with the signal was Ivon, with the assistance of Georgie White, the militia bugler, whose blast was to set the young men marching through the town. Georgie stationed himself on the steps of the old Town Hall, and when the moment arrived, gave what amounted to a call to arms with such a blast that it was heard all over the district. A short time later the regular soldiers, fully armed, were seen advancing along North Parade and did not discover until they reached the top of Great Darkgate St. that the bugle call was not meant for them. Poor Georgie was brought before the Mayor, John Evans of Commerce House, and severely reprimanded. The attempt at early closing then collapsed. A more effective attempt was made three years later when the signal for the start of the procession was the ringing of the old bell in the Town Hall, but that, too, failed to secure early closing.

John James was born c. 1830 at Pantgwyn on the Nanteos Estate, a farm which is said to have been in the family for over 400 years. In time he started work as a pupil teacher under Thomas of Penparcau School but didn't like it, and became apprenticed to a grocer in Bridge St., David Jones, probably the bank manager. He disliked this, too, and went to London where, for a short time he found himself at a disadvantage because of his poor English. It was not long, however, before he overcame this and opened his own grocery store. Soon he opened a second, then a third and in a surprisingly short time John James became the owner of twelve grocery stores, all doing well. He began to take part in public life, parochial and municipal, and became a member of the Stepney Board of Guardians. He also established stores in Birmingham.

In 1864 he bought property stretching from North Parade along Terrace Rd. as far as the premises now used by W. H. Smith, and reaching as far back as Bethel in Baker St. The corner with North Parade was then the site of a two-storey house owned by David Jones the Bank, and used by him as another grocery store. In 1872 James came to live in Aberystwyth and began developing his site. He pulled down the corner shop, and in its place he built a large, handsome store called the London and Provincial Stores along North Parade. Further along Terrace Rd. he built a large covered hall known as the John James Market Hall. It was twice burned down and twice rebuilt. It was on the site now occupied by W. H. Smith and, before that, by the Cambrian News works and offices built by John Gibson in 1895. (The initials JG and the date are still to be seen on the building.)

As stated earlier, Aberystwyth was then a very untidy place, especially on market days, when street sellers, potato carts etc. obstructed both pavements and highways. It was hoped that by providing covered market halls, the streets would be cleared. But the people concerned refused to leave the traditional selling places and John James's hall was half empty. He then allowed the National Provincial Bank to have the corner site and moved his grocery and wine store into part of the hall, using the remainder as an entertainment centre. The bank moved there in 1880. The post office at that time was in New St., an inconvenient site for a town spreading so rapidly eastwards. There being an empty space next to the bank, John James offered it to the Post Office, which moved there in the early 1880's, to the site now occupied by Liptons and Dewhurst.

There was no more active man in Aberystwyth than John James, there was not one public movement of which he was not a member. He became a town councillor within a few months of coming to the town, was made an alderman and served as Mayor in 1884 and 1885. When he joined the council he found its finances in disorder and succeeded in getting a borough accountant appointed, an act which put that body on a firm financial footing. In the water supply controversy between the advocates of pumping and gravitation he came down firmly in favour of the latter, and assisted materially in securing the Llyn Llygad Rheidol and Pumlumon estate. He was also of great assistance in the settlement of some **Corporation leases questions. At the end of** his second term as Mayor he was presented with a silver plate worth £100 in recognition of his public services. He became a J.P. in 1885 and sat at Llanilar and Llanbadarn, was a member of Downie Trust, one of the promoters of the Public Baths Co. and a large shareholder in the Aberystwyth Steam Packet Co. He was also on the Bronglais Board of Guardians.

When the County Council was formed in 1888, John James became one of Aberystwyth's first representatives. When he was made chairman of the Police Committee, Dr. Enoch Davies is believed to have said, "Now Cardiganshire will be free." He held the chair throughout the investigations leading to the dismissal of Major Bassett Lewis, the appointment of Sgt. David Evans which was vetoed by the Home Office, the appointment as Chief Constable of Howell Evans, as well as during the attempted enquiry by the Home Office into the proceedings of the Police Committee.

The University College had a good friend in John James, he was one of the members of the original College Council and he fought hard to retain the College in Aberystwyth. One of his last acts before he died was to sign the documents for the transfer of the College from the Trustees to the Incorporated Institution.

During his stay in Aberystwyth he acquired a considerable amount of property. After purchasing a farm called Bryncrwys, he entered into a protracted and expensive lawsuit with Nanteos and won. He farmed Brynamlwg (now a College Social Club) and turned it into a profitable venture. He even started a milk supply in the town, opening up stores for that purpose in Terrace Rd. and Great Darkgate St. A few years before his death he took out an auctioneer's licence, opened an estate agent's office next to the bank and conducted a number of very profitable sales. He was also connected with

a coachbuilding and saddlery business and with the meat market in St. James Square. Rising every morning at about 4 a.m., he exercised personal control over his businesses and his death closed one of the most active and most useful lives in Aberystwyth.

Sir John Williams Bart., was born in Bailey, Gwynfe, Carmarthenshire, the third of four sons born to David and Eleanor Williams of Blaen Llynant. His father was both the minister of the local Congregational Chapel and a farmer. John Williams was born on 6 December 1840 and was educated at a local school before being sent, in 1855, to the Normal School in Swansea to

Sir John Williams Bart.

begin his training for the ministry. During his two years at the latter he became very interested in science and went from there to study this branch of learning in Glasgow. In 1859 he returned to Swansea and became apprenticed for two years to two medical men there—W. H. Michael and Ebenezer Davies. He next went to study medicine at the University College Hospital in London where he stayed six years, gaining his M.R.C.S. and M.B. in 1866, and the M.D. the following year. John Williams then returned to Swansea and set up as a general practitioner in that town.

After a few years he was appointed to the staff of his old hospital in London and became a Professor of Obstetrics of London University. He soon became one of the capital's leading medical men. In 1886 he began serving the Royal Family, especially at childbirth, and in 1894 was made a baronet by Queen Victoria and was also honoured by the King of Denmark. He published a number of works on obstetrics. During the Boer War he helped to establish a Welsh hospital in South Africa and worked hard with those fighting tuberculosis in Wales. He was now a wealthy man and in 1903 he returned to live in Wales at Llanstephan House where he lived happily for six years, becoming a J.P. and High Sheriff of Carmarthenshire.

John Williams began collecting books in Swansea, but the opportunities for doing this were much greater in London, and his membership of the Cymmrodorion Society there brought him into contact with people of similar tastes—J. H. Davies, Gwenogvryn Evans and Henry Owen. After he came to Wales he continued to collect books, manuscripts, oil paintings and old maps. Before returning to his native country he had already been told that the Peniarth MSS would be his when the brothers Wynne died.

He was interested in the National Eisteddfod and was at the one held in Mold when he first became actively involved in the movement for opening a National Library in Wales. After a great deal of hard work on his part, he and others secured for Wales not only the right to have its own library, but also succeeded in having it located in the place which Sir John favoured —Aberystwyth. In 1909 he moved to a house on Victoria Terrace and became President of both the University College

The plaque on Blaenllynant, Sir John Williams's home in Victoria Terrace

and the National Library, offices which he held until his death in May 1926.

In the very month that the library opened at the Old Assembly Rooms, January 1909, the Peniarth MSS came into his possession and he presented them to the National Library at once. In all, he gave the N.L.W. 1,200 manuscripts, some of them almost priceless, and over 25,000 printed books, apart from the many, many books and journals on medicine and related subjects. He also gave to the two institutions of which he was president, oil paintings, maps and some fine 18th century furniture. They have cause to be very grateful to Sir John Williams.

Caleb Morgan Williams was a native of Whitland in Carmarthenshire where he was born in 1853. After being educated locally he was apprenticed to the drapery firm of James Howell in Cardiff. In 1874 he came to Aberystwyth and opened a drapery shop, first in 9, Eastgate where Daniel Thomas later had his business, and then in Pier St.

He began to take part in public life almost as soon as he arrived in the town and in a few years had become the most prominent man in Cardiganshire. There was no Aberystwyth or county institution of which he was not or had been a member. As was said of him when he died "His record of public service was so great and so varied that it became a byword, an object of admiration or the subject of reproach. Public work became a religion, his passion for it knew no bounds, his zeal and devotion were nothing short of marvellous and only his most intimate friends had any idea how

heavy were the sacrifices he made in the discharge of his many, many, multifarious public duties. Beginning as a servant he ended up as a slave—to the public. So wide was his experience and so great was his reputation for thoroughness that no public body in Cardiganshire could be considered complete unless C.M. was a member of it. His prevailing influence on public bodies was due not to a gift of speech but to the mastery of facts. Though the most prominent figure for years in the public life of Cardiganshire, no man in the county did so much work out of sight as C.M. That he ruined his own business in attending to that of the public (was) a notorious fact for some years. His 45 years service on the Aberystwyth Town Council, and 39 years on the County Council constitute(d) a fine record. He was the most progressive member of the Town Council, not an idealist, but he excelled as an administrator, especially in the realms of health and education."

He was a staunch Liberal, the president of the County Liberal Association in 1892, when he was also made a J.P. He deserves always to be remembered for his work during the tithe riots of the 1880's. Because of the refusal of tenants to pay tithes, there were often forced sales of their goods, events which were sometimes attended by outbursts of violence. C.M. often accompanied the police on these occasions and by his reasoned eloquence was able to quell the riots. He drove many miles in his old-fashioned high trap to the wilds of Cardiganshire in attempts to keep the peace, and saved the bailiff from many a rough reception. When an inquiry was held, he was invited to London to give evidence on behalf of the rioters.

C.M. was elected a member of the Police Committee as soon as it was established and was its chairman in 1893 and 1910. With Peter Jones and John James he took a leading part in the acrimonious discussions which led to the dismissal of Major Bassett Lewis as Chief Constable over the importation of large numbers of police from neighbouring counties to deal with the rioters, and the use of the police to protect private estates.

When the Quarter Sessions ceased and the County Council was formed, C.M. was among the first county councillors and became its chairman in 1896 and 1924. He was very methodical, kept an excellent filing system and was able to silence many an opponent by his knowledge of the history of the subject under discussion. As chairman he presented the address of welcome to the Prince and Princess of Wales in 1896. As mayor of Aberystwyth in 1889 he did the same to Queen Victoria in Wrexham.

On financial matters he believed in the greatest efficiency at the lowest cost and had the farming community firmly behind him. They respected him also for his extensive knowledge of agriculture. As member of the committee for the Joint Counties Mèntal Hospital at Carmarthen, he saved Cardiganshire thousands of pounds. His rigid economy led to a teachers' strike when he persuaded the education authority to refuse to implement the improved salary scales for teachers.

C.M.'s interest in education ranged from the university to the village school, being a member of the Court of Governors of the former and of the local education authority looking after the latter. He showed great interest in small village schools, and for some years he gave silver watches to those pupils who had never lost a day's schooling. There are probably some of "C.M.'s watches" still in being. He was for many years a member of the Governing body of Ardwyn County School and its chairman for 13 years. His views on patriotism during the 1914-18 war led to the dismissal of one of the school staff, a conscientious objector, and the pupils then staged a protest demonstration against C.M.

As member of the Poor Law Guardians, he was very critical of the unfair load borne by Aberystwyth as compared with the rural areas, but was just and sympathetic with the poor and often gave relief out of his own pocket where it would not readily be given by the relieving officer.

C.M. worked hard to secure the National Library for Aberystwyth and was a personal friend of Sir John Williams. He was a trustee of the Downie Bequest, a member of the Management Committee of the Aberystwyth Infirmary and a Commissioner of the Land Tax for the county from 1893 onwards.

In religion he was a member of the Portland Street English Congregational Church, where he was a deacon, treasurer and Sunday School teacher for over 20 years. He was an active supporter of the Band of Hope.

After many years in business, C.M. closed his shop in Pier St. became an insurance agent, and moved to Laura Place.

He died on 11 September 1928 at the age of 75.

Sir David Charles Roberts was born in Loveden House, Bridge St. in 1850 and was educated at the Liverpool Institute and the University College, Aberystwyth. He was only 21 when he was elected to the Town Council and he remained a member for well over fifty years. He became a county councillor as soon as the County Council was formed in 1889 and served that body, too, for half a century. He was the first chairman of the County Education Committee and held the office for a long period, acquiring an interest in education which he never lost. The financial side of public life also attracted him, not only was he chairman of the county finance committee, but also became the treasurer of both the University College and the National Library. He was

Sir David Charles Roberts

made a J.P. in 1895.

His family had strong religious convictions and he was a devoted member of Tabernacl all his life. Not only was he a deacon there for thirty years but he also became Moderator of the South Wales Association in 1929, and treasurer of the Central Fund. Such devotion was not surprising, for his father formed Tan-y-cae Sunday School and on his mother's side he was a great grandson of David Charles, brother of Charles of Bala, founder of the Sunday School in Wales, and one of the founders of the British and Foreign Bible Society. David Charles was the composer of many hymn tunes, among them the well-known "O Fryniau Caersalem" and "Rhagluniaeth Fawr y Nef."

A Liberal in politics and a hard worker for the party, D. C. Roberts was invited to stand for Parliament, but refused. In 1906 he was appointed High Sheriff of Cardiganshire and made president of the Aberystwyth and Cardiganshire General Hospital. In 1936, he received his Knighthood, had conferred on him the honorary degree of LL.D., and was made a freeman of the borough of Aberystwyth.

Both in the setting up and running of the National Library of Wales, he gave unstinting service. With H. C. Fryer, Peter Jones and C. M. Williams he helped to secure for the Library the Grogyddan site. He was a member of the Council of the library and the chairman of its finance committee from 1913 until 1935, when he was elected treasurer in place of the late Lord Gladstone of Hawarden. He held this office until 1939 when he was forced to resign because of ill health. He was a

generous contributor to the library building fund from the beginning.

Sir David Roberts was mayor of Aberystwyth on three occasions, he had an extensive timber business and owned a considerable amount of property in the town. He died on 19 February 1940 at the age of 89.

Sir George Fossett Roberts was born and bred in Aberystwyth and had a real affection for the town and its people. He came of a family which had a record of almost a century of municipal service. His grandfather, John Roberts the tanner of Mill St., became a member of the Town Council when it was first formed in 1835, he was also made one of the Town Improvement Commissioners. His father, David Roberts was a town councillor for 40 years and mayor on three occasions. Sir George himself served the same body for 25 years and was mayor twice. In 1935 he was knighted for his services in the field of politics—he was a staunch Conservative—and in public life generally. He had previously been awarded the OBE (Military Division), been made a C.B. and had conferred on him the honorary degree of LL.D. of the University of Wales.

Sir George did devoted work on behalf of the Aberystwyth General Hospital. The welfare of that institution was one of his major concerns. For many years he was chairman of its Committee of Management and later its president. When the National Health Scheme came into operation in 1948 he was made the first chairman of the Mid Wales Hospital Management Committee but had to resign for health reasons in 1951. He later served as honorary member.

Two other institutions to which he gave untiring service were the National Library of Wales and the University College of Wales. He served as vice president of the latter from 1940 until his death in 1954. His association with the National Library extended over more than 40 years. When King George V and Queen Mary visited Aberystwyth in 1911 to lay the foundation stones of the Library, Captain G. F. Roberts, as he was then, being High Sheriff, figured prominently in the proceedings and was among those presented to their Majesties during the ceremony.

His official connection with the Library began in 1914 when he was made a member of the Court of Governors, an office which he held until his death. In 1919, soon after his return from active service in World War I, he was elected a member of the Council and served in turn on the Finance and Book Committee, the Building Committee and the Records Sub-Committee. He succeeded Sir D. C. Roberts first as chairman of the Finance Committee in 1936, and as Treasurer of the Library in 1939. Five years later, on the untimely death of Lord Davies, the Court of Governors turned to Sir George as the man who would most worthily uphold the dignity and traditions of the presidency; he held this high office until his death on 9 April 1954.

George Fossett Roberts was made a J.P. in 1906, High Sheriff in 1911 and Deputy Lieutenant of the county in 1929. Among his other offices was the chairmanship of the Borough Advisory Committee set up by the Lord Chancellor, membership of the Governing and Representative Bodies of the

Church in Wales, membership of the County Council and the Cardiganshire Police Committee, and for many years Vicar's Warden at Llanbadarn Fawr. He also served as president of the Cardiganshire Conservative Association, chairman of the Cardiganshire Territorials Association, District Commissioner of the Boy Scouts, president of the Aberystwyth Football Club, chairman of the Golf Club, member of the Aberystwyth Chamber of Trade, a member of the Board of Guardians Assessment Committee for 20 years and its chairman for 8 years, and president of the Cardiganshire Branch of the R.S.P.C.A. from 1935 until his death.

Sir George was for many years a strong supporter of the Army Territorial movement. In 1902 he was made the commanding officer of what was then called the Cardiganshire Artillery Volunteers and was responsible for the building of the Drill Hall. He was on active service throughout the first world war and, after 1919, commanded the 102 Field Brigade Artillery, later becoming its honorary colonel. He was awarded the Territorial Decoration.

Sir George Fossett Roberts was a man of high principles who was respected everywhere for his kindness, generosity and unfailing courtesy to all and sundry. His connection with the brewery in Trefechan (he was managing director from 1890 until he retired in 1935) possibly prevented him from pursuing a political career in Parliament, for it aroused the total opposition of the large and powerful temperance group in the county. But he never allowed this to affect his attitude to his fellow townsmen.

He died in Glanpaith at the age of 84 in 1954.

The Rev. John Williams was a Methodist minister without a church, an active man who became involved in a number of good causes in the town. It was he who founded the Band of Hope in Aberystwyth, and helped to establish the Sunday School known as *Ysgol Skin*, by letting his little chapel in Skinner St. be used for that purpose. He built the Temperance Hall in North Parade as well as several private houses in the town. When the Lifeboat Institution was formed in Aberystwyth, he became its local secretary, he also served on the School Board and collected much money for the University College. As stated above,

The Rev. John Williams (bottom right) with the Aberystwyth Life Boat Crew

| JOHN EDWARDS. | ALFRED WORTHINGTON. | JOHN WILLIAMS. | THOMAS JONES | CAPT. T. WILLIAMS (COXSWAIN). | CAPT RD. EDWARDS. | JOHN COLE. | JAMES DANIEL. | REV. JOHN WILLIAMS (Local Sec) |

he was an ardent advocate of total abstinence and gave the drinking fountain on the old Town Clock.

Professor Mary Williams (b. 1883) was the daughter of the above mentioned Rev. John Williams. After graduating with honours at the University College of Wales, Aberystwyth, she became one of the first holders of a University of Wales Fellowship. She then went to study at the Sorbonne in Paris and, later, held an appointment there. Her next move was to Durham University as Professor of French and Romance Languages, one of the first women in Wales, if not in Britain, to hold a university chair. A few years later, Dr. Williams was appointed Professor of French in the University College of Swansea where she taught for many years. Such was her reputation there, that a number of rooms and a modern Hall of Residence have been named after her.

Dr. Mary Williams was a first class teacher and a distinguished scholar, an acknowledged authority on the Arthurian legends both in their Welsh and French settings. She was also an adventurous person and never lacked courage. While a student in Paris she visited a fair where Bleriot was offering trips in his flying machine. Dr. Williams bought her ticket and flew round and over Paris with him, two years before he flew over the English Channel.

On retiring she returned to live in Aberystwyth at a house in St. David's Rd., once the home of Professor Edward Edwards, one of the most popular teachers of all time. Professor Williams died in October 1977 at the age of 94.

ABERYSTWYTH CELEBRITIES CARICATURED BY MATT

From the Sunday Graphic, 31 August 1930

The Old Town Revisited

Great Darkgate Street

Until the 19th century, there was very little building in what is now called Upper Great Darkgate St. When the Castle House was built in 1789, apart from the castle, the church and its graveyard and some taverns above the old Town Hall, the whole area west of Pier St. and Bridge St. was open land. After Castle House was built for Sir Uvedale Pryse the field behind it, used for circuses, markets, fairs, football and some militia training, was called Cae Bach Judith (Judith's Little Field) after Pryce's housekeeper. The entrance to the graveyard then consisted of a triple arch which was later demolished and replaced with a more modest affair, further back.

The area now occupied by St. James Square and the surrounding buildings was also used for fairs, and in particular, as a market place. As was to be expected in such an area, early in the 18th century there were several taverns, the *Angel, Ship Aground, Three Jolly Sailors* where St. Paul's Church now stands, the *Ship Launch* and the *Swan.* In the building which is now the *Farmers Arms,* there was a large merchant and grocers business kept by John Jones. It was in existence c. 1790.

In the 1820's the Assembly Rooms, Laura Place, the Meat Market in St. James Square and other houses were erected and by the early 1830's the area was built up. The portion of the main street from the Old Town Hall to St. James Square was then called Bow Street, and the remaining section to the graveyard named Church St.

At the junction of Bow Street and Weeg (Pier) St., was the Old Town Hall facing

The Angel Inn in the early 20th century

The present-day Angel Inn.

Aberystwyth c. 1860, possibly the oldest photograph in existence. The Castle Hotel, pier and Queen's Hotel had yet to be built. The old Customs House, with a garden between it and the sea, stands at the corner with Pier St. The narrow promenade (widened later) had been extended to Constitution Hill. The purpose of the excavations shown in the bottom left hand corner is unknown.

Bridge St., and across the road on the Bridge St. corner was a house which was to become the home of R. S. Hughes, a very well-known Welsh musician. It was later an ironmongers shop kept by "Doughton Town Clock".

Padarn Hall, formerly the Lion Royal and before that the Gogerddan Arms, was built about 1727, its portico and curiously incised keystones still give it an air of distinction. It was kept in the 1750's by a man who is believed to have been a member of the company of soldiers sent down to guard a lead mine when some local land-owners were trying to rob the Crown of its mineral produce. In the 1760's the inn-keeper was Alexander Gordon, a colourful character, four times mayor of Aberystwyth twelve times one of the bailiffs, and coroner for thirty years. But though pledged to uphold the law, he sold ale without a licence, failed to clear the street in front of the inn of the mixen (manure heap) which regularly accumulated there and assaulted officials sent to serve a summons on him. The Court Leet and the Quarter Sessions some-times met at this inn, especially while the Town Hall was being rebuilt in the 1770's. Its yard was occasionally used by Non-conformists to hold services in the early 1800's.

The marked increase in trade which occurred when the Gogerddan Arms be-came a leading coaching inn during the first half of the 19th century, led to its being extended along both Great Darkgate St. and Bridge St. The break in the old inn's roof line shows the extent of the alteration in Great Darkgate St.

A few doors down was Parry's House, a tall Tudor-style structure with its top half overhanging the street. In return for allow-ing the house to be demolished to widen the street in the late 18th century, Parry was given a free grant of a strip of Penmaes-glas common which enabled him later to build part of what is now High St. Scandrett the chandler's premises came next and below that, where the Cooperative Stores now stands, was the house where the Calvinistic Methodists formulated their articles of faith in 1823, as the plaque testifies. Taylor Lloyd's chemist shop occupies the site form-erly held by the *White Horse Inn* and below that there were two other taverns, the *New Inn* which had a yard stretching to Queen St., and the *Brittania* kept by the Rees fam-ily which gave its name to the hill behind the Roman Catholic Church—*Banc Sion Rhys*. They were for many years the town's chief carriers of timber from Radnorshire, for shipbuilding.

The narrow, arched passage alongside the

A very old portion of the town in St. James Square between the Meat Market and St. Paul's Chapel. It once housed the House of Correction and gaol

shoe shop above the post office, was formerly the entrance to Brittania Court, a rabbit
warren of small houses inhabited mostly by
people of the same blood. Though shunned
by law-abiding people, it housed the Morgan
family which kept there Aberystwyth's first
post house in the early years of the 19th
century. It was at the back of this court,
in Queen St., that the indomitable Azariah
Shadrach had his Independent chapel in a
building which later became a slaughterhouse.
The court is now completely covered by
Post Office buildings.

Back at the old Town Hall, the vacant
site at the corner with Pier St. held an old
building where some 17th century work was
discovered when it was demolished in 1964.
It was for many years a grocers' shop, last
in the occupation of Silvanus Edwards.
David Evans the jeweller's shop and the one
above are typical of the two-storey plus
a dormer type of building which were very
common indeed in the town in the past.
These two shops together were formerly the
Miners Arms kept by the redoubtable Mali
Rees. They, too, contain some good 17th
century woodwork.

Part at least of Howell's drapery store was
built on the site of the old Talbot Inn which,
with its yard, coachhouses and stables,
covered a large area extending back to
Eastgate. Its main and side entrances were
in Great Darkgate St. and many a religious
service was held by the early Nonconformist
in the yard and, occasionally, in the Long
Room.

The Talbot was well liked by visitors and
on its staff was a remarkable man known as
"the doctor", a barber by trade who also

*The premises where the Methodists formulated their
articles of faith 1823*

*Great Darkgate St. showing the arched entrance to
Brittania Court*

received a small salary for keeping the keys
of the castle. According to one visitor in
1791 he was shaved by this man who:

"had then attained his one hundred and
seventeenth year, stood erect and had a
ruddy complexion and an unwrinkled
brow... Four years before, he had undertaken, for a small sum of money, to ride
from the Talbots' Head to Machynlleth
...and back, without resting, but on
condition that he should be allowed
twenty drams before he started, and as
many on his return. He took them seated
on his horse, and felt but little fatigued
from his journey."

The landlord of the Talbot in the 1780's
had been round the world with Lord Anson
"in quality of quartermaster".

In 1830 this fine old coaching inn was
demolished, and the present hotel built in
the new Market St. which was created out
of the old yard. The street, opened in
1832, housed the Corn Market and five
taverns,—*Number Eight, Prince of Wales,
White Hart, Market Tavern* and another.
The corner site, now Cecil Jones, the optician's premises, was the Humphrey's
Medical Hall, a public dispensary. Almost
next door down was the *White Lion* at the
back of which Dr. Lewis Edwards, later
Principal of Bala Methodist College, and
father of the first Principal of the University
College of Wales, kept a school in 1827
underneath the room first used by John
Cox for printing.

Further down still was the *Heart of Oak,*
a tavern which also served as a dispensary
in the 1830's under the direction of Dr.
Richard Williams. At the bottom of the

Terrace Road, 1910.

street was the House of Correction for North Cardiganshire, built in the 1790's. The Old Dark Gate with its two round towers had then disappeared except for a portion of one of the towers.

Other taverns in this street were the *Queen's Head, Crown, Eagle, Golden Lion, Red Lion* (also a circulating library), *Union* and the *Raven*.

Well away from the remainder of the town, next to Seilo Chapel and worthy of attention, is Sandmarsh Cottage, the only dwelling on Sandmarsh Lane, now Queen's Rd., until well into the second half of the last century. This attractive, well-preserved Regency house has double bow windows which were once common in the town. Whenever a lease expired the Town Council insisted on improvements before granting a new lease. Unfortunately among the improvements insisted on around 1900 were bay windows instead of flat or bow windows and, as a result, the town lost most of its handsome old windows. The difference can be seen at the National Milk Bar near the sea end of Terrace Rd. It is composed of two houses, one of which was "improved" while the bay window bye-law was still in force.

The Milk Bar showing the difference in the windows

Sandmarsh Cottage

Some fine stone houses in North Parade c. 1820, and similar to some in Bridge St.

Bridge St. (*Heol y Bont*)

This was Aberystwyth's leading thoroughfare until well into the 19th century for it was not only an important business centre but also contained the homes of some of the leading families in the district.

In the early days, the river end would have had a gate and portcullis flanked by two round towers and the town walls. The gate was removed in the mid 18th century because it proved dangerous to heavily laden wagons, and the walls did not long survive the gate.

At its junction with Mill Lane there was a long, low house owned in the 18th century by Richardes of Penglais. About 1800 it was bought by Capt. William Williams of the ship *Lively* who came from a family of mariners. His grandfather John Williams, born in 1740, was involved in an abduction which attracted much attention in the mid 18th century. After serving a long apprenticeship on his father's ship John decided to become master of his own boat and set out for Radnorshire where most of the timber for shipbuilding was then bought. While inspecting some trees at the farm of Beili Noyadd, near Rhayader, he met and fell in love with the daughter of the house and proposed marriage. The daughter agreed but her parents were strongly opposed to the union. The young people had other views and the lady ran away from home to marry young John Williams. Not long after the birth of their first child they set out on a coastal trip northwards leaving the baby in the care of John's parents. Off Harlech a violent storm wrecked the ship and both were drowned. They were found in close embrace on the beach at Llandanwg near Harlech and were buried in the churchyard there in 1768.

As the town grew, the close proximity of Capt. Williams Williams' house to the new bridge proved so inconvenient to traffic turning into Mill Lane that the Corporation asked the captain to allow them to take a yard off the house to widen the road. In return they gave him, free, a portion of Penmaesglas, then an open common, where the Parish Hall and Vulcan St. now stand. It proved a very profitable exchange for Williams.

A few yards further up was *Carrog House* the home of the philanthropist, the Rev. Thomas Richards of Carrog, near Llanddeiniol. At Carrog House he often entertained his former fellow students at Cambridge, Thomas Clarkson and William Wilberforce, who together fought so hard to abolish the slave trade. Among other friends who stayed in Bridge St. were the Rev. John Keble, Professor of Poetry at Oxford, after whom Keble College is named, and Isaac Williams of Cwmcynfelin, two of the four originators of the Tractarian Movement in Oxford. It was while John Keble was staying in Aberystwyth that he visited the source of the Severn and was inspired to write the hymn "Go up and see the new born rill" and, after seeing the sun sinking behind a bank of cloud over Cardigan Bay, he composed the hymn which contains the words "Sun of my Soul, thou Saviour dear". Carrog House now houses the local branch of the Royal Air Force Association.

Further up at what is now the entrance to Powell St. were two very old, low-roofed houses demolished to make way for the new street in 1864. The upper one was occupied by Lewis Hopkins, builder and rate collector, The lower house was the home of David Owen, Cowkeeper, known locally as Deio Goch dwfn (Red David the deep one) because of the colour of his hair and the depth of his trickery and scheming.

At the corner with Back Lane (Gray's Inn Rd.), was a handsome stone house which now has a stucco facade. The heiress to Gogerddan, Margaret Pryse, married Edward Loveden of Buscot Park, Berks. Their son, Pryse Loveden, changed his name to Pryse Pryse and was M.P. for the county boroughs from 1818 to 1849. It was he who built the place in Bridge St and named it *Loveden House*. Though it also served as the Gogerddan town house, it became the permanent home of Pryse Loveden's crippled sister, hence the local name *Ty Miss Loveden* (Miss Loveden's House). She used a sedan chair to go to church, apparently the last person to use one in Aberystwyth. For going round the town she had a specially-made wheel chair drawn by a well-trained and well-caparisoned donkey led by a liveried servant. She died in 1855. As stated above, the house was later used in turn, as a militia depot and inhabited by Sergeant Major Stott and his family, as the Liberal Committee Rooms during the turbulent election of 1868 when Evan Matthew Richards was elected to Parliament as a Liberal, and as the home of the parents of Sir D. C. Roberts, a noted man in the public life of Aberystwyth. It afterwards served for a few years as a Baptist College before becoming the offices of the

Welsh Gazette in 1899. It is now a local government office, hence the present name of "Ceredigion".

Higher up is the *Black Lion*, built about 1700 and a busy coaching inn before the Belle Vue was built in the first quarter of the 19th century. The cobbled stretch in front is all that remains of the town's cobbled streets which were macadamised by the Town Improvement Commissioners in 1848. The Black Lion was the birthplace in 1801 of John Lloyd Davies, a poor boy who went as a clerk to a solicitor's office in Newcastle Emlyn, studied law, and married Mrs. Lloyd, Gallt yr Odyn, He later became M.P. for Cardigan Boroughs.

At the corner with Queen St. is a shop, now the Art Gallery, formerly called Commerce House where Lewis Pugh, the controversial Wesleyan Methodist of the early 19th century kept a draper's shop. He was followed there some years later by "Ivon" Jones a grocer. Later still came Hollier, a blacksmith, whose family kept a most interesting haberdashery much loved by the ladies of the town. A few yards further up was the side entrance to the Lion Royal, a glass door on which was etched in Welsh "God Bless this Bar" (*Duw a Fendithia'r Bar Hwn*).

Almost opposite was the "Shades" the temperance tavern described above. The entrance to Princess St is described below. Opposite the Black Lion is an attractive double bow-fronted stone house of a type once numerous in the town. Further down is *Westminster House* where the Pughs of Henblas, Abermad had their town house. Below this was the Nanteos residence, a very

old house which was greatly neglected and became the home of several poor families. It was mounted by a long flight of steps of good breadth, projecting well into the cobbled pavement.

Lower down is the Old Bank House, the home of the first bank in Aberystwyth, if not in Wales. Nearer the bridge and almost opposite Carrog House is No. 51, the handsome house occupied by Dr. Rice Williams described below, and at the very bottom of the street below the bridge is McIlquhams china store, a grain storehouse in the 18th century, a theatre in the 1820's and possibly a Nonconformist chapel before that. At the corner of South Rd., then called Shipbuilders or Shipwrights Row, was the *Freemasons' Arms* on the site of a very old house indeed. This was one of six taverns in Bridge St., the others being the *Carpenters Arms, Farmers Arms, Hope, Nag's Head, Star,* and the *Shades*.

One of the most interesting people living in Bridge St. in the early part of the 19th century was the above-mentioned Dr. Rice Williams, believed to be descended from an ancient family of physicians who practiced healing for many centuries and were connected with the Welsh legend of the *Meddygon Myddfai*.

This tells of a beautiful maiden, member of a people who lived beneath the surface of a lake in north east Carmarthenshire. She fell in love with a local farmer's son and promised to marry him on condition that he never touched her with anything made of iron. He agreed, they married and had three sons. To the eldest of these, Rhiwallon, she imparted her great knowledge of

A house in Bridge St.

Westminster House

The Old Bank House

McIlquham's China Store 1886

the healing qualities of herbs and other plants and showed him where to find them. He became known as the first of Meddygon Myddfai (the Physicians of Myddfai).

It is possible that the maiden represented, in folklore, the Stone Age people who hated and feared the later Bronze and Iron Age inhabitants of Wales. Whatever the truth of this, the story is that Dr. Rice Williams was descended from these physicians and was believed to be the last. However, Sir John Williams, Queen Victoria's "beloved physician" and the founder of the National Library, was also from Myddfai and could also claim to be last of the Physicians of Myddfai.

Dr. Rice Williams was a skilful surgeon with a taste for fine furniture and paintings, including a fine portrait of the Duke of Newcastle. His services were much in demand in Cardiganshire and elsewhere and he was for many years the coroner for North Cardiganshire. Dr. Rice was medical man to the Corbetts of Ynysmaengwyn in Merionethshire and often rode there on horseback, using the ferry from Ynys-las to cross to Aberdyfi. Woe betide any ferryman who failed to answer his summons promptly.

In Aberystwyth he was active in many ways and was always generous to charitable causes. The act for which he was best remembered was the building of Penbryn House, known as the Bath House, on the northern part of what came to be Marine Terrace and described under that title.

Princess Street, formerly Rosemary Lane, is in part a very old street. At its lower corner with Bridge St. were two houses, one above the other, the upper part being reached by stone steps from the pavement. The lower part was once an ironmonger's shop. The upper part of the building was known as the "Smuggler's House", built for the purpose and one of a number in the town. It contained secret passages, hidden doorways and staircases, hiding places galore and double walls, all to conceal contraband and fugitives. In the 1820's it was used for printing by Samuel Thomas and, later, for the same purpose by Esther Williams.

On the opposite corner was the *Old White Lion* built in 1727 and once one of the town's chief hostelries. The story is told that in the second half of the 18th century, two young Scottish packmen visited Aberystwyth regularly, and made this inn their headquarters. When they went their rounds they left their spare stock of goods and money with the landlord. One evening the packmen went for a walk towards Pendinas and were never seen again. It was generally believed that the landlord and his two sons had followed and murdered them, but their bodies were not found and no enquiries were made concerning them. Their goods and money were said to have been stolen by the landlord. Early in the 19th century, some labourers digging on Pendinas found the skeletons of two men. The discovery created a sensation in the town and it was taken for granted that these were the remains of the Scotsmen. But nothing further could be done, for the landlord and every member of his family had died.

In the early 19th century the old inn was converted into a shop kept by Peggws Jones and known as "Siop Peggws". It sold some groceries, but most of its trade was in an Indian commodity, indigo blue, a dye then much in demand in town and country alike for colouring wool and other materials.

Princess St. also housed a glazier, draper, a tanner and currier, the sexton of St. Michaels — a noted singer, and two sisters who scraped a bare living at *crimpio capiau*—crimping ladies caps. Further on was the *King's Arms,* a tavern much in favour with heavy drinkers and gamblers at cards. It was said of this inn that very late one night a notorious group of gamblers and drinkers were thinking of going home when they heard the ringing of a bell and the cackling of a gander, sounds which apparently heralded the approach of His Satanic Majesty. Rooted to their seats the four gazed fearfully at the door and saw the Devil himself. He then disappeared but they remained unable to move, until next morning. Despite its being told by men known to be drunkards, the story was believed in the town. After that the tavern was said to be haunted and fell empty. It was later taken over and converted into a grocer's shop and residence by David Jones the Bank and his brother Ivon. Lewis Pugh had his saddlers shop in this street, it later became the home of Griffiths the cooper.

The corner house with St. James Square, also a tavern in former times, was turned into a book shop by a retired Peninsular

Old Princess St.

War sergeant major. It was later a bakery and behind it in 1840 worked two nailers who failed to make their business pay and had to move elsewhere. Another house was occupied by John Lewis, a chandler more noted for the high price of his candles than for their quality. The street still retained some attractive old properties until recently when they were demolished to make way for a far from attractive car park.

High St., first named New St., then Castle Lane, was built in an area known as Castle Green in the 18th century. The name "High St." did not become official until about 1815 but it was used some years before that. It was the home of John Evans, born there in 1812 when the street was only partly built. His father had been a sailor in a man-of-war and wore a queue, the plait or twist of hair worn by sailors of that time. On his return to Aberystwyth the father took to plying small craft around the coast.

Old High St.

John was apprenticed when 12 years old to William Jones y Cab, a cabinet maker who had his workshop opposite the Assembly Rooms, on the site of Grafton House. The boy became an outstanding craftsman, his woodcarving became so admired that his fame spread into England, and he was employed to do fine carving at a number of manor houses in Shropshire and elsewhere. He lived in Shrewsbury and Liverpool for a while. He also worked in Pembroke Dock doing carving on ships until that port had so declined that the Navy, wishing to use his services, put him on the establishment and sent him to work in Chatham. On his return to Aberystwyth he went to live in the Bath House on the Terrace and had a workshop behind the Old Bank House in Bridge St. Unfortunately no example of his work is known to have survived.

At the bottom of High St., on the vacant site in South Rd., and overlooking the old shipbuilding area, was one of the first foundries in the town.

Pier St. (Heol y Wig)

Wig (Weeg) being the Welsh name for the bay towards which this thoroughfare leads, it was known to everyone as Weeg St. until the building of a stone pier about 1810 on the rocks where the pier now stands, led to its being named Pier St.

It seems likely that in medieval times, because of the town wall, there was no outlet to the beach until part of the old wall was demolished, probably in the 15th or 16th century. In the 17th century the street contained very few houses, part of it was arable land and in 1631 a section was called "Parke y ddeyntir" which suggests that there was, or had been a fulling mill there.

At the seaward corner of Pier St. and Eastgate, in the 17th century was *Ty Mawr*, a large house owned by Gogerddan and let in 1675 to Thomas Powell of Llechwedd Dyrus, sergeant-at-law and father of

The Regency House in Pier St.

the first Powell of Nanteos. It later became the property of the Richardes family of Penglais. How much of it was built in the 18th century is not known. Its attractive doorway can still be seen in Eastgate. Part at least of the house became the National Provincial Bank in the 1840's. The whole corner as far as, and including the older part of Galloway and Morgan's bookshop was included in the old house.

An examination of the facades of the street's buildings, above the shop fronts, shows evidence of some handsome building. The outstanding structures are now the Customs and Excise Offices and the attractive three-storeyed bow-fronted Regency House facing the bookshop.

The first Customs House was built in 1773 facing west, at the eastern corner of Pier St. and King St., and had an attractive walled garden between it and the sea. The

H.M. Customs and Excise Offices

first customs officer to live there was Edward Locke and the house was called Locke's House. Locke was a prominent man in the town, he and Job Sheldon were sworn enemies and there was a story told that when Locke was seriously ill Sheldon went to see him. Locke is then reputed to have said "Hello Sheldon, very good of you to come, but remember if I get better, this visit must not be held against me." With John Matthews, Locke led the revolt against the church rate being levied on Nonconformists during the rebuilding of the second St. Michael's Church.

There were only two taverns in the street in the early 19th century, the *Skinners Arms* and the *Unicorn*. The former was behind the Old Town Hall and to its front was fastened the town stocks in 1821. The space in front of the tavern was part of the old market place and was used by stallholders until well into the 1950's. The old "Skinners" is now known as the *Tavern in the Town*. The *Unicorn* was at the corner of New St. and Pier St.

No. 4 Pier St. was once the workshop of William Evans, then the best known clog-maker in Mid Wales. In 1874 the street also housed a Deaf and Dumb Institution.

No. 11 Pier St. was named Compton House where, in a small ill-ventilated room, the town's first free library was housed. After a spell in Terrace Rd., the library returned to Pier St. to *Ty* Mawr, to the premises formerly occupied by the National Provincial Bank.

New St. housed the North and South Wales Bank in the building now used by the Pentecostal Church, and in a house directly opposite was the town's first proper post office until the 1880's. Above the post office in the same building, was the Savings Bank established by the Rev. Thomas Richards of Bridge St. John Cox the printers' works were also in New St. and his shop was at the corner with Pier St., opposite the *Unicorn* tavern.

Eastgate. For centuries this was known as Little Darkgate St. because it led to a small gate in the medieval town wall. The gate was known as the Felon's Gate, for it was through this opening that condemned criminals were led to be executed at the gallows to the north of the town. The last person to be hanged was an elderly woman who poisoned her employer at a house called the Cupola in Trefechan early in the 19th century. The Welsh name for the street in the 16th century was *Heol y Cryddion* (Shoemaker's Road.). The change to Eastgate is said to have followed complaints from tradesmen that the name "Little" Darkgate St. was a hindrance to trade.

At the top of the street, next to the old Penglais town house with its lovely doorway are the Downie Vaults once owned by Joseph Downie whose generosity to the town should always be remembered. A few doors away is the Prince Albert Hotel which retains some of its 18th century features, particularly the strong-looking rain

The Theological College, formerly the Hotel Cambria

The Tavern in the Town, formerly the Skinners Arms

water head marked in the fashion of that time. Another 18th century building, set back from the street behind railings, is Crynfryn House, once the home of the Derbyshire man, Sir Thomas Bonsall, who made a fortune out of lead mining in North Cardiganshire. He was knighted in 1796 for presenting an address of welcome, signed by 600 prominent Cardiganshire people, to King George IV. The house once had gardens extending to, and along the sea cliff top. It became a hospital in the late 1850's and was until recently the Social Security Office. Just below is a tall mid 19th century warehouse complete with its vertical loading bay and dormer, newly converted into a Tourist Information Centre. Next door is a garage on a site once occupied by some of the Talbot Inn stables. Early in this century they were used first as stables and later as a garage for Jones Brothers' horses, carriages, buses and charabancs.

At the bottom of the street at the junction with Baker St., which is on the line of the old town wall, there is a figure head of Queen Victoria mounted on the wall. Now an office, this building was once the Victoria Tavern and behind it, reached by the narrow passage alongside Slater's shop are the remains of the little chapel built by David Jenkins for the Methodists about 1808.

The site now occupied by the Pantyfedwen Trust Offices at the corner with Market St., was occupied by Aberystwyth's first cinema, first named Cheetham's Picture Palace and then the Palladium. It was previously the site of two successive corn markets.

Eastgate has more courts than any other

A 19th century warehouse with loading bay

The figure-head of Queen Victoria

street in the town—Laurel Place, Gateway Buildings, Albert Court, Windmill Court, and one if not two others. The most interesting in the town is Windmill Court near the top west side of the street. It was once the site of a short-sailed windmill used to grind corn. When in use it was open to the sea and surrounded on two of the other sides by low-roofed houses. It ceased to operate about 1740 and the machinery was used to construct Morfa Mill (Melin y Mor) behind Tanybwlch beach, under Pendinas,

on the site now used to stable horses. The latter mill was demolished in 1860.

When it ceased to operate, the Windmill court structure was turned into four apartments reached by circular stone stairs around the outside of the building. The rent paid by the occupants decreased with the height of the apartment above ground. A number of stories are told of the old mill's inhabitants. Very early in the 19th century, the top floor was occupied by a very poor family of many children whose mother had died when they

Windmill Court after the mill was converted into apartments c. 1860

were young. The father, a feckless spend-thrift came home late one Saturday night to a house empty of food. Having no money to buy any, he decided to keep the children in bed until Monday, if possible. He carefully blacked out the few small windows and refused to allow the children to get up by pretending that it was still too early. On Monday morning he was able to beg food in return for some service. One of his sons, Charlo, who became a shoe-maker, was later noted for his ability to entertain people and was in great demand at local taverns where he amused the customers in return for drinks.

Another unusual resident was Thomas Robert, also a shoemaker and never seen without his leather apron. Thomas had two great loves, beer and Calvinism. Unlike the majority of his fellows he could read and write with ease and was well versed not only in the Bible but also in the religious con-troversies of the day, especially the Armen-ianism versus Calvinism debate. It was his custom to work hard at his craft for a spell without drinking any ale, and then to spend all his money on strong drink. At the end of the spree he usually had to take to his bed to recover.

His wife Nans was a sensible hardworking old lady who, to keep the wolf from the door, sold things of her own making. These were set out on a stall in Eastgate at the entrance to the court and consisted of "pop", ginger beer, rock, small cheeses and cakes. It was said that once, when Thomas was ill after a bout of drinking, on taking a visitor to see him, she asked her husband how he was feeling. He replied that he was dying and so Nans asked if he was certain of that. On being answered in the affirmative she asked him who would he recommend her to marry when he was gone. This upset Thomas who told her to go to the devil. She then replied that this would not be possible, for the law forbade a widow to marry her former husband's brother.

Evan Owen, one of the leading deacons of the Welsh Wesleyans, a total abstainer and a godly man, also lived in Windmill Court, then said to be the haunt of the un-godly and the "Sons of Belial". Evan Owen in Windmill Court was compared to "Lot Gyfiawn yn Sodom", a Saint among Sinners.

Between Eastgate and the sea, and running at right angles to the former is **Crynfryn Row, a row of cottages built by** Sir Thomas Bonsall in his garden in 1792 and reached along a road alongside the Public Library. They were first called Bonsall's Row. Behind them, and built later, is another row of houses parallel to Eastgate, once known as Crynfryn Court and now Crynfryn Buildings. Crynfryn Row leads to a steep line of steps known as *Stepys Mawr* which, being very near the

Gateway Buildings, Eastgate

Old Crynfryn (Bonsall's) Row. The crumbling wall in the foreground may have been part of the old town wall

The White Horse window

junction of two of the old town walls, may have been an ancient access to the beach.

It is interesting to note that before being set up at the above mentioned Crynfryn, the first Aberystwyth Hospital was in Alfred Place, in the building now occupied by the solicitors, Humphrey Roberts and H. D. P. Bott.

The White Horse Inn at the junction of Upper Portland St. and Terrace Rd. with its handsome, tiled bow window was owned first by a Mrs. Drew who previously owned the White Horse Inn in Great Darkgate St., and before that the Lord Hill which stood just below the alley leading to the old Wesleyan Chapel in Queen St.

MAYORS OF ABERYSTWYTH BOROUGH

c.1450 William Vaughan
early ʃSir Rice ap Thomas
1500's⎰William Herbert
1615 Richard Pryse
1659 Maurice Vaughan
1661 Sir Richard Pryse
1665 Maurice Vaughan
1668 Thomas Prise
1669 Richard Pryse
1671 Riceus Lloyd
1678 Sir Thomas Prise
1679 Francis Vaughan
1681 Sir Thomas Prise
1682 Evan Evans
1684 Riceus Lloyd
1685 Carbery Pryse
1686 John Pryse
1688 Edward Pryse
1689 Evan Evans
1690 William Williams
1692 Rice Lloyd
1693 Edward Pryse
1694 Edward Pryse
1696 Evan Evans
1697 Edward Pryse
1699 Roderic Richard(e)s
1700 Roderic Richard(e)s
1702 Thomas Pryse
1703 William Williams
1705 William Price
1708 John Jones
1710 Roderic Richards
1712 David Jones
1717 Thomas Lloyd
1720 Thomas Pryse
1721 Walter Lloyd
1722 James Parry
1724 George Jones
1728 Rice Lloyd
1729 Lewis Oliver
1730 Alexander Gordon
1731 William Jones
1732 Richard Parry
1733 James Evans
1734 Matthew Evans
1735 Evan Watkins
1736 Griffith Morgan
1737 James Davies
1738 Thomas Pryse
1739 Griffith Morgan
1740 Evan Watkin
1741 Alexander Gordon
1741 Thomas Williams
1742 John Evans
1743 Alexander Gordon
1744 Griffith Morgan
1745 Alexander Gordon
1746 David Morgan
1747 Evan Watkins
1748 David Morgan
1749 Richard Hughes
1750 David Morgan
1751 Evan Watkins
1752 David Morgan
1753 Iltid Evans
1754 David Morgan
1755 Evan Watkins
1756 David Morgan
1757 Evan Watkins
1758 David Morgan
1759 John Jones

1760 Matthew Evans
1761 John Jones
1762 David Morgan
1763 John Jones
1764 Evan Griffiths
1765 John Jones
1766 John Parry
1767 John Jones
1768 John Parry
1769 Thomas Lloyd
1770 John Parry
1771 John Jones
1772 John Parry
1773 John Jones
1774 Peter Lloyd
1775 Thomas Lloyd
1776 Thomas Lloyd
1777 Peter Lloyd
1778 John Parry
1779 John Pierce
1780 John Hughes
1781 John Pierce
1782 John Jones
1783 Robert Owen
1784 William Poole
1785 Robert Owen
1794 John Jones
1795 William Poole
1804 Job Sheldon
1807 John Jones
1808 William Poole
1809 Job Sheldon
1810 William Poole
1811 Job Sheldon
1812 George Bonsall
1813 Job Sheldon
1814 Job Sheldon
     Job Sheldon
1815 John Jones
1816 Henry Benson
1817 Thomas William Williams
1818 Job Sheldon
1819 Thos William Williams
1820 Job Sheldon
1821 George Bonsall
1822 Job Sheldon
1823 James Morice
1824 Job Sheldon
1825 Morris Davies
1826 Job Sheldon
1827 Morris Davies
1828 Job Sheldon
1829 Henry Benson
1830 Morris Davies
1831 Job Sheldon
1832 Henry Benson
1833 Job Sheldon
1834 ʃMorris Davies
     ⎰William Williams
1835 William Williams

Elected Mayors
1836 ʃJames Hughes
     ⎰John Hughes
1837 John Hughes
1838 John Roberts
1839 John Hughes
1840 Richard Owen Powell
1841 Thomas Jones
1842 John Evans
1843 Lewis Jones

1844 John Evans
1845 David Edwards
1846 David Edwards
1847 John Miller
1848 John Miller
1849 William Williams
1850 William Williams
1851 John Hughes
1852 John Hughes
1853 John Miller
1854 John Hughes
1855 Thomas Jones
1856 F. Rowland Roberts
1857 F. Rowland Roberts
1858 George Fossett
1859 Robert Edward
1860 Robert Edward
1861 Griffith Thomas
1862 Thos. Owen Morgan
1863 Thos. Owen Morgan
1864 John Davies
1865 John Davies
1866 Richard Roberts
1867 Richard Roberts
1868 John Matthews
1869 John Matthews
1870 Thomas Jones
1871 Thomas Jones
1872 Thomas Jones
1873 Philip Williams
1874 Philip Williams
1875 John Watkins
1876 John Watkins
1877 David Roberts
1878 David Roberts
1879 Peter Jones
1880 Peter Jones
1881 Peter Jones
1882 John Jones
1883 John James
1884 John James
1885 George Green
1886 George Green
1887 David Charles Roberts
1888 Caleb Morgan Williams
1889 Griffith Williams
1890 David Roberts
1891 William Kenneth Palmer
1892 William Thomas
1893 Thos. Davies Harries
1894 Thos. Davies Harries
1895 Thomas Griffiths
1896 Robert Doughton
1897 John Jenkins
1898 David Charles Roberts
1899 Caleb Morgan Williams
1900 Edward Pryce Wynne
1901 Richard Jenkin Jones
1902 Evan Hugh James
1903 Isaac Hopkins
1904 William Thomas
1905 Thomas Doughton
1906 Robert Doughton
1907 Caleb Morgan Williams
1908 J. T. Davies
1909 Edward Pryce Wynne
1910 Thomas John Samuel
1911 Daniel Thomas
1912 George Fossett Roberts
1913 David Charles Roberts
1914 Edwin Morris

1915 John Evans
1916 Caleb Morgan Williams
1917 Thomas Doughton
1918 Edward Pryce Wynne
1919 Prof. Edward Edwards
1920 Rufus Williams
1921 Joseph Barclay Jenkins
1922 Edward Llewellin
1923 David Davies
1924 Rhys Jones
1925 Llewelyn Samuel
1926 John David Williams
1927 George Fossett Roberts
1928 Thomas Henry Edwards
1929 Hugh Hughes
1930 Griffith Ellis
1931 Walter Diver
1932 Peter Bremner Loveday
1933 John Lewis Evans
1934 David Edwards
1935 Jenkin J. Humphries
1936 Llewelyn Rowlands
1937 J. Barclay Jenkins
1938 John John
1939 Llewelyn Samuel
1940 Thomas Morgan
1941 Thomas Lewis Old
1942 Frederick T. Foulkes
1943 Benjamin Pryse
1944 Griffith Davies
1945 Arthur W. Miller
1946 Hubert G. Pickford
1947 T. Llewelyn Thomas
1949 J. Arthur Hughes
1950 Richard Jenkin Ellis
1951 David Thomas
1952 John Lewis Davies
1953 William Gray Pryse
1954 Ernest Wm. Roberts
1955 Wm. George Rowlands
1956 Rowland G. Pickford
1957 Evan Jenkins
1958 Chas James Williams
1959 John John
1960 Henry Ifor Owen
1961 Wm. Gwyrfai Kitchin
1962 Clifford Knight
1963 Ryland Kenneth Clues
1964 Richard Jenkin Ellis
1965 Henry Cecil Owen
1966 Ernest Wm. Roberts
1967 Ronald Glynne Pickford
1968 Ceredig Jones
1969 John Caleb Edwards
1970 Henry Ifor Owen
1971 Samuel Lewis
1972 David Leslie Evans
1973 Bryn Davies

The Town
1974 Ceredig Jones
1975 Merfyn Jones
1976 Joshua Richard Thomas
1977 Ryland Kenneth Clues
1978 Mrs. Mona Rachel Morris
1979 Miss Katie Alice Jones
1980 Graham Thomas Parry